MW00452649

Champagne

...and Real Pain

Champagne

...and Real Pain

CELEBRITIES IN PARIS
IN THE FIFTIES

Maggi Nolan

Mosaic Press
A David Applefield Book

Oakville, Ontario • Buffalo, New York

Copyright @ 1998 by Margaret Claughton Nolan

All rights reserved under International and Pan-American Copyright Conventions.
No part of this book may be reproduced or transmitted in any form, by any means, electronic
or mechanical, including photocopying and recording information storage and retrieval systems,
without permission in writing from the publisher, except by a reviewer who may quote brief passages.

All the photographs in Champagne...and Real Pain *belong to ©Collection Maggi Nolan.*
The author, however, wishes to acknowledge the following: p.16 ©Marie-Claire Montanari,
p.149 ©Susannah Torem, p.171 ©Paul Foucha, p.186 ©Jean Fargeas, p.183 ©Gérard Décaux,
p.256 ©Alain Gagnez, p.329 ©Jean-Luce Huré.

Published in Canada by Mosaic Press, P.O. Box 1032, Oakville, Ontario, L6J 5E9, Canada.
Offices and warehouse at 1252 Speers Road, Units #1&2, Oakville, Ontario, L6L 5N9, Canada.
UK trade distribution handled by Calder Publications.
United States trade distribution handled by Midpoint Trade.

Canadian Cataloguing in Publication Data

Nolan, Maggi, 1923-
Champagne–and real pain: celebrities in Paris in the fifties
ISBN 0-88962-665-0

1. Nolan, Maggi, 1923- 2. Gossip columnists – France – Paris – Biography.
3. Celebrities – France – Paris. 4. Paris (France) – Social life and customs –
20th century.
I. Title.

Mosaic Press (Canada)
1252 Speers Road, Units #1&2
Oakville, Ontario L6L 5N9
Tel:/Fax: (905) 825-2130

Mosaic Press (USA)
85 River Rock Drive, Suite 202
Buffalo, NY 14207
Tel:/Fax: 1 (800) 387-8992

Email: cp507@freenet.toronto.on.ca

For all orders and inquiries **outside** of North America, please contact:
Association Frank, 32 rue Edouard Vaillant
93100 MONTREUIL/France
Tel: (33) (1) 48 59 66 58 / Fax: (33) (1) 48 59 66 68;
within France: Tel: 01 48 59 66 58 / Fax: 01 48 58 66 68
Email: david@paris-anglo.com

Online direct ordering available at:
http://www.paris-anglo.com/maggi

Printed in Canada

Book design: Christiane Charlot
Cover photo (*detail*): Maggi Nolan at Maxim's, 1957.

FIRST EDITION

Champagne...and Real Pain
is dedicated to my daughters
Cathy and Janne

Acknowledgments

With thanks and love to these special ladies
who helped me when I was in distress:

Maître Suzanne Blum
Olivia de Havilland
Gweneth Dulles
Drue Mallory Heinz
Princess Grace of Monaco
Dorothy de Piolenc
Maggie Vaudable

...and, especially, my sister, the Sister

I am grateful to my editor David Applefield for his belief in this book
and for keeping alive the great tradition of Americans publishing
in Paris today. I also thank his editorial team, Susan Bernat,
Tanya Leslie, and Christiane Charlot for transforming
a big manuscript and some vision into a real book.

And, finally, a heartfelt special thanks to my dear friend
Susannah Wilshire Torem, who, in the memory of her husband,
the late Charles Torem, and those glorious years in Paris,
helped make this book a reality.

Maggie

The imperious Monsieur Albert, director of Maxim's in the fifties, was very nice to me.
I called him *Papa* and he called me *Ma fille*.

Preface

*P*aris in 1949 was like another world when I first set eyes on fellow American, James Nolan, in an office on the Rue de Berri near the Avenue des Champs-Élysées in the Herald Tribune building. We met, worked together, married, had children, bought a home and became full-time Parisians in the world of yesterday. It was good—while it lasted.

Imagine a life without television, video, stereo, plastic bags, paper cups, fast food and quick service, to say nothing of pressing-while-U-wait. A gourmet cook in the kitchen without slicers, dicers, mixers, blenders, freezers, micro-ovens. No built-in machines to wash dishes or clothes. Imagine an office with no computer, no fax, no photocopier, no nothing but a rusty, dusty mechanical typewriter to clatter up a racket and break your fingernails on its keys.

Imagine the Avenue des Champs-Élysées as it was in the early fifties with barely any traffic except official government and diplomatic vehicles and ancient taxis driven by vintage White Russians who bellowed Volga boatmen songs as they rumbled down the Avenue. Then, of course, a procession of pretty girls breezing by on bicycles, their floral dresses flowing out behind them.

This was the scene from the Étoile's Arc de Triomphe right down to the Rond-Point where there was a line of horse-drawn carriages you could rent for a promenade up the "Champs" and down the Avenue Foch to the Bois de Boulogne and back again.

Ladies looked lovely everywhere they went in made-to-order coats, suits, and dresses from the grand houses of fashion and/or whipped up by little seamstresses who had learned their trade in the workrooms of famous designers. Ladies wore custom-made hats and slick gloves for all occasions and carried lace and linen handkerchiefs in their sleek leather handbags.

Those were the days of luxury ship travel from the USA to France. Visitors brought their steamer trunks, countless suitcases, hatboxes by the pile for the "season" that sometimes lasted for months. It was chic to stay awhile and really get acquainted with people, places and things. (Some, like John Ringling North, the circus king, brought a limousine and chauffeur, as well.) People were ready to live it up every moment; the names were big and the prices were small. People-watching was wonderful and you never felt like fainting when you looked at your check.

In the fifties I had ideal occasions for top people-watching as the wife of Jim Nolan, whom Howard Hughes hired to handle European public relations for Trans World Airlines from Paris, and later when I wrote a twice-weekly column about people in Paris for the New York Herald Tribune's Paris edition.

Those were the days when sophisticated Parisians and their American counterparts did a lot of socializing in elegant bars of the best hotels. Any day or evening a collection of diplomats, business executives, top-flight journalists and assorted celebrities gathered at every table or perched on every bar stool. Just everyone knew everyone else: if they didn't it wouldn't take long for one regular guest to chat up another after a few times of elbow-to-elbow bending.

People staying in the hotels did their entertaining in the bars as well; these were the times before mini-bars and maxi-machinery upstairs. The same faces were seen on the scene every year. There were familiar faces in the haute couture crowd in Paris to order or report the latest fashions: another set showed up for the big racing events at Longchamp and all the parties before, during and after; then a steady stream of chic, elite socialites passing through Paris en route to castles in Europe or villas in the south of France. All could be found socializing downstairs in the bar.

Hotel barmen were masters of their trade. They made an art of their métier which was considered a lifetime career. Young beginners took pride in learning from their elders and knew they'd gain prestige as they progressed. Barmen were "personalities" known by name down through the years. Personally pleasing their paying guests gave them pride and pleasure. They knew names, favorite drinks, habits both good and bad, and the right spot to seat everyone who spent time and money there. Habitués had high old times telling their troubles, offering opinions, asking for special cocktail recipes or just gossiping the hours away.

At the Ritz, day after day, there were celebrities all over the place like the pert Paulette Goddard sitting next to me. She could always make me laugh; when she looked up at the hunting scene decorating one wall and asked me what kind of beasts they were supposed to be, I told her "wild boars" and she answered that she hoped that they were the only "wild bores" we'd see that day. Once Linda Christian swept by in sables, not noticing that she brushed by "Papa" Hemingway, standing at the bar with his back to us. In a corner, you'd see Humphrey Bogart lighting Lauren Bacall's cigarette just as Aly Khan came by the door surveying the scene before going upstairs to see his father, the Aga Khan III, who lived in a master suite with his wife, the Begum Aga Khan, his cocker spaniel, his parrot and an entourage fit for a king. Of course, Charles Ritz, son of the founder, would scurry by loaded down with fishing tackle and all the paraphernalia for his favorite pastime. Added to this there was a perennial parade of chic society ladies and fashion folk to keep you up to date on what was going on, sometimes printable and sometimes not. All this and it was only lunchtime!

At the cocktail hour over at the Hôtel Raphael on the Avenue Kléber, you could sit in front of a wood-burning fireplace and spot Audrey Hepburn with Mel Ferrer; William Holden just in from Kenya; Cary Grant meeting David Stein, the local Music Corporation of America agent; Roberto Rossellini in animated conversation with a fellow Italian film maker while his wife, Ingrid Bergman, was taking care of their twin baby girls upstairs. The Raphael looked like an Italian palazzo and was the favorite of Roman film makers; it was also the choice of MCA for their top clients because David's private mansion where he often entertained them was right around the corner.

Meanwhile, over at the George V, head barman, Rudolph, was like a star to the stars. Among his regular clients: Maurice Chevalier and the fighter, Georges Carpentier. Or you'd see Darryl Zanuck and Jack Warner holding court; a marvelous Marlene Dietrich floating by in chiffon; gorgeous creatures like the sleek Katharine Hepburn in an elegant pantsuit or a bubbling Ginger Rogers in snowy white from head to toe.

Paris had American celebrity residents as well, like Betsy Blair and Gene Kelly. Gene had filmed An American in Paris here and then his "reel" life became his "real" life. He'd often be seen prancing down the Rue de Berri to meet his chums at the star-studded Hôtel Lancaster, just a few steps from the Paris Herald Tribune.

Over in the most elegant residential section of Paris, Olivia de Havilland settled down to life as the wife of a Frenchman. The legendary "Melanie" of Gone With the Wind was raising her son and baby daughter in Paris and was always busy with American-Parisian activities such as the library, hospital and church. Olivia was always "news" whether it was making films like The Ambassador's Daughter and The Proud Rebel or calling in the local builders to "raise the roof" on her house to make more room for her family. (Little did I know when I first wrote about her, that she'd become a lifetime friend.)

One American in Paris was a pal of mine before he became a celebrity. J. Paul Getty was just another ambitious American businessman making deals from his top-floor hotel room at the George V. When he gave launching parties for the tankers he was building in France, I went to these festive affairs, writing about him and his cronies before he was declared "the richest man in the world" and long before his bandwagon got so crowded with strangers.

If you were around in those days, you'd remember the Paris Herald Tribune. It was like a small-town American newspaper–a Paris-based "daily" printed in English and read by everyone in the English-speaking community. It was written by American and French journalists on the spot and edited by British-born Eric Hawkins. He was like a bantam rooster when he got his feathers ruffled. Reporters admired and feared him as they went out to do their own stories from start to finish: ideas, interviews, fact finding and fact checking to the actual writing, which was not altered on the news desk unless Eric gave the order.

Tough if Eric found mistakes in the copy; there was only one person to blame. Too bad for me when readers called in about a mistake I'd made in the day's column: I had given the title "Princess" to someone who was not entitled to a title. Eric wouldn't have caught my error if he hadn't had those calls. Readers were sacred to him and mistakes were serious. Another time, I didn't put enough "ns" in Minnelli (or was it "ls?") I really got hell for that and these were the days of Vincente with an "e" before Liza with a "z."

"Don't you know it's an insult to a person when you spell a name wrong?" he said in a voice that sounded more like sorrow than anger. I learned that lesson so well that today when I see misspelled names, they seem to jump up at me right off the page.

We had a tacky newsroom, rickety chairs, rationed supplies and pre-war type-writers, (heaven knows WHICH war). We got itty-bitty paychecks with no such thing as fixed hours or paid vacations, but we had fun. Eric had a way of making us feel that we were all part of a family and the paper belonged to us. Our rotten income was a source of chagrin but we often laughed it off; jokers in the newsroom would never ask you how much money you were making but rather "How much is it costing you to work here?"

Readers seemed to feel that the Paris Trib belonged to them as well. The fact that it was located right off the Champs-Élysées attracted many visitors, drop-ping in just to say "hello." In those days the whole staff worked in the same large newsroom, but not all at the same time; the huge half-moon-shaped news desk was manned in shifts. I had the right to use Eric's desk in the a.m. as long as I was out before teatime. Only Art Buchwald had his own desk, but that was both good and bad. Good because he was lucky to have a desk of his own and bad because it was located just inside the main door where everyone went barging and banging in and out. Often strangers would stick their heads in and ask Artie for directions to wherever they wanted to go. He got pretty fed up with this, especially at the deadline time when he was polishing a story. More than once he threatened to direct the next person who asked for the publisher's office straight to the mens' room down the hall.

You just never knew who'd come through the door. Once when Artie wasn't there, Around the World in 80 Days producer, Mike Todd, came bursting in with his hat on the back of his head and yelling "Where the hell is Buchwald?" I was happy to be able to tell him that he'd find Artie playing chess across the street in the bar of the Hôtel California.

Alas, the old Paris Herald Tribune we knew and loved is no more. It's gone forever. There's a newspaper now called the International Herald Tribune and it's quite impressive and worldly. The IHT is co-owned by the New York Times and the Washington Post with offices located on the outskirts of Paris in Neuilly-sur-Seine. It's a big business venture using columns, editorials, articles and news bureaus of both papers plus a steady flow off of the wires from agencies like Associated Press and Reuters. Although it's edited in Paris, the IHT is printed all over the world at the same time as in Paris.

No tacky offices like the Rue de Berri; they're elegantly installed with the lat-est up-to-the-minute equipment. One of the first oldtimers to see the new setup was the drama critic, Thomas Quinn Curtiss. "You wouldn't believe it, Maggi," he said. "It's incredible. They do everything by machine and they even have RUGS on the floor."

Like I said, Paris in the fifties was another world.

Maggi Nolan
Paris, 1998

Chapter One

When I first arrived in Paris on May 20, 1946, there was only one person I knew and one French phrase I could say without looking in a book. My friend was a former co-worker on New York's Madison Avenue, Dorothy Scher Schoenbrun, and my only French phrase was "*je ne parle pas français.*"

Dorothy had arrived almost a year before I had the proper papers in order to get permission to cross the ocean. Dorothy had the same pile of documents to fill out, but an easier time of it because of her past international fashion connections plus a husband awaiting on the other side of the Atlantic. I seemed to flounder around before I could wangle press accreditation, writing assignments and credentials acceptable to the proper authorities, but the big day arrived and I was on my way.

Travel from New York to France was by ship; luxury liners which had been turned into troop ships were being put to use to sail civilians across to Europe. Passengers were assigned bunks, one on top of the other from floor to ceiling with no such thing as a stateroom and barely enough room to breathe. I didn't care, I'd been dreaming about France for years and I was on my way.

In Paris Dorothy and I had a date to meet as soon as I arrived. She said her husband's office was the easiest to find as it was just off the Champs-Élysées on the Rue de Berri in the Paris *Herald Tribune* building known to everyone. Other American offices were there like the *Associated Press* and *Newsweek* as well as the editorial and business offices of the newspaper and their basement printing presses.

David was not yet famous for his CBS connection; he was a reporter for a tiny, unknown outfit called Overseas News Agency, which he managed in Paris after his war work with the Office of War Information was over. He had a miniscule bureau with one other reporter and a secretary and had just started part-time broadcasting for CBS Radio. (The world of television was not yet a reality.)

The minute Dorothy introduced me to David, I felt I'd known him all my life. Although I was taller than he, he instantly became my big brother. When I confessed that I didn't speak French except for my five-word phrase, he shook his head in brotherly disapproval, saying I had to add that I was sorry not to speak French, otherwise the French might think I didn't want to speak their language. So we added, "*je regrette beaucoup*" to my "*je ne parle pas français*" and I truly appreciated this bit of advice I got on my first day in France.

Dorothy and David immediately took their "little sister" in hand, starting by showing me around the recently-liberated sites of Paris. There were bullet scars everywhere, which gave me the shudders, but D. and D. were so used to them they didn't seem to notice. At that time things were scarce and hard to come by but David managed to get enough gas for his little ant-shaped Citroën to arrange thrilling excursions that newcomers such as I could never have known without him.

Times were unforgettably moving, like the night they took me to hear the incredible singer, Édith Piaf, who was straight off the streets and still unknown. Piaf was a tiny, bird-like creature with a giant-sized voice. As the little "sparrow" stood before us, her songs could bring tears to your eyes whether or not you understood the words. Her heart and soul seemed to come out with her songs in a voice that seemed to start from her toes.

A favorite stopping-off place for D. and D. early in the evening was a picturesque wine café on the 16th-century Place des Vosges, where Richelieu, Victor Hugo, and the Marquise de Sévigné once lived. The bar called Ma Bourgogne was run by a lusty fellow whose name was Louis, but he was nicknamed Louis the Burgundian. He was famous among wine experts all over the world and his bar was a place where wine lovers would gather to discuss vintages like they were talking about poetry. Fine wines were hard to come by in those early post-war days but Louis dug up part of his precious pre-war stock that he had hidden during the Occupation and international wine connoisseurs were coming back to Louis' door, where they'd always find him with his wife, son, dog and a cuddly cat.

Today, Louis the Burgundian has long gone from this world but Ma Bourgogne still stands on the Place des Vosges.

In my very first days in Paris I wore a gray-blue uniform I'd bought in Macy's with U.S. insignia sewn on the sleeve, because I'd been told that the insignia were necessary. Ready for my life as an American in Europe, I thought it looked quite spiffy and I was surprised when I noticed that I seemed to be the only non-military American wearing my U.S. emblem. Then, when I noticed "U.S. GO HOME" scrawled on walls around Paris, I was shocked that the city I wanted to love didn't love me back, after all that France and America had been through together. Then one day when I got up enough nerve to go into a bakery and point to the sugary bun in the window that I wanted to buy, the woman came from behind the counter waving a long *baguette* at me, while shouting furiously. All I understood in her tirade was *les Américains* and I walked out feeling like I'd been punched on the nose.

David explained her fury: our government had sent corn flour to replace their scarce or non-existent wheat flour. When bakers used the flour for classic *baguettes*, the result was a gray, pasty and tasteless disappointment. "But *I* didn't do it, David," I whimpered, and he pointed to the U.S. on my sleeve. I got the message, unsewed the emblem and from then on people looked at my face instead of my sleeve.

Of all things about France I learned from Dorothy and David during first moments in Paris, my introduction to champagne changed my life. Although I loved going to parties, I had a habit of saying "I don't drink" when I was offered a cocktail, just as I'd say "I don't smoke" when the cigarettes were handed around.

David insisted that sipping champagne was NOT drinking as I had known it where I came from and, besides, it was invented by a monk in a monestery in the 1600s who described the consumption of his nectar like "drinking stars." My very first sip was of Pommery & Greno, dated 1936 on the bottle. It was delicious and had nothing like the smell of bootleg gin or homemade beer in a barrel that I remembered from back home.

From that day on I became a champagne sipper learning how to tell the excellent from the ordinary by looking at color, texture and how the bubbles rose from the bottom of the glass.

The accreditation I had from Farrell Publishing Corp. allowed entrance to many events plus a press pass to the 1946 Peace Conference (complete with a dove-decorated press pin designed by Picasso) at the prestigious Palais du Luxembourg. International journalists crowded together each day to report what went on with the world's statesmen with household names like Britain's Attlee, America's Byrnes, Russia's Molotov, France's Bidault and Belgium's Spaak. It was very impressive but I knew immediately that I was out of my depth; I didn't know beans about world politics. Never mind, I thought, I'll just watch and listen while I didn't dare write a word.

Then, one day, I saw words written about me or, rather, about my hat. I'd created a turban for myself out of black net decorated with two white doves I plunked on top. (There were hatshops all over Paris where you could buy the makings for your own creations.) Every morning I'd put on the turban, knowing that I wouldn't have to worry about what my hair looked like underneath. No one commented on my creation until I heard a journalist say, "Here comes Maggi-the-hat" when I walked into the American Press Club. Joe Dynan, the club's president, jumped up and handed me a page from a French newspaper full of Peace Conference photo *actualités* and there I was with my hat smack-dab in the middle of the page.

"So which of these birds is Molotov, Maggi?" he laughed and then added, "the one on the left I suppose."

After that, I showed up at the Peace Conference in the same black net turban without the birds. One day I saw David Schoenbrun with a group of journalists surrounding General Bedell Smith. I walked over to David, who introduced me to the General when his impromptu press session was over. The General looked me over, smiled broadly and asked, "Are you the lady` who covered the war for *Harper's Bazaar?*"

Champagne...

Dorothy and David Schoenbrun were the only people I knew in Paris when I arrived in 1946.

That did it! I never went back. Fortunately for me, it was just at this time that I was contacted by Eleanor Darnton, former women's editor of the *New York Times*, who asked if I'd be a stringer for her newly-organized Women's National News Service, which supplied articles to women's editors in newspapers all over the United States. She wanted me to do a series of reports about women and children in post-war Europe.

What luck! The perfect assignment to justify my existence after my fiasco at the Luxembourg Palace. I started sending stories from Paris immediately about French women getting the vote, their increased numbers attending universities, lack of everyday needs in the market, etc. The feature about a beautiful escapee from a concentration camp who came back to head women's organizations was the hardest; I had chills when she showed me a camp number tattooed on her arm.

Packing just one suitcase for my travels, I stored everything else I owned in the basement of the hotel and off I went, with my typewriter in one hand and the suitcase in the other, little knowing what I'd find for American women's pages in newspapers in the countries where I'd be going.

The easy part was checking in with Information Officers at U.S. Embassies, where I'd get names of key women to talk to for my stories. The hard part was seeing for myself devastation everywhere and the privation of innocent women and children. Articles were mailed from Italy, Greece, Yugoslavia and Czechoslovakia, after my first ones from France. They were full of facts, statistics and figures straight from official sources but never went into the painful, miserable scenes I saw like baby beggars in rags roaming all alone. Nor did I have the heart to write about a young girl who lost both feet when they were frozen during her life as a partisan for Tito in the mountains of Yugoslavia.

Oh, there was plenty to write about , like the fact that Italian women had just gotten the right to vote in 1945–there were 25 women holding seats in the Assembly–that women were discouraged from seeking higher education which cost them more tuition than it did Italian men and were even discouraged from leaving their kitchens or the fields because they'd be considered "bad." Most of the homes in Rome didn't have running water but women would be arrested if they tried to wash their clothes in public fountains.

In Athens, through the U.S. Embassy, I received a cable from my sister that my father had died after his 44th birthday and my mother was returning to her mother. It seemed unreal, like my whole past was wiped out as though it had never existed. Sadness and depression settled heavily on me and, instead of sleeping, I'd stay awake remembering how rootless I'd felt as a child–rootless and unwanted.

I was born in California of a mother from Colorado and a father from Alabama. They'd married in Denver where my sister was born and I came along a year-and-a-half after when they wanted a boy. From the very first, I felt unwelcome and unloved; they called me "Sister" as though I didn't have a name (I was given my mother's name on my birth certificate). Two brothers were born two and four years after me before we moved to Seattle, Washington, where I went to school. That is "schools" because we changed addresses many times while my father moved up the ladder in his career.

He had only a high school education but, as a real go-getter, he went from office worker to book-keeper to top salesman in an air reduction company. He was a money-maker during a time people called The Depression. He liked saying, "we're living high-on-the-hog" when he entertained his friends endlessly, serving basement-made gin poured over lime sherbet in stemmed glasses.

My feelings of "unwantedness" were especially painful on New Year's Eve, which was my birthday. No one remembered or, if they did, they ignored it. It was party-time for my parents; extra help was hired to put up special decorations, blow up balloons, unpack the confetti, funny hats, streamers and noisemakers, plus prepare all the fancy food to be served. It was not for me; I was told to stay out of the way.

I was a loner from the beginning; writing poetry, swimming in Lake Washington, earning pocket money with chores so I could buy notebooks for my poems or go to the movies on Saturday for specially-priced matinees. When I was not quite 16 I left home and married a man 20 years older than I, but a few months after that I was divorced. At 17, I had my first office job, assisting the editor of a little poetry magazine called *Tumbleweed* in Portland, Oregon. And that led to a job writing copy for a local advertising agency when World War II began, thus inspiring me to try my luck in New York.

Still in my teens, I arrived in New York with writing samples under my arm and high hopes in my head. Jobs were easy to find and so were young, attractive men

Champagne...

who wanted to get married. I found myself saying "Yes" to a naval engineer who left after our courthouse ceremony and a romantic weekend in the country. It was unreal; he sailed away on a ship without a name to parts unknown. We never lived together and I went to work as usual, wondering why I had been so foolish. Later we agreed to a "friendly divorce."

Writing light, insipid, advertising copy during the war gave feelings of guilt which I tried to abate by working for the Red Cross and war relief organizations, but these were days of discontent, knowing something was missing but not knowing what it was. Another marriage followed: a brilliant Yale man called away on a secret mission to Los Alamos. He managed to get back to New York to spend time with me in our hotel suite on lower Fifth Avenue, but he was secretive, moody and jealous of imaginary rivals, refusing to realize that his only "rival" was my work.

I was in the middle of this marriage failure when Dorothy Scher Schoenbrun became so important in my life. It was a joy working with her as a team at Lester Harrison Associates at 44th and Madison. She was the art director and I was the copy chief, despite our tender years. We didn't kid ourselves that we had top executive jobs because of our outstanding genius. Women got positions such as ours in those days because the men had gone off to war–while advertising went on in slick magazines as before.

Dorothy didn't know it at the time but she was inspiring me to make my way to France after the war. Every day, after our conference on ideas, layouts, artwork, copy and final proofs, she'd talk about her husband and their plans to settle in Paris. She'd show me letters, cards and photos David Schoenbrun managed to mail from wherever he happened to be with the Office of War Information. She had endless stories to tell about her life in Europe before the war, studying art, attending Parsons School of Design on the Place des Vosges, her marriage to David in Vienna and their flight from there just before the war began.

One day before she left for France, I confessed that I had decided to go to Paris and would see her there as soon as I could get the right papers filled out and, no matter how long it took, I'd be there despite the fact that there was no one waiting for me. She laughed and said, "You never know, Maggi, you never know."

My sleepless nights in Belgrade and Prague took my thoughts through my unhappy childhood to the very moment I received the cable from my sister. If I felt "rootless" before, what was I now that my father was dead and my mother living in a city I'd never visited with a woman I didn't know. Facing assignments from the Women's National News Service with a letter from Eleanor Darnton delivered in Belgrade, saying my stories were good and enclosing a check, I knew I had to finish my assignments, and I did, but my heart wasn't in it. All I wanted to do was get back to Paris–and STAY there.

In Paris, three years after my arrival, I was back to the starting point: looking for a job. Top on my list of visits to make was David Schoenbrun's office to see what was happening on the Rue de Berri. David had not changed his business address but he had certainly improved his surroundings. He had roomy space for a buzzing staff separated from his private office behind glass panels. He was now a full-time broadcaster for CBS Radio, like Ed Murrow in London, with promise of CBS Television right around the corner. His background, experience, contacts and knowledge of France made him the perfect man for the job.

David greeted me in a big-brother manner, looking me up and down. "Well, if it isn't the fancy-tailed Maggi-bird," he said, referring to my suit with its pinched-in waist and a jaunty flounce in the back. He motioned me to sit down, brought me up-to-date on Dorothy and their new baby, Lucy, plus their new apartment that I hadn't seen yet. Then I excused myself for taking up his office time and confessed that I was looking for a job and hoped he'd give it some thought.

"You shouldn't have any trouble, Maggi-bird," he said, "if you'd just stop flitting around." I got up to leave and we were saying goodbye when I looked out the window and saw a strange sight in an upper office across the courtyard.

"David," I asked, "am I seeing things or is there really a crazy Frenchman standing on his desk while he dictates to his secretary?" David looked up with a lusty guffaw.

"He's not a crazy Frenchman, he's a crazy American, " he laughed. David forgot that we'd just said goodbye as he started to explain the man upstairs was Jim Nolan, Promotion Director for the *Herald Tribune*, from Pennsylvania and a very nice guy whom I should get to know. David took charge now, picking up his phone to call Jim's secretary. When he told her that Mr. Schoenbrun wanted to see Mr. Nolan right away, we saw Jim jump off his desk and within minutes he was standing at David's door. He had a smile that I can only describe as ear-to-ear, readily admitting that he had been peeping into David's office from his perch, wondering who that French girl was down there. David loved this; he couldn't wait to tell Jim that I thought he was a Frenchman although, being a diplomat, he didn't mention the word "crazy."

Jim and I started talking a mile a minute about nothing at all while David just stood there beaming. I decided, right then, that Jim was full of charm and good humor and was even good-looking, despite his thick glasses. I also noted that he looked at my pinched-in waistline as he talked.

"This is FATE," announced David. "You two really ought to get together." This brought me back to reality with a jolt.

"David," I said between my teeth, "I'm looking for a job."

"Looking for a job?" Jim chimed in. "Well, if you know anything about advertising, there's a job for you upstairs." He went on to explain his project was to get out a special supplement for the paper on the Marshall Plan. He needed someone who knew copywriting and could make rough layouts. David seemed to be bouncing up and down now, rattling on and on about my big-time job in New York City as a copy chief and blah-blah-blah, until I felt my face was on fire.

Jim listened intently, then looked at his watch saying he was late for an appointment but if I'd show up in his office the first thing in the morning, he'd tell me all about the job. Then he was gone as fast as he'd come in, leaving me staring at the door. But David was all over me like an Indian blanket, not about the job that I apparently had, but pouring out every reason there was for me to marry this fellow who was perfect for me in every way. "He's the guy for you...single...near your age...runs around a lot and should settle down...you too, Maggi...."

As soon as I got a chance to get a word in I reminded David that I wasn't looking for a "crazy American," I was looking for a job and it looked like I might have one for which I'd be forever grateful. Amazing, I thought when I left, less than thirty minutes had passed since I stepped into David's office and it looked like I had a job in his building.

In my room at the Hôtel Duminy, around the corner from the Place Vendôme, I went to bed early with curlers in my hair and determination to be on the Rue de Berri the first thing in the morning. Setting out my clothes, I picked my most businesslike black suit with a high-necked black blouse which I'd brighten up with my pearl necklace. This was like my Manhattan career girl's uniform complete with gloves and a little black felt hat, not forgetting a shine on my shoes, which I got with face cream because I didn't have any polish.

After my *café au lait* with a crusty roll and jam the next morning, I was on my way to the Rue de Berri and arrived just before nine o'clock, which to me was "the first thing in the morning" but when I stepped into Jim Nolan's office, a formidable-looking creature looked up from her desk, without a smile, and informed me that Mr. Nolan never arrived before ten-thirty, and sometimes later.

This was my first look at Hélène Surewitch, a Polish-born Parisian of a certain age, who would have had the power to frighten the daylights out of me if I hadn't been so interested in getting a job. She gave me a look that might ice over a volcano when she announced that I could wait if I wished. She was wide in her chair, had brownish-grey hair pulled into a bun on her neck, and a hard look on her face that seemed to tell me she was ready to loathe me the minute I came in the door.

I stood around awhile, looking at piles of papers, proofs, layouts, folders, and typical material in advertising departments everywhere. Then I looked out the window to get an idea of the angle from which Jim had first set eyes on me the afternoon before. Standing around some more, I finally had enough of this waiting game and got the nerve to say so to this unfriendly creature.

"Look," I said, "I was told yesterday to come here the first thing in the morning and, to me, that is now. I just came to see what the job is and to decide if I can handle it." These must have been magic words to her because she immediately stopped what she was doing, assured me that "the boss" would be in soon, and actually looked me in the eye as she talked.

What followed made it clear that she knew exactly why I was there. She motioned me to sit down while she explained that the person who was supposed to write the text of the Marshall Plan supplement had gone back to America and they needed immediate help to fill in the space that had already been sold. She took out folders to show me where everything stood at the moment, but while she was explaining, I could tell by her face what she was thinking: she was certain that I couldn't handle the job.

Never mind, it wasn't the first time that I had to prove myself professionally to someone who hadn't worked with me before. I could tell that she had made up her mind that I was overdressed and undertalented, just by the way she was looking at me and saying things she was certain were over my head. But then, like magic, she changed when we began to discuss the actual work at hand. We were talking business–her business–and we were managing very well. I knew I'd made real progress when she told me I could call her Surey.

Still sometimes her voice would reveal that she still thought the job was too difficult for me as she spread page after page of the supplement layout on the desk, indicating what was missing: "Here's the coal mining page...here's the steel page...here's the space for petroleum." If she expected me to faint at the task, she didn't know what writing jobs I'd done before stepping through the door. Wartime advertising agencies spent a lot of time on institutional advertising and I had written about optical product designing, industrial progress, diamond cutting, wartime factories, plus the series I'd recently finished on postwar problems facing Europe. So I knew that if I had enough facts on any subject, I could put it all together in the allotted space.

(Ah, but I have to admit I wrote some real lulus such as the series on girdles that started "Diana, the Daintiness Girdle with the Detachable Crotch," and a series for Bali Bras when they introduced different cup sizes. One advertisement read "A is for ALICE, tiny and slight. B is for BETTY, just about right. C is for CHARLOTTE, not quite so small. D is for DOTTIE, more ample than all.")

Facing the frown on Surey's face, I took one page of the supplement layouts in hand, asking questions that any copywriter would ask the account executive before taking on an assignment. She was really thawing out now and by the time "the boss" breezed in she seemed almost warm.

Jim was in an exuberant mood and his spirits seemed to soar even higher when he saw that Surey and I had been discussing the Marshall Plan project. After he shuffled through his morning mail and messages, he asked me if I'd already started to work. No interviews? No résumé? No filling out of forms? Thinking back, he must have been desperate to get the job done. And the look on Surey's face, plus the big build-up David had given me, seemed to be enough for him to give me a try. Now it was up to me to show him and Surey that I knew what I was doing.

Chapter Two

We became a miniature advertising agency with Jim as the account executive, Maggi, the copy chief, and Surey, the office translator/manager/secretary. Artwork and photography came from freelancers as they were needed. We had a primitive office with two-and-a-half desks, a drawing board that could be folded to stand behind a door when not in use, and two mechanical typewriters with a French keyboard for Surey and an American one for me. Our rickety chairs looked like odd rejects from other *Herald Tribune* offices.

You can learn a lot about people working an elbow away, day after day. Surey, I was certain, had a crush on "the boss" and would work herself to a frazzle to please him. It didn't take long to figure out that Jim was an expert contact man with enough charm to sell the proverbial iceboxes to Eskimos. But, oh, if it came to follow-up or attention to detail, he wasn't there. He liked to come into the office announcing the space he sold and to whom, and it was up to Surey and me to do the rest.

I didn't care. I was doing work I liked and getting compliments plus a little beige-colored envelope every week, that gave me enough to live on. In those days, my spacious top- floor room at the Duminy, overlooking the orange chimney pots on rooftops for blocks around, was one dollar a night and that included my Continental breakfast with coffee, milk, sugar, roll, butter and jam.

Jim followed a certain fixed routine on the Rue de Berri. After he checked into the office and looked over the mail, he would disappear for awhile. Surey could always find him if she needed a paper to sign, a decision to make, or if there was missing information on a contract or for text and all those things that only "the boss" could handle. First she'd check the bar of the Hôtel California to see if he was playing chess with a young newcomer to the *Herald Tribune*, Art Buchwald, straight out of military service. The bar was just across the street from the paper and was like a home away from home for all.

If Jim wasn't there, she'd check a little Italian restaurant around the corner called Tangage, where he might be twirling spaghetti with novelist Irwin Shaw, photographer Bob Capa or dancer-actor Gene Kelly. If "the boss" was neither here nor there, she'd send a messenger over to the Champs-Élysées to a sidewalk café, where most of "the boys" from the Rue de Berri liked to sit in cane chairs and watch the girls going by on foot or bicycle. Jim, more often than not, was located right there oggling the hours away through his horn-rimmed glasses. When I knew him better I said his glasses should be called "horny-rimmed" and he should be careful not to make a spectacle of himself.

After countless hours of hard work, we had our Marshall Plan supplement ready for *Herald Tribune* distribution. The ink had barely dried on it before we were busy on a series of promotional and institutional advertisements to appear in the New York edition of the paper, presenting such products as French perfumes, cognacs, and champagne from Champagne, the place on the map where the monk invented the drink. This was the beginning of the Champagne country's campaign to keep wine producers from calling their drink "champagne" even if it didn't come from Champagne. Alas, they lost.

Surey was an excellent co-worker, totally unafraid of long hours of toil. Working with Jim was more difficult as his moods changed often without explanation. Surey knew him well. One day when he was very low, for no reason, I thought, Surey explained as soon as he went out, that he was searching for a new gimmick for the next supplement, and hadn't come up with an idea. New York advertisements kept us busy but there wasn't enough profit for Jim to keep his interest. His worry was what to do for an encore after the Marshall Plan.

During the day, I wracked my brains trying to think of something, and before worktime was through I thought of something he might like, which I wrote down on a piece of paper and set out on his desk for him to find when he came back from wherever he was. I typed: "NEXT YEAR–1950–WILL BE THE 2000TH ANNIVERSARY OF THE CITY OF PARIS. DO YOU THINK THAT IT WOULD MAKE A GOOD THEME FOR A SUPPLEMENT?"

When Jim came in at the end of the day, he read my note and gave a big rodeo-type "YAAA-WHOOO" while he started to do a jig. I was amazed by his quick change in mood, but pleased that he obviously liked my idea. Surey didn't bat an eyelid; she was accustomed to these outbursts. "What do you think of this, Surey?" he asked. "What about a supplement to celebrate the 2000th birthday of Paris? Would THAT sell ads–boy, would that sell ads." He left the office to go upstairs to the newspaper's executive suite to check out the idea with the directors, without telling Surey where he got the brainstorm that made him holler.

He didn't have to tell Surey; she knew. We laughed about it when he was gone and I told her it didn't matter where the idea came from as long as it gave us work to do. "And puts the boss in a good mood," she added.

Jim wasn't gone very long and when he came back it was obvious by the look on his face that the project had been approved. In high spirits, he invited me to join him and Art Buchwald for a drink at the California Bar and then accompany

Champagne...

him to the Hôtel Lancaster up the street, where the owner, Émile Wolf, was giving a little cocktail party for Americans staying there and for favorites from the *Tribune* building.

Of course I accepted. Jim was in such a good mood that I enjoyed his company. It seemed that everyone we met was told the big news by Jim, but he neglected to say where he got the idea. Never mind, when he asked me what I wanted to drink, I raised one eyebrow and said, "I drink only champagne."

From then on, Jim and I often lunched together, talking shop and sometimes joining journalists across the street for drinks after work. The conversations and chit-chat were always jovial, never serious or personal. After shop-talk, it was joke time with lots of laughs. And then he asked me out to dinner. I'd been expecting him to do that, as we seemed to be getting along so well without really getting a chance to be ourselves, by ourselves. He always gave me the impression that he was busy in the evenings when he got calls from ladies during office hours, and turned on some heavy verbal charm when he got on the phone. When he was out and Surey had to take messages, she really got on her high horse, showing contempt for her task and grumbling "another silly fool" when she hung up.

For our first dinner date, I asked Jim to meet me in the bar of the Hôtel Lotti on the Rue de Castiglione down the street from my hotel, because I didn't want gentlemen appearing at my door. My hotel was a small family hotel, run by Monsieur Duminy himself, who was always at his desk and knew everyone by name. I remember taking special care to be glamorous that night, picking out a black dinner dress I'd bought at Molyneux during their sale of original models, sold for next-to-nothing because they had paraded in a collection for weeks. This unusual number had a stand-up collar in the back, but in the front it had an inch-wide divide showing skin right down to a wide, waist-pinching belt. Decked out in this little dream I added some droopy earrings, completing the total change from my usual sedate office attire. I remember this so clearly because of Jim's reaction when we met and sat at a corner table for a drink.

He sort of stumbled into a chair leg when he sat down, mumbled our order to the waiter and didn't stop staring at my neckline to the belt. It was just too much for him; he finally blurted out, "How the hell do you keep that dress together?"

I probably sounded like a dressmaker or a seasoned seamstress as I tried to explain that *haute couture* was an art, the work of an architect, ingenious designs that started on the inside of the dress. By the time you had hooked up all the inner hooks, snapped all the snaps and zipped up the zippers, it was like wearing two dresses when the outside dress was fastened. He either wasn't listening or didn't understand, because he just kept staring until his glasses looked like they were steaming over.

Jim picked out a little bistrot in Montmartre for dinner. We drove in his Citroën up the winding, narrow streets to a place near the Sacré-Coeur, that looked like it came out of an old French movie setting with red checked tablecloths, candles in wine bottles, the menu written in chalk on a blackboard, waiters wearing big, dark blue aprons and *le patron* behind the bar bursting into song every once in a while.

After a delicious dinner and several glasses of heavy red wine, we strolled all around the top of Montmartre, and around and around the stark white Sacré-Coeur Basilica that stood like a giant wedding cake, reaching toward the black sky. The cobblestone streets and tiny old buildings looked like Utrillo paintings brought to life. Walking back to the car, Jim pointed out a garage-like structure which he said was an art gallery run by a character he knew called Hervé, who'd been in the French underground during the war, but now sold paintings done by local outdoor artists from the Place du Tertre, a few steps away.

(This man became Hervé Odermatt with an elegant art gallery on the fashionable Rue du Faubourg Saint-Honoré, selling masterpieces to collectors, discovering and promoting new painters, and being seen in the company of socialites and celebrities in exclusive places down through the years, even to this day.)

Back in the car, we drove around Montmartre, passing the Moulin de la Galette, the 13th century windmill on the winding Rue Lepic, which had inspired

"Maggi the Hat" printed on the front page of Paris Actualitès, covering the Peace Conference, August 1946

La mode a fait valoir ses droits : voici un chapeau bleu « up to date ». Il supporte deux blanches colombes de « la Paix » qui éclairent le sourire de cette brune ravissante.

artists like Renoir and Toulouse-Lautrec. We turned around and around some more until we were back at the peak of the Butte again. Jim parked the car with the church behind us and all of Paris below. This was the first time I'd seen this spot at night, totally deserted as not many people had automobiles and, if they had, gas was not easy to get.

The scene was breathtaking. We stayed there for heaven knows how long. Jim started to talk and didn't stop, as though he wanted me to know everything there was to know about his life before the evening was over. Starting from the beginning when he was born in Reading, Pennsylvania, 34 years before, he listed the fancy schools he'd attended. Then he went on about how he'd loved his wartime public relations stint in the U.S. Air Force, stationed in London, because it gave him the chance to hang around the big brass and be in on top secret information.

It was clear that he was out to impress me and I found his efforts quite touching while, at the same time, I was inspired to tell him a bit about myself in sharp contrast. So I told him I never finished high school, but I was a good swimmer and once I'd won a posture contest. However he was so serious that I felt ashamed at trying to tease him about his place-and-name dropping, so I let him continue the story of his life.

Before the evening was over up there on the hill, I found myself confiding in him about my life and telling him things I'd never put in words to anyone. I dug deep, confessing my rootless feelings and then, yes, confessed I'd been married, not once, but three times. He chuckled and said that I was "one up" on him because he had been married twice himself. He never asked me the details of 1, 2, and 3, brushing them off as "wartime hysteria" and "teenage mistakes," which was not exactly accurate, but I found his conclusions very touching.

He didn't ask any more details, but went on telling me about his own life. His first wedding was a gigantic, very social affair in a Catholic Church in Philadelphia with hundreds of relatives, friends and acquaintances in attendance. Receptions, dinners, cocktail parties for days and plenty of reports in the newspapers' society pages. "You know, all the damned trimmings." The second was to a New York beauty, also a society girl, whom he met in a supper club where she was singing, more for amusement than money.

When he was talked out, he took my hand when he saw a sad look on my face. In a lowered voice he told me not to worry about the past because all that mattered was the future. His words soothed me and his reaction to my confessions of marriage mistakes made me feel like a great weight had been lifted from my shoulders. Here's a man who accepts me as I am, I was thinking, and David's words about Jim being the man for me came rushing through my head.

Jim started up the car to leave this lovely spot, but first leaned over on the steering wheel to look down at Paris by night, twinkling with star-like lights. "Look at that," he said, "Paris at our feet. Great things awaiting us down there."

I think I just said, "Mmmm," in reply. I didn't know what the future would hold but I did know one thing: I was smitten.

After our first evening on top of the world at the Butte Montmartre, Jim and I spent much more time together and began to accept invitations as a twosome from married couples at the *Herald Tribune* and the Schoenbruns, who were doing more and more entertaining. Then Jim would get together with Art Buchwald for chess games, followed by dinners with me and Art's new girlfriend. She was a pert and lively blonde, Ann McGarry, from Warren, Pennsylvania, and had a Paris public relations job for Pierre Balmain.

During office hours, we were the same as before, sticking strictly to business. I doubt if Surey, smart as she was, knew what was going on. After hours was different when we both started making pointed remarks on the importance of settling down, having a family and living a real life. Jim often referred to mutual friends who seemed so happily married, while I'd point out how ideal a couple Dorothy and David were, now that they had little Lucy.

It wasn't long before Jim asked me to marry him, which I expected because we'd seemed like two halves suddenly become whole, working and playing together day and night. (Not ALL night because Jim wasn't allowed in my family hotel and his bachelor apartment in a Left Bank gatehouse had no room for two.) The marriage proposal happened when we were having a late lunch at the favorite Italian hangout around the corner from the *Trib*. We'd had a business meeting with an important French executive who'd been tough with me at first, but charming at the end of the encounter. Jim complimented me on handling a fellow who obviously didn't think a lady could write his industrial copy. I laughed and told him I was used to that and repeated what General Smith had said to me at the Peace Conference about covering the war for *Harper's Bazaar*.

As we were both chuckling, he wrote something on the back of a business card and put it on the table in front of me. "Dear Maggi–Will you pls. think about marrying me? Yrs very truly, J. Nolan–PS Katlick Kids."

I looked at the card, gulped and swallowed a few times and then picked it up and added on the bottom, "Kommie Kids." He laughed and added "OK" and so I was engaged to be married, taking the proposal seriously, but leaving the PS as a joke coming from a twice-married man who never went to Church. It might sound unromantic, but we shook hands on the deal and went back to work.

Back in the office I tried to keep my mind on our projects but my head was in a whirl and I wanted to run down to David's office and tell him the news. "This is real. We think alike, we work as a team, we'll have a family and build a good life. He knows all about me–no secrets. He's eight years older, just the right age, and we know the same people, have the same interests. And we work well together," I kept repeating, "we're a team. That's what matters. This is reality, not an escape, and it means roots, my very own roots."

When Jim left the office on an afternoon errand, I could feel Surey staring at me, so I finally looked up and met her eye-to-eye. She gave one of her very rare smiles that she kept for special occasions and said, "*Alors*, when are you two going to get married?"

In Paris, then as now, agreeing to get married and getting it done are two different matters. I'd heard that it wasn't easy, but we found out it was impossible for us. Americans had to have resident permits and post their intentions for two weeks in the public office in their residential district. Although I had press cards and *laissez-passer* permits, I had no *carte de séjour* to declare that I was an official resident of Paris. Jim had nothing but his American passport, which gets nowhere when you want to get married in France.

We were told it would take weeks, maybe months, to get our papers in order, but Jim was having nothing of that. He was convinced that, with all the important people he knew in England, we could get married in London without any delay. So off we flew to London with high hopes that we'd be married immediately, with the help of his friends. The idea was fine by me; I looked forward to a ceremony in English instead of French.

Jim's charming friends opened the doors of their beautiful home to us, served cocktails in the garden, lunch at a long, highly-polished dining table, which was absolutely delightful. By afternoon our host, a very important man in the government, had made inquiries and came back to us with a long face and a short report, "Impossible."

It was a lovely visit despite our disappointment and at the end of the day we headed back to the air terminal to fly back to France. That night, however, all flights had been cancelled because of bad weather and we were stuck in Kensington's Majestic Hotel, next to the terminal, until the next flight out in the morning.

I have special reasons why I can never forget the name of the Majestic Hotel: it was the first time we'd ever spent the whole night together; it had gotten so cold that you could see your breath in front of your face, the only heat in our room would come from an antique heater if it was fed shillings. But neither of us had any shillings, so Jim said we'd just have to go to bed and stay there until time to take the plane. That's what we did and that is the night we made our first baby.

(More than eight years later when I passed that hotel with my two daughters, Cathy looked out and said, in French, "Look, Mother, there's a hotel called Majestic. Does that mean they make magic in there?" I said something like "perhaps" and vowed to tell her the story one day.)

Back in Paris Jim began to gather information about other places in Europe where officials might be easier on Americans wanting to be husband and wife. Several friends told us the same story: Vienna, Austria, was the best place if you had a valid passport and, if you'd been married before, you had to present your divorce papers. That sounded fine with us so we made plans to go as soon as we could. Before we'd gotten our train tickets, Jim began to get moody and silent, which made me think he'd changed his mind. Upset as I was, I knew I had to get at the truth, so I faced him with my fears.

He confessed, a bit sheepishly, that he really did want to get married, but he also wanted to go skiing. I laughed, relieved that this was the only problem, and suggested that he easily could do both by skiing first, while I finished up some work with Surey and I could meet him in Vienna afterward. His mood changed immediately, and he was like a little kid going about making the skiing and travel plans. After he was off on his skiing holiday, Surey told me that he went skiing at the end of every year until he met me and probably missed going as it was now February.

Everything worked out beautifully. When I arrived in Vienna he was waiting at the train station to meet me and had already checked into our hotel. But he was in a strange mood again and I had to talk him into telling me why. He finally told me he'd had some bad spills and ended up being black, blue, purple, yellow and green, up and down half of his body. I told him he ought to be thankful that he was still around and in one piece. Cheering up, he joked that we'd have a colorful wedding.

When we got to the hotel I had a problem of my own. I was experiencing half a "curse," a whole "curse" or no "curse" at all, which was something that had

Vienna turned out to be the easiest place for Americans to be married in Europe at the time. Jim and Maggi Nolan: husband and wife.

never happened to me. I confided my upset and we ended up just holding hands in mutual sympathy.

Following the advice of fellow Americans who'd married in Vienna, we started the step-by-step procedures. When I brought out my divorce papers (only the last one was necessary) I was surprised to see Jim didn't have his. "I'll just say I'm Catholic," he announced, and when I asked him why he hadn't told me to do the same, he said he didn't think I could lie convincingly. Thinking back, that was probably a left-handed compliment, but I was upset at the time, especially when the hatchet-faced lady making out our official papers gave me a black look as she handed back my Final Decree, translated into German for the occasion.

After a few days, we had a civil wedding ceremony in a business office in the German language. All I had to do was say "Jah" or "Yah" when the time came, which I knew by the expressions on faces and the little nudge that Jim gave me. If we hadn't been given a certificate to prove it, I couldn't have believed that we were really married.

Back in Paris we checked into the Hôtel California to be together while hunting for a place to live. Jim's bruises were disappearing and he seemed his happy, charming self, but my trouble went on and I was upset to be starting a marriage this way. Jim was very sweet and husband-like, driving me to the American Hospital in Neuilly to see a doctor recommended by friends at the *Herald Tribune*. The doctor was a specialist for women, and as we discussed my condition he smiled knowingly and asked if my husband worked at the *Herald Tribune*. When

Married in Vienna.
No time for a honeymoon; we had
to get back to the *Herald Tribune*.

I told him we both worked there, he put his pen down and predicted that we were going to have our first child.

"Do you know I've delivered about a dozen *Herald Tribune* babies? You all seem to be having babies over there."

After the necessary tests and examinations, I was told that there was a baby on the way, despite other symptoms, and that if I'd go to bed for awhile everything would be all right. I didn't tell him that I had so much work waiting on my desk that I couldn't stop.

Back at the hotel directly across the street from the office, Jim agreed that I should keep working but take it easy. A few times during the following weeks, I'd go back to the hotel from the office, fearing the worst. Finally Jim said, "Don't worry, if you lose this one we'll have another." But all I could say was that I wanted THIS one.

It wasn't long before we moved into a furnished apartment; the first in a series of rented, furnished homes. Each place had a crazy story of its own. The first was a duplex on the Boulevard Gouvion Saint-Cyr, where the widowed owner lived in servants' quarters just off the kitchen. We never saw her but Anne-Marie, the maid Jim brought from his bachelor apartment, saw the woman too much and she wasn't happy every time this intruder passed through "her" kitchen. It was an invasion of her territory and she didn't hesitate to let us know of her outrage every day.

We tried to placate her but it didn't help; she took to talking to herself in a loud voice that could be heard all over the apartment. "That woman" had marched on the scrubbed floor before it was dry, "that woman" had stolen a piece of chicken, "that woman" had put her finger in "my apple sauce." We didn't know if her accusations were true, nor did we want to ask the landlady so we let Anne-Marie rave on.

Jim had a good friend living in a huge studio across the street: an American composer named Alexander Matlowsky, whom he called Sandy. He visited us a lot, playing on our baby grand piano, spending hours over a chess board with Jim, or sharing our Anne-Marie-cooked meals, which were simple but delicious. When he wasn't with us, he often invited big crowds to his spacious studio, where he served wine and cheese. Once he had a friend staying with him, Eartha Kitt, a singer-actress who was in Paris to appear in a play with Orson Welles. She loved to wrap a cotton turban around her head, put on a great big apron and cook up a storm in his kitchen. We could see her from across the street.

Sandy's wine and cheese parties brought together musicians, artists, journalists and actors of various nationalities. It was at one of these get-togethers that I noticed Art Buchwald and Ann McGarry were getting serious, and there was a real romance going on. I never dreamed that I'd go in and out of business with Ann the following year.

Chapter Three

In the early days of our marriage, Jim was very candid with me about his past unhappy relationships with women. While telling me, he'd always assure me that he'd do better this time. His sentiments pleased me but sometimes his confidences were hard for me to take when he talked about his relationships with men. He told me that he'd been attracted to men since he was very young, especially men of talent. He showed me an old photo of him when he was very young, in a boat with a very virile, handsome fellow, whom he described as a prize-winning sportsman he'd known at school. "I really had a crush on that guy," he told me, leaving me shocked and wondering why he found it necessary to tell his pregnant wife such things.

When I was older and wiser, I understood that this is a phase in a man's life that is not unusual, part of growing up and finding himself. But I never understood why he told me during a difficult pregnancy. Then I found myself wondering whether Jim still had crushes on men. The thought wouldn't go away as his friends, neighbors and fellow workers paraded through my head. I remembered a day in the office when a freelance artist came in saying Jim told him he'd leave a package for him. I didn't know anything about it, but Surey did. She opened a drawer, brought out a box from an expensive men's store and handed it to him without a word.

The young man opened the box in front of us and seemed girlish with pleasure. I watched him pick up the ties to admire, to stroke and hold up for us to see. He was young and slim, with an angelic smile on a face framed in silky blond hair. He was a good artist, whose finished work I'd always found satisfactory. I hadn't studied him as a person before Jim told me about his attraction to talented men; now I saw him in a different light. Surey had always said that she couldn't stand this fellow, but she'd never told me why.

It was around this time that I was in for another shock. One day at lunch Jim reached in his pocket, took photos out of an envelope and slid them across the table to me, saying "Look at these. Isn't this the spitting image of me?" The pictures were of a little boy about five years old, who looked exactly like a baby Jim without glasses. When I looked up at Jim he announced, "That's my son in England."

How I kept calm I don't know because I was feeling betrayed. I kept saying to myself, "He has a son, he has a son," while Jim went on matter-of-factly, explaining that the little boy was a love child he'd had with an English girl whose husband was away in the service. Jim said the husband had agreed to accept the boy as his own. If this was so, I wondered why the mother was sending photos to Jim; but I didn't ask. All this time I thought our child would be Jim's first. I was devastated.

Upsetting thoughts were easily put aside in those days with so much to do, interesting people to see and charming places to go. After a busy, successful work week, we'd often take off in Jim's trusty Citroën for jaunts around the countryside to "change our ideas" as the French say. Jim made our plans for trips to favorite places he'd visited many times in his childhood. Whatever he suggested was fine with me as I hadn't seen anything of France and enjoyed Jim's pleasure in showing me around.

Sometimes we'd take a quick trip to Versailles and be back by the end of the day, sometimes we'd weekend in Normandy and, when we could take enough time away from work, we'd go to Brittany's Quimper and Dinard, where Jim had spent youthful summers. Deauville, in Normandy, was our frequent destination, where we could check into the Hôtel Normandy and take sidetrips to Trouville and Honfleur.

A trip to Dinard stands out in my memory because of the beginning of Jim's endless stories about his father, whom he'd nicknamed "the old man." Driving to Dinard, I got acquainted with Jim's father through Jim's talk. J. Bennett Nolan, the Pennsylvania historian, author of books, member of prestigious organizations, friend of the famous, recipient of medals and citations galore. At the same time, I saw another facet of the man I'd married when he'd report the many disappointments he'd heaped on his father, especially the schools from which he'd been expelled down through the years. Every time he'd get kicked out of boarding school, he said, his father would pick him up and enroll him in another.

This sounded to me like his father guessed in advance that Jim would be expelled, and was ready with a new school. As for Jim, it seemed to me that he had been a little boy trying to tell his father that he'd rather be at home. Listening without comment was easy for me until we were walking along the Dinard beach and Jim showed me where he'd often played. He said he didn't have playmates as he was always with "the old man," but on the days that his father had card games with grown-ups, Jim was on his own. He bragged that his favorite pastime was running up and down the beach to find kids building sand castles. He said he got a big thrill jumping right in the middle of the castles, stomping them flat and then running away.

"Oh, Jim, that's awful," I said and he shot back that it was not awful but fun; the bigger the castle, the more fun it was.

This saddened me. All I could see was an unhappy little boy trying to draw attention to himself. With all his paternal stories, he never talked about his mother except to answer my questions with "Yes," she was alive and "Yes," she'd been on all his childhood holidays. I felt I had a picture of his father but couldn't imagine what his mother was like.

At first I thought that Jim had moved to France to live a life of his own away from his father but that proved wrong; J. Bennett Nolan was in the habit of visiting France at least once a year by ship for a few weeks' stay. In early Spring he was on his way to Paris with a free ocean voyage in exchange for ship lectures on subjects such as Benjamin Franklin's life during his diplomatic post as first American Ambassador to France.

Jim said that he'd be arriving for his usual stay at the Hôtel France et Choiseul on the Rue Saint-Honoré, but he didn't say exactly when, so I was taken aback one morning in the office when a short fellow in a rumpled jacket, tennis shoes and a visor cap stepped in the door announcing, "I am Mr. Nolan." "This can't be J. Bennett Nolan," I thought. After all I'd heard about him I expected a tall, distinguished gentleman in impeccable clothes with a little rosette in his lapel, showing that he was high-ranking in the French *Légion d'Honneur*. So much for my image of "the old man."

When Jim came in, I was amazed to hear his father talking to his 34-year-old son like he was a child, making Jim a little boy again. From their conversation, it was plain that Papa planned to take over our lives during his stay. He wanted to know exactly what we were doing, where we were going and with whom, as though it was understood that he'd be included in everything, instructing Jim to pick him up at the hotel every day so he wouldn't have to bother about transportation.

As soon as he left I asked Jim if he always went around in the outfits like the one he was wearing. "Naw," Jim laughed, explaining that today's clothes were those he wore when he went to old bookshops to make bargains or to the flea market in search of brick-a-brack to ship home. Nevertheless, in those days of careful attire, his get-up was shocking in our neighborhood and he must have looked like a strange *numéro* to everyone on the Rue de Berri.

From the time his father arrived in Paris, Jim fell right in with his wishes, which was sometimes inconvenient if not downright annoying. Happily, however, several times our adventures with "the old man" turned out to be amusing. We lunched in a château of an ageing American heiress who'd married a titled Frenchman no longer on the scene. Baroness Eva de Gourgaud was a real *numéro* with white doves flying in and out of her bedroom windows, which she welcomed because "I like their company." She wore flat, brightly-colored sandals which she said she bought by the dozen in a shop on 42nd Street in New York, because they were the most comfortable shoes she'd ever had on her feet and you could get them in more colors than there were in a rainbow.

Her château was crowded with treasures in furniture, art, porcelain and silver. When we entered her dining room for lunch, she called attention to the exquisite rug on the floor, saying "I had to take it back from the Louvre Museum; my other dining room rug was all worn out."

Another *numéro* in Mr. Nolan's collection was a cousin of a certain age named Marie Stewart McGrew, married to a distinguished-looking fellow named Tarn. When we went to cousin Marie's ornate apartment on the Quai de Béthune, the routine was always the same. Marie had her butler, Henri, serve a martini to every guest, whether or not it was wanted. Then, when she'd see someone's glass nearly empty, she'd screech in fractured French, with a Pennsylvania accent, *On-ree, On-ree, donnay lui on dee-vee-dund, see-voo-play*. Of course dear Henri understood perfectly that he must fill a guest's glass with a "dividend" or "bonus" of martini.

Marie's apartment overlooked the Seine and had one of the most coveted views in Paris, but she had placed giant rubber trees in front of every floor-to-ceiling window. When I asked her if she didn't mind hiding the view, she said, "What view? There's nothing there but a river."

Although Marie had lived in France for almost 20 years she still didn't speak French, explaining that if anyone had anything important to tell her they "damn well better say it in English." Guests on the Quai de Béthune were at her mercy. Martinis were followed by saltless food with no salt and pepper in sight, because that's the way she wanted it. Once she stopped a guest at the door and sent him away because he'd brought his little dog. "But, Marie," he protested, "I remember that you had nine dogs at your house in Joinville."

"Yes, and I had nine servants to take care of them," she answered, and refused to let him in for lunch.

Our kitchen drama between the maid and the widow-lady didn't let up. Jim finally went downstairs to the concierge of the building, asking if there might be another apartment available in the same building. She said there was nothing at the moment but that she would let us know as soon as there was. One evening soon after that, we were entertaining fellow *Herald Tribune* folks, Lydia and Mike Horton, when the doorbell rang. It was the concierge to tell us that an apartment had become available upstairs. The occupant had just hanged himself.

We moved soon after, but NOT upstairs. Our next home was a furnished house with a big garden in Le Vesinet, just outside of Paris. Jim found it through *Herald Tribune* friends while I was having another check-up at the hospital. Many of our friends were convinced that out-of-Paris living was ideal, especially if you were starting a family. It seemed like everyone lived in places like Châtou, Orgival, Bougival or St. Cloud. And today, somewhere in this world, there are Americans born in Paris in the fifties with names like Horton, Attwood, Perlman and Cook, as well as Nolan.

Champagne...

The house in Le Vesinet was the second place, but not the last, that Jim signed up for without showing to me first. I didn't mind; he convinced me that it would be great and it did seem charming. Anne-Marie agreed to come and work for us every day, but she refused to move in, saying, "If I wanted to leave Paris, I'd go back to Brittany."

During the first months of pregnancy I was still going to the office with Jim every day, but now I set up a little *bureau* at home. Jim brought the drawing board from the office and I dusted off my trusty portable to continue working on our *Herald Tribune* projects. Jim would bring me work from Paris and take it back with him when it was ready; I'd be on the phone with Surey several times a day and she'd tell me how much she missed my happy face. I was very touched and told her that now I had a "fat happy face." The only difference in my working at home at first was that those little beige envelopes holding my pay were no longer forthcoming.

I fretted and fumed for a while before I got the nerve to bring it up to Jim. It was painful for me to point out that work was work and should be paid for: it had nothing to do with our personal life. He was grumpy about it but paid me for my labors from then on without comment.

Immediately I put my earnings into baby clothes, crib, hampers, baskets, baby scales and all those things that made up a nursery. When the maid, our unforgettable Anne-Marie from Brittany, watched what I was doing, she said, "What are you doing all that for? What if the baby is born dead?"

Many years later, I learned that this is a popular belief among many French people who wouldn't think of buying anything for a baby until it's born. That day, however, I thought that Anne-Marie was being cruel and it hurt.

Dorothy and David Schoenbrun were in our lives a lot; David was thrilled that his two "crazy Americans" had finally gotten smart and Dorothy was doing endless little things that a new mother can do to help a mother-to-be. One of the BIG things that she did for me while not intending to was the day she took me to see the Pierre Balmain fashion show. After sitting through an absolutely beautiful collection, Dorothy took me through the salon to find the *directrice*, Ginette Spanier.

She was a bubbling ivory-skinned, black-haired lady full of life and in love with high fashion. Ginette had promised Dorothy that she'd pick out some model coats for her to try on, so she led us into a spacious dressing room, asking how we liked the show. I said it was superb but, patting my front bulge, I wasn't exactly in shape to have a Balmain creation at the moment. She put her finger to her lips and said "Shhh," and disappeared to get the coats for Dorothy.

Ginette came back with her arms piled high and plunked all the coats down on a chair. In the middle of the pile of black wool creations was a beautiful, burgundy-red, brocade cocktail coat that buttoned all the way from neckline to hem. She explained that the coat came from a collection several years back; there had been a stick-slim dress under it but that was sold and the coat was left behind. She held it up to me explaining that I could wear it all buttoned up right away and then wear it with sheath dresses later. I thought it was just about the most beautiful thing I'd ever seen, and Ginette assured me that she could give it to me for "next to nothing" if I would only promise not to tell anyone that Pierre Balmain made maternity clothes. "He'd have an absolute FIT," she said.

Of course I bought the coat and it became the most practical purchase I have ever made. I had such a success with it that Dorothy took me to a little dressmaker to copy the model in several different fabrics and colors. She made a coat in green-and-gold satin, in brown taffeta, in Chinese brocade, plus a daytime coat in beige linen with black frog-closings. And the investment could be considered totally amortized insofar as a second baby followed the first and I wore the same coats for years.

Preparing for the arrival of the baby, I bought every book I could find at the English bookstore on the Rue de Rivoli, so I'd have an idea of what I was doing. I picked out the second bedroom and bathroom on the landing for the nursery. The bedroom had its own terrace at the back of the house and a staircase leading down into the garden. I was already imagining sunny afternoons when we could put a playpen among the trees and flowers on the grass. The nursery was large, with a place for everything. Going by the book, I even made a weighing chart to put on the wall above the table scales. When Dorothy Schoenbrun first got a look at what I'd done, she laughed heartily. "This looks like an advertising agency," she commented.

While I was on clouds planning our blessed event, something was happening to Jim. Surey said that he was getting bored with his job, that he'd lost interest in supplements even though they'd been successful. He was frustrated trying to find someone to handle follow-ups and follow-throughs, which he refused to do. Surey joked that although she was a genius, it was impossible for her to handle everything that we'd been doing. Although I did all the work Jim brought home to me, it wasn't the same as being on the spot with Surey, and while the idea for the 2000th Paris Birthday supplement was mine, I couldn't travel back and forth to Paris for researching editorials, contacts with advertisers, getting okays on texts and all details I'd handled before. I didn't mind as I had a project much more important than facing businessmen who didn't take me seriously. But Jim was dejected and morose.

One fine Fall morning I announced to Jim that I had to go to Paris with him because I knew the baby was on the way. There were ever so slight contractions giving me signals that today was the day. Poor Jim looked weak in the knees as he took my overnight bag to put in the car. I told him I wanted to go to Elizabeth Arden first for a shampoo and manicure. The whiter he got around the gills, the calmer I wanted to be. Insisting that he drop me off at Arden's and we'd meet at the Ritz two hours later to go to the hospital from there, assuring him that I knew what I was doing.

Elizabeth Arden, in those days, had their six-floor headquarters at number 7 Place Vendôme, run by Elizabeth Arden's sister, Mme de Maublanc. Here one could get head-to-toe treatment by international experts. Everyone who worked there seemed in awe of the great Miss Arden, if not downright scared of her imperious ways. (Little did they know that she had invented herself. Born Florence Nightingale Graham, she never finished school but set herself up on borrowed money and her made-up name, describing herself as a beauty expert.) When she arrived on her Paris premises, she was treated like a queen, while clients were treated as mere princesses.

My usual ladies in their pretty pink and white uniforms were cheerful and charming, as usual, but when I told them that "today is the day," they stepped up their work with notable speed. They certainly didn't want such a happening in their salons. I reached the Ritz Bar in plenty of time to have a club sandwich before Jim came to pick me up. The barman looked concerned until Jim arrived, although I'd assured them they had nothing to worry about. How did I know? I don't know how I knew, I just knew.

For someone having a first baby, I was certainly sure of myself when I said there'd be a wait before the birth. But I didn't realize how long that wait would be. Something was going wrong. It wasn't until 8:30 the next morning that Catherine Elizabeth Nolan came into the world–by caesarian.

Never mind the details because I don't know what they were. When the doctors saw what was NOT happening, they scheduled an operation for the first thing the next morning, when they wheeled me down the hall and into the operating room. Back in my room, when I opened my eyes all I wanted was to see the baby the nurses said was a "perfect little girl." One of the nurses handed me a glass of champagne, saying "We always give champagne to new mothers; it's the best medicine there is."

When they put the tiny bundle in my arms, I was thrilled beyond words to see the most beautiful baby I'd ever seen in my life. One of the nurses standing there, admiring the baby with me, said that caesarian babies always look beautiful at birth because they don't have to struggle to be born. I was hoping Jim would arrive to see the baby before they took her back to the nursery at the end of the hall, but he didn't appear until the middle of the afternoon, saying he'd been "out with the boys" the night before and had a giant hangover. He plunked down a pile of gifts from fellow parents and friends at the *Herald Tribune*, looked out the window, walked the floor and announced he'd have to be going because he had a lot of work to do.

What was going on in his head that day I will never know but I did discover that he was confused about exactly when our daughter was born. Years later, when Cathy was grown, she told me her father said she was born in the evening. After that, I saw her birth certificate filed by Jim while I was still in hospital, declaring our daughter's time of birth as 8:30 p.m. instead of a.m. Maybe it doesn't matter, but there are certain things a mother can never forget.

Cathy and I had several visits before we left the hospital, starting with Dorothy

Schoenbrun, Sandy Matlowsky, and then David Seymour, the Polish-born American photographer known as Chim, who took bedside pictures of mother and child. He was a wartime friend of David Schoenbrun, who had founded Magnum Photo Agency with Bob Capa and Henri Cartier-Bresson. Every time he came back to Paris after an assignment, it seemed there were more Paris-born American babies to photograph, which he loved to do, saying he'd rather take pictures of babies than war fronts.

Leaving the hospital we took a Swiss nurse with us back to Le Vesinet, to help me get accustomed to caring for a brand new baby. She was a fat, bossy creature who frightened me with her don't-do-this and don't-do-that orders, until I forgot all I'd learned in the books I'd bought. But she did seem to have the baby's interests at heart, so I tolerated her manner as best I could in my new mother/post-operative state.

One afternoon Jim came home from the office earlier than usual and motioned me to come upstairs to our room, as he had something important to discuss with me. He had a grim look on his face as he closed the door, announcing that it was time to discuss the religious upbringing of our child. At first I grinned, thinking he couldn't be serious about such a thing when Cathy was only a matter of days old. The awful scowl on his face wiped the grin off mine. "You promised to have Catholic children," he stated, still standing as I sat on the edge of the bed.

I reminded him that I had done nothing of the sort, and if he was referring to the little card stating "Katlick" and "Kommie," did he think I was serious. Further, how could he expect me to take him seriously when he'd been divorced from his Catholic wife and didn't even go to church. All the time I thought I was reasoning with him, the look on his face told me that my efforts were wasted. He was so determined to argue that it got on a low level of "I did not," "You did too," until I was shaking from the ordeal. When time came to nurse the baby, I had no milk.

For the first time I felt really glad to have the Swiss dragon there to help me with the formula to feed the baby. She didn't waste time upbraiding Jim for causing "Mummy" to lose her milk, saying she had heard everything we said through the door.

It wasn't long before I knew why Jim was acting that way with me. His father was bombarding him with letters, nagging him regarding his "obligation to the Church." Never mind that Jim never paid any attention to religion, never mind that he'd been divorced, never mind that we'd been married in an office and not a church. All that seemed to matter to Jim now was pleasing his father by doing what his father told him to do.

The rotten mood Jim was in and his unrelenting tirades finally wore me down and I told him I didn't see any harm in a christening ceremony if that would keep peace with his father but, as far as upbringing was concerned, I had made no promise and he knew that as well as I did. Jim seemed jubilant: he could now announce to his father that he had arranged for a christening at St. Joseph's on the

Avenue Hoche. On the day of the ceremony we met Ann McGarry and Jim's friend, Neil Osborne, in the bar of the Hôtel California before the christening and then joined others in Surey's walk-up apartment in Pigalle for a celebration.

Baby Cathy smiled in the California Bar, screamed in church and slept all through the party.

Back in Le Vesinet changes were taking place. Anne-Marie decided not to take the train to us anymore and quit without notice. She hated to travel but wouldn't live outside of Paris; she resented intrusions and detested the Swiss German and English-speaking nurse whom she called fascist and *boche*; she even continued her complaints long after the nurse had gone to join another family with a new baby needing her professional care. There was peace with both Anne-Marie and the Swiss nurse gone, but finding help where we were was neither easy nor satisfactory. There were countless young girls in the community who wanted work, but they knew less about housekeeping than I did. To add to this, Jim's unhappiness with his job manifested itself when we were alone, no matter how charming he was when others were around.

Who knows how long we would have endured this sorry out-of-Paris existence if I had not seen a rat under the radiator in the baby's room. Not a mouse, mind you, but a rat!

I had the baby on the changing table and quickly wrapped her up and ran downstairs to Jim. He grabbed a broom to chase the beast onto the nursery terrace and down the steps to the garden. There was an empty house on the edge of the property, which must have contained the rat's nest from whence he came. Lord knows how big a family he had over there, but we decided not to hang around to find out.

We moved to Paris the next day, checking into the Hôtel de la Trémoille, and a sun-filled suite with room enough for the baby's crib and all the new baby equipment I had collected, leaving our excess baggage in storage while starting a search for a proper place to live.

It was just at this moment that luck came knocking on the door. Howard Hughes' Trans World Airlines was opening up all over Europe and wanted an American "charmer" with impressive credentials to head the first European TWA Public Relations office from Paris, setting up others in London, Rome and Madrid. This sounded like a dream come true for both of us; they stressed the importance of a presentable wife, because social entertaining with important people would be a vital part of the job. Jim and I had already worked well as a team so it seemed like a made-to-order job.

Chapter Four

Jim was in a state he called "sweating it out" during the short time TWA directors took in making him a firm offer for the job. At this time the president of TWA, Warren Lee Pierson, appeared in Paris with his wife, Eleanor, and invited us to dine at the Ritz. They were bright, amusing companions interested in everything and everyone in Paris. When dinner was over and we were walking down the hall toward the Place Vendôme entrance, Eleanor asked me straight out if I'd like "my" work if Jim got the TWA job, adding that they always looked over the wife when they hired the husband. I assured her I'd be delighted but she couldn't have imagined how pleased I'd be, believing so strongly that marriage was teamwork.

When we told our French friends of Jim's possible job in public relations they didn't know what we were talking about. Trying to explain didn't get us very far either because no one had ever heard of *relations publiques*, which came to be called *relations extérieures* at TWA during that time. In those days, in the USA public relations was in its infancy with listed companies in New York numbering in the low hundreds, while in Paris there were no listings at all.

It didn't take long for TWA to confirm their offer, which came before we'd found a place to live. Jim jumped with joy at the news, saying now the most important thing for him to do was find a suitable home in keeping with a TWA public relations image. While he took care of that, he said, my project should be finding a babies' nurse like Dorothy and David had, so I could devote time to TWA projects.

"The first damn thing I have to do," said Jim, "is find a theme for TWA to celebrate the 5th anniversary of starting up in Europe." It came to me like a flash: a TWA Kids' Party. Everyone we knew had children. A party with balloons, ice cream, cake, clowns, all the stuff that's festive, colorful, photogenic. And, of course, I was thinking of myself, showing up with Cathy at her first party for a good cause.

"We're in business, Maggi," said Jim gleefully. I couldn't wait to tell Surey that

Champagne...

"the boss" was in good humor once again.

After registering for a babies' nurse in an agency the Schoenbruns had used, I spent several afternoons in the hotel suite interviewing a parade of applicants, one after the other. Most of the ladies wore crisp white uniforms under flowing, navy blue, ankle-length capes. They looked down their noses as they requested minimum hours with maximum wages and holidays. Not one asked to see the baby. On about the third day of interviews I was losing hope.

Then an applicant named Catherine arrived. She was henna-haired and wore a gray coat with matching skirt and a crisp white blouse closed at the neckline with a tiny enamel bird pin. She asked right away if she could see the baby. Peeking through the slats of the crib, she asked her name. When I told her, her face lighted up and she started a barrage of questions: age, diet, sleeping habits. Not bad, I thought, she really seems human. Then when I asked her what salary she wanted, she answered in old-fashioned third person French, "As *Madame* wishes." And that's how Catherine (nicknamed Catina as soon as Cathy could talk) came to live with us for 13 years.

I didn't want to see the rest of the applicants after spending just minutes with Catherine, but there were a few interviews already scheduled. Before she left, she gave me a copy of the letter she had from her last employer and the address where she could be reached. I wanted to tell her right away that she had the job and could start as soon as we had a place to live, but felt I'd better talk it over with Jim first so we shook hands and she was out the door.

As it turned out, Jim wasn't interested in talking it over; he came bursting into the suite with that ear-to-ear smile of his, announcing that he had found the perfect place for us to live. It was a private mansion in Paris' exclusive residential district, the 16th. "Just wait 'til you see this place," he said, "full of masterpiece paintings...great for parties...Bechstein piano, parquet floors, crystal chandeliers all over the place, period furniture and even a Madame Récamier couch...."

When I could get a word in I asked about basics like the number of bedrooms, bathrooms, proper accommodation for nurse and baby; but Jim was vague and a bit impatient. Then, when I asked when I could see it for myself he told me we could move in right away while he waved a sheaf of papers under my nose. "I've got it," he announced, and that was that.

His description of the *hôtel particulier* was enthusiastic and sincere, and when I looked at the inventory I couldn't help but be impressed. Rembrandt and Rubens on the walls, period furniture from Louis XIII to Louis XVI and so on. "This place must cost a fortune!" I gasped, but Jim just waved a hand in the air, assuring me that we could afford it. He hadn't told me what his salary and expenses would be and I didn't have a clue about his finances; I was happy to take his word that this mansion was within our means.

What a shock when we arrived at our new "home." What Jim had said was certainly all true, but he forgot to mention that the daughter of the owners was going

TWA's 5th anniversary party in 1951 was the occasion
of Cathy's first social engagement at Ledoyen.

to keep her room on the top floor and share a bathroom with our nurse and baby. He neglected to tell me that she also had a snarling bulldog forever by her side. Another detail he overlooked was that we were stuck with a maid-of-all-work who was too old for general housework, but good at keeping the coal furnace burning and sweeping the front stairs and sidewalk in exchange for her room and board.

I knew I had to go along with this; Jim was already projecting us into the future parties we'd have and the people we'd impress. He'd memorized a list of celebrities who were on their way to Paris at that very moment: Faye Emerson, former wife of Elliot Roosevelt, now married to the top bandleader, Skitch Henderson; Johnny Meyer, PR man for Howard Hughes in Hollywood; former Elliot Roosevelt sidekick (later with Onassis), Bing Crosby, on his way over to prepare a film and so on.

The baby's nurse surveyed her situation on the top floor and calmly set about to organize her space. I was embarrassed and upset at the quarters given her, but she said not to worry, she had seen worse. That's when she told me she'd been a nurse in a Jewish family during the war, when they had to hide and "make do" in very difficult times.

Our private mansion soon became the stopping-off place for countless celebrities arriving in Paris by TWA, many through the courtesy of Howard Hughes. The outstanding caterer at the time, Georges Rosell, was kept so busy he could have opened an annex next door to us. His work was like magic: tell him how many guests were expected and he'd set the whole beautiful party up in no time at all. Little did our festive guests know what was going on behind the scenes, as it all looked so effortless and elegant.

While I acted the part of the glamorous Mrs. Nolan in the salons, I tried to hide the misery of living in that house. It was four stories high and wasn't practical or comfortable. The kitchen overlooking a weed-filled back garden was always full of people, such as the daughter with her visiting friends (and the snarling dog who snatched food off the counter and gobbled it down); the aged maid with people she said were her relatives; the maid we hired by the hour who stayed to feed her husband our food because he had helped her shine the crystal chandeliers. And I worried constantly that the nurse was not getting proper attention upstairs.

Once, during a party, I saw the maid on the staircase going to the top floor with a tray. "The nurse's dinner," she announced as I stared into a plate of spinach. I took the tray to the buffet table and filled it with cocktail goodies like smoked salmon squares, *foie gras* on toast, ham slices, cheese and a mixture of miniature pastries. Catherine had a hot plate upstairs so I left the spinach for good measure. She seemed so pleased and grateful that I went down once more to the bar and found a half-bottle of champagne to go with her dinner.

This was the same night that Faye Emerson was screeching in the downstairs hall that her Aleutian was missing. "My Aleutian–my Aleutian, I've lost my Aleutian," she was bellowing. Her "Aleutian" was found under a pile of coats in the entry and that's how I learned that Aleutian Island minks were the most expensive, exclusive coats of the day.

These were the days when Jim was in his glory; he never stopped reminding me that our house and celebrity-studded parties were the talk of Paris and that every TWA executive he talked to in the USA was impressed and pleased with the progress and prestige achieved in Europe. At the same time, he made it clear that he thought I was being petty when I complained about our household problems. I wept when he laughed about the snarling bulldog snatching our veal cutlets. "So we'll go out to dinner," he said, forgetting about the nurse upstairs.

Paris had more than passing movie stars at the time; directors and producers showed up in droves to spend film money that had accumulated in France during the war and remained frozen. After unsuccessful bids to get their money out, film folk decided to come to France and spend it on the spot. Films were being made, villas were being purchased in the South of France along with apartments in Paris, while champagne and caviar evenings at the Tour d'Argent and Maxim's seemed *de rigueur* as a natural thing to do.

One of the first film star celebrities we spent a lot of time with was Bing Crosby, who came to France to make a film called "Little Boy Lost" for Paramount. We entertained him at home and in restaurants and then went to visit him in Montfort l'Amaury while he was shooting his film. His lunch break with the cast and crew was in a luxurious *auberge* belonging to the restaurant/club man,

Maurice Carrère, where a stately chestnut tree grew majestically right in the middle of the dining room.

After lunching with Bing and the Paramount people at long trestle tables set up especially for the film makers, Bing told us to get back in our car and follow the make-up trailer that he was taking back to the film set. On the side of the trailer was the name Perc Westmore, and as Bing climbed in he said, "See you later; between here and the set I have to grow a head of hair."

Throughout his stay, Bing counted a lot on being entertained by Jim at Maxim's, which was an "in" place to dine at the time with fellow celebrities at every table, and then on to Maurice Carrère's nightclub on the Rue Pierre Charron, l'Orangerie, decorated with genuine orange trees. (Singers like Édith Piaf and Yves Montand entertained here with unknowns like Eddie Constantine, an American from California who became a number one film star in France.)

Bing was ready to go everywhere and see everything, so he was easy to entertain. He loved picturesque spots on the Butte near the Sacré-Coeur, and to watch the outdoor artists around the Place du Tertre as they painted the familiar scene. Jim introduced him to Hervé at his indoor/outdoor art gallery, where Bing spent hours and hours during several visits, looking at all of the works of art for sale, but he never bought one.

Bing really enjoyed the good life and seemed completely relaxed wherever he went. Once, after a hefty lunch with heady wines at the Berkeley near the Rond-Point des Champs-Élysées, we walked over toward the six fountains surrounded by grass and flowers. He stepped over the ankle-high fence around the grass, sat down and then lay down on the lush green lawn and promptly went to sleep.

High life went on in our art-filled private mansion while Jim continued to look upon my complaints as highly exaggerated. He had set speeches about showing more appreciation of the success we were having with our entertaining, which was such an important part of his new job. Sometimes I felt so frustrated that I'd hide in the master bedroom, fall on the ornate gilt bed and stare up at the hand-painted cherubs floating around the pink and blue clouds on the ceiling, wondering what I had done to merit such misery.

One evening during another super successful reception, a British art curator was among our guests. We didn't know him, but he was brought by a girl named Barbara Potter from Philadelphia, who had told us he was brilliant and connected with a London museum. He seemed to be totally fascinated by the paintings and stopped for a close look at each and every one. When he got to the largest one that took up almost the entire wall next to the piano, I joined him and asked, "Do you like that Rubens?" "Yes," he answered, "but who painted it?" He wasn't joking; he stated emphatically that we could take his professional word that all of our paintings were fakes. "Nice fakes," he added, "but fakes all the same." I thought this was very funny but Jim was so furious that I didn't dare laugh. Jim's fury didn't subside; he hated being taken in and was probably worried that everyone would know this awful truth. From then on, every time I told him about something that went awry in the house, he'd add, "And the paintings are FAKES!" which was far more important to him than anything else.

Jim was determined to break our rental agreement and get out as fast as we could. I was so delighted when he told me this good news that I giggled in bed that night before the lamp was turned out. "What's so funny?" Jim asked, and I told him that I bet the ceiling above us with its cherubs floating in a pink clouded sky was listed on our inventory as genuine Michelangelo. Despite his fury at falling for fakes, he laughed as we snuggled down to sleep.

One morning before we left that awful house for yet another furnished rental, Jim told me to expect an unusual visit that day. He was given enough money by his mother to buy a mink coat for me; the furrier would be over to show me different shades of mink. All I had to do was pick the color and the style I wanted, and the mink coat would be made-to-order for me. It seemed like a lovely idea and I was truly grateful to have such a marvelous mother-in-law, who showered me and the new baby with endless gifts. She wrote to me over and over about how thrilled she was to finally have a grandchild. At 74 years old, she thought she'd never be a Grandma.

When the "mink man" arrived, I showed him into the parquet-floored salon and to a satin chair next to mine. He had a large portfolio in his arms, which I thought had the color chart and coat styles. But he announced that another gentleman was on his way up with the samples. The second man arrived with a giant case that looked like a linen trunk. Together they opened it and began to spread huge bundles of matching mink pelts on the floor. They must have put out half a dozen piles of pelts, each pile in a different shade. I was appalled; it looked like piles of dead rats all over the floor. Those poor dead creatures bunched together like that made me feel sick. It took all the nerve I had to tell them that I'd changed my mind and did not want a mink coat, after all.

Afterward, I was really frightened that Jim would be mad at me when I told him what I had seen and how I had felt. Surprise! He seemed to understand and said, "Look, my mother sent you a million francs; you can do what you wish with it." A million francs didn't mean that I was a millionairess; it was worth about 2,000 dollars at the time. That was enough for a first quality, made-to-order mink coat.

The first important purchase I made with my "mink money" was a set of Lalique champagne glasses for Surey. She had done so much for us beyond the call of duty; she had taken our baby in arms to have her photographed for my passport before I was well enough to do so myself; she had given the christening party for Cathy in her tiny Pigalle apartment; she had shown in so many ways that she cared about us. When she gave us a wedding gift of a giant Lalique ashtray, she mentioned in passing that she had always dreamed of owning Lalique champagne glasses. When I mentioned that to Jim and said we should get them for her, he said, "What a waste!"

But now I had some money I could spend as I pleased. I could do it. Surey was so thrilled with her Lalique *flûtes*; you'd think I'd given her the moon. It didn't bother me that she thanked Jim more profusely than me. There was no need to go into the story of my "mink money."

It didn't take long to decide what I wanted to do with the rest of my loot. Around this time, when Dorothy and David, Ann McGarry, Jim and I were together, the subject of the total lack of professional public relations in France invariably came up. It was just at the time when Ann was going through a double crisis: she was fed up with her low-paying, unappreciated press work at Balmain and frustrated with her on again/off again romance with Art Buchwald, which didn't seem to be going anywhere. She didn't have a dime, she was discouraged, and she kept saying she'd just have to go back home.

The more we talked about PR in Paris, the more it seemed natural for us to open an office with Ann, Dorothy and I working together. I offered to put up Ann's 1/3 partnership and David said he'd put up 1/3 for Dorothy. (Art Buchwald was out of the picture at that time, no matter what he claimed later.) We went to the best-known American lawyer in Paris, Charles Torem, of Coudert Frères on the Avenue des Champs-Élysées. He was not only smart and efficient, he was also the tallest lawyer in town, so he towered over all the others in every way.

Dorothy and I were the ones to insist that we call our company Ann McGarry Associates, after playing around with McGarry, Nolan and Scher and McGarry, Nolan and Schoenbrun.

We played around so much with the names that we were writing down nonsense like McNolan and Scher. Choosing Ann McGarry Associates seemed the most practical thing to do: Ann had contacts from New York's Celanese Corporation to Texas' Neiman Marcus. From the beginning it was clear that Ann was going to be the first to bring clients to us. Before I'd found our office space to rent on the Avenue Président Wilson, she'd already lined up Norma Geer of Celanese to be our first account. Norma was a brilliant woman promoting acetate fabric in American fashions; now her site was France.

In no time at all we were in business. Dorothy dreamed up the letterhead for our new stationery and was destined to do all layout and artwork; my job was writing everything from letters to elaborate presentations to press releases and text plus captions for photographs, while Ann drummed up business. We needed a French secretary immediately for office work and business correspondence in French, so the search was on. I started to interview a number of young ladies who didn't have any idea of what we were doing.

Trying to explain public relations to young ladies in Paris, 1951, was not easy. When I'd show them photos and text in newspapers and say that we had done that, they'd say, "Oh, you're photographers," and I'd say, "No, we placed the material." And then they'd say, "Journalists?" "No." "Work for the newspaper?" "No." "Well, then, how can you say you did that?" Most of them probably thought we were all out of our heads, but when a lady said frankly she didn't know how it worked, but she'd like to find out, she was the one for us.

The first important campaign we had was to convince top French dressmakers to design at least one creation in acetate fabric made by Celanese. We promised (1) their exclusive use of the bolts of their choice at no cost; (2) free photographs of their creations posed by top models; and (3) free placement of photos and press releases in the French and American press with guaranteed credit to the dressmaker.

Despite all of the above, it was not easy to talk *haute couture* geniuses into using a fabric that wasn't pure silk, wool, linen or cotton. Their standard argument was, "We've never done that before." Slowly, several agreed to give acetate a try. Each one would look at the fabric from all angles, feel it, test how it draped on a mannequin and conclude, "What have I got to lose?"

This campaign meant long hours of hard work but it was worth it. We earned our fees, Norma Geer had one of the biggest hassles of her life shipping fabrics to France, but she was thrilled to see the fashion clippings piling up on her desk in her suite at the Hôtel Lancaster. We were getting recognition and compliments galore, we even received a little note from the most famous public relations practitioner in New York, Ben Sonnenberg. To me this was the greatest compliment we could get as he was unique; he had started with accounts like Texaco, Viking Press, Sam Goldwyn, Elizabeth Arden and Helena Rubenstein way back in the Depression years.

A few weeks later he came to Paris and I met him at the July 4th party in the gardens of the American Embassy. He was a short, fat man with a walrus-like mustache. He said very nice things about our new enterprise and then asked, "And as one of the partners, what is your claim to fame?"

"I'm the tallest," I said, and he laughed so heartily that his tummy jiggled.

On the home front, Jim lost no time in finding us yet another furnished home; this was heaven compared to the hell of the monstrous museum we'd been in. There were many places available then. Paris was full of furnished apartments owned by upper-class Frenchmen with country homes to go to while renting to "rich Americans." Jim took us to our new apartment on the Rue de l'Assomption. When I saw the roomy, clean comfort, I hugged him right in front of the owners. The new place was ideal for both impressive entertaining and comfortable family life. The foyer was a room in itself, connected by double doors leading into the salon and dining room. Doors could be opened up to greet more than a hundred guests. Down a wide hallway lined with cupboards, closets and drawers were three bedrooms, two baths and a sunroom after an immaculate kitchen and servants' quarters with back entrance and elevator. The apartment was carpeted throughout and although the heavy Louis XV furniture decked out in chocolate-colored satin might be far from ideal, it was adequate.

Of course there's always a catch: the owners wanted to rent to us strictly month by month with no contract. They warned that they might want their apartment back on short notice. We didn't care, it was perfect for us then and there. The hourly maid we'd had in the mansion moved in with her husband and they became our cook and butler installed in the cozy quarters next to the kitchen. They had pleasant dispositions but when Jim's shirts and sweaters went missing and my silk umbrella disappeared with several pairs of nylons at the same time, we had to replace them (not the missing items but those so obviously responsible for the loss). Next we found a very sweet couple, refugees from Hungary, who were far from perfect but their honesty and effort made up for the rest. The nurse liked Ferdinand and Sidi immediately, which counted a lot for peace and tranquility behind the scenes of our hectic social life. We were organized and content; the only drawback was the monthly visits of our landlord. As he counted his cash for the rent on a table, we never knew if he was going to ask for his apartment back on the first of the next month.

Jim's work was going beautifully from his very impressive offices on the corner of the Avenue des Champs-Élysées and the Avenue George V, where he had a panoramic view. Workmates were American for the most part (then) and happy to be in Paris. They worked hard and played hard; the money made went a long way toward a wonderful life. Business was moving fast in an upward swing and hardly a dull happening to mar the precious moments. Every TWA airplane arrival brought a load of celebrities, VIPs and socialites to keep everyone on their toes, especially Jim.

The legendary Lou Walters, owner of New York's nightclub, The Latin Quarter, was met by Jim at the airport and asked to have a tour of the top (and topless) nightspots. That's not all: before flying back to Manhattan Lou had also asked Jim to find a lady passenger on an airplane going back to New York to take his suitcase full of *haute couture* clothes; he knew he couldn't get through customs if he took them himself. He said that the beautiful dresses were for his daughter, Barbara, but Jim thought it more likely that he was going to impress some show-girls in his club with exciting Paris fashions.

One day Jim had Barbara Hutton on his hands (and in his arms!). She was a frequent TWA air traveler by then and could never seem to get off the airplane and into her limousine without getting hysterical. Jim had to carry her while he sweat-ed and Barbara bawled uncontrollably. She borrowed Jim's breastpocket handker-chief to wipe her tears and still had it covering her face when he left her. Later a liveried chauffeur delivered an immaculately-laundered handkerchief to our door with a bouquet of beautiful spring flowers.

By that time Jim and I were settled comfortably in our new home and enter-taining with ease and enjoyment. Ann McGarry Associates was going strong. Agenda entries from the beginning were dates with top mannequins for photos by American-Parisian, Gene Fenn; rendezvous with hotel officials to plan a campaign for the Hôtel George V; press presentation of CBS color television for Smith, Kline

Champagne...

& French; work meeting with executives from the leather industry, a linen promotion, and so on. Day to day worksheets in the office were full of photo sessions, printer appointments, press release writing, proof readings, French translating, Franco-American mailings...

In the middle of everything, we took on the advertising and publicity of Art Buchwald's first book, *Paris After Dark*. When the *Herald Tribune* executives refused to publish the book, Jim Nolan and his Pan-American pal, Clem Brown, put up the money to back it and made their investment back several times over. For Buchwald we did our job at Ann McGarry Associates for love, not money.

Flushed with the success of our Celanese campaign with Paris dressmakers, we next had a fashion and film project for Columbia Films. They had a movie coming out called *David and Bathsheba*, and we publicized top French dressmakers who agreed to create Bathsheba-inspired dresses. Results were marvelous and everyone was happy: film company, dressmakers, top models, photographers, fashion journalists and, of course, Ann McGarry Associates as we pocketed our well-earned fee.

Everything was looking up and I had something else to be happy about: it seemed another baby was on the way. I giggled to myself thinking at least something GOOD had come out of that awful house full of fakes on the walls and cherubs on the ceiling. The doctor confirmed my expectations but I was surprised at his disapproval. He reminded me that he had told me to wait two years, and Cathy was only five months old. I shrugged and smiled but he went on making undoctorly remarks that perhaps he should have put a zipper in place of the *haute couture* on my stomach. I didn't care, it thrilled me to think another little Nolan was expected.

I felt marvelous and kept right on with my life at home and in the office, although I was getting rounder by the minute. No morning sickness, no change in routine except sitting up all night with Cathy a few times when she was cutting her teeth. Jim was taking it all in stride as well, never once reminding me that pregnant women made him sick. But there was one unforgettable evening when he made it obvious to everyone at a dinner party that he preferred someone else's company to mine. That night, all dressed up in my hide-a-baby cocktail coat-dress by Pierre Balmain, Jim and I went to dine with Dorothy and David Schoenbrun in honor of CBS "star" Ed Murrow. By now David had moved way ahead with CBS as Radio/Television Chief in Paris, with fancy penthouse offices on the Champs-Élysées. The Schoenbruns had a luxuriously-furnished apartment on the Avenue Bosquet, not far from the Seine River and with a view of the Eiffer Tower from their corner windows.

This evening they were entertaining us in one of their favorite restaurants, Vert Bocage, top-rated at the time and a must for gourmet diners. There was fine food and divine wines for the eight of us: Schoenbruns, Nolans, Ed Murrow from New York, Howard K. Smith from London, international photographer Bob Capa and his tall, blonde date from Norway.

Jim was seated across from Capa's Nordic beauty and made it clear to everyone that he was pretty pleased, pouring out the blarney for all to hear, but he didn't seem to see or hear anyone else. I tried to keep my eyes off the dress she was wearing; it was a lot like the tiny-waisted dinner dress that I had worn on my first date with Jim. His attention to "Miss Norway" from aperitifs to café and cognac was so upsetting to me that I kept staring into my plate, feeling fat and ugly and quite unable to look anyone in the eye. Dorothy saw what was happening, I knew, but she could do nothing about it.

Much more important things were going on at the table that evening. These were times when television was taking hold of communications; the table talk was about CBS projects like the "See It Now" series, followed by "Person to Person" programs linking important personalities from different countries in live discussions. This was more important than Jim making a tennis date with the sexy lady across from him before the dinner was over. Why am I writing this down after so many many years have gone by? It's because of that incredible creature, Bob Capa. After dinner, when we all got up to leave, everyone was busy gathering hats, coats and scarves when Bob Capa came over and stood directly in front of me and stayed there until I looked him in the eye. With a big smile he said, "I just want to tell you that I think pregnant women are the most beautiful women in the world." And with that he leaned over and kissed the front of my coat on the 7th tiny button, just where the huge bundle I was carrying began to show.

Bing Crosby wined and dined at Maxim's where François poured the house champagne.

Champagne...

What a lovely man he was. The world-famed action photographer known as a high-spirited adventurer with endless exploits of courage and daring in front-line wars was a different kind of hero to me. He dared to show himself as a kind human being who knew what to say to whom as well as why and when. Three years later when I read on the front page of the Paris *Herald Tribune* that Bob Capa had been killed by a land mine in Indochina, I cried like I'd lost my best friend, though I hadn't seen him since the Schoenbrun dinner.

I wasn't always jealous and unhappy when Jim made dates with other women. The night he got all dressed up to escort Clare Boothe Luce to a formal dinner, I even helped him with his black tie and considered that evening as part of his job.

"Try to have a good time," I told him as he went out the door. But that dinner party turned into a whole night on the town with this enticing creature. Jim didn't come home until the wee hours of morn. He was stumbling and mumbling as I helped him out of his clothes and into bed.

"She's so beautiful, beautiful, beautiful," he kept saying. Now, I had heard that she didn't care for the company of women and I had heard that she was just crazy about men, but I hadn't heard that men were crazy over HER.

Pondering that a bit in my pregnant fat-and-sassy mood, I still wasn't jealous. I wrote a little verse and put it on Jim's breakfast tray:

> *I made a truce*
> *With Clare Boothe Luce*
> *I gave her all my men*
> *And now we're friends again...*

When Jim woke up he was bleary-eyed but in a good humor when he read my four-liner. He put it in his pocket, still chuckling when he went out the door. Later he told me that he gave it to C.B.L. and she laughed. I worried about how she'd act if we ever met, but I need not have fretted at all. A year or so later when we were introduced at the American Embassy residence, her eyes twinkled when she heard my name. We shook hands and she gave me a huge, cheery smile.

Chapter Five

Several times in the next few months awaiting the arrival of our second baby, Jim and I talked about possible names. He asked me what I thought about James Bennett Nolan, if it was a boy; I said that would be fine with me. Then he suggested that if it was a girl, why not Christine, as it was expected around Christmas time. I said "maybe" and then invented a girl's name that I liked. "What about Janne–that would be a combination of Jim and Anne?" He seemed to prefer his choice but nothing was decided. In those days you didn't know whether your baby would be a girl or a boy until it arrived.

I told Ann about my Janne inspiration. She seemed to be flattered but had so much on her mind that it was hard to tell. Business was booming and she was busy night and day. She found an assistant, a tall, bouncing, bubbling blonde who had worked for the American edition of *Vogue*. Things were going so well that it even seemed possible that Dorothy and I would be able to draw salaries soon. To date, Ann, the French secretary, models, photographers, printers, and now Ann's assistant, were being paid, but Dorothy and I were working for fun and not thinking about money.

It looked like our little business was destined for big times. Everyone was in an expansive mood and we were gathering printed proof of our successes. But I kept worrying about Ann. Our business carried her name and she had not yet taken steps to get her personal papers in order. It didn't matter if you were just another American tourist hanging out in Paris for a while, but when you had a business with your name on it and were heading for success–no telling what might happen.

I hinted, I suggested, I tried to sit her down to talk about it but she'd shrug with a big smile and off she'd go on another of her endless rendezvous. She was having a good time proving her worth and couldn't care less about boring details. I understood that but nevertheless, in my corner of the office taking care of the business side as well as press releases, I couldn't help worrying that with every success we had came the danger that someone might want to make trouble for us.

Champagne...

Nagging at every chance I got, I finally told her that if she didn't get her papers in order she might be put out of France. She laughed merrily at that one. "Don't worry," she said, "if it comes to that, I can always marry Buchwald."

Little by little I was learning a lot about Ann. She was a tiny blonde dynamo–bright, cute and witty on one hand, secretive and cunning on the other. She came from a huge Irish Catholic family in Pennsylvania and must have struggled against a lot of odds to get anywhere at all. Once Jim introduced her to a tall, dark and handsome friend from Reading, Dick Bortz, who was not only a bachelor, but was taking over the family candy factory that was doing very well. This attractive fellow took me aside on his next visit and accused me of putting Ann up to romancing him. I was flabbergasted; such a thing never entered my head. Then he went on to say that she "came on like gangbusters," closing in on a couch and giving him sweet talk that was too sugary even for him.

"She's just not my type," he insisted, "not my type at all!" How true that was. Later he married a six-foot-tall brunette horsewoman. They had five handsome children and lived happily ever after.

One day in our office when everything seemed to be moving along smoothly for all, Ann got Dorothy and me in a corner to convince us that it was time for her to make a business trip to New York. Her reasoning seemed solid and she didn't have to insist. We agreed. Ann was doing a good job getting business and, after all, she had a lot of clout with her name on the letterhead and the reputation that Ann McGarry Associates was earning. Arrangements were made and she went merrily on her way to Manhattan.

It must have been about ten days later that she returned bubbling over with her report of important contacts and promised projects in the making. I'm certain that everything she said was true, but it didn't cushion the shock I got when the cancelled checks from our dollar account came in. She had taken blank Ann McGarry Associates checks with her to New York without telling me and some of the cancelled checks that came back were for fancy clothes bought in an exclusive 57th Street shop.

I stared at the "evidence" I held in my hand and couldn't believe that she would do such a thing. She had check-signing rights on co-signed checks but never the right to do this. I tried to call her aside to talk about it but she said she didn't have time. When I insisted, she got angry and announced, "I needed clothes," in a voice that made me the culprit for denying her necessities.

I felt sad and betrayed when I told Jim about it and wasn't ready for his reaction. He calmly stated that it wasn't very much money so I shouldn't get upset about it. "Jim, that's not the point–what about PRINCIPLE? If someone can do this behind your back, what can happen next? Isn't confidence in one another basic in a partnership?" Oh, I know, I went on and on, getting all my hurt out. This inspired Jim, in the first of many tirades, to accuse me of being "nothing but a Calvinist."

Obviously one can't remember arguments word-for-word, but this went on so many times that it was almost like a script. "You're talking like a Calvinist," he'd state as though I should know better.

"I don't even know what a Calvinist is," I'd say. Jim picked out that label to pin on me when I told him that my father's name was Calvin, which was also the name of one of my brothers. I didn't have a definite religion you could put a tag on, and when he first asked me what Church I went to when I was young, I answered, "The one nearest to where I lived." Jim's insistence that I was a Calvinist inspired me to look up what it meant; and when I learned that a man named John Calvin emphasized the doctrines of pre-destination and salvation only by God's grace, and that it was associated with a stern moral code, that didn't sound so bad to me.

Future accusations that I was a Calvinist didn't bother me.

The first Franco-American public relations company in Paris, Ann McGarry Associates, was growing all the time with more business coming our way every month, but my relation with Ann was at a low ebb. I continued to go through the motions of working with her; we had a lot of projects on our desks requiring partners to work together. My heart wasn't in it and my head was deliberating exactly what I should do. The answer came straight to me at a Franco-American reception I attended a short time later. An American banker from our bank told me that he'd had a visit in his office from Art Buchwald and Ann McGarry to discuss Ann McGarry Associates business.

"Art Buchwald," I gulped, "what has he got to do with our business?" The banker seemed a bit embarrassed but he went on to explain that Art had come with Ann to warn the bank that she was having trouble with one of her partners, so the bank should be careful not to let anyone come in and close down the account. My heart was beating fast when I heard this. How could Ann know so little about me that she feared I'd do such a thing behind her back?

Funny how things turn out. I never had any intention of telling anyone about our troubles. Here I was telling the banker, who was also a friend, exactly what had happened and how sad I was about it. Then I realized I knew what I had to do. No one ever has to worry about my touching our account, I told him, but I did plan on going to the lawyer who set up our business and see how I could get out...gracefully.

All I wanted was my third of the original investment–never mind what I had put in for Ann. She could consider that my farewell present. Jim's father was in Paris on the day I had an appointment at Charles Torem's office to pick up my Ann McGarry Associates check and he went along with me. He seemed quite pleased that I had gotten my money without a problem and I didn't dare tell him that Ann's investment was mine as well, as it would have been ample proof to him of what a lousy businesswoman I was. I was still upset about Buchwald's part in all of this; when I first met Art I liked him. In those early days, he was full of funny jokes, original ideas and enthusiasm to share his GI-American-in-Paris experiences. In addition to that, his life story touched my sentimental side. In boyhood he had been in and out of foster homes and he had lied about his age to get into the Marines during the war. Things were better for him after the war when he could profit by the GI Bill, which enabled him to be a student in Paris at the Alliance Française with a living allowance, gas ration coupons and a student's card giving him discounts on everything from the subway to the Paris Opéra.

To make ends meet, he said, he'd sell his gas coupons to the highest bidder and he got a job at *Variety* for eight dollars a week plus free movie and theater tickets. Then he wangled a job at the *Herald Tribune* by telling one editor that another editor had hired him when editor number one was out of town. His work was read, laughed at and loved by all. After Clem Brown and Jim Nolan came up with the cash to publish Art's first book, *Paris After Dark,* Artie never looked back.

A perfect explanation of why I was no longer an associate of the Associates was the imminent arrival of another little Nolan. No waiting around a day and a night for this one; the doctor had the arrival scheduled for early in the morning of December 28. Before Christmas I bought little Cathy a miniature baby carriage, an exact replica of a real baby buggy, built by the makers of the genuine models. When the butler saw this tiny vehicle, he seemed worried and suggested perhaps it would be too small for a new baby. I laughed and explained that it was for Cathy and her dolls so that she could wheel them up and down the halls and not be jealous of the other "doll" in the bigger carriage when it came on the scene.

Three days after Christmas, Janne Émilie Nolan was born in the same maternity wing of the American Hospital of Paris where Cathy was born just a year and two months before. The atmosphere was still quite château-like and the champagne served was delicious. Jim was there soon after, at ease this time and ready to discuss the name of our new daughter. He still wanted Christine and I still wanted Janne. "But I thought you were mad at Ann," he said and I explained that my upset with Ann was much too petty to influence me to change my mind. Jim was the one who had to go over to the *mairie* in Neuilly to register the birth and I thought for a long time that he might have written Christine in the books, but he let me have my way and, after all, the "J" in Janne was in honor of Jim. And, for Janne's birth, he didn't make a mistake about the hour of arrival: nine in the morning, not at night.

Janne was two days old when my favorite photographer, David "Chim" Seymour, showed up at the hospital to see the new arrival. He loved to take baby pictures and was kept busy taking photos of many new American-Parisians coming into the world at that time. What a lovely man he was. How sad that he didn't just keep doing what he was doing in Paris. But he was an action photographer who had survived world wars, always off to some trouble spot. Before Cathy and

Ann and Art Buchwald
with me in the days
when I thought
Art was funny.

Janne were old enough to know him, he was shot dead by trigger-happy patrol
guards at Suez while reaching for his passport in his breast pocket.

When Janne came home from the hospital, little Catherine Elizabeth Nolan
was just beginning to stand on her own. She promenaded her dolls up and down
the corridor, weaving from side to side and bumping into closet doors, but always
arriving at her destination in the salon to show off her dolls. She was beginning to
talk at the same time and with the usual mama-dada-baby, she added something
that sounded like "cat-na." We figured that out pretty soon. She was trying to say
"Catherine," which she heard often when I called the nurse in the hall. Cathy soon
perfected "cat-na" to "Catina," which became the official name for Catherine from
then on.

Cathy gave her sister a nickname as well. From the time she peeked into the
baby's basket, she called her "Kiki." No one figured out where she got that but it
stuck to Janne Émilie Nolan until she went to school. As soon as she learned to
write, Janne penned a note and handed it around like an official announcement
declaring that her name was no longer Kiki, thank you very much.

The new baby was about three months old and it was a fine Spring day when
Jim announced that we were going to take a flying trip to the U.S. to show our family to everyone in Reading, PA., USA. "The whole family?" I asked. "Are we taking the nurse?" He said that was no problem at all; the company was very generous in allowing air travel for employees and there was more than enough room in
the Nolan home.

Breaking the news to Catina and convincing her that she ought to try flying in
a plane wasn't easy. She'd never been near an airplane before and the idea of crossing the Atlantic high in the sky terrified her, she said. When she realized that we'd
be going *en famille* whether or not she was with us, she changed her mind.

The TWA airplane in those days was roomy and comfortable with only four
seats in each row, separated by the aisle. Jim and family were given the first row

seats across the front with plenty of room for a baby basket and all the essentials needed for the trip. And because the plane was far from full, Jim was given another two seats in the second row. As a TWA executive with lots of charm, Jim enjoyed VIP attention all the way. In those days, flight time could be anywhere from 17 to 20 hours, with a stopover for refueling at Shannon, Ireland, or Gander, Newfoundland. When the plane took off Catina looked like she was going to faint but as soon as we were airborne she busied herself with the children and forgot all about her fear of flying. Up in the air, she was fine but every time we had to take off or land, I thought I might have to call for smelling salts or whatever they had to revive a passenger who'd passed out cold.

Arriving at the Nolan family home was an adventure. Grandma Nolan was so thrilled to have the visit of her grandchildren that she couldn't stop following us around and making sure, with her housekeeper Bessie, that we had everything we needed to make ourselves comfortable. She even told Bessie that in France people had breakfast in bed, so she'd better get out the proper trays.

The huge house was located right in the city but had its own back and side gardens connecting the property with another house on the next street belonging to Grandpa Nolan's sister.

The Nolan house looked like a mixture of museum, antique store and curio shop. It was filled, bottom to top, with European furniture, paintings, prints, maps, tapestries, urns, leather-bound books and art objects of every size and description in every nook and on every shelf and table. All the way up the staircase were fitted shelves holding miniature French soldiers set in battle scenes, looking like they had marched right out of history books. I saw all of this, in passing, and knew it would take weeks to see everything in that unusual house.

The next morning brought me an example of how different Reading was from Paris. Bessie, the maid, came bursting in without knocking and said, "Morning, Maggi. Have a good sleep?" and plunked a breakfast tray on the table. I giggled, remembering the third person manner of servants back home where, after a discreet knock, they'd enter and say something like "Would *Madame* desire to have the curtains opened?" Looking at the tray Bessie left brought another contrast; there was so much food there that I couldn't look at it.

Later, I took the tray down to Bessie in the kitchen and told her I'd be coming down to the dining room from now on as all I wanted in the morning was coffee and toast. I liked Bessie, but was surprised when I went into the kitchen to see that she had a little black and white, spotted, mongrel dog chained to a chair. "I didn't know you had a dog, Bessie," I said, thinking I'd give him a pat on the head, but Bessie stood in my way, warning me that he might snap at me. Then she explained that it was Grandpa Nolan's dog who stayed right there where he was except when the master came to take him on walks.

I didn't think that was much of a life for a little dog but Bessie said that it had always been that way since she'd been there. There had been other little mongrels before this one; they were all called "Doolie" and as soon as one died (or escaped and ran away) the master would just go out and get another one.

While Jim's father was out that morning, Jim showed me through the various suites of rooms in the house. I was surprised at the contrast between Grandma's simplicity and austerity in her bedroom, bath and sun porch and the outright opulence of Grandpa's rooms across the landing. He had French period furniture with a Louis XVI bed and an ornate inlaid desk fit for a French tycoon. His bathroom featured a wall of elaborate mosaics created with old stones imported from Italy. Further along the hall was Grandpa's library with books on floor-to-ceiling bookshelves. There were piles of maps, prints, and giant leather, gold-tooled folders holding historical papers on a huge center table lighted with a spotlight. He had enough chairs, lamps and end tables to fill a shop plus an oversized easy chair with footstool and a couch against the wall for his afternoon naps.

I was allowed to take a good look at the library but Jim told me it was off limits for everyone unless Grandpa was there and extended an invitation. At the end of the house, by contrast, was Grandma Nolan's sunroom full of greenery, overlooking the back garden. Visitors were always welcome. When I think of her, I can see her sitting quietly in her wicker chair with the sun streaming through the leaded windows. That's where you'd find her every day, sitting and sewing. She liked to mend whatever needed attention and very often, she'd be darning gentlemen's socks using an odd, old-fashioned, egg-shaped object. She'd put the sock-mender inside a sock, placed just under the hole so she'd have perfect control of her work. Do people still use these things today? I don't know but in those days that olive-tree wood, egg shape with its silver handle was a must in Grandma's life. She worked so meticulously that you couldn't see where the hole had been.

Catina and the babies seemed to be getting along so well and I enjoyed being with Grandma so much that I would have been quite happy to stay right there in the house for our entire visit, but Jim and his father had social plans for us every evening. They liked to go to the Country Club where the other members crowded around and gave us a lot of attention. Grandma told me, between us, that she didn't care too much for that social scene, but agreed with the plans without a word. She was ready and waiting downstairs in the hall before anyone else.

Our visits to the Club gave me a new insight into the Reading world. The first thing I noticed was an animated lady, outstanding in the crowd, who looked like a middle-aged kewpie doll to me. Grandpa was paying her a lot of attention and she was gushing all over the place. When Grandma and I were alone at our table, she said very sweetly that she'd be happy if I didn't find time for "that woman," nodding toward the curly-headed kewpie doll still batting her eyelashes in Grandpa Nolan's face. I patted my mother-in-law's hand to show her I understood and it was never mentioned again.

When I asked Jim who this person was, he said "Just a friend of my old man." I was still curious so Jim added that she and his father had a lot in common. "She collects things," he explained. I wanted to say "like other ladies' husbands?" but I didn't.

It was obvious to me from the first evening that although J. Bennett Nolan was treated with respect to his face, a lot of fellow members of his Club were quick to "do him in" behind his back. The first one to add to my knowledge of my father-in-law asked me if I had read any of Mr. Nolan's books, which he had to publish himself. When she saw my surprise, she added, "Oh, didn't you know he pays for the printing of his books out of his own pocket?"

Another told me the story of the Nolan marriage like it was a momentous event in Pennsylvania history. It was the talk of the town in the old days, she said, when Grandma married Grandpa. It was the luck of his lifetime, marrying all that money so that he never had to earn his own way. "Imagine never having to work for a living," she said with a wide, sweet smile. Added to this were any number of people who casually asked me what I thought of the animated kewpie doll. I was ready for that one, I simply told the truth: "I don't know her."

A surprising fact about the family came directly from Grandma herself when she told me that although everyone thought they were Irish because of the name, both sides of the family were more Pennsylvania Dutch (the name given to German settlers long ago). I laughed and said that Jim would always be as Irish as Paddy's Pig to me, with all the blarney and shenanigans that went with it.

Chapter Six

On the airplane coming back to Paris, Jim announced quite casually that he thought the time had come for us to buy our own home, either an apartment like the one we were renting or a town house. I was thrilled with the idea but couldn't help asking how we could possibly afford it. He assured me there was no problem. "Mom'll help," he said in his bored, don't-worry-about-it tone of voice. There was plenty of room in our apartment for our growing family but we were constantly harassed by the owners month after month. Jim started lining up places for sale for us to take a look at. I was included this time as buying something was much more serious than renting. I was grateful but soon discouraged at the terrible shape most of the apartments and houses were in. Most had been neglected since the war and many of them had beautiful salons and frightful conditions behind the scenes. It was hard to believe that people greeted you in luxurious living rooms and then showed filthy, antiquated kitchens and bathrooms with broken-down plumbing.

One place we looked at seemed high above the average and when we started to talk to the owners seriously, they told us that old-time servants were installed in the servants' quarters and couldn't be put out. "Oh, no, we can't have that," I said and the lady selling the apartment remarked, "Oh, but Madame, they're very old." In other words, they'll kick off soon, you see.

After that lady's suggestion to buy her apartment with its "death watch," I asked Jim if we ought to have a little respite; the apartment we were in seemed like a palace in comparison to those we'd been seeing.

Jim was flying on short business trips to London, Rome and Madrid by then. Hardly a week went by without a three-day absence from Paris. I'd gone to Rome with him once to attend a TWA celebration, but wasn't scheduled to take another trip with him until the following year when TWA would be flying airplane loads of celebrities to the opening of Conrad Hilton's Castellaña-Hilton in Madrid. Once when he hadn't been away from Paris for a while, he announced just before the weekend that he was called to Rome and from there he'd go to Madrid. "May I borrow your typewriter for the trip?" he asked. The request seemed a little odd to me; in all the times we had worked together I'd never seen him in front of a typewriter. I took my portable out of the closet and dusted it off for him to take along with his luggage, not giving it another thought. When we said goodbye I expected him back the following weekend.

Alas, in the middle of the next week Jim's secretary called to tell me that the lady from Hollywood who borrowed my typewriter had just brought it back. She asked if I wanted it delivered to me or if I could wait until Jim got back. After getting my breath, I tried to be casual when I asked her if she was sure the lady wouldn't need it any more. "No," I was told, she'd come back from Rome and was now on her way back to Hollywood. I told the secretary I could wait for my machine until Jim got back. "Thank you, anyway," I said, and hung up feeling like I'd been hit on the head.

Jim came bouncing in on Sunday. With his luggage he carried a large, flat box. With a big smile, he put it on my lap and said, "Here, try this on for size." In the box under lots of tissue paper was a luscious red silk evening gown by Rodriguez of Madrid. Jim couldn't wait for me to try it on so I went back to the bedroom while the butler brought him some coffee. The dress fit perfectly and I went trailing down the hall to show him how it looked. "Wow!" he said, "I can't wait to show you off in that," and he kissed my bare shoulders.

This was hardly the time to talk about my typewriter; I wasn't even thinking about it. We had an invitation for a formal dinner party at Maxim's coming up and this was an ideal gown for the occasion. Jim was in an expansive mood, telling me all about TWA progress in his PR offices and then going into the details of buying the dress. The PR lady he'd hired in Madrid had taken him to see the fashion collection, helped pick out the dress and then talked the saleslady into selling the model gown although their showings were far from over for the season. I said "thank you" several times.

The next week we had our "typewriter talk" but it was Jim who started it when he came in carrying my portable. Obviously his secretary had told him about our conversation. He dumped it on the floor and started. "Listen, I knew if I told you it was for some dame, you'd get mad."

"Jim, I'm not saying anything."

"Yeah, but I know what you're thinking."

"I'm thinking you went to Rome with her, is that true?"

"So we were on the same plane. So what?"

"So I'm thinking what you think I'm thinking."

And on and on. He claimed that she was an important journalist writing travel stories and he had to do everything possible for her. Everything? Anyway, he knew that being a professional, I would readily have lent my silly typewriter to a journalist had I been asked. Not being asked suggested his relationship was more personal than professional.

This incident passed over quickly; we were too busy to bicker. I pouted a bit but soon bounced back like a rubber ball. We were meeting so many people day and night that sometimes it was hard to remember where we had dined the night before and what we had eaten, let alone the first and/or last names of the people around the table. One fellow I really liked from the very beginning was TWA President, Warren Lee Pierson. He was smart, relaxed and witty, and his wife, Eleanor, matched him. They were hard-working people by day (she wrote articles for magazines like *Town & Country*) but they were amusing and fun after dark. Once we went to dinner with them with handsome Jack Heinz (of the 57 varieties) and an Irish beauty, Drue Mallory, who had stunning auburn hair and sparkling green eyes. After dinner we decided to go to L'Éléphant Blanc, which was now the top all-night spot, but Drue disappeared without a word. When Jack Heinz realized she was missing, he excused himself and hurried off to find her.

Warren laughed and said that Drue had been pulling that trick since they'd arrived in Paris. "If Jack keeps chasing Drue, she's going to catch him," Warren chuckled. And, of course, Drue and Jack did get married and stayed married forever after.

Another evening, Warren, Eleanor, Jim and I were dining at the Ritz. Warren asked me if I'd like to suggest a wine to go with dinner and I said, "Just champagne will do." He looked up and grinned, saying he hoped TWA was making enough money to pay for my choice.

Another time at Maxim's, Jim asked me if I'd help him choose a champagne. I picked out an outstanding one on the wine list which I'd gotten to know when dining there. Then I went upstairs to powder my nose and when I returned, champagne was already poured in my glass. I tasted it and tried very subtly to whisper to Jim that they were giving him the wrong champagne; it was nothing like the one I had selected. Everyone at the table laughed and gave me high marks; Jim had deliberately ordered another, wondering if I'd notice.

Champagne, by now, was my favorite beverage and I knew if that's all I drank during an evening, I'd never get a headache or feel the least bit woozie. I learned that good champagne never gives you a headache; inferior brands are the ones to watch out for. There weren't many bad bottles in those days; today you'd better beware. There are a lot of awful bottles around. I call them "instant headache" brands.

It wasn't long after I'd declared time-out on apartment hunting that Jim came home excited, elated and animated. "Eureka, I've found it," he announced, grabbing me around the waist to twirl as he sang out his news. He'd found a house–a real house with a garden and a wall around it–and it was just around the corner from where we were. "The house belonged to a doctor who was getting married and moving away and wanted to get rid of it. Bedrooms and bathrooms for all and a wine cellar in the basement with a big key that must be a foot long." He said all this barely taking a breath. When he stopped dancing and chanting, I looked him in the eye and said, "You bought it."

Indeed he had. He was afraid that someone else would get there if he didn't take it fast. I was fearful until early the next day when he took me around to see it. We rang the bell at the iron gate and the door was buzzed open by a maid in the house. My first look gave me a funny sensation, that feeling of having seen the place before. The house was what the French call a *petit pavillon* set back in the garden. There were three rooms on each floor and more bathrooms, showers and WCs than we'd ever seen in a house in France. They were modern and they were all in working order, which deserved a special citation in those days.

The ground floor had a living room the length of a house with a picture window overlooking the garden and a smaller window overlooking the back terrace. There was a huge kitchen with pantry, a picture-windowed dining room and a linen closet as big as a room itself. One flight up, there were bathrooms on both sides of a master bedroom with a dressing room any lady would like. The next floor was a nanny's dream. A huge room as big as the salon downstairs that made a fine nursery with Cathy's furniture; a small room for a new baby, Catina's room overlooking the garden with one wall fitted with cupboards and closets. The top floor had servants' rooms with oval-shaped windows overlooking the garden. And a back room for luggage and storage. The servants' floor had running water and a WC; a modern shower had recently been installed downstairs in the neatly-cemented cellar. On the opposite side of the *cave* a special room had been built for wine; it looked like a little prison and had a huge key to open the heavy wooden door.

I went around the house several times. I looked and looked and looked some more. "Jim," I said, "it's great." Of course, when chipped paint and discolored walls and worn-out carpets caught the eye, it was obvious there was a lot of work to do but it still was a dream come true.

How can I ever forget that moment when Jim and I stood in that little garden overgrown with weeds. We turned around together and looked at that funny little *pavillon* which seemed to have our name on it. Before leaving, the giant chestnut tree cornered in the garden just inside the wall caught my eye. I went over and gave it a pat on its bark. It was like an old friend.

In 1952, the Rue du Docteur Blanche was picturesque and unique. If you visited it today it would be hard to imagine how it was in the fifties. As soon as you turned the corner of the Rue de l'Assomption, it looked like country living. Each house had a garden in front; most houses and gardens were enclosed by walls except those like the cottage-studio of American sculptor, Herbert Hazeltine, at the opposite end of our *pavillon*. The sculptor's home didn't have a wall and his garden was so overgrown and wild that you felt like you were making your way through a field to get to his door. Here he specialized in sculpting thoroughbred racehorses in solid gold for his horsey clients like Winston, Diana and Raymond Guest.

Our street was named after alienist Dr. Esprit Blanche, born in 1796, who died exactly 100 years before we moved into his street in 1952. His son, Dr. Émile Blanche, lived and died at number 19, where Dr. Esprit Blanche's grandson, Jacques-Émile Blanche, writer/painter, lived until he died in 1942.

Our house at number 50 had about a ten-foot wall in the front with two heavy iron doors. The bigger door was the "masters' entrance" leading into the garden; the smaller one was the service entrance opening onto a narrow pathway going around the side of the house to the pantry door through a tiny back garden. A high wall on one side separated our garden from the next-door neighbor but the other side had no more than a shoulder-high fence. Anyone could have climbed over it if they wished but people didn't do things like that in those days. These were days before double locks, alarms, security guards and all the things that became necessary later.

We were in the process of moving into our own home when Christian came into our lives. He was a street cleaner for the City of Paris, stationed on the Rue du Docteur Blanche; a huge man proud of his job and interested in all residents on "his" street. He took an immediate liking to *les Américains* and offered to help us to get our garden in shape. In no time, he became our unofficial handyman, first clearing all the weeds and cutting the straw-colored grass, which made an immediate improvement. He spent so much time in the morning talking to Jim about what had to be done and then again in the afternoon about what had been accomplished that I worried he might get into trouble with his City of Paris superiors but he never did. His street was always impeccable.

I can still see the tall, distinguished-looking Christian in his neat midnight blue uniform with his natty matching cap. He carried a handmade broom crafted out of tree twigs for his street cleaning. Today there's quite a difference: frog green overalls, plastic jackets and bright green machine-made twiglike brooms of pure plastic. (Ah, but in addition to these frogmen, there are bright green machines of all sorts, watering , scooping, and sucking up debris all over town.)

The next project Jim gave to Christian was to put in a pink brick surface for an outdoor parasol-covered table with chairs. Then he started on indoor projects as well, like building shelves from floor to ceiling in the linen room off the kitchen. What a neat idea that turned out to be. On one side of the room were shelves for each floor of the house: the bottom shelf for table linen, next the monogrammed linen for our floor (thanks to Jim's mother), then the pink-and-blue trimmed for the nursery and green trimmed for the top. The other side of the room held shelves for the servants' uniforms, kitchen towels, etc., and there was space to hold the vacuum cleaner, ironing board, household supplies, etc. Christian had every reason to be proud of that project.

Jim and I had the time of our lives "playing house." Every Saturday morning we'd get into the car for a cross-town trip to the flea market. It was a treasure trove of incredible bargains. On the way to the second-hand open marketplace we'd

Champagne...

The *petit pavillon* I loved
at 50 rue du Docteur Blanche.

decide in advance what we should concentrate on, otherwise one could get lost in the maze and end up exhausted and empty-handed. One day we'd be on the look-out for a chest of drawers, another we'd be hunting for dining room chairs or else "How about checking out marble-topped tables?"

Of course, one could still get side-tracked. One Saturday I saw an oil painting of an ancient Italian scene which gave me that "déjà-vu" feeling with tingling on the back of my neck. I stared at it, walked away, turned back and stared at it again. Tugging Jim's sleeve, I said, "Please, let's get that." He thought it was an awful, dirty mess but he had just passed up a set of six sizes of pewter mugs which I said were terrible, so before our Saturday jaunt was over, he had his mugs and I had my painting.

By a series of mini-miracles, I still have that painting which two "experts" insist is a work by Hubert Robert (1733-1808), but I haven't tried to prove it in the Robert room of the Louvre Museum. I like it. A few years ago the Austrian painter, Heidi Beer (widow of the conductor, Sydney Beer) restored it for me and we discovered two little figures in the background I didn't know were there.

Oh, what a lot of "stuff" we bought. Silver trays, candlesticks, firebacks for our three fireplaces, a gilded clock that never worked but looked lovely on the mantel, lamps, end tables with secret drawers, partial sets of crystal glassware, odd silver goblets, soup ladles, cigarette boxes and so on.

Jim was so anxious to start having parties that we didn't even wait until the salon was furnished. Our neighbors, Jesse and Liz Jones, who lived on the tree-lined, unpaved Square du Docteur Blanche, lent us a couch, chairs and little tables from the large array of leftovers stored in a room of their four-floor home. The Jones' house was one of the most popular party places in Paris. Jesse headed the promotion department of *Newsweek* and his wife, Elizabeth Flanigan Jones, was the daughter of an American admiral.

The upside down house that the Jones called home was designed and built by the outstanding and controversial Swiss-born French architect Charles Edouard Jeanneret, known as Le Corbusier, who seemed to like shocking people, as did other creators of his time like Pablo Picasso and Gertrude Stein. The Jones' house looked like a blockhouse from the front. Guests came in through a side door and had to climb three flights of stairs to get to their hosts. The living room and entertaining area with a large terrace were on the top; dining room and kitchen just below; bedrooms and baths under that and then the servants' quarters and storage space on at street level. Once you got up to the roof and began to enjoy the incredible hospitality of Jesse and Liz Jones, you never wanted to leave. (A wag around Paris said he bet there'd still be guests up there if the house hadn't been turned into a Le Corbusier museum a few years later.)

The Jones introduced us to two services that American-Parisians couldn't live without in those days: the American Commissary and the American Diaper Service. The commissary was a must for baby food in jars, tissues and toilet paper, peanut butter, whiskies, beer and soft drinks, cigarettes and all sorts of cocktail snacks unheard of in France. In the days before disposable diapers were invented, the American Diaper Service was a family's best friend, delivering stacks of gleaming cotton diapers and taking away a canvas sack of soiled ones. With the great number of American-Parisians being born, plus the increasing number of French parents who learned about the service, they must have made a fortune before plastic came to town.

Having Jesse and Liz Jones living on the Square, across the street and down the road, was a blessing on many occasions when Jim was away and I had no plans for the evening. Their door was always open to their Nolan neighbors. Liz, too, often dropped by on sunny afternoons to sit under the parasol in the garden and watch her son, Robin, playing on the brick floor at our feet. One day, however, he gashed his knee on an uneven edge of brick. "You'd better do something about that brick," Liz told me as she rushed her little boy home. I told Jim about it but he didn't think it important enough to comment on. I repeated what Liz had said and pointed out that the same thing could happen to our children.

"Keep the kids off it," was his comment on that.

He said "Keep the kids off" another time a little later when he came home with two wooden horses he'd found which had once adorned a French park's carrousel. He placed one on each side of the pathway and repeated "Don't let the kids around these; they're antiques and they cost a fortune." (Cathy and Janne came to call them *les "da-da" de Dada*, which showed they understood that they were hobby horses belonging to their father.)

When the butler told Jim that he had worked for a man who'd been sued by a guest who'd slipped on a garden pathway while coming to a party, Jim announced that he was going to have the garden landscaped by professionals from the neighborhood. Although I didn't think a fancy project was necessary, I kept quietly happy with the thought that the dangerous brickwork would be taken away.

Jim's enthusiasm over the garden planning put him in a good mood as he pored over the elaborate proposals. "Fountains? Oh, no, Jim," I dared say one day and he grabbed the landscapers' layout out of my hand. (*Ye gads*, I've done it again.) "Sorry dear," I added, "its up to you. I'll like anything you decide." I was getting to dread his bad moods, especially when they seemed to be caused by me. My apology soothed him. He bounced back smiling and told me about a Chinese artist that Louis and Maggie Vaudable, the owners of Maxim's, had told him about. Zao Wou-ki was coming up in the art world, though he was only in his early thirties. Jim wanted to take me to his atelier to choose something. He seemed to have completely forgotten his outburst.

Jim ordered his garden, *sans* fountains. The table and chairs were placed outside the picture window of the dining room, a two-seated swing stood under the chestnut tree. Lots of bushes that didn't need much tending were added and in place of the brick floor, stood a giant cement kidney-shaped basin for flowering plants. Jim was quite pleased with his landscaped handiwork, so I certainly didn't tell him that Liz Jones said she thought the basin looked like an outdoor bathtub.

A short while later, we went to Zao Wou-ki's atelier where Jim said I could choose what I wanted. I loved the work of this Chinese-Parisian on sight and wouldn't have minded owning them all. I selected two, two-foot wide lithographs: one a Surrealist rendition of the six towers of Paris, and another of a bottle jug. The Vaudables had huge Zao Wou-ki paintings in their collection, but I thought smaller lithographs suited us in our *petit pavillon*.

Our new world in our own home seemed a wonderful place to be until Jim's father came back to town. Actually he traveled with Jim's mother this time on the same ship, but she checked into the Hôtel Lotti on the Rue de Castiglione, while he took his usual room at the Hôtel France et Choiseul around the corner. Jim's father was the first to arrive at our new home late afternoon before Jim was back from the office. He didn't waste a minute in letting me know that he disapproved of buying such a big house in the most expensive neighborhood in Paris. Then he took a tour of the downstairs rooms, barely furnished at the time, and said it was obvious that we had frittered away a fortune on "doodads" that we could live without. He walked around like a master of the house and I couldn't wait for Jim to get home to tell his father to mind his own business.

When Jim came home his father repeated his *réflexions* but Jim ignored him. Not once did he try to argue or even answer back. Later, when we were alone, I tried to get Jim to talk to me and explain why he didn't stand up to his father, but he turned his back with a shrug. "Forget it," he repeated. "I told you to forget it."

When Jim's mother came over the next day, she arrived by herself in a taxi. The driver helped her with her packages, boxes and shopping bags full of fancy surprises. She smiled, kissed me and said she loved it when I called her Grandma Nolan. We sat in the sparsely-furnished living room while she showed me the lovely surprises she'd brought from America. There were pink and white sweaters, caps and mittens for the babies, one-piece snowsuits impossible to find in France at that time, plus enough toys to start a shop. For me, there were two satin-and-lace nighties from Vanity Fair and two beautiful, antique tablecloths. She said they'd been in her family and that we should have them here in Paris. For Jim she brought undershirts and socks in just the right colors and sizes. I was touched by her generosity and pleased with her impeccable taste. She took my hand and told me once again what it meant to her to have grandchildren.

And then she added with a laugh, "All my friends have gold bracelets with medallions for each grandchild," she said. "Now I can have one myself."

Cathy and Janne as babies in French pram.

Champagne...

She moved around the rooms, admiring the house while saying how pleased she was that her son had finally settled down. She kept repeating, "And now I have grandchildren." When the babies came in from their afternoon *promenade* in the double baby carriage, Grandma had tears in her eyes as she looked out the picture window and saw them being wheeled through the gate. After a visit, they were taken upstairs, but before Catina went up Grandma put an envelope in her hand and told her to buy something nice for herself.

We had tea before Grandpa and Jim showed up around cocktail time. Grandma Nolan asked that I take all the packages upstairs before Grandpa Nolan came in. "No need to mention this in front of Bennett," she said, knowing that she didn't have to say any more. All the goodies were out of sight as we sat waiting for Jim and his father. The austerity of the scene didn't keep Grandpa from taking up his monologue of the day before. Jim ignored him as he got out the cocktail glasses and Grandma didn't seem to hear him. Later I discovered her trick: when he'd start to rant and rave she'd close off her hearing aid with a switch–a little disk attached to the front of her dress. I discovered this when I said something to her and I saw her switch it on and ask, "What did you say, dear?"

I couldn't ignore everything Grandpa Nolan said; I wasn't immune like Jim or armed with a switch like Grandma. I heard him and it hurt.

Grandpa Nolan could be counted on to criticize everything we did, all the people we knew, and especially, everything we bought for the house, the children and ourselves. There was one *réflexion* he loved to repeat: every time he saw me sipping champagne he'd remind me not to get accustomed to drinking champagne because I'd only get beer when I moved back to America.

Chapter Seven

Tirades by "the famous Pennsylvanian historian, J. Bennett Nolan," my father-in-law now called Grandpa Nolan, upset me more and more. Often when Jim came home from the office after one of Grandpa's visits to our house, I'd plead, "Can't you tell your father to leave me alone? Can't you remind him that he's not paying our bills? Why don't you tell him that TWA picks up the tab for the wine cellar?" But Jim would only repeat that I shouldn't pay any attention to "the old man."

Fate is funny! With all the tirades against Jim's spending habits, it was his father who instigated the greatest expenditure in our new home when he arranged our lunch in a country château as guests of a Parisian *antiquaire*, Maurice Chalom, of the Place Vendôme.

One Saturday, we were obliged to accompany Grandpa to a château belonging to a man he'd met on the ship coming to France. Grandpa was never one to refuse an invitation to lunch and he had arranged for us to come along so Jim could drive him back and forth. He got full directions on how to get there from the host and handed them to Jim before even checking whether or not we had other plans.

Our host was totally charming in greeting us and making introductions to his guests who seemed to be other Americans of various ages, sizes and accents, probably shipboard acquaintances like Grandpa Nolan.

Monsieur was not very tall, quite bald and had a dramatic black patch over one eye; he reminded me of the actor, Erich von Stroheim. Since the end of the war, he had been buying broken-down châteaux from impoverished French families and then fixing them up to sell to the best customers of the moment: rich Americans.

He only did one at a time and actually lived in each one as he repaired, replenished and redecorated. Then he gave a series of luncheons *chez lui* with the idea of selling the château out from under himself. He didn't have to worry about being homeless as he had a luxurious garden apartment on the Rue de l'Élysée, right across the street from the Palais de l'Élysée, where the President of France takes up residence, within walking distance of the Place Vendôme.

Champagne...

Putting Grandma and Grandpa Nolan on the boat-train. Jim held their
new TWA flight bag filled with Paris souvenirs.

M. Chalom was a delightful and generous host on this beautiful day when we lunched under the magnificent trees in the gardens of his latest masterpiece. Afterward, with the other guests, the host took us on a tour of house and grounds. (Jim's father had fallen asleep under a tree.)

Jim was in one of his expansive moods, charming our host with the story of our recent purchase in the best section of Paris and all we'd done so far to fix it up. When he said that we'd just about finished but had left the living room until last because we wanted it to be an extra special place for entertaining VIPs, I peeked at our host's expression. His face lighted up with a big grin and there was a glimmer in his only eye. He invited us to come to his salons on the Place Vendôme to "get ideas" for our decor anytime we wished.

One day soon after, when we had accepted an invitation to a cocktail party at the Ritz, Jim suggested that we leave for the Place Vendôme early enough to pay a visit to Maurice Chalom. When we arrived we were greeted with open arms like we were long-lost friends. His headquarters in the corner at number 17, Place Vendôme, stretched way back to a garden and were piled high with French furniture, oriental rugs, Chinese screens, paintings of all sizes. I was overcome by the sheer mass of furniture crowding my eyes but every once in a while my attention was drawn to a chair, a table or a certain piece of fabric and I commented on each object that attracted me. Maurice listened and finally commented, "You are drawn to Louis XVI."

I laughed and told him I didn't know one period from another, but he pointed out that each and every one of the things I had admired was from Louis XVI. I thought I was crossing him when I said, "Ahh, but I also love Chinese screens," and he shot back, "Again, Louis the 16th decor."

We had a nice visit, shook hands and Jim invited him to come around and see us the next week when we were having a few people in for cocktails. You can bet he came! While chatting with fellow guests, he was checking out the rooms and he stayed until he was the last one in the salon. Before he left, he had even taken a tape measure out of his pocket when Jim had asked in passing if he had any idea of the measurements of the windows.

It wasn't long after that Maurice Chalom called and said he wanted to visit us again. This time he had fabric samples to show and he was bringing a beautiful inlaid Louis XVI desk which fit perfectly in an alcove near the back windows, saying he wanted to lend it to us just to see if we liked it, with no obligation to buy, of course.

Maurice was a clever salesman. He convinced us that we should have made-to-order settee and chairs in a Louis XVI style as the cost would be very little in comparison to the real thing. It wasn't long before we had a "Chalom salon" with couch, chairs, marble-topped tables, a coffee table made out of a section of a Chinese screen and, of course, we didn't send the desk back.

That lovely desk in the alcove became my "headquarters" where I kept engraved stationery, invitation and calling cards, thank-you notes, datebooks, greeting cards, gift lists, guest lists and all those necessities having to do with the hectic but happy times on the Rue du Docteur Blanche.

One of our first guests in our new home was a charming Frenchman, Jean de Gourcuff, from the Paris TWA office. Jean was quite knowledgeable about food, wine, furniture and everything in France pertaining to good living. He had a beautiful wife named Alix and they lived in a tasteful town house on the Rue de Berri, next door to Elsa Schiaparelli. (Alas, the buildings have now been torn down and there's a glass and steel complex in their place.) At the end of our first luncheon with Jean, when we were getting up from the table, he looked over at the huge fireplace in the far end of the room and asked if we planned to keep it painted as it was.

"Why?" we asked. "Don't you like the color?" and he said he thought it a shame to paint over marble. It had never occurred to either of us that there was marble under the paint or even that anyone would think of such a thing. Jean went over to the fireplace and took a tiny knife out of his pocket, saying "Permit me?" He scraped a tiny patch off the top revealing deep, burgundy-red marble underneath.

Champagne...

"It's beautiful," I said, nodding for him to chip off some more which revealed burgundy-red marble delicately veined with white. It took endless hours of toil by Christian, the street cleaner (now called "the gardener") and the butler to scrape, chip, clean and polish to perfection. The fireplace turned out to be the majestic highlight of the room, and strangely enough, the burgundy carpet we had selected to put down before we knew about the fireplace blended in as though it had been planned.

The Hungarian couple we had with us then, Ferdinand and Sidi, were sweet, hard-working people and it was a sad day indeed when Jim told me we'd have to replace them. We would be inviting very important people to dinner and needed a gourmet cook and a butler who served in the formal French style wearing white gloves. It was horrible having the duty of telling them they'd have to go after they'd been so helpful during the settling, when we seemed to be living gypsy-style in a half-empty house. I seemed hesitant in facing the facts that Jim put before me; he repeated that it was our job to cater to very important people "...and for God's sake, we've got to do better than goulash."

Cook and butler couples were available in numbers in those days. But to find the right ones was something else again. Each couple we took on trial brought surprises, disappointments and adventures; sometimes it seemed like a parade of weirdos were moving in and out.

One couple recommended by Max Blouet, director of the Hôtel George V, had newly arrived in Paris from Marseille. They had excellent references, but the cook insisted on putting garlic in everything and refused to discuss cooking without it. Another couple had loud arguments in the kitchen that seemed to be turning into genuine battles and you could hear their goings-on in the far corner of the garden. One cook was excellent, but her husband was obviously crocked when the time came to serve the cook's perfect meals. This fellow was also a master at breaking our best porcelain. We had to say "goodbye" to yet another couple when we discovered they went out for jaunts in Jim's car every chance they got. And this was only one of a number of disappointments with them.

A few days after paying them off to continue our parade of misfits and n'er-do-wells, Jim's car was stolen from the street right outside our house. By this time he had sold the Citroën and bought a brand new, silver gray Chevrolet which looked pretty fancy on Paris streets in the fifties . It was rare indeed for a car to be stolen in those days and I was certain that the butler had done it. I gave Jim a paper with the butler's name, social security number and even the references he'd given us, but Jim wasn't interested. "Forget it, I'll get another car," he said.

He reported his loss to the police but didn't offer them any clues. The *gendarmes* proved that they were on the look-out for a spiffy, gray Chevrolet: a few days later they stopped Arnaud de Borchgrave of *Newsweek,* at the Porte de St. Cloud. He was at the wheel of a twin of Jim's car which he had bought at the same time from the same dealer and could present ample proof that he was not

Cathy and Janne in the Parc de Saint Cloud wearing American-made
snowsuits from Grandma Nolan.

a car-stealing culprit. Jim's car was never seen again.

Just about the time I had given up hope of ever finding "Mr. and Mrs. Right," when it seemed that I had as many different-sized white jackets on my shelves as they had in a store, Pierre and Anna came into our lives. Pierre was tall, white-haired and quiet; Anna was short, round, red-faced and jolly. They were proud people, sure of themselves, and content to have made a career of their jobs. They had worked many years for a European diplomat who'd left France. They knew their duties well.

Pierre and Anna owned their own little apartment in another part of Paris but they lived on our top floor during the week and went home every Saturday evening until Monday morning. This was fine with us; we had the house to ourselves during weekends and could run in and out of the kitchen as we pleased. Weekdays the kitchen and pantry might as well have had "No Entry" signs as that was forbidden territory. Catina was welcome to trot in and out; she had trays to return, baby bottles to heat, clothes to press or the baby carriage to get from the back for her daily outings. Maybe, sometimes she just went there to chat; she liked Pierre and Anna because they were good at their job and had respect for themselves and the people around them.

Before we'd been in our dreamhouse for six months Jim's longing for end-of-the-year skiing trips came up as before. It was a blow to my fragile ego when Jim took off on a skiing trip by himself on my 30th birthday, which was New Year's Eve as well. I couldn't believe that he could be so uncaring of my feelings but he just announced he was going and left. I had reminded him at Christmas that it was the first birthday of our second child in three days' time and he told me she was too little to know what day it was, "So why make a fuss?"

I wanted to say, "but what about ME?" but I knew it was a waste of time to argue with him when he'd made up his mind. I sat around feeling sorry for myself; the Jones family had gone away for the holidays, so I couldn't cheer myself up with them. But before my day was over Harriet Morrow Boudet called from her apartment around the corner on the Boulevard Suchet to wish us Happy New Year. Harriet was the sister of Bill Morrow, Bing Crosby's Hollywood writer and good friend. She married Pierre, a sweet and very smart Frenchman who was on his way to making millions in a way no Frenchman had thought of until then: importing American chewing gum for the French market. I learned about his endeavours in an unusual way when the Boudets were attending one of our celebrity parties and one of the guests, Virginia Warren, daughter of Chief Justice Earl Warren, couldn't get a taxi to take her back to her hotel and Pierre offered to drive her if she didn't mind his "business vehicle." The next day it seemed all of our guests had heard of Virginia's experience of the night before, which offered them giggles and chuckles. On both sides of Pierre's car, in giant lettering, for all the world to see was "Wrigley's Chewing Gum."

Harriet was a kind, firm friend and I found myself blurting out my tale of woe about New Year's Eve, my birthday, being "abandoned" by Jim and, worse yet, I wailed "I'm THIRTY years old." Harriet hung up, saying that she was going to come over right away, and within three minutes she was ringing the bell at the garden door.

My friend and neighbor insisted that I would celebrate my birthday with her and Pierre at Maxim's with two friends from Chicago. They had a table for four but it could be stretched to five. I didn't want to go (my face was fat from crying) but when Harriet and then Pierre insisted, I dressed in my red Rodriguez and off I went.

Jim must have had a rotten time on his skiing trip because he came back sad and sorry. He never told me where he went skiing or who was in his party, but he was down in the dumps and didn't have a bruise on his body so I knew he hadn't had bad spills as he had just before we were married. My intuition told me to try to forget my end-of-the-year disappointment and I was doing pretty well. Then he actually acted jealous when I told him I'd been to Maxim's with our neighbors.

It wasn't long after this that a king came for cocktails at one of our celebrity parties on the Rue du Docteur Blanche. Egypt's King Farouk was still on his throne and in good stead with the world. When he came to Paris he took an entire floor of the Hôtel Royal Monceau for himself and his entourage.

Neighbors Harriet Morrow Boudet (sister of Bing Crosby's writer, Bill Morrow) and her husband Pierre, who put Wrigley's Chewing Gum on the market in France.

Champagne...

Jim told me that King Farouk might come to one of our parties one day but I didn't give it much thought. Those days, in addition to his frequent trips to London, Rome and Madrid, Jim had added trips to Cairo with the top TWA executives who were conferring with the King to open TWA Airways to Egypt. Jim always came back with fabulous stories about his visits and how interesting a man King Farouk was. This was before all of the horror stories appeared about the King. Jim found him highly educated, amusing and an enthusiastic admirer of the United States of America.

The King signed the deal with Trans World Airlines to make Cairo a TWA destination and Jim came back jubilant that he had not only signed but said he'd be coming to Paris and would be happy to pay us a visit. I laughed and said we'd better not count on it, but Jim insisted the King was crazy about America and knew more about our country and its history than many native born Americans.

"We'd better get in a supply of Pepsi Cola, too," Jim added, saying that was all he drank. King Farouk had made a deal with that company to give it marketing rights in Egypt. I was still skeptical but Jim bought a whole case of Pepsi the next time he went to the American Commissary and put it in the wine cellar to await the King.

One evening soon after, everything was ready for another of our cocktail parties. Our remarkable Monsieur Rosell was there in person setting up the buffet table, hiding champagne in pails of ice under the table to replenish those in silver coolers on both ends of the buffet and arranging endless goodies like pastry boats filled with crab, smoked salmon, caviar, ham and cheese chunks, cheese sticks. In addition, Anna had prepared a few dozen of her special deviled eggs that always had party success.

Just before the guests began to arrive, Jim hurried in late from the office and while running up the stairs to change, he called out, "Farouk is coming over tonight."

Quickly, I found Pierre and told him to bring up the Pepsi Cola from the wine cellar because King Farouk was coming. Pierre turned as white as his hair and disappeared into the kitchen. At the time, I must confess, I didn't expect to meet a king that night and by the time quite a few guests had arrived it was completely out of my head. Jim and I were standing in the doorway when he gave me a little poke in the ribs, saying, "Here he comes." A huge personage came through the gate with a big smile on his face as he made his way up the garden path. "Golly, how do I address a king?" I asked. But Jim was already down the three steps to greet the King on the pathway.

The night King Farouk came to our house was long remembered on the Rue du Docteur Blanche. He arrived with a fleet of eight automobiles carrying his entourage because our party was to be a short private visit before he went on to an official affair. I didn't see the cars and I didn't see anyone with him except his gentleman assistant who came inside with him; the others waited outside. According to the butler, the entire street was jammed, the neighbors were more impressed than angry when they saw official flags on the automobiles and countless cooks and butlers came out to see the show.

I didn't have to worry about having a monarch in our midst; he immediately made himself at home, acting more American than some of our U.S. guests. He smiled, laughed, chatted and shook hands all around and then picked a corner of the dining room by the window as his spot to "hold court." He really seemed appreciative when Pierre arrived with a gleaming crystal glass and an opened bottle of his favorite drink. Pierre was marvelous in his white gloves, holding a brilliantly-polished silver platter covered with a lace doily. (It was our fish platter that Jim and I had found in the flea market but Pierre had decked it out for a King.)

Farouk seemed quite happy in his corner where he could see everyone coming and going and taste every tidbit that was passed his way, but when Pierre brought over a platter of Anna's deviled eggs, Farouk motioned him to stay right there. I've never seen it before and I'll never see it again: while chatting with guests, Farouk managed to eat every one of the eggs. When the platter was empty, Pierre backed away and went off to the kitchen to fill it up again.

Just then, Catina appeared in the doorway with Cathy in her arms. Ah-hah, that was a new one. Catina, who never batted an eyelid over celebrity guest lists and never came downstairs during parties, arrived on the scene supposedly on her way to the kitchen. When King Farouk caught sight of the baby his eyes sparkled and he gave her a big "hello." The nurse approached him, answering his questions about name and age. Farouk leaned over, tickling Cathy under her chin, and called her *petit bout de chou* which could mean "little cabbage" or one of those whipped cream pastries, *chou à la crème*. (The American expression would be something like "sweetie.")

The garden gate was barely shut after Farouk's departure before everyone began talking at once about what a nice fellow he was, how friendly and natural, how kind and amusing, how well-spoken he was in French and English. That was before he lost his kingdom and before scandalous stories were written about him. Shortly after, Jim gave me some pale green prayer beads Farouk had given him to commemorate the birth of his first and only son, Prince Fouad. (Maybe Farouk gave out a million of these souvenirs but I was pleased to have mine and happy to be able to show it to his son in Paris 30 years later.) After Farouk's first visit to the Rue du Docteur Blanche, he came over every time he was in town. He joked that his entourage was getting smaller every year and we could tell how important he was by the number of cars parked outside the door.

It's hard to remember the "who's who" at the party that night of Farouk's first visit. Of course, there was the wife of Maxim's owner, Maggie Vaudable, who often came and sat in the same rose satin Louis XVI chair the entire evening. She always wore something sensational by her friend, Christian Dior. Another guest one can't forget was the inimitable Carol Channing, who looked like a giant pixie. She was

Champagne...

famed for her Broadway character "Lorelei Lee" in Anita Loos' classic *Gentlemen Prefer Blondes*, followed by *Let's Face It, Lend An Ear,* and *Wonderful Town.* That evening in Paris, she was so relaxed that she kicked off her high-heeled shoes and proceeded to entertain a group of guests with an impromptu routine. Little did she know that another guest was doing a bit of entertaining behind her. Our favorite tall, dark and handsome candymaker from Reading, PA., Dick Bortz, couldn't help trying on Carol's shoes. They fit!

A trio of late arrivals showed up at the end of the reception, missing the King as well as Carol's unique performance. Zsa Zsa Gabor and Porfirio Rubirosa appeared in the company of Earl Blackwell, founder of Celebrity Service, Inc. We had no more deviled eggs to offer but there was still champagne, tidbits and chit-chat before they left for a formal dinner at Maxim's.

The morning after King Farouk's visit to the Rue du Docteur Blanche, the bell at our garden door didn't stop ringing. Every time Pierre opened it, another florist arrived bringing another bouquet. There were eleven in all and the biggest one came from the King himself. There were two dozen red roses with the longest stems I had ever seen.

I was accustomed to receiving little bouquets after dinner parties but never such a mass as this after a mere cocktail party. Anna and Pierre were beaming as the little notes and cards were read out to them and they bustled about trying to find the right vase, urn or pot for every offering. The King's roses presented a problem: they were almost as tall as little Anna and we had nothing suitable. Pierre solved that problem. He took a bottle-green enamel wastebasket from beside my desk, put it under the picture window in the salon, and brought a huge steampot full of water from the kitchen to hide inside the wastebasket. Then Anna took the roses, saying, "If *Madame* will permit me," and began to arrange the roses one by one and very slowly. I watched her as she made the roses look like those arrangements you see in florists' windows. I learned a lesson that day that I've appreciated ever since. She helped me with all the bouquets, first spreading a thick covering of newspaper on the dining room table and arranging each bouquet in a vase, placing one bloom at a time. What a difference from my way of plunking everything in at once and then trying to make it look even and pretty.

Maybe everyone knows what Anna knew but I didn't until watching her handiwork and admiring the results. I tried a few flower arrangements myself and was so pleased to see the results of her one-at-a-time-and-slowly method. For some time after that I'd look at the bottle-green enamel wastebasket and picture the beauty of the King's roses and remember the day I learned how to arrange bouquets.

Chapter Eight

Everything was going so well for the Nolans that I began thinking and dreaming about having another baby. The idea thrilled me, now that Janne was big enough to be out of a crib and share the nursery with Cathy. Maybe this one will be a little boy, I thought, but I'd be just as happy with another little girl. Never two without three, as the French saying goes. I was ready to discuss it with Jim when he handed me a letter on pale blue stationery, saying, "Tell me what you think about this." It was a letter from the lady in England who had a son "the spitting image" of Jim. She wanted Jim's help with the boy's education. I did a double-take when I saw her signature, Margaret, the same name as mine. I wished that he hadn't shown it to me but he had and he was standing over me to get my reaction. I can't remember what I said, word for word, but I tried to tell him that he, and he alone, could make a decision on what he should do but it shouldn't be to the detriment of his other children.

After that, every time he flew off to London I wondered if he was seeing the lady named Margaret. He'd taken me to Rome and Madrid but never to London since our premarriage flight. Much later, observing him and his habits, I didn't think it was a Margaret luring him to London. He was attracted to new faces. He liked to charm the pants off sexy strangers. Jim never told me what his decision was about the boy's education and I never asked. The subject of bringing a new Nolan into the world did not come up either.

Life in the *petit pavillon* took on a certain set routine with Catina, Anna, Pierre and a little old lady named Madame Luleu, who came to sew for us every Wednesday afternoon. I got up early every morning, put on a cozy housecoat and went up one flight to breakfast with Cathy and Janne at their low nursery table where they sat in pint-sized chairs. Catina, in her crisp pink or blue pin-striped uniform, sat down with us when Pierre brought up the breakfast tray. The nursery would be filled with a marvelous aroma of fresh coffee and hot toast, and the sounds of children's chatter and the clatter of cups being plunked on saucers. Anna always put a *soupçon* of chicory in her coffee. To this day a whiff of that in

Champagne...

passing brings a vision of the Rue du Docteur Blanche.

Breakfast with the babies was Catina's ideal moment to tell me everything that HAD to be done. Leak in the bathtub, broken drapery cord, light out in the hall, children need new shoes. Every day I went away with a mental list of what had to be seen to on the nursery floor. She spoke in the third person, saying things like, "Perhaps Madame will have a moment today to...." But that polite, old-time French manner still held the urgency of a direct request. Sometimes Jim would appear on the staircase ready to go off to work, but most times he was just rubbing his eyes and having coffee from a tray by the bed when I returned.

Jim was a night person and often quite grumpy in the a.m. I knew better not to bother or bore him with mundane affairs. I learned the hard way. Have you ever asked a night person early one morning what he'd like for dinner that evening?

After Jim was off to his *bureau*, Anna would come into my dressing room to discuss menus, number of guests, special requests. She shopped every day on the Avenue Mozart a few blocks away, carrying her leather satchels out the door and returning loaded down about an hour later. There was no such thing as a supermarket. Items were selected and purchased one at a time. Anna went to the *crémerie* for milk, butter and cheese; the *poissonnerie* for fish and "fruits of the sea" like oysters, lobster and crab; the *boucherie* for meat; the *boulangerie* for bread, *brioche* and croissants. Then there were other shops for fruits and vegetables; a place called *marchand de couleurs* for household needs plus another *marché* for flowers and plants. There was no such things as paper bags or plastic sacks. Cooks' lightweight leather satchels were a necessity.

Everyday shopping probably stemmed from the lack of refrigeration in kitchens, at first, but it was then a tradition. Cooks and chefs in our neighborhood did a little socializing at the same time. I was told that Anna and Pierre were among the big shots of the neighborhood after King Farouk came to call.

Anna was an enthusiastic cook, always full of marvelous menu suggestions. And if I'd suggest serving something that was not in season, she could be counted on to point it out to me, in third person French, of course. Her brain was like a computer under her hair; she remembered what we had served to whom on their last visit and you never had to tell her more than once when a certain guest didn't eat a certain dish.

Even the simplest dishes that came out of Anna's kitchen looked like works of art. A roast of veal appeared looking like an Easter basket. She'd slice the roast and put it back together in place amid a nest of multi-colored spring vegetables. Steamed cauliflower arrived whole in a sea of lemon sauce and sprinkled with fresh parsley. You could slice it like a cake; it was steamed to perfection. Even the ordinary eggplant looked lovely when Anna presented it. She skinned it, sliced it lengthwise and fried it to a golden brown. (I, the eggplant hater, found Anna's eggplant delicious.)

Sometimes, when she was certain that guests would show up on time, she'd prepare a soufflé with truffles to start dinner. At other times when we'd invited guests who were notorious for their lateness, she'd make a soufflé for dessert instead. Her specialty was a pink soufflé concoction made with huckleberries. Another *merveille* was her wonderful upside down apple pie made in a skillet, the tart caramelized on top the second she turned it over onto a plate. It was served hot with clotted cream.

You'd think one might get fat on Anna's cooking, but one never did. The menu was always varied, the portions were small and you left the table satisfied, not stuffed. Wines from our cellar then had names like Volnay, Chambertin, Châteauneuf-du-Pape, St-Émilion and Pomerol. A glass and a half during a meal was quite enough.

My desk work after breakfast right up until time to think about lunch was like a job I'd often have to go back in the afternoon to finish, especially when Jim surprised me with instructions for our next reception. It would be for Mr. so-and-so from such-and-such coming to Paris in a week or so and we'd have to get "the American list" together to please and/or impress him. On our list were top American-Parisian businessmen, diplomats, journalists and fellow airline executives totalling about 125 people, which was our capacity on the ground floor with the double doors of the salon and dining room opening into the foyer. Invitation cards written, addressed, stamped had to get to the post office without delay, telephone calls made, the caterer engaged, orders given to the servants, plans made for the flowers. This in addition to paying bills and filling out salary forms; the invitations received had to be properly accepted or declined and thank-you notes went out for parties, gifts and flowers. The job was looked upon by Jim as a "big nothing" if I dared mention the time spent or tried to answer him when he'd ask, "What the hell did you do all day?"

The household and I had an unspoken agreement that I'd be out for lunch as it was simpler for everyone in that busy household. Catina lunched in her room, Pierre and Anna at their kitchen table, and they didn't have to set up and serve in the formal dining room for me all by myself.

Sometimes I organized a ladies' lunch at Maxim's where I invited TWA executives' wives. Sometimes I had luncheon meetings concerning American Hospital projects (like a fund-raising movie night in the presence of a star). Sometimes I had dress, hat or shoe fittings and would be happy with a snack and a cup of tea at the elegant Ladurée, a landmark on the Rue Royale since 1862, with hand-painted ceilings and lots of gilt. There were other days when my old pal, Eve, would show up from her house in the country to take me out for lunch. How can it be that I have written all these pages already and not told you all about Eve?

The first time I set eyes on Eve was in a customs shed in Paris where travelers came to claim their trunks arriving by rail after their ship trip across the Atlantic. We started to chat. She was an American from New York with a job modeling clothes at Patou. I thought she was the most beautiful creature on earth: short blonde hair, long neck, slim and trim form, looking like she'd stepped off the pages of *Town & Country Magazine*.

But she was more than that. She made me laugh, she made the customs officers laugh. We had a pleasant talk but, strangely enough, didn't exchange names and telephone numbers. Never mind, when I was flying off to London with Jim trying to get married, she got off the plane right in front of us and we chatted and laughed like we were old friends. A few months after that we ran smack dab into her in the casino at Deauville. Jim and I were married then and invited her to our home in Paris. Next thing you know, she was married herself, to the director of the slick magazine, *Realities*, Alfred Max. They bought a house at Les-Loges-en-Josas and Eve Max came into my life to stay.

Several times a week, Eve would zoom-zoom her Citroën into Paris, screech to the curb in front of the house, jump out and buzz the garden doorbell three times before getting back into the car to wait for me to come out. If I didn't come out soon enough for her, she'd buzz-buzz again, push the heavy door open and yell my name loud enough for the whole house to hear.

By this time, Catina would be peering out through the curtains on the nursery floor, hence Eve took to calling her "Mrs. Danvers" from Daphne du Maurier's classic *Rebecca*.

Eve and I loved to lunch at the Ritz but it was always a hectic ride to our destination. Eve was an excellent but very fast driver. She got impatient with the less skillful. She could cuss them out in such language as to make a truck driver slump down in his seat. I understood the English expletives, of course, but I didn't know where she'd picked up the vivid French swear words that made the other drivers' mouths drop open.

Eve, who'd acted like a foul-mouthed truck driver behind the wheel became someone else the minute she stepped out of her car in front of the Ritz. She was allowed to leave her car right in front of the door and she'd get out looking an absolute dream in her sweeping, nearly ankle-length mink coat, swinging her Hermès handbag and clinking her stylish shoes on the cobblestones. She wore medium high heels and her ankles reminded me of the thoroughbred horses at the Longchamp racetrack.

We always arrived at the Place Vendôme entrance of the Ritz and then walked all the way down the long hall lined with showcases to the Cambon Bar and the Ritz Restaurant, a block-long distance on luxurious carpet. What a greeting we got from each and every barman; they were all fine fellows known all over the world. There was Georges, Bertin, Louis, Jacques and the young *chasseur*, Claude, who became more famous than all. In the beginning Claude was a 17-year-old bellboy wearing a chocolate brown and beige uniform. He went on errands for everyone, picking up train and ship tickets, organizing theater dates, making phone calls and learning to fib to some wives calling for their husbands. "*Monsieur* has just left, *Madame*," he often had to say for a customer leaning on the bar chatting up

Georges. His father worked in the depths of the Ritz on the heating installations and his mother was a seamstress at Gabrielle Chanel's workshop across the street. Claude became head barman of the Ritz for many years, right up to the eighties.

The fifties were the years when the Ritz was really the Ritz. Madame César Ritz would often sit in the grand, Louis XVI lobby with her cane propped against her chair and observe everyone and everything going on. Few people knew what she looked like, if they even knew that there was such a personage. She was a perfectionist and missed nothing. This regal creature had a son, Charles, who was always there as well, though his interest in the hotel business was far from dedicated. He preferred to go fishing every chance he got and when he wasn't out with rod and tackle, he was reading or writing about fishing. It was he who instigated the building of the Espadon Restaurant, featuring a fishy decor. One thing he did insist on at the Ritz was said in an expression he learned from his father: "The customer is always right." At the Ritz employees practiced what he preached.

Eve and I would have a drink while we decided about lunch. She liked whisky and I always ordered a split of champagne. Depending on how much time we had, we'd lunch in the restaurant or have a club sandwich at a banquette table right in the bar. Eve often had a dress fitting at Christian Dior or Balenciaga. She was the one who took me to my first Balenciaga fashion collection and drove me over to see a new designer, Hubert de Givenchy, who was working from an apartment on the Rue Alfred de Vigny.

The dressmakers had house models working every day so you could see a collection in peace and quiet with plenty of elbow room just about any afternoon you wanted. I began to covet Balenciaga creations long before I got acquainted with saleslady Madame Alice, who helped me spend all my money every time there was a sale.

When Eve and I had enough time to have lunch in the Ritz Restaurant, it was always an event to remember. Lunch was leisurely and the food divine. There were fashionable folks at every table. It was here that I first took a close look at the Duchess of Windsor, who was just a table away with an American thoroughbred racehorse owner named Mrs. Howell Jackson. The Duchess looked beautiful in a royal blue suit with a diamond and sapphire pin that seemed to light up the corner where she sat. As I was feasting my eyes on her dazzling appearance, I heard her talk and was shocked to learn that she had a voice as raucous as a rowdy barmaid. Later, when I got to know her, it didn't bother me a bit, especially since she was so nice to me that I could forgive her a lot, but I can't forget that day. How could such a horrible voice come out of that elegant creature?

One day when Eve and I were walking down the long hall back to her car, Eve had her slinky mink over her arm but she let it slide down as she walked and finally held it by the collar and let it drag slowly along the floor behind her. I was walking with her but dropped back to get a better look at this intriguing *tableau*. She reminded me of a mighty hunter who'd just bagged an exotic beast in the jungle.

Champagne...

She was unaware of all this as she glanced into every showcase of jewelry, porcelain, silver, scarves, handbags and the rest. When she noticed that I had fallen behind, she told me to hurry up and asked what I was doing. When I told her that I'd never seen such a scene before, she denied dragging her mink, insisting, "I did not," and to this day, she still denies it.

Every afternoon in Paris those days found me back at home, usually in a cozy hostess coat in my dressing room, waiting for the children to come home from their outing and spend some time with me. On Wednesdays, I'd go down to the salon because the sewing lady stationed herself in my dressing room where she had a lot to do, mending, altering, replacing buttons for the children, Jim, or taking care of household linen and servants' uniforms. From the salon, I could see the children coming into the garden and I'd go to the door to take them from Catina while she wheeled the huge two-seater carriage around to the back of the house. Sometimes Catina would join me for a Dubonnet in the salon, but most times she'd go upstairs to prepare for the evening. This was fun time for me; I'd listen to Cathy and Janne chattering, singing songs and I'd watch them dancing around. I let them do all sorts of *choses défendues* things like opening cupboards, taking the phone off the hook, and pulling books off the shelves. When the time came to be serious, they were very reasonable. I'd say to Janne, "Hey, if the phone stays off the hook nobody can call us," and she'd put it back. Then I'd suggest that we put Pierre's bottles back on the shelves because he might not like it if we broke any of "his" bottles, and back they'd go. Maybe some books stayed scattered on the floor, but fun was had and no harm done.

Soon Catina would come to collect the children for their evening routine. I'd go back to Madame Luleu to talk over her future work, pay her for her time and accompany her to the door. Later I learned that she would say goodbye to me at the front door, go around the house to the servants' entrance, chat with Pierre and Anna, and have a nip from whatever bottle was opened. She loved to gossip, she worked by the hour in several homes around the neighborhood and knew inside stories of interest to all who cared to hear that sort of thing. When I was told all this, I laughed and wondered why she didn't pass through the dining room to get to the kitchen, especially in bad weather.

I really enjoyed going out as "Mr. and Mrs." with Jim. We'd spend time with the top executive of the *Herald Tribune*, Geoffrey Parsons, and his actress wife, Drue, in their château at Milly. We'd go to Liz Miller's penthouse apartment overlooking the Seine. It was always a heady occasion at Margaret Biddle's private mansion for lunch or dinner, where the silverware was gold.

Every time we went to some incredibly impressive home full of fabulous paintings, Versailles furniture and priceless porcelain, I'd get an extra thrill returning to our little house behind the wall, decorated little by little, mostly from the flea market. It looked so sweet, solid and real that it made me feel that I had roots, after all.

Our *petit pavillon* seemed to become a stopping-off place for countless Americans coming to Paris, and we had a perpetual open house for TWA travelers of note. Mixed in with celebrity guests were New Yorkers who liked to stop in to see the house, have a drink and visit Cathy and Janne in the nursery. There was one lady named Leona Shattuck who brought carton after carton of Schrafft's Ice Cream packed in dry ice. Catina loved the exotic flavors and called Leona the "ice cream lady" like it was some sort of special title. Leona admired Cathy and Janne; she told us they looked like little Renoirs sitting in their chairs. (Later, when they were old enough to make jokes, Cathy said to Janne that they ought to find the ice cream lady and tell her that the Renoirs had turned into Picassos.)

Another visitor was Nathan Cummings, owner of a canned goods company called Consolidated Foods. He'd send us carton after carton of his products, which our household declared inedible, especially the canned corn. "In France we grow corn to feed pigs," said Anna. Catina agreed but later admitted that she liked the tiny green peas he sent and she took to calling Mr. Cummings *"Monsieur Petit Pois."*

Nate became quite a man about Paris, giving dinner parties at Maxim's and the Tour d'Argent, and then all night parties on excursion boats floating up and down the Seine. He'd fill a whole boat with guests, have an elaborate sit-down dinner served, and hire a lively orchestra to play for all-night dancing. One night he even arranged for fancy fireworks to go off from a certain bridge as his boat approached. Unfortunately for the genial host, the fireworks operator miscalculated his arrival and fired off everything for a tourist-filled *bateau mouche* before Mr. Cummings' boat was anywhere near the site. Nate was furious, running up and down and waving his arms.

Another time Doris and Jules Stein (MCA founder-owner) were on Nate's boat for a cocktail but had not realized that his sailing parties lasted so late; they had a party of their own being given by their daughter, Jean Stein, and didn't want to miss it. Doris was in a vile temper, cussing against Nate so all could hear. I tried to make light of it, saying something like, "Can you swim, Doris?" and she turned her fury on me a minute or two, making me realize that you didn't try to be funny when Doris was mad.

Nate loved to go out with gorgeous girls in Paris, especially famous ones he could talk about later. He couldn't help telling everyone about his night with a movie star he took to an exclusive, expensive bordello. The lady lost her diamond bracelet between the satin sheets. She was heartsick because she didn't dare go to the authorities to declare her loss and was certain she'd never see her treasure again. Lo and behold, the bracelet was returned to her in a discreet package, left with the *concierge* at her hotel the next afternoon.

"How's that for honesty?" said Nate.

Champagne...

Jim brought more than guests home for the family to take care of, starting with a dog when Cathy was a few months old. The scrawny puppy must have been the runt in a litter of Breton spaniels. We called him Bret after Breton, not the Hemingway character. From the very beginning Bret didn't seem to like ladies or babies. He was definitely Jim's dog. Catina took Bret on walks every afternoon with the children, but he'd show his appreciation by chewing her slippers or overturning her waste basket or pulling clothing off of hangers. When Jim was around, Bret followed him around like a little gentleman, but most of the time he was a four-legged devil. Yet Jim didn't have much time for him; he'd come home and open the garden gate to let Bret out on the street to run up and down. When I said it was dangerous and he should keep him on a leash before he got killed by a car, Jim said if anything happened to Bret he could always get another one.

The next little beast that Jim brought home came in a tiny cardboard cracker box. It was a newly-hatched black bird that a pilot brought back on a plane. There was half a banana in the box but it was obvious that the poor little fellow was too young to eat by himself. Pierre and Anne seemed disgusted, I was upset, but Catina immediately took the bird in hand and started to feed it through an eye dropper. Jim was chattering away that a lot of pilots brought back these birds

Cathy and Janne's baby nurse stayed with us for 13 years. Her name was Catherine but Cathy nicknamed her Catina.

because they could learn to talk just like humans. It was a Mynah bird which everyone doubted would survive, but Catina put him on a towel in the nursery bathroom and fed him day and night until he was standing on his feet and opening his beak every time he heard her voice.

Jim suggested to the children that the bird should be called "Clarice," but Cathy objected, saying that since the bird was not a "clare" color, but black, he should be called "Noirice" (like "Blackie") and so Cathy named yet another member of the family.

I looked up everything I could about Mynah birds, but every time I told Catina that these birds could learn to talk like humans, she'd give that "Catina look" that meant that she didn't think I knew what I was talking about. Noirice was getting so big and beautiful that Christian built him a cage big enough for a flock of birds. It was on wheels and could be placed anywhere. One morning when I came upstairs for breakfast, Catina was in a terrible state, saying Noirice was sick and that I must call the vet immediately as she didn't know what to do. How did she know he was sick? Because he was coughing. When I told the vet that the bird was coughing and asked what to do, he sounded very bored when he told me it was impossible for any bird to cough. "Birds can be caught in a current of air and die," he told me, but it was impossible for them to catch a cold and cough. When I told him it was a Mynah bird, he got a big laugh out of that and said the bird was just repeating the noise that someone in the house was making. When I hung up, I told Catina that we now knew that we had a talking bird; the butler had a cold and Noirice had heard him coughing. Proof came a bit later when we heard Pierre coughing again and Noirice doing the same right after.

This was the beginning of Noirice's very verbal existence. Hearing the telephone ring, he'd say "Hello" in three different voices. When you'd wheel his cage to the window where the sun was coming in he'd say, in French of course, "Oh, it's so nice here," and when he'd see a plate of food coming his way, he'd say, "that's good." Catina let him come out at certain times and he liked to sample bits of butter on her breakfast tray. When she didn't open his cage door fast enough for him, he'd sit next to the opening and say, "*Tu viens, viens–tu viens*," which meant something like "come here–you come here." He also had a habit of calling "Bret" and whistling in such an authoritative tone that poor Bret would come racing up the stairs to find nothing but a big black bird in a cage. Of course he called Catina, Cathy and Kiki all day long and had tones of voices from soft and sweet to shrill and angry. Cathy and Kiki tried to teach him to whistle *Au clair de la lune, mon ami pierrot...*, but he could only whistle half of the line and grunt as though he could do it, but didn't want to.

How can anyone know what goes on in a bird's brain? When I'd tell people that I was certain that Noirice knew what he was saying when he said it because all his remarks fit the situations, they'd shrug and shake their heads. But early one evening when the servants were away and Catina was feeding the children in the

Champagne...

kitchen, I was in the salon when I heard Kiki crawling up the stairs with little snif-
fle noises. I knew she'd probably done something naughty and was being sent
upstairs. I wanted to come out and give her a cuddle but I didn't dare interfere. As
she got further up the stairs, I distinctly heard Noirice saying in a sweet, comfort-
ing tone, "Kiki, Kiki," and the little one answered, "Yes, Noirice, I'm sad!"

Chapter Nine

A lthough I was well aware that Jim loved to turn on his charm with attrac-tive ladies, I wasn't ready for evidence of shenanigans coming from the servants. Catina informed me that Anna and Pierre were remarking about lip-stick traces on *Monsieur*'s shirts and handkerchiefs which seemed impossible to remove. They washed, scrubbed and boiled to no avail. What a careless creature Jim was. He'd come home from trips and fill his laundry hamper in his bathroom with everything he'd worn on his travels; it was plain to Pierre and Anna that they weren't trying to remove *Madame*'s lipstick from his clothes. I was embar-rassed in the household and hurt that I was apparently a has-been in the heart of my husband.

There was more to come. One time a friend called asking if I was feeliing bet-ter and I said I wasn't sick; why did she ask? She said that Jim had told her I was-n't feeling well when she saw him at Maxim's the night before. I hung up, startled and shaking. I didn't tell her that Jim had taken his bag and briefcase the day before, telling me he had to go to Rome. Then, he came back with bag and brief-case in hand, as though he was just returning from a business trip. Before I could decide whether or not I wanted to have a serious discussion, he announced that he had commissioned an artist to paint my portrait.

I couldn't imagine a sillier idea and told him so.

"Listen, Maggi, everybody who is anybody is having his wife's portrait done," came first followed by, "this man is a good portrait painter and he needs the work." And then, "What the hell have you got to lose," cinched by "so tell me what you've got BETTER to do with your time?"

I agreed to pose for the painter. It changed my routine. Although I was depressed over Jim's behavior, I had to keep going in the "show must go on" atmo-sphere. We had the house, the family, the animals, the duties of going out and invit-ing people in. I had the responsibility of the servants, writing invitations, sending gifts, flowers and thank-you notes enough to give me writer's cramp. In addition, I was volunteering to help with charitable campaigns as Mrs. James Nolan, along

Champagne...

with other wives of American businessmen in France. I didn't have time to worry or fight. Now, every morning right after breakfast in the nursery, I had to return to my dressing room to fix my face, arrange my hair, and put on an evening gown. Those were the days before hairspray and electric hairdryers, blowers, curlers and all those things ladies take for granted today. I had long hair, further down than my waist, so I just shampooed it in the shower, dried it with towel after towel, brushed it all flat and wound it around and around in a coil, or bun, at the back of my neck and fastened it all snugly with giant hairpins. It looked quite elegant in those days, especially with long earrings of which I had quite a few. (If I wore my hair like that now, I'd look like a bag lady on a bad day.) Make-up was no problem: I wore a little lipstick and touched the tips of my eyelashes with mascara and sometimes I'd wave a powder puff over my nose if it looked too shiny, so I was soon downstairs to meet the portrait painter in the salon.

The Czech refugee artist painting my portrait, Vaclav Neubert, was a tall, slim, hollow-cheeked fellow who rarely spoke. He'd set up his easel in silence, placing me exactly as I'd been the day before, and start to work.

He smoked horribly smelly French cigarettes that discolored to a dirty yellow before he'd smoked down to the stub. I hated the look and stench of them. Pierre would bring a tray with coffee for him but he wouldn't drink it until he was through for the day. He didn't want the coffee reheated: he drank it as it was.

The dress I selected to pose in was the red Rodriguez Jim had brought back from Madrid after his fling in Rome with the "typewriter lady." This was the dress I'd worn to Maxim's when he left me alone to celebrate my 30th birthday. And now, after he had told me he was flying to Rome and stayed in Paris with I-don't-know-whom, I wore it for the portrait I didn't want painted. This saddened me but I tried to behave as a lady should; it wasn't the painter's fault. Little by little, he told me his wartime story. Before he finished the portrait, I wasn't minding his cigarettes; after all HE'd been through, the least I could do was tolerate some smoke.

I don't remember how long it took to finish the portrait. It seemed like forever. He had two of his paintings on display in a gallery on the Avenue de l'Opéra. I peeked in and saw portraits of Ava Gardner and the Duchess of Windsor, which I recognized immediately as his. He worshipped the Spanish painter, Diego Vélasquez, and was very pleased when I told him I was wearing a dress by a Spanish designer.

When his work was ready for framing, he took it away and said he'd deliver it to Jim in his office when it was ready to be hung. We shook hands and as he went away the only thing I was thinking was, "now I'm going to be framed."

Words are strange things. Just when the artist said that he was going to have my portrait framed, Catina started her third person comments about *Monsieur* taking advantage of our *joli cadre* in the nursery by coming in with strangers at odd hours, unannounced and often inconvenient.

She went on to say that although she understood that *Monsieur* considered his house and his children in a *joli cadre* (that could mean "pretty framework," "love-ly atmosphere," "agreeable background"), it would be better if he let the nurse know of visits in advance.

So, she too felt "framed" up there. I said I'd see what I could do and I certainly didn't tell her what "being framed" could mean in English. The next thing we knew Jim brought a photographer to the house late one afternoon and said he was going to have some pictures taken of us with the children in the salon. Catina threw up her arms but started opening closets and cupboards to dress them prop-erly. She took her own curling iron and tried to create some curlicues on their heads while I went to my dressing room to put on the dress and earrings I'd worn to lunch. It was hectic but we arrived back in the salon and posed for typical fam-ily photographs to show the world our ideal *cadre* on our Christmas card that year, which I signed, stamped and sent just as Jim was taking off on another skiing hol-iday by himself.

Although I saw so well how beautifully Catina, Anna and Pierre did their work when they knew in advance who'd be coming through the door, I couldn't con-vince Jim of the importance of announcing plans. Late, impromptu visits on the nursery floor with animated strangers upset Catina. Bouncing in with any number of people at cocktail time and never telling Anna and Pierre if they'd be staying for dinner put the kitchen in a tizzy. I found myself trying to excuse *Monsieur* as he was just doing his job. It only angered Jim when I asked him to be more consider-ate with his household. He liked to say, "What the hell are they being paid for?"

A few times when guests would come bouncing up the stairs to the nursery floor landing wanting to see the children at bath time or bedtime, Catina would stand like a royal guard at the landing and not let anyone pass. Disgruntled guests suggested that Catina be replaced immediately by someone more amiable. Jim would heartily agree with the guests while they were there and then agree with me after they left when I'd say a nurse was for babies, not guests.

Once he brought a New York newspaperman home with him long after the babies' bedtime. The man was carrying a stuffed doll that looked bigger than him, and he was also a bit stuffed with booze himself. He tried to go upstairs to present his gift in person but this time it was I who stood at the bottom of the stairs block-ing his way. Jim kept saying, "Ahh, let him go...what harm will that do?...come on, be a sport...," and it was obvious that Jim had had a few drinks before he'd come home. I stood there until they were convinced that I meant it. The gentleman dropped the doll, telling Jim that he wanted to go back to the George V. As Jim took his car keys from the table, he turned to me and hissed, "bitch," and was out the door, which he slammed behind him.

I was feeling like a hag, nag and a bore as well as a bitch at that point. Instead of giggling and gossiping with Eve the next time she came around to take me to lunch, I started telling her my troubles. She always had an original answer to everything and this was no exception. When I got through with my tale of woe, she leaned over the table and gave the hat I was wearing a not-so-gentle tug.

"Listen, you," she said, "you need an OUTLET." Then she gave my hat another tug because she hated it. (She hated all my hats and refused to wear one herself, even though everyone wore hats to lunch in those days. Eve had a sleek, short haircut and her yellow hair was cut to a point in the back. She called it her "duck's ass" hairdo.)

"Your outlet should be PHYSICAL," she told me, going on to explain that she, too, had felt frustrated and unhappy until she started going horseback riding every day. That's what kept her going, exercising all the anger out of her system.

I could see her point for herself, but I didn't know how to ride and I didn't have any riding clothes. These were days before jeans and before you could walk into any department store and ask for the sportswear division. Eve had the answer to that as well. She knew a place where they made riding outfits fast, efficiently and at a reasonable price and she, herself, could pick me up to take me to the country and show me the right way to ride.

Jim seemed enthusiastic when I told him about Eve's idea. He urged me to follow through as soon as possible and insisted that I have the proper clothes. Both of us were thinking the same thing, I'm certain–maybe an outlet like that would make me more relaxed in my home *cadre*.

The day my riding outfit was delivered, Jim's father was sitting in the garden. When the messenger came through the gate and handed the box to the butler, Grandpa Nolan was by his side to see who was sending what to whom. By the time Jim came home from the office, his father had had his ugly outburst with me and I was upstairs in my dressing room. I saw Jim standing by the garden chair where his father was still seated and "the old man" was waving his arms and smacking the table with the palm of his hand.

Jim let him finish and went away. I vowed not to try on the new outfit until Grandpa Nolan had left Paris. Jim didn't mention riding or the clothes. Our first conversation of the evening had to do wih what his father had planned for the following Sunday. I reminded Jim that we were invited by Nate Cummings to go to the Grand Prix horse races at Longchamp and we had a date to meet him at the Plaza Athénée on Sunday.

Besides that, I reminded him we were going to see his father on Monday; we had a date to go to Cousin Marie's for cocktails and dinner. Jim insisted that we had to go with his father on Sunday as well and I insisted that we had to keep the invitation we'd accepted. The upshot: Jim spent Sunday with his father and I got decked out in "Grand Prix" attire in a beautiful suit that Eve had bought for herself from Balenciaga and then thought it would look better on me.

This was the first time I defied Jim's wishes to adhere to his father's orders.

That Sunday of the Grand Prix at Longchamp, the American food king, Nate Cummings, had three other guests with him: Ethel LeVane, a nervous, jumpy

"Maggi Nolan," by Vaclav Neubert, oil on canvas.

creature everyone called Bunny; a funny fellow known to be a financial wizard, J. Melville Forrester, whom everyone called Jack; and a tall, slim, quiet business-man from Oklahoma introduced as Paul. (Later, Jack told me his full name was Jean Paul Getty.)

The five of us piled into Nate's long American convertible that looked like a low-flying airplane and went off to the races. Longchamp, in those days, was about the chicest place to be on that traditional last Sunday in the month of June—the highlight of thoroughbred races for the year, the "Grand Prix."

Elegant champagne lunches were served in a ground-level, glassed-in restau-rant surrounded by grass and flowers, in sight of the gravel path where the horsey set could be seen passing by. When the races started, you crunched along the grav-el to your seat in what looked like the bleachers at a football game. The crowds were small and elegant; gentlemen in gray top hats and ladies looked like old-time royalty at play. Everyone seemed to know everyone: Aly Khan, by himself (but you always knew he had ladies waiting for him not far from where he was); André Dubonnet, the French aperitif king, with his Texas girlfriend, Elyse Hunt; the cir-cus king, John Ringling North, with his starlet lady-of-the-moment, (after he broke off his romance with French movie star, Martine Carol); the part-time Parisian from Oregon lumberland, Elizabeth Miller, who became Mrs. Theodore Weicker before becoming Mrs. Anastassios Fondaras (through all the name changes Liz kept the same penthouse apartment in Paris, where she entertained her horsey friends after the races–and still does).

After the races, I invited everyone back to the Rue du Docteur Blanche for pink champagne. The servants were away so I settled my guests in the salon and went to the kitchen for champagne and snacks. When I came back, they were all standing under my portrait. Ethel, by now, had told me that she and Paul had written a book on art collecting which she'd send to me. I already knew that Nate collected paintings by the dozens to ship back to America so I was a little embarrassed at their rapt attention to my bare face staring down at them.

I honestly didn't like the painting. I truly didn't like my looks with pug nose and I knew I had crooked teeth even though they didn't show. I also thought it was plain to see that I hadn't wanted to be painted in the first place. The only thing I liked about my features was my forehead and maybe that's why I kept pulling my hair away from there. But as my guests sipped their champagne and started to discuss the painting, they weren't discussing me but rather the quality of the work of the painter. "Look at it as if it's a painting, not a portrait of someone you know," Nate said.

Tall, quiet Paul sipped his champagne, nodded his head thoughtfully and said, "Yes, it's a fine painting."

When Jim and his father came back, the only guest they knew was Nate, who drew their attention to the portrait and repeated what everyone had decided. Father and son said very little at the time but they knew that Nate collected paintings every year and was always making the rounds of art galleries in Paris. After the guests left Jim's father announced, "We should sell that portrait to Cummings to pay for those riding clothes."

The next day we were at Cousin Marie's on the Quai de Béthune, sitting at a huge, round dining table being served by Henri, when Grandpa Nolan got on the subject of selling my portrait to Mr. Cummings. If he didn't buy it, he added, it would be a good idea to put it up for sale.

Marie, by then, had had more than her share of pre-meal martinis. She leaned over her *consommé* and cackled in my direction. "Be careful, Maggi, they start by selling your portrait and they end up selling YOU!" She thought that was very funny and said it more than once.

My hurt was so intense that I couldn't sleep that night. I kept running over in my mind how I'd posed for the portrait to please my husband. I'd ordered riding clothes with his blessing and enthusiasm, and yet he stayed silent no matter what his father said. Over and over I told myself that he didn't care about me anymore and might even be enjoying the punishment and hurt his father was doling out to me.

The next day I took the painting down from the wall and slipped it under our double bed where there was just enough room for it to fit in and not be seen. Until this drama was over, I thought we ought not to have this picture staring down at us in the salon. I figured the empty space on the wall might start Jim thinking about the importance of what he was putting me through. Think again, Maggi!

Jim had a temper tantrum the minute he saw the wall. He accused me of stealing his property. He said he had ordered it, paid for it and could do with it whatever he wanted. He continued his tirade throughout the evening and into our bed, where we were sleeping above his precious "masterpiece."

It didn't take long for me to realize I'd taken our battle too far, but I kept my fighting stance. If Pierre and Anna knew my secret, they didn't mention it. The night-time accusations went on after I had called the artist to come and take his painting away in exchange for a second one I'd pose for, in another evening dress. When he arrived to roll up the canvas he was very sympathetic to my story and seemed to appreciate the compliments that had been paid by art collectors in our midst.

More weeks of posing, more cigarettes, but with a subtle mutual understanding of my project. Jim, by then, didn't seem to care. He was living such a full life away from me, the children, the house. With his father back in America, the least of Jim's interests seemed to be the portrait no longer on the wall and, later, the one taking its place.

When he needed me to attend an official function or co-host an event, he'd tell me and I'd follow through. Once he had a whole TWA plane load of American journalists arriving in Paris. To entertain them he hired a boat on the Seine, invited a group of local guests to join the party and told me that I was expected to come along. This was the first party he had ever planned without my help on guest lists, invitations, and follow-up telephone calls. I was just another guest on the boat during this fancy party with loud music, loads to drink and piles of food on every table.

There were several pretty girls there–a sure way of having an attractive, successful party. As I sat at a table, one of the ladies was introduced to me by a newsman I knew. When she heard the name "Nolan" she asked me innocently if I was related to Jim Nolan of TWA. "Hey, she's his wife," the newsman bellowed. The poor young thing looked like she was going to swallow whole the *canapé* she'd put in her mouth. I wasn't angry; I felt sorry. It was obvious that Jim had been making his big pitch to her, neglecting to tell her that he had a wife. And it was plain to me that my husband didn't want to be married anymore.

Jim's unique Paris job went to his head from the beginning. There was no way that he would have admitted that TWA public relations was teamwork, as Eleanor Pierson had explained it in the long hall of the Ritz.

From the time he went golfing with Bing Crosby in St. Cloud, mentions in American newspapers about Jim Nolan's Paris exploits began to appear. It seemed like a marvelous thing because, after all, Trans World Airlines and TWA operations in Europe were always cited and I, as a professional public relations practitioner, knew the value of that. Clippings came in from Ed Sullivan's column. Leonard Lyons, Bob Considine, a fellow named Irv Kupcinet in Chicago and another in San Francisco named Stan Delaplane. Stan wrote about his friend, the "Boulevardier" of the Champs-Élysées, and forgot to mention TWA. As the clippings piled up Jim began to break the basic public relations rule that forbids you to believe your own publicity. He strutted around wearing a bowler hat, using his expensive umbrella like a cane. The picture: the King can do no wrong.

Champagne...

Sometimes when Jim was supposed to be *en voyage*, friends would tell me they could swear they had seen him at L'Éléphant Blanc or the late night piano bar, Calavados. Once a visitor from Hollywood called me when Jim was supposed to be in Madrid and said he was calling Jim at home because he'd tried the Baltimore as Jim had told him to, but he wasn't there. I took his message and then looked up Baltimore in the telephone book. It was a hotel on the Avenue Kléber.

After that, every time Jim announced that he had to take a trip, I'd want to ask him if he was "going to Baltimore," but I didn't dare. Once, in my misery, I called that place and asked for Mr. Nolan and they told me he was out but I could leave a name and number and he'd certainly call me back. I hung up wondering why I was taking so much trouble proving something I already knew and increasing my feeling of martyrdom on the Rue du Docteur Blanche.

Franco-American projects helped me keep my serenity (and sanity?). I helped with the publicity for the fund-raising campaign to benefit the American Hospital of Paris, the first such project they'd launched since 1937. Then I was on the program committee when the American Friends of France had a gala première of the film, *Sunset Boulevard*, starring Gloria Swanson. She wasn't able to appear in person because she was playing on Broadway in *Twentieth Century* with Jose Ferrer, but she arrived in Paris to vacation and celebrate soon after.

George Abell, *Time* correspondent in Paris, gave a reception in his town house for the glamorous Gloria. She was so surrounded by gentlemen that I didn't get a chance to say more than "hello." Still, it was the beginning of a very long acquaintanceship with that unusual lady.

First we'd see each other and chat at the Hôtel de Crillon where she'd stay in the penthouse. She was always in a hurry to get into her Rolls Royce to pick up her "beau," Lewis Bredin, who stayed at the Traveler's Club on the Champs-Élysées.

Years after that, back in Paris, she was staying with her daughter, Michèle Farmer Amon and her film producer husband, Robert. Gloria was getting a bit on in years then and could be a rather tiresome houseguest. Michèle asked me if I'd take her mother "off our hands" one evening. I suggested that she might like to come to the Club Interalliée, which now had a health bar and I knew Gloria liked that kind of food. The only problem, I said, was that there were many steps leading to the swimming pool where the health bar was located. I need not have worried, she was up and down those stairs faster than I. We had a marvelous time. She filled her plate several times and could tell me the nutritional value of everything we ate. She had a fit when I ordered wine with my meal and gave me a long lecture. She wasn't against wine, she was against drinking anything at all while you ate. "Don't drown your food, my dear!" she told me sternly.

She was a good sport. Before we left she not only autographed a menu for the waitress but sketched a little portrait of herself on it as well. "Keep this, young lady," she told her. "Some day it may be worth a lot of money."

Chapter Ten

During my Franco-American projects, I got acquainted with an American-Parisian of long date, Margaret Benedict, founder of The Junior Guild of the American Cathedral in Paris and breeder of champion pug dogs she kept in rooms of their own in her home in Passy. The ribbon and cup winners had all their trophies displayed on marble mantelpieces over fireplaces in their head-quarters.

Margaret's mother was lesser known but had her claim to fame dating from the 1920s. Mrs. Le Grand L. Benedict founded the Benedict Bureau on the Rue du Mont Thabor, around the corner from the Place Vendôme, with a British partner, Captain Basil Throckmorton, and her daughter Margaret. They were dedicated to helping wealthy clients with shopping, steamship and train tickets; it was the best place to hire private motor cars for special excursions, and offered the best buys in real estate.

Margaret's mother worked long, odd hours and had most of her meals around the corner at the Ritz, where she got to know the chef, Georges Auguste Escoffier, before he became known as *le plus grand cuisinier* of his time. One day, a Sunday, Mrs. Benedict arrived at the Ritz too late for breakfast and too early for lunch. (These were the days before anyone had heard of brunch.) Escoffier came on the scene at the door of the dining room and promised he'd come up with something, insisting that she sit down and start with fruit.

Miss Margaret told me her mother had barely finished her grapefruit when the chef reappeared and placed a dish before her. There was a toasted English muffin on the bottom, thin slices of ham, two poached eggs topped with hot *hollandaise* sauce and generous slices of truffles. When M. Escoffier was asked what this deli-cious concoction was called, he said, "Eggs Benedict," because he'd just created it for Margaret's mother. This grand happening was in the twenties and became a favorite with Ritz *habitués* long before it ever appeared on any menu. (Today it's on menus all over the world but sometimes called "Eggs Benedictine" as though it was inspired by monks or laced with liqueur.)

Champagne...

One afternoon, when I had been to an American Women's Club luncheon, I opened the garden door and a big glob of yellow caught my eye. The maintenance men who kept up the garden had been in while I was away to fill the cement basin with yellow pansies. Jim paid them a retainer to change the plants there when it was necessary and I had always liked their mixtures of blooms, especially when they filled the space with pink tulips and white daisies, but this all-yellow spot reminded me of a tub full of scrambled eggs. "Ah, well," I said to myself, thinking it wasn't worth worrying about.

When Catina faced me, asking what I was going to do about the *honte* in the garden, I didn't know what she meant. Why was it a disgrace to have yellow flowers? She explained to me that in France, yellow is the color of infidelity. She added that Pierre and Anna were very upset and had stood in disbelief when they saw the flowers being planted there. I tried to smile the whole superstition away. I told her we were Americans, after all, and whatever plants were there today didn't matter as they were only temporary. But my mind was racing to Jim's lipstick-stained clothes, his disappearances and all my other worries including the word "pansies."

I teased Catina, telling her she'd already taught me too many superstitions, like not handing a knife or scissors to someone because you'd sever friendship, and never trimming your nails on Sunday because that brought bad luck and so on. Still, those yellow pansies became like an enemy. I didn't discuss the garden with Jim anymore, so nothing was said, but I could never shake my dislike for yellow flowers after that. Those were the days when I recognized a certain pattern in Jim's behavior. When he'd had what he considered a fine time *en voyage*, he'd come back in an exuberant mood with an armful of presents for me. But I was ungrateful. All I could think of was the "typewriter lady" and my red dress from Rodriguez. Funny, he never brought back anything for the children or Catina, only for me, when he'd had what he called a "good trip."

I could always tell when Jim had not had everything his way *en voyage*. His face would be set in a scowl, he'd be moody and grumpy until I'd try to make him laugh or tell him about the invitations and projects we had to look forward to or repeat compliments about him that I'd heard from friends. He'd get out of his bad mood and even seem to want to cuddle when the lights were out.

It's amazing how much one can take in a situation like this and still pop up smiling. Jim was living another life and getting by with his lying and cheating because we had so much to lose if I faced him and decided to fight. I came very near to outbursts when friends would call and give me reports of where they'd seen Jim and with whom because this was too humiliating to bear. Of course, he knew many of his French friends had mistresses, but French men were champions at the game; they knew discretion and consideration. They never took a mistress where a wife was known, for instance, whether it was a restaurant, club, jeweler or dressmaker. Jim was so indiscreet that it seemed he was deliberately presenting himself to show what a lusty ladies' man he was. One time David Schoenbrun cornered him at a party where he'd shown up with another lady, but Jim told him there was nothing he could do about his behavior because "Maggi doesn't excite me anymore." When David told me that, I had just heard that Jim had been misbehaving in a nightclub known for exotic dancers who'd sit at the tables with the customers after they'd done their shows.

"Maybe I ought to take up belly-dancing," I said to David, feeling like laughing and crying at the same time.

More and more often I seemed to be dining alone at a brilliantly-polished table for eight. Sometimes it was because Jim was *en voyage* but other times he just didn't show up at all. After waiting past the dinner hour, I'd tell Pierre that I'd dine by myself as *Monsieur* must have been delayed by very important people arriving on TWA. Pierre and Anna were very smart; they knew exactly what was going on but they never faltered in their work.

Then came an evening at home with a mixture of Parisian friends, airline executives and visitors to Paris invited for a buffet dinner. Liz and Jesse Jones brought an American girl visiting Paris who was extremely stunning and vivacious. I always welcomed pretty girls; they made a party sparkle. But Jim, in front of everyone, began his number one pitch. I tried to give him black looks but I was ignored as though I didn't exist. When Liz and Jesse were leaving, Jim insisted that their friend stay and announced that he would drive her back to her hotel.

Jesse agreed that it was a good idea. His Porsche was at the end of the private road but Jim's car was parked right outside our door. When he left with her I was seething. How long would he be away this time? How dare he bring his skirt-chasing right into the house and under my nose? I decided I couldn't take it anymore. I wasn't going to stand around and watch him foul up our nest.

It was less than an hour later when I heard Jim come back, slamming doors and banging the cocktail cupboard open and shut. When he came upstairs he had that I-had-a-lousy-time look on his face. He was so obvious that I found it disgusting. He'd made a pitch but it didn't work this time. Not all the tootsie-pies fell for his charm, especially when it was poured out in his own home in front of his wife. This time I didn't feel like cheering him up or telling him that guests said they had a great time at our party. "Let him stew," I told myself as I took my place in our bed as far away from him as I could get. This was the first time in our marriage that I pushed him away when he tried to get near.

I wasn't ready for his tantrum. He started cursing like I'd never heard him curse before and, emphasizing his fury, he gave me violent kicks that pushed me to the floor. I was more humiliated than hurt, went into my bathroom and locked the door. My shame at this ugly scene kept me from going downstairs to sleep in the salon because I didn't want the servants to know. After a while, I went into my dressing room to get a blanket, returned to the bathroom and slept in the tub until I heard morning noises and went upstairs to have breakfast as usual.

Jim was up and out of the house before I came back downstairs. Not a word to me but he did tell Anna and Pierre to expect him back for dinner. He was no later than usual that evening; the children were in bed and I was in the salon. I asked Jim if he wanted to have a talk before or after dinner. "What about?" he asked. "If it's about last night, I've forgotten the whole thing."

Pierre announced dinner and we went in as usual, Jim chatting about whom he'd seen and what plans we'd be making for upcoming parties we'd have and invitations we'd accept. Before the end of dinner, I announced that I still wanted a heart-to-heart talk, not about last night, but about us. I'd been thinking about it all day and I wanted to get it out. I assured him that I, too, could forget about last night and all the other nights when I'd been upset if we could straighten out our basic relationship which was getting out of hand. He said he didn't know what I was talking about but he would listen to what I had to say if I insisted and we went back to chit-chat until after dinner when we were back in the salon.

He had that "do we really need this?" expression as we sat in two straight chairs with a little marble-topped table between us, as far away from my portrait as possible, which was now a straight-faced creature in a green dress. If you happened to look up at her, she'd stare right back. It could give you the creeps.

I had trouble starting my speech and was probably pretty corny beginning with that night we looked down to Paris at our feet from where he'd parked the car at the Sacré-Coeur. How wonderful it was, being a team, building something together. We had everything going for us. Jim's expression told me he was getting bored, his attention span was nearing the end. Then, he sat up like I'd smacked him across the face when I got on the subject of his skirt-chasing escapades. I tried to assure him that I understood his having to prove his manhood but this wasn't the way to go about it. I was being hurt and humiliated and it was getting to be too much for me. Finally I got to the point I was trying to make. "Proving your manhood doesn't come from adding up how many dames or babes you can charm the pants off, but rather what kind of husband and father you can be."

To clinch it, I repeated the "be a husband to me, be a father to your children, be the master of our household and, for God's sake, take care of your little neurotic dog!" If I expected him to take me in his arms and say he was sorry, and we'd have a new start as of right now, I didn't know my husband. He let me finish my speech and then got a bored, superior look on his face. "What do you think you're doing, Maggi?" he asked with a half smile, "trying to play the psychiatrist?" He got up and walked to the door, turning around before going out and saying, "Don't you know you have to go to SCHOOL for that sort of thing?"

Not long after the heart-to-heart talk I'd wanted to have turned heartless, Pierre and Anna gave their notice. They said they had a chance to go and work for a diplomat and, after all, that was the life they liked best. I nodded that I understood, but I must have seemed so saddened that Pierre said he and Anna would stay until I found replacements if I wished.

I let them go as soon as they told me of their intentions. I didn't blame them though I didn't really believe they had a new job lined up. They knew a sinking ship when they were on it and they wanted to save themselves. I could have kept them but I didn't want them to see me go through that miserable search for help again. I also thought of the possibility of Anna and Pierre talking to new recruits, telling them about lipstick on collars, lateness and disappearances of *Monsieur* and, worse yet, yellow pansies in the cement "outdoor bathtub."

For a time we were without anyone cooking in the kitchen and running the house. This all happened on the eve of the annual vacation time in France, which meant two whole months of July and August when Paris shut down and Parisians disappeared. Every year we had rented an apartment in Deauville or Trouville, where there were so many friends coming and going that it was like Paris-by-the-sea. Catina loved these summers and didn't take a minute away from the children. This year we found a roomy apartment right on the boardwalk of Trouville, over-looking the beach.

There was room for everyone including a guest room and bath, but Jim barely stayed any longer than it took to dump us with our load of luggage, the dog and the bird in his cage. By now Jim had the most ostentatious automobile of all: a huge, back-finned, ivory and beige monster, which he had bought from an army colonel returning to the USA. No more discreet black Citroën, no more four-door, family-style Chevrolet; now he presented himself to Paris in the most vulgar vehicle one could find. "It was a bargain," was Jim's explanation for owning such a monstrosity.

In Trouville, Liz Jones zoomed up almost immediately in Jesse's Porsche with her son, Robin. Catina took the little ones with Robin and the dog across the boardwalk and down to the beach to their place in the sun and sand under a colorful parasol. By the time she left, Liz knew for sure what she had suspected–things were pretty bad between Jim and myself. She was sympathetic but there was nothing she, or anyone else, could do.

When Jim returned to Trouville to take us back to Paris, we loaded babies, nurse, bird and dog with bags and baggage, looking like country bumpkins in a giant, two-toned car that seemed like Hollywood-on-wheels.

I was shocked to see the state of our home. Although Jim had said that he was going to do like the French did and shutter up the house during the summer, he had done no such thing. The house was in a mess and it was obvious that he had been "batching" it in our absence. All the beds were unmade and awry with soiled linen. Jim said his father had used Cathy's bed and a friend named Steve had been in Catina's room. I didn't want to think about the master bedroom. I hurried upstairs to strip the beds while the children were still in the garden with Catina.

The kitchen was full of dirty dishes, glasses and empty wine, whisky and beer bottles; someone had burned a hole in our dining room table; the salon had unemp- tied ashtrays everywhere and stains on the carpet. I looked up at my portrait and wondered if it had been removed or turned toward the wall in my absence.

I set to work trying to get the house in order, knowing that I couldn't begin to think about hiring help until I got a little order in my head as well. Jim was very good about unloading the car and getting the bird and cage upstairs in the nurs- ery with all the bags and baggage, but then he was off in his car again, saying he had some things to do. It was Saturday and he hadn't even stayed around long enough to see that we had supplies for the weekend. Worse yet, I had no money on hand and couldn't run out to buy anything until I asked Catina if she had a lit- tle to lend until *Monsieur* gave me the household cash.

Soon after the summertime fiasco, Jim got even more careless about turning over enough money to me every month to run the household and take care of the children's needs. He'd come in and out of the house so fast and leave on trips with- out telling me where he was going or for how long. And when I'd stop him in the middle of the garden and have to plead, it sickened me to be in such a position as he so obviously resented having to reach into his pocket. I'd have to ask him every month for money to pay the bills. I'd suggest to him that he put enough aside every four weeks as I could tell him pretty accurately in advance what was required, but he'd only smirk, dig into his pockets, and hand over enough for our needs, some- times with a shake of his head and a snide remark about how I seemed to be able to gobble money down like cornflakes.

I was extremely sensitive to this "money misery;" I had made my own living all my life and hadn't ever had to ask for anything except my paycheck. Now, Jim was not only making it hard for me to get household bills paid but he was making snide remarks in front of others.

One evening we had guests in for cocktails and they admired our little salon, saying that the things we'd selected were perfect for a *petit pavillon* in Paris. I said we were quite pleased with Monsieur Chalom, who seemed to us about the best in Paris. Jim laughed at this and said, "Maybe not the BEST, but certainly the most EXPENSIVE," giving me a glance as if to say that it was I who was responsible.

Except for the times that Jim needed to use our home as his *joli cadre*, he spent little time with me and our children. He'd still announce when we had to have a cocktail party or a buffet in honor of someone important coming to Paris, and take a list out of his pocket of the Parisians he wanted me to invite, mail cards to if there was time, or telephone each one when the party was impromptu. For these events we had our trusty Georges Rosell to do a fine job and his helpers who'd leave our house spic-and-span.

In the next few months I tried to find the perfect housekeeper, with a promise from me that I'd pitch in when needed. So began the parade of hired help whose names I would certainly have forgotten if I hadn't had my yearly "agendas" to remind me; names like Germaine, Raymonde, and Hélène. One afternoon, Catina

A happy family on the Christmas card was really something else behind the scene.
Jim went skiing by himself again!

said she'd seen our old Hungarian couple, Ferdinand and Sidi, on the street and they wanted to come by to see the children in the garden the next afternoon. I said, "Of course," and to invite them for an aperitif as well.

The next day I was in the house when they arrived and I went down to visit with them. Ferdinand and Sidi were between jobs again, but I told them that I could hire only one person instead of two. Ferdinand chatted in Hungarian with his wife and then turned back to me to say that they'd work for just one salary if I'd take them back. I was just about ready to get rid of Madame Hélène, who seemed to be marking purchases in her daily book of things we'd never seen on the table, asking for more money for the kitchen than Pierre and Anna had ever spent when we were entertaining.

Even though Jim was not staying at home those days and nights, I knew I had to discuss taking back Ferdinand and Sidi. He shrugged as if it didn't matter to him, but he couldn't help adding he didn't know I liked goulash that much. His insult turned into a challenge for me. I bought a beautiful French cookbook in English with full-page, full-color photographs of what each dish should look like, and spent time every day reading in English, translating into French for Ferdinand, who translated into Hungarian for Sidi. We had some lovely dishes from our combined efforts and I learned a bit about cooking in the process. Our meals were far from gourmet fare, but delicious. Before Ferdinand and Sidi came back to the Rue du Docteur Blanche, I'd had the unpleasant task of counting the laundry to be picked up every week and had seen for myself the lipstick smudges on Jim's clothes. What shades. Ugh! Magenta, burnt orange or ultra violet. Now I could mention it to Jim; before I had been careful not to let him know that I had heard from the nurse who had learned about it through the cook and butler when clothes were laundered at home. And yet I said nothing, knowing that words got me nowhere and only put him in a filthy mood.

Martyrdom was my middle name until I began to learn that Jim was being seen with the same girl night after night, and she seemed to be a steady date instead of his usual once-and-done affairs. Each and every person who mentioned her to me said she looked just like me. Even Dorothy Schoenbrun couldn't help commenting that this girl with Jim looked like me, though "out of focus." Thomas Quinn Curtiss said he saw Jim in the early hours of morning at Calavados with this girl. "At first I thought it was you," he told me.

One afternoon, when I'd gone to see the Christian Dior collection, I was crossing the Avenue Montaigne when I saw Jim's car cruising down the avenue toward me. As it came nearer I saw a dark-haired, white-skinned lady driving the car. Yes, she looked like she might be me, but she wasn't. The car, however, was definitely Jim's big "bargain" in ivory and beige.

The first chance I got, I asked Jim to take the time for a talk and we were back in the salon. This time, I didn't waste words. I told him what I'd seen with my own eyes and how all of our friends were telling me about the same girl and treating me in that "poor little Maggi" manner that I couldn't take any more. Yes, I mentioned the humiliation of having to handle his dirty laundry covered with lipstick. He let me finish until I said if he didn't change his ways I was ready for a divorce. He got up, going to the door to deliver his unforgettable exit line. "Fuck off, Maggi, you've never had it so good!" (The "F" word sounds like nothing today, but in our world of the fifties it was the lowest possible insult.)

I was devastated. His remark about never having it so good really showed how little Jim understood me. He was weighing and measuring everything in a totally different way from me. His idea (which he repeated many times) was that I was nothing more than a poor working girl living in a lousy little hotel room when we met and, now just look at all I had. But I felt I had nothing without being part of a team building a life and sharing in the great experience of parenthood.

The miracle of children has never ceased to amaze me. They were "little people" from their first days. Sometimes I'd be frightened of the great responsibility one had bringing babies into the world. Every day was a fascinating experience going upstairs for breakfast, spending time with them in the afternoon, taking care of them on weekends, holidays and during the vacation months. Their imagination intrigued me. They'd come back from their walks in the park with stories they'd made up about imaginary people they'd met. I asked Catina, "Who is this *Madame* they keep talking about?" and she'd shrug and say it was just another character they'd invented. Once I heard them talking together about someone I thought they called "Monsieur Johnny Marr," but it turned out that they had given this nickname to their father when he came upstairs one day and found out that Janne had pulled a mobile decoration from its suspended spot. He had lost his temper and announced "*J'en ai marre*," which means "I've had enough." He spent little time with his daughters, which seemed a pity for him to be called "Mister I've Had Enough."

Chapter Eleven

E ve came up with yet another good idea to help me through this dreadful time. It was her suggestion that I begin to invite some of my favorite people over for cocktails and maybe even dinner. She pointed out to me that I needed to just be myself and see the friends who meant something to me rather than a constant parade of strangers.

The first friends coming to the house were neighbors Pierre and Harriet Boudet, and the Jones of course, plus a lady I'd become acquainted with at Elizabeth Arden's, Dorothy Thorp de Piolenc. She was a bouncing, buxom American textile heiress who'd married a French marquis. Her Frenchman wanted to live in America and she wanted to be a *Marquise* living in Paris, so they traded countries. Dorothy was a darling, full of good humor. She could brighten anyone's day just by showing up. Through Dorothy I met the most charming Frenchman I'd ever known, Roger Dann, who was an actor-singer in stage musicals and had appeared in Hitchcock films. Elegant, gentlemanly and amusing, he was like a French Cary Grant. (Today he is over 80 years old, still elegant, gentlemanly and amusing. He can be seen on those late, late television programs showing old movies like *I Confess* with Anne Baxter and Montgomery Clift, or *Two For The Road* with Audrey Hepburn and Albert Finney.)

Now most of Jim's time was being spent with his "Maggi-look-alike" and I received so many reports of his activities that I wondered just how much more I could stand. Jim was home only when he needed to present the picture we made to the outside world of visiting TWA executives and celebrities passing through Paris. I felt like I was chained to a chair like the little Doolie dog in Reading, PA.–awaiting the master–ill-humored and ready to snap.

My friend Eve's visits were precious to me because she was the only one I could confide in and put into words all my misery that I bottled up inside. At first she sympathized. As time went on and my reports got more heated, she brought an elegant society lawyer with her one afternoon. It was teatime but we had cocktails while Eve and I filled him in on my problems. This was the beginning of a new era–Maggi was no longer the doormat suffering in silence.

This time I announced to Jim that I meant what I had said. If he didn't act like a husband and father I was ready for a divorce and had already consulted a lawyer. He only half-listened, glancing several times at his watch before he shrugged and went on his way. He was so careless and sure of himself that he emptied a pile of papers from his pockets and piled them onto the mantelpiece in our bedroom. That's how I learned his girlfriend's name on a doctor's bill which had been addressed to him at their Left Bank apartment and stamped "paid."

Grandpa Nolan didn't hesitate to get involved in our marriage problem. Appearing on the scene he let me know that Jim had told him I was threatening divorce. Making me sit down at the garden table under the parasol, he announced that I should be aware of a few "facts of life." First of all, he wanted to make it clear just where I stood in the family. Did I realize, he asked, that a Protestant mother was considered merely the vessel by which the children were brought into the Catholic Church, and if I divorced his son I would lose my children? I scoffed, saying that I was the mother, after all, as I started to go. He had more on his mind, insisting that he was warning me and I'd better make an effort to understand "before it is too late." As he threatened again that my children would be taken away from me, I sat down again and told him a few truths about his son going days and sometimes weeks without even going upstairs to see our children or take them out or even ask how they were. His reply to this was that they'd be better off raised in a convent.

This was too much. I said what happened to my daughters was my business and I was going to do my best for them and try to give them everything I hadn't had, like loving care and education. If his son didn't want to do his share then I'd just have to do more. I tried to sound like I was sure of myself, but I was trembling inside and furious with Jim that he didn't face me himself, or at least warn me that he'd told his father of our marriage problems, knowing his father would come directly to me with a warning that if I didn't stay in my corner and be quiet I'd suffer the consequences.

As soon as Grandpa Nolan left Paris I was ready for a real showdown with Jim, but he arrived on the scene with a friendly face, saying that he hoped his father's visits hadn't been too difficult. I probably stood with my mouth open with surprise as he went on saying he didn't think we had to pretend anymore, and that I was right about the divorce being necessary. He confessed that he'd moved in with this lady I'd heard so much about. Now he saw no reason why I shouldn't go right ahead with legal proceedings.

In a light-hearted mood before leaving, he pointed to the cement basin in the garden, asking what I'd like to plant there next time. I suggested evergreens that wouldn't need anything but watering and trimming. He was charming, complimenting me on my taste, and that day didn't have to be reminded to leave the household money.

Champagne...

The lawyer Eve brought to the house began his work for me. I was a very confused creature through months to come. My children and their progress and everyday joy they brought was all that kept me together. I felt they had been put in my care by a higher power and I had to prove that I was worthy. If that sounds corny it's because one can get that way when the chips are down.

I was often alone in the garden waiting for Catina and the children to get back from their afternoon excursion. I felt the strange sensation of having a powerful friend in the giant chestnut tree, standing magnificently in the corner of the little property with half of its branches shadowing the garden and the other half over the wall and onto the sidewalk. Never having told anyone this for fear of being thought a bit dotty, I dare say it now because I've heard of many others in many lands having the same feelings. I touched the trunk and felt strength from it as I entertained very heavy thoughts on the responsibility of bringing children into the world.

I needed faith and strength to do right by those little people who were on earth because of me and had their whole lives before them.

It was in the beginning of these trying times that an American-Parisian, David Stein, telephoned. He announced who he was and I immediately thought he wanted Jim and said he should try Jim's office at that hour. "I don't want to talk to Jim. I want to talk to YOU." Then he went on to explain that he had been seeing Jim around socially lately and figured that we were separated. Then, the night before, he had actually gone up to Jim and asked for permission to invite me to dinner.

I laughed in disbelief at first, saying, "Oh, so you asked my husband for permission to take me out, and so what did my husband say?"

"Well, to tell you the truth, Maggi," David said, "He patted me on the back and said that would be very, very nice of me!" I didn't answer right away while this scene settled in my head. Then I said something rude like it seemed to me that I could make up my own mind who got "permission" to take me out but David refused to be insulted. He chatted on about parties that were taking place and people who could be amusing.

I finally said, of course, he could call me the next week if he wanted and "Thank you" for calling. David Stein was a nice fellow who ran the Paris office of the Music Corporation of America (MCA), which was founded by his brother, Jules Stein. They were agents for top movie stars and David often entertained MCA clients in his mansion near the Arc de Triomphe. We often saw David at fancy French-American parties and in the best clubs and restaurants, always in the company of celebrities. He'd been to some of our receptions, always bringing a very pretty singer, dancer, actress or model. In my present state of mind I didn't see why he wanted to ask ME out. In my eyes I was unattractive if not completely ugly and besides, I was a failure.

The first time I went out with David, he took me to a cocktail party in a Left Bank mansion belonging to a tycoon, Daniel Saint. The minute I stepped into the luxurious salons, I forgot about my feelings of inferiority. André Dubonnet, the aperitif "king" shook my hand graciously, but then leaned over and whispered that he was happy to see me out-and-about and looking so well. (I knew that meant Jim had been spreading stories of my "illness," but never mind.) Then Sir Charles Mendl shuffled toward me, telling me that I had very, VERY beautiful shoulders and I didn't feel ugly anymore.

David was very sweet to me and even mentioned that he thought Jim was out of his mind to leave me at home. He added he wished I'd come out with him again and mentioned he had a party at his place in a few nights' time, which he hoped I could attend. It seemed like the tonic I needed right then and I accepted while joking that perhaps he should ask permission from Jim.

"From now on, it'll just be between you and me," he laughed as he left me at the gate.

Too bad this isn't a novel. I'd be happy to write that David and Maggi fell madly in love, got married, had a lot more children and lived happily ever after. Alas, sweet, attentive, thoughtful and generous as he was, David seemed to have worse problems than I. He lived in a beautiful town house full of fabulous furniture, fine paintings and everything a man about Paris could ever dream of; yet he was living two separate lives. His outside existence as the magnificent man of the world was quite true except when his brother and sister-in-law came to town.

Jules Stein was the self-made tycoon married to an ambitious woman, Doris Jones Stein, who appeared on the Paris scene to take over the mansion like the Dowager Queen Doris arriving at her summer palace. David had to vacate his master bedroom, dressing room and bath for the royal visit. He was exiled to a top-floor room like a houseguest in his own home. From the self-assured master of his mansion when he was on his own, David became little more than a flunky in the lady's presence. Big brother Jules was good to every member of his family and did much to see that they were well-off financially, but when it came to adhering to his wife's wishes there was never any question as to whether she'd have her way.

If prizes were ever given out for snobbishness, Doris could win every one. From the minute she appeared in Paris, she got parties together that looked like the guest list had been copied straight from the social registry, mixing them with top star celebrities from Hollywood who happened to be in Paris at the time. David hopped around to make certain that the servants were on their toes and everything was lined up for successful social gatherings in Doris' name.

Even if you didn't know when Doris and Jules were in town, you could have sensed that something had come over David. He'd become nervous, insecure and sometimes seemed hopelessly lost in confusion. Then when they were gone he'd be on his own again, Master of the mansion and in charge of his life once more. The difference was disturbing to people who cared about him, but there was nothing anyone could do because one dared not mention such unpleasant subjects, and David was never known to complain.

Champagne...

David Stein was the perfect host, but he had to vacate his mansion suite when his sister-in-law came to town.

From the first evening David Stein took me out with permission and a pat on the shoulder from my husband, he introduced me to countless celebrities, not always in crowds but on evenings when he entertained people who shunned parties, like the moody actor Montgomery Clift. He was in Paris at the Plaza Athénée with his girlfriend, Libby Holman, and David asked me to join him at dinner with them at the Coq Hardi. Monty was on vacation before starting a fim called *Miss Lonelyhearts* with Marlon Brando. He made it clear to David that he'd dine with him if there wouldn't be more than four of us, and he added emphatically, that no press was to know that he was in Paris with Libby (fifteen years older than he, but a torch singer with still a lot of fire aglow).

We picked them up at the service entrance of the Plaza Athénée because they wanted to avoid being seen, and off we sped on the highway to the Coq Hardi. Monty Clift was a difficult man to talk to because he stared straight into your face with piercing blue eyes and never smiled, even when he said things like, "What's the name of this place? Hardy Cock? That's a funny name for a restaurant." David told him *coq* meant rooster, but I'm certain Monty knew that as well as we did. On our way back to Paris they asked to stop at the side of the road where there was a grassy slope. They got out, walked a bit away and lighted a cigarette which they shared. It was years before I realized that they smoked "grass" on that grassy slope.

Of all the world famous movie stars David introduced me to, Cary Grant was the most outstanding. Indeed, he became a lifelong friend. Today it's hard to believe that I turned my back on him the first time we were introduced. I must have been *blasée*, as Paris was full of Hollywood stars. While out and about with

Eve in the daytime and David in the evening, I'd seen Burt Lancaster with Tony Curtis, Audrey Hepburn and Mel Ferrer, Gene Tierney with Aly Khan, and Clark Gable with several TWA executives. Then, attending a star-studded cocktail party on the Place Vendôme with David this evening he introduced me to Cary Grant at the very moment that I caught sight of Myrna Loy in the crowd. She'd been a favorite of mine since I was about 12 years old and I couldn't take my eyes off her. After shaking hands with Cary, I turned to zero in on Myrna Loy, who was just elbows away from me, surrounded by a group of guests.

"Wow," I thought, "now I can get a real close-up of a star of stars." Never mind that she was almost as old as my mother.

I had seen some of her films enough times to know certain scenes word for word, and sometimes I'd go home, lock myself in the bathroom and try to imitate her crinkly-eyed smile in front of the mirror. I even tried her voice–which I considered very special like a "voice with a grin in it"–but I couldn't come near to sounding like that incredible creature.

Myrna Loy was in Paris with other actors who were also there that evening: Edmond Arnold and the not yet known actor, John Forsythe. They were filming with American-Parisian Olivia de Havilland, in a movie called *The Ambassador's Daughter*, also co-starring Adolphe Menjou (whom everyone thought was French but was born in Pittsburgh, PA.). Excited to be in the same room as Myrna Loy, I inched my way closer to hear what she was saying but it was disappointing. She was complaining bitterly about French studios and how inferior they were to Hollywood ones. With every word she seemed to grow more agitated and animated, waving her arms around while she talked, even though her right hand held a very large martini.

Our hostess in Paris that evening was Verna Ostertag, a long-stemmed American beauty who had been a partly-clad showgirl at the Lido nightclub until she changed all that for a very rich husband and *haute couture* clothes. Two marriages later she became the very well-kept mistress of a wealthy French businessman who was seldom on the scene. She loved to entertain lavishly when he wasn't around. And when her friend, David Stein, helped her with the guest list, she had star-studded parties and served giant-sized cocktails. Tonight, here was Myrna Loy holding a "deep-dish martini" in her hand when I was successful in sidling up very close to my goddess, but before I knew what was happening I felt cold martini sloshing around in one of my satin shoes. I said, "Oops," stepping back, but Miss Loy moved forward, still sipping, then dripping and telling her sad story of filming in France.

I managed to back away and went squishing around the salon a while, feeling like the party was over. I found David Stein, who'd invited me to go to dinner after the cocktail party, and asked him if he thought it might be time to go. He seemed delighted that I wanted to leave because, he said, Cary Grant didn't even want to come in the first place. That was the first I knew about plans to dine with Cary

Champagne...

Grant. David invited another couple to join us, a pretty French mannequin and her American boyfriend, and off we went to dine in David's favorite Left Bank cellar.

Across the Seine at number 1, Quai Bourbon, was Au Franc Pinot, a favorite wining, dining and dancing spot of the fifties , where you'd find chic socialites and celebrities. Borah Minevitch, old-time entertainer and *bon vivant*, had taken over one of Paris' oldest caves dating back to the 1600s and turned into a mirrored paradise on several levels below the street.

Au Franc Pinot, the historic watering hole of French revolutionaries, became a showplace with amusing, original decor, like chairs from the flea market that had once been seats in horse-drawn carriages in the bar on the street floor. Descending into the cellar, you were in another gilt-edged, antique-mirrored world with gleaming linen, polished silverware and sparkling crystal glassware gracing every table. Romantic music from a small orchestra played for dinner, livening up later for all night dancing.

Borah had really put his heart into this spot as well as the money he made in America playing harmonica on stage and on radio programs with a group called "Borah Minevitch & the Harmonica Rascals." When he took over Au Franc Pinot, it was a pile of rubble. He spent all of his days and nights there from the cellar-digging right to the grand opening. Once when he thought the workmen were too slow digging into the depths of the cellar, he slipped a few old gold coins in the dirt where they would surely be dug out. The findings stirred the diggers on to greater depths in record time. To Borah, that gold investment was money well spent.

David was our host for dinner and placed Cary Grant right across from me, the French mannequin across the table from himself and the young lady's date at the end of the table. I didn't notice this unfair seating until the dinner conversation didn't include the man on the end as much as it should have. What really brought the situation to my attention was David taking the girl to the dance floor at the end of the dinner at coffee and cognac time. David and the lovely damsel stayed away so long that the gentleman had downed at least two after-dinner drinks and was getting a bit restless in his chair.

Cary seemed to sense the tension and started to tell us some funny stories about his teenage circus days. He was such good company that I had long forgotten my woes. He was so funny and made me giggle so much that my wasp-waisted girdle was beginning to pinch. The American businessman got up without a word and we saw the back of him as he made his way up the stone staircase.

"Guess he doesn't like circus stories," said Cary and I assured him it wasn't because of his stories that the fellow's tail was in a knot. He nodded, "I know, I know," and I confessed that I might have been a little jealous myself because David was supposed to be my date but, thanks to Cary, I was laughing more than I had in a long, long time.

When Cary said he thought that he could now ask me to dance, I shook my head. "No, not right now," and then it was his turn to laugh. He told me he was glad that I didn't want to dance as he, frankly, danced like he was playing football and might even break something. So he continued his funny routines, which I was later to call his "Archie Leach Acts," because they were learned when he was Archibald Leach of Bristol, England, before he went to Hollywood.

Before our first evening was over, I became acquainted with his old vaudeville routine called something like "The Day the Balloon Went Up," which he seemed to remember word for word. The act is between an old man and a young boy waiting at the fair grounds for a Jules Verne-type balloon to take off. Cary took both parts—the old man all hunched over who can't straighten up so he stares at the floor, and the young fellow who keeps looking upward, wide-eyed and excited. I can't remember the words of the original routine but it was hilarious and when finally the balloon goes up and the man and boy are heading homeward, the little kid asks the old man why he can't straighten up and he says, "I don't rightly know, maybe suspenders buttoned to my fly." Then he adds that it'll be easier going home "cause it's all down hill."

I laughed so much that Cary was laughing at me laughing and the more funny jokes he seemed to remember. Finally, he said I was such a good audience that he'd have to polish up some more routines for future occasions. I was unaware then of what his balloon act would mean to me—or what balloons already meant to him.

After dinner at Au Franc Pinot with Cary Grant, David and I dropped him off in front of the Hôtel Raphael with the usual glad-to-have-met-you and see-you-soon. I didn't dream at the time just how soon that would be. Cary showed up the very next afternoon in the *petit pavillon* on the Rue du Docteur Blanche.

It was Sunday as usual with the cook taking off after breakfast and Catina and I sharing our day with Cathy and Janne. I'd invited a few American-Parisians to drop by, have a few drinks and raid the refrigerator when they felt like it. David was expected and promised to bring my favorite champagne. Before he came, he called and asked if it was okay to bring Cary Grant with him, saying, "Just talked to Cary and he isn't doing anything." Sure enough, a little while later, I saw Cary with David, sauntering through the garden up to the door. He looked quite dapper in casual clothes with an elegant ascot instead of a tie.

There were six or seven friends lounging around in the salon. Cary went up to each and every one of them, shaking hands and saying, "Hello, I'm Cary Grant." Before taking a place in an armchair, he said he was expecting a telephone call from his wife, Betsy, and that he had transferred the call to my number. I told him I'd show him the way to the kitchen pantry; there was a wall phone where he could take his call in private. He seemed appreciative, for though there was a phone right at his elbow, it was near more than a dozen ears as well.

The phone rang soon after and I motioned Cary to come through the dining room and into the pantry. It was indeed California calling so I handed the phone to Cary and went into the kitchen to fill the empty ice bucket.

Champagne...

After his short and sweet talk with Betsy Drake, he came into the kitchen and sat down at the cook's table, asking if there was any old thing he could eat as he hadn't had any lunch. I opened our giant-sized refrigerator and pointed out an assortment of "goodies" we always had ready for Sunday snacks. Roast veal? Vegetable salad? Apple tart? But Cary had been eyeing the sliced American brown bread on the counter and asked if he could have a lettuce sandwich on brown bread and a glass of milk. I laughed and told him that he was asking for what had been my lunch every summer of my young life at Seward Park on Lake Washington in Seattle many, many years before. While I fixed his "lunch" he told me he knew a lot about my part of America, having toured all around there in vaudeville, "before you were born, Maggi."

We were getting along so well that I dared ask him why he thought it necessary to say to everyone, "I'm Cary Grant," when we all knew exactly who he was. He smiled and said, "If you'd been called Gary Cooper as many times as I have, you'd do the same as I do!"

He went on to list various common sense reasons for announcing your name. It's good manners, it avoids drawing blanks or calling someone by the wrong name, it can prompt the other fellow to give his name. Then he told me how happy he was to have talked to Betsy, and how talented and great-to-be-with she was, and what a marvelous sense of humor she had. He took a letter from his pocket and let me read a paragraph she'd written about some characters who came to their house to do some work but had tangled everything up. It was funny. Her report on workmen in their house could have inspired a Marx Brothers movie.

I discovered that Cary had a remarkable way of getting me to talk about myself. He'd ask a key question and show he was really interested in the answer to the point where I was saying things to him that I hadn't even put into words before. I was still in shock at what was happening to my life, full of feelings of failure and fear for what was to come. His comments were general, not personal, but they meant a lot to me. He said most people don't know the importance of getting to know themselves. Self-love is necessary before one can love another, one person alone is not to blame in a relationship, and he punned, "It takes two to tangle." He told me about himself, as well. When other kids were making go-carts out of apple boxes, he was cooking his own meals and washing his own socks, while mastering the song-and-dance or comic routines to earn a living.

He told me that he, too, had hang-ups over his parents. When I told him about my mother bragging that she had slapped my left hand when I was a baby because I was favoring the left instead of the right and no child of hers was going to grow up using the "wrong hand," he laughed and said that he had gone through the "right hand–wrong hand" thing himself, but that we should be glad, not mad, because we were probably ambidextrous. "And that can come in handy sometimes," he added. I was giggling and said "I'll shake on that," and we both held out our left hands and shook hands the "wrong" way.

We seemed to have so many things in common that I felt like we were related in some way, and when he put his hand to his forehead I noticed that we had the same hairline with a marked "widow's peak." That was before he deliberately changed his hair style, which hid it from view.

Before our talk was over, we discovered that we were both born under the sign of Capricorn and I told him I understood that meant the last part of our lives would be better than the first. "Just think what a lot we have to look forward to," he smiled, just about the time that David came through the swinging door from the dining room saying, "You've been out here for an hour–and where the heck's the ice?" I didn't think we'd been away from the salon very long but when I looked at the amount of ice that had melted in the sink, I knew everyone must be wondering what we were up to out there.

A few weeks after our first meeting Cary Grant was back in Paris on his way to Spain to star in a film with an unknown Italian actress named Sophia Loren.

Cary called David Stein as soon as he'd checked into the Hôtel Raphael and they made a dinner date for the following Saturday "at the house," as David called his impressive mansion which was a stopping-off place for countless Hollywood celebrities. (David secretly housed some of them, like Marlon Brando, in a third-floor hideaway.) David called me to ask if I'd like to dine at the house with him, Cary and a pretty American singer named Florence. I accepted, of course, feeling very much at home with David and comfortable with Cary, who made me laugh when he wasn't saying things that made me delve into my thoughts.

Chapter Twelve

The day before David's dinner for Cary Grant was Good Friday and when I was walking down the Avenue Mozart, I stopped with a gasp in front of a pastry shop window. The display was entirely Easter inspired with chocolate bunnies, fish, decorated eggs, *bonbon*-filled baskets and all that, but hanging above it was a giant, all chocolate balloon decorated with white, squiggly Montgolfier designs. Hanging down from the balloon was the passengers' basket, filled with yellow chicks peeping over the side. It was a work of art that took my breath away and I just knew I had to get that balloon for Cary. I could imagine it already hanging between the dining room and the salon in David's house.

I went into the shop ready to pay whatever the super sugar chef might ask but, alas, he had no intention of parting with his masterpiece at any price. Not even the President of the Republic could make him change his mind, he said, shaking a sugar-coated finger in my direction. He offered all the bells and bunnies and fish I could carry away but his balloon–"Never!" The more I looked at it, the more I knew it was for Cary but I had to walk out of the store without it. I stood staring through the window, so close to the pane that I bumped my nose but the chef stood behind his balloon, shaking his head, *"Non, non et NON!"*

Walking up the avenue, feeling pretty low, I saw a magazine stand in front of a newspaper store. Cary's picture was smiling at me from the cover of a weekly magazine. I bought a copy and scooted right back to the chocolate genius. He gave me that "oh-no-not-you-again" look, but I thrust Cary's photo under his nose and asked him if he wouldn't like this *Monsieur* to enjoy having a balloon. His shop helpers (ladies, all) crowded around him and seemed to be clucking like Easter hens. I was an instant celebrity in their eyes if I was a friend of Cary Grant's.

Mr. Chocolate Man was melting, "Ahhh, if it is for this *Monsieur*, perhaps it is possible," he said, and we started to make plans for him to come in person with the balloon. We made a date at David's the next afternoon and I warned David's maid, butler and cook of what to expect. The sugar chef wrapped his prize in miles of cotton until it looked like a moon-sized cocoon. He loaded it into a special pastry delivery van with no other *bonbon* on board and rode beside it all the way from the Avenue Mozart to the Étoile to make certain that no damage would be done.

He flushed with pride when he heard the servants assure him that his masterpiece was for Cary Grant. He carried it upstairs and supervised the trio as they hung the Easter balloon in its place of honor above their heads.

That evening, Florence arrived right after I did, but before Cary. She was amazed that we'd be only four for dinner, saying that she had expected a crowd to be gathered in honor of this top star. David always had a bevy of beauties and their slick dinner-jacketed escorts, except for Cary, who didn't like that. Poor Florence was flabbergasted and said she wouldn't know what to say or how to act with this idol whom she adored from afar for so long. We were downstairs and I motioned her upstairs to the salon and dining room with me. I showed her the *pièce de résistance* and told her she could break the ice with Cary immediately when they were introduced downstairs by saying, "Do you know what time the balloon went up?" And I assured her that the rest of the evening would take care of itself. She didn't know what I was talking about, but then she was a good sport. When she met Cary, she spoke her line perfectly.

Cary looked at both of us slyly and asked me if I'd been doing his routines behind his back, and I just laughed and said, "The balloon went up at four o'clock this afternoon," and Florence and I rushed upstairs ahead of David and Cary to station ourselves near the grand piano where we could see Cary's reaction. We were acting more like six-year olds than the super sophisticates we were supposed to be. Cary stopped still in the doorway, sighting the balloon straight away. He stared, approached slowly and then seemed oblivious to everything as he looked up at his surprise.

The butler came in with a big silver cocktail tray and got our attention, but when I looked at Cary again, he had his back to us and was still looking at the balloon. I walked over to him and he turned, looking into my eyes and taking my hands in his. Never in a million years would I have expected such a dramatic reaction. His eyes were inky black and it looked like there might be tears there but they didn't dare fall. "Maggi, my love," he said, and that was all, but it was enough to see the sentiment and pleasure he felt.

To lighten the moment I giggled and said, "Hey, don't stand under that contraption. It might fall on your head and it weighs more than ten pounds!" Right with it, Cary said, "And I bet it COST more than ten pounds, too!"

We had a delicious and marvelously-relaxed dinner. Cary was in a mellow mood back in the salon and asked David if he had a camera as he thought we ought to have a souvenir shot of our Easter Eve evening. David was thrilled. He wouldn't have dared ask Cary to pose for a photo during a private evening at home, no matter how much he might have wished it. David practically stumbled over himself getting the camera, but Cary very calmly supervised the picture-taking under and all around the big balloon. Finally Florence laughed and said, "You don't want pictures of us, you're sweet on that ten-pound hunk of chocolate hanging up there!"

Years later, Cary told me the balloon story that had been an unforgettable part of his life. He said when he was a toddler, his father taught him a poem called something like *Up In a Balloon So High*. That was okay but one night his father woke him from a sound sleep, took him downstairs where a noisy party was going full blast and made him recite his balloon poem while being held up above his father's head. Little Archie Leach bumped the ceiling as he tried and failed to remember his lines to please his father. He said he could never forget the misery of that moment.

We dined once more before Cary Grant flew off to Spain and there were only four of us once again. This time, David invited the aforementioned long-stemmed American beauty from the Place Vendôme, Verna Ostertag, as Cary's "date," and it was she who insisted we end our evening at L'Éléphant Blanc, where everybody-who-was-anybody could be found every night and until the wee hours of morning. Cary was a good sport about it and agreed but when he added that he couldn't think of a better way to spend his last night in Paris, he was careful not to look at me because he knew we'd laugh out loud at his terrible fib.

There was the usual magnificent mob scene at the nightclub with its sardine-packed dance floor and the orchestra playing full blast. David was received with open arms by the manager who took us immediately to the reserved table in Cary's honor as David had called, promising the appearance of the biggest star of Hollywood. When we were seated and my eyes got adjusted to the lighting, I spotted local and visiting celebrities all over the place like Bob Hope at a table next to the aperitif king, André Dubonnet and then Betty Lanson, the American heiress who'd married into a French champagne family and then the Italian playboy, Prince Jean Caracciolo, with a party of titled-entitled guests and then, in the doorway, Errol Flynn, obviously plastered to the eyeballs, coming in with a bevy of very young blondes.

That night when Cary asked me to dance, I thought I ought not to refuse. It was so crowded that we could have just stood there and had a conversation except that we couldn't he heard over the loud music. We discovered that Bob Hope COULD be heard. As he danced past he yelled that now he knew how it was to dance in the subway during rush hour.

We made our way back to our corner and tried to talk. Before David and Verna came back to the table, Cary said some things I'd never forget. He was talking generally, as usual, and the point was that sometimes when a man and a woman were attracted to each other, they made the mistake of starting a big romance. The trouble with that method was that an affair had a beginning, a middle and an end. Friendship with someone you really cared about was better. "Friendship goes on forever."

Cary Grant had tears in his eyes when he looked at the chocolate balloon I got for him-but the tears didn't fall.

I've always hesitated to tell about that conversation because I thought my friends would interpret it in ways I wouldn't like. "He was just telling you he was-n't interested in you romantically," I could hear one saying. Then, "Ah-ah, I knew he didn't like girls." But I believed I knew exactly what he meant and our friend-ship lasted from 1956 until he died in 1986, while my romances fell by the wayside so often that I had trouble remembering names. As for his liking girls, I knew he loved them and spent a lot of time proving it.

A pretty American girl I knew was in Spain at the same time as Cary when he was filming with Sophia Loren. My friend couldn't wait to tell me the details of her romance with Cary and, believe me, she had no complaints. She went on and on telling me what a romantic lover he was and couldn't help adding "and we made love for 45 minutes!" I listened politely, thinking how upset Cary would surely be if he knew what a blabbermouth this attractive lady was.

Anyway, I calculated that my friend's affair with Cary was going on at the same time as he was getting acquainted with Sophia Loren and still married to Betsy Drake. Twenty years later when Sophia's book, *Living and Loving*, written with A.E. Hotchner, came out saying that Cary had been in love with her and had asked her to marry him, Cary was asked to comment. He refused politely, saying "Ask Sophia; it's her book, not mine." I don't think he ever discussed romances and I know he didn't care for folks who'd kiss-and-tell.

It was when Cary was shooting *The Pride and the Passion* in Spain that I first discovered that he loved to talk on the telephone. He called me several times from there just to chat and find out what was going on in Paris. He seemed interested in everything from whom I'd seen the night before, to the latest *bon mot* of my daughters, what the weather was like and so on. He liked to listen and always had interesting comments. One time I told him I was fed up with everything and thought maybe I ought to move back to America. He said people should solve their problems right where they were because when they packed their bags, they packed their problems at the same time and took them along to wherever they went.

It's hard to believe that Cary Grant could be truly interested in all the things I filled his ears with during our telephone conversations, but I could always tell that he was listening because of the remarks he made afterwards and the opinions he put forth.

When I told him about being hurt by the words of someone, he said words can't hurt. People who try to hurt you have a problem. Recognize it–understand it. But don't let THEIR problems hurt YOU.

I told him about Jim bringing up my lack of education. "Never mind, people like us never stop learning." Then he added that our whole lives are dedicated to listening and learning and every day is an adventure in education. You're not dictated to by scholars, you learn for yourself. No one gives you rules to follow, you think things out for yourself. So you don't have diplomas to wave in front of people to show how smart you are. You have to BE smart."

He always seemed interested in the latest news about the children. One time I told him that Cathy walked just like her father–toes slightly inward–and I guessed that we'd have to live with that as it was probably inherited. "Don't be so sure, try dancing lessons," he said, but I thought her too young. "No one is ever too young to dance," he said. I asked the baby doctor and he said it was a fine idea. It's a good thing I talked to the doctor about dancing before I talked to Jim about the money for dancing lessons. Jim didn't like the idea of extra expenses but when I told him the doctor said it was a good idea, he didn't hold back. (I could just imagine what he would have said if I had quoted a movie star's advice.) I took Cathy to dancing class every week after that on the Avenue Georges Mandel. The results were amazing and she has those baby dancing lessons to thank for her straight forward walking today.

Years later I tried to thank Cary for pointing me in the right direction and he said he didn't do any such thing because it was MY decision, not his.

Life in the *petit pavillon* separated into two parts: daytime routine of mother/housekeeper and glamorous evenings as a guest in David Stein's mansion. After a day of supervising grocery shopping, cooking, cleaning and sharing the children's walks in the afternoons with Catina, I'd go to my room after their bedtime to transform myself into *haute couture*, high heels and long earrings for an evening at David's with interesting people, fine food and wine, plus marvelous music. Often I wore my favorite Christian Dior dress that had a white satin tunic over a matching sheath, making the dress look the same from the front and the back (a model that I'd gotten on sale). I had a big success with that dress because it was different. When Jack Benny and Mary Livingston were at David's one evening, Mary told me she thought my dress was divine and asked me where I had found it. Then she called Jack over to see the dress, making me turn around while she said, "Look, Jack, it's Dior, it's Dior." Jack took a long look and quipped, "Great, but I can't tell the front Dior from the back Dior."

During this time I started to write words to some music David composed, which he often played for guests after dinner. He was an accomplished musician. I thought it a pity that he didn't use his talent more seriously and spend less time worrying about the pressures of big business and a bossy sister-in-law, but nothing ever changed *chez* Stein.

Sometimes the little ditties I wrote for his music stayed in his head and as soon as dinner was over, he'd sit down at the piano while guests were having coffee and cognac to entertain them with our latest creations. One song, however, was too long for him to memorize so I typed it for him to look at while he played. His music was based on an old Russian ballad and my words were based on what I was feeling toward life and love at the time.

I FOUND MY PARADISE
WHEN I LOOKED IN YOUR EYES
I FELT A THRILL THAT I
HAD NEVER KNOWN
AND SUDDENLY TO ME
DREAMS WERE REALITY
AND I KNEW I WAS YOURS
AND YOURS ALONE

I FOUND MY PARADISE
WITHIN YOUR WARM EMBRACE
AS HAPPILY I ROAMED
THAT HEAVENLY PLACE

Champagne...

AND YET I SHOULD HAVE KNOWN
THAT AFTER SUN COMES RAIN
AND PARADISE ONCE FOUND
CAN BE LOST AGAIN...

Although I reached the point where I knew a serious relationship with David was not to be, we got along beautifully and were perfectly at ease with each other. Sometimes when we were alone I'd call him by his real first name, Herman. When I thought he was being too stuffy about someone or something, all I had to say was "Now, Herman" to get his attention. He'd look attentive and listen to what I had to say after answering, "Yes, Margaret."

Jim was installed with his "Maggi look-alike" on the Left Bank, but reports of his doings didn't bother me anymore, though our relationship fluctuated depending on his moods. He seemed so anxious to be free, on the one hand, that he signed all official papers the lawyers put in front of him and rarely came over to the *petit pavillon*. But when his father was in Paris, his visits with him were frequent and upsetting. Grandpa kept up his ranting, raving and threatening while Jim made no attempt to answer, telling me after his father had gone that I should have learned by now not to pay any attention to "the old man."

Once, however, he sided with his father during his tirade over the outrage of Maggi having three servants. "Yes," said Jim "it is outrageous." I tried to explain that Ferdinand and Sidi really counted as one, worked faithfully, were worth taking care of and needed their job. Grandpa was furious but I went on saying I never would have taken them back if Jim had not agreed. Jim said nothing, but when he went out the door with his father he said, "Get rid of them, Maggi."

It was heartbreaking.

All the months between the original filing of divorce papers and getting a final decree seemed like a lifetime. Accompanying soul-searching was agony. I'd failed. My partner-in-life had left me for another woman. I must be ugly, stupid and inferior. Then I had to try to convince myself that I was okay, after all I'd been an advertising executive, a world-traveling journalist, a Paris hostess and, don't forget, the mother of two "little Renoirs."

Sometimes I'd stand alone in the garden under the spreading chestnut tree, hoping for strength as I touched its trunk. Once I put my nose up close, touching the bark, and whispered, "I wish I knew how to pray," and I could swear I heard the tree say to me, "You ARE praying."

During these days of household chores and mental anguish, Cary Grant called for lengthy chats from wherever he happened to be. Our talks were more about ideas and ideals than movie making and party going or Paris gossip. After each conversation I'd feel lifted, renewed and certain that I had it in myself to make a good life for me, Cathy and Janne.

One of our telephone talks was about religion. It was after I'd received a letter from my sister telling me she was entering a convent as she wanted to become a nun. I was stunned. The last time I'd been with her the only thing she was worrying about was the color of her nail polish and whether it clashed with the dress she was wearing. Mixed emotions about my sister becoming a Catholic bothered me. Would she become like Grandpa Nolan? But then I reminded myself that Grandma was Catholic and like an angel to me. Cary was very positive on this subject when I told him of anti-Protestant Catholics in my life. He seemed to have a ready-made speech, reminding me that there were good ones and bad ones in all religions, nationalities and skin colors, so it was impossible to condemn *en masse*. Then he voiced his own opinions that his religion was his business and nobody else should be concerned just as others' religions were no business of his. One thing he couldn't stand, he said, was someone using his religion as an excuse to be unkind to others.

After my painful parting with Ferdinand and Sidi, once again I was on my own except for Catina on the nursery floor. We worked out a makeshift schedule while I looked, once again, for a maid-of-all-work. I was determined to continue having friends come to call because it seemed to be a tonic for me. Entertaining by myself was different now. It couldn't be on the same scale as Jim's festivities in the name of TWA. In the first place, there was no way that I could afford to get Monsieur Rosell on the telephone and turn everything over to him. I gave cocktail parties with snacks from the American Commissary instead of fancy canapés, and then dinner parties featuring simple fare instead of gourmet feasts, but no one seemed to mind.

A couple of times I asked young Claude, the *chasseur* and novice barman of the Ritz, if he'd like to help me with my cocktail-buffets and make a little pocket money on his day off. He was excellent, setting up everything on the sheet-covered dining room table and arranging the food beautifully on our silver flea market platters so well that it looked absolutely elegant. I got a lot of practice arranging bouquets, as well. Flowers cost so little in the open stall on the Avenue Mozart that I could select a variety of blooms to mix and match for the buffet table and salon.

Sometimes when I was out of cash I'd have to turn the giant key to the wine cellar and take a bottle of red or white from what was left. One evening an actress, Carol Sands, who'd come to dine, was astounded to see a bottle of precious Volnay being poured to accompany veal stew. "Maggi, what extravagance," she gasped. I had to say "I'm sorry, but that's all I have."

The pressure from Jim to get rid of the servants after his father's objection was followed by another unhappy situation. One day Grandpa flatly stated that I should be ashamed of myself "sitting on a fortune."

At first I didn't know what he was talking about and thought he referred to my having a lot of money in the bank. I told him I couldn't possibly sit on a fortune insofar as I didn't have a dime except what Jim gave me for the children and the household. No, he didn't mean that. "Don't you realize that the money paid for this house could be invested?" he asked, not expecting an answer because he went on with his monologue about money-wasting and criticized every detail of his son's affairs–that is to say, all of his son's affairs except the one he was having with Miss "Out-Of-Focus," which came too close to his own affair with his kewpie doll.

Jim took up his father's idea about getting rid of the house to have the money to invest. He didn't repeat that I was "sitting on a fortune" but he might as well have, as it was obvious that he was parroting his father's latest abuse. I reminded Jim that his children needed a home and that a family was something you just couldn't cancel out. He dropped the subject and I thought I'd won my point.

Maybe I'm imagining it, but I believe the house sale was forced by Jim's father after he came around to the Rue du Docteur Blanche one sunny Saturday afternoon and walked into an impromptu garden party where about ten happy guests were having a very good time. The gathering was a "fence-painting party" which came about when the wall between our house and the property next door was torn down and a temporary rough wooden fence was put in its place. Jim had given his permission to destroy the wall which had dual ownership with neighbors who were tearing down their mansion to build an apartment building. David Stein saw the structure and said it was the ugliest thing he had ever seen. I agreed and said it was too bad we weren't Tom Sawyer and Huckleberry Finn; and that's how the painting party came about the next afternoon.

David said he'd get white paint and brushes and a lot of beer and snacks. He said he'd bring a visitor to Paris, Phil Silvers, whom he'd already entertained at Maxim's and the Tour d'Argent, and he'd surely get a kick out of something like this. I told him I had my New York friend, Barbara Schick, with me and I'd bet that a Schick Razor heiress would be amused by such an event as well. Then we thought Borah Minevitch and his wife, Lucille, would be fun. Of course, I invited Dorothy de Piolenc; I could hear her giggling over such an adventure before she actually did. Neighbors from around the corner, Harriet and Pierre Boudet, came over plus David's best friend, Bill Richmond, from the Embassy and his actress friend, Carol Sands.

The afternoon painting party started out with lots of beer and juicy hot dogs from the American Commissary, complete with mustard and pickles. When Catina took the children out for their daily jaunt, Bill and Borah took the paint and started to scrawl some rude words on the fence, laughing their heads off all the while. Of course we knew that their daring handiwork was temporary because they were going to cover it over with a solid white paint job right after having their fun, so we all laughed at their antics. All except Phil Silvers, who looked like he was in shock.

I wonder if there's anyone around who remembers Phil Silvers? He was a Brooklyn-born comedian with a career in vaudeville and burlesque before having one of the most successful television series in the fifties , playing a rascal called "Sargeant Ernie Bilko." You'd think he'd take rough language in his stride but he was very disturbed and dipped a brush into the paint, covering over the bad words as fast as the "naughty boys" wrote them. Poor Phil was so overwrought at their performance that he even managed to change the scribbled "U.S. GO HOME" to read "U.S. WELCOME."

Phil was a dear person. He practically jumped for joy when the fence painting was completed. The job looked professional, without a trace of bad words or a splash on surrounding bushes. The children returned delighted with the project and the party continued. When Grandpa Nolan came through the gate, he glared at everyone as though they had no right to be there. Whe he saw beer bottles, full and empty, on the garden table, it looked like he did a doubletake, as though he was thinking that I hadn't waited to return to the USA to give up drinking champagne.

He sat on a chair away from everyone, obviously annoyed at seeing guests enjoying themselves. I went over to him asking if he'd like to have a beer and he seemed to resent this even more. He left soon after, not bothering to bid anyone "goodbye." Catina was very observant from her post at the nursery window upstairs. Later she stated simply that she thought *Monsieur le père* was "crazy with rage." I said I didn't notice, but I knew she was right.

The next time Jim came to the house, he announced that he was selling "the property" and further discussion was out of the question. Three months before the final divorce papers came through, Jim was sending prospective buyers to see our home. At first I asked him not to do so because it was upsetting the children to see this parade of strangers at all hours, to say nothing of Catina and myself. He still insisted that the sale was serious but he would compromise and turn the entire matter over to an agency. The gentleman in charge then made specific appointments before bringing prospective buyers to the door and I'd try to schedule them at hours when the children would be in the park.

News of the sale got around among our Paris friends and I started to get calls from the curious. I actually had an afternoon visit from a good friend, Maxim's owner, Maggie Vaudable, who lectured me on my "stupidity." "It's YOUR home!" she insisted, and she wanted me to promise her that I would never allow the house to be sold right out from under me and my children and, above all, "Stay right where you are and don't you dare budge!" I was touched by her concern but told her she didn't understand the pressure I had on me from Jim and his father. I just couldn't live like that.

Jim was in and out, picking up clothes, books and personal belongings a little at a time and changing his address so often that I couldn't keep track of where he was except through his office. Once his lawyer called my lawyer looking for him, saying he'd lost track of his whereabouts and the secretary wasn't being cooperative. I told my lawyer that I was certain she'd give Jim the message to get in touch with his lawyer because rule number one at TWA was that Jim be available at all times in case of airline emergencies.

Another time, before Jim's customary end-of-the-year skiing vacation, he dropped over to the house to pick up winter clothes that were still left in his

Champagne...

cupboards and closets. Before he left, he took some photos of me with the children in the garden as we were on our way out to the park. When we came back I discovered that Jim had forgotten to leave the monthly household money in its usual place on my dressing room table. The memo I'd made for him about upcoming repairs and gardening bills for the house was still there. I called his office and was told that he had already left and the secretary didn't know where he could be reached. I let that pass, thinking she'd tell him I'd called and he'd remember what he'd forgotten.

After days went by without a word, I called his office again and, this time, told his secretary of the urgency because I had absolutely no money. She let me finish and then in a sarcastic tone of voice said, "Don't worry, Maggi, we won't let you starve." This verbal slap in the face from Jim's secretary made me wonder what kind of tales he was telling her about me.

Jim returned with a sun-and-snow tan and a big smile, bringing the household money to me as though it was natural to have disappeared and be late in giving me cash for the house and children. He didn't bother asking me how I'd gotten along without funds or mentioning my telephone calls to his secretary. I said nothing, happy to be able to pay Catina her salary plus the amount she had lent me.

Chapter Thirteen

The next time Jim was off on a business trip he said that he had given the roll of film with the children's photos on it to his secretary to be developed and I could pick up the prints at his office at the end of the week. When I went there to get our pictures, the secretary handed me the undeveloped film, saying that she hadn't had time to get the photos made, but she said "YOUR photos," handing me the roll as if to say, "Do it yourself."

When I had the film developed there were more photos of Jim's sexy lady in skiing clothes than there were of me and the children in the garden. This was the first time I had a close-up of "Miss Out-Of-Focus" and I could see a slight resemblance to me, but she was smoking a cigarette in every photo. I'd never smoked in my life and I always thought that Jim didn't care for ladies who did. She must have been exciting enough for him to overlook the matter.

Finally the divorce papers came through. It was official: Jim and Maggi were no longer man and wife. Jim seemed elated. He didn't mind that I had gotten full custody of the children and the maximum amount of maintenance allowed by French law at the time. He wanted his freedom more than anything else. I doubt if he even read the final judgment. The amount of money granted to me legally was just about the same as that which Jim was accustomed to giving me for the household but couldn't cover extras like repairs, gardener, vacations or anything for me. I was ready to find a job but knew I couldn't keep the daytime schedule I had and be a working girl at the same time.

Even though the right to stay in the house was granted, every day it became clearer to me that I'd have to leave this dream home which was becoming a nightmare to manage. The French Court couldn't help me when Jim was late in his payments or didn't agree to pay for "extras" or ignored little things like roof repairs and a crumbling chimney. I was haunted by his father's words–"sitting on a fortune"–and losing a lot of sleep trying to figure out what to do.

One morning, I was at the garden door, loaded down with groceries, when I saw Eric Hawkins coming toward me. Eric was the editor of the Paris *Herald*

Champagne...

Tribune who'd been to our *petit pavillon* for celebrity parties. He looked a bit surprised to see me in a raincoat carrying a cook's shopping bag. I saw his expression and laughed, "The glamorous Maggi Nolan before your very eyes." It was plain to see that he'd expected me to be sitting in a salon, dressed in *haute couture*. He explained that he was in the neighborhood a few blocks away and just took a chance that I might be there because he wanted to talk to me. I invited him into the salon while I dropped my shopping bag in the kitchen and shed my raincoat.

While sipping his aperitif, he told me what was on his mind: he wanted me to work for the paper, writing a "society" column. I'm certain my mouth dropped open in surprise but then I said I didn't think I could do that sort of thing as frankly, I couldn't stand columns with a bunch of phoney titles and names that nobody knew. He agreed, admitting that the lady doing it at the moment was attracting that sort of criticism and that's why he wanted to change.

"But what could I write about?" I asked, and he had his answer for that as well.

"Write about the people you know, the people you see, what they're doing. You know so many interesting people."

I told him I'd think about it but I wasn't certain I could handle a job and the house at the same time. But suddenly everything seemed to be happening at once. Jim had a serious buyer who wanted to pay him cash for the house and expected to finalize the sale without delay. He solved the problem of where I was to move by finding an apartment to rent for me not far from where we were living.

The furthest thing from my mind at this time was to insist on staying in the house, no matter what I was told were my "rights." It was too big to handle and I had no money to keep it up. An apartment where there'd be no upkeep and where I'd be able to take a job would be the answer, and Jim's two-year advance payment on the rent freed me from the heaviest burden. Despite the deep pain of breaking up our home, I had high hopes of a new life of peace, and work that I'd get paid for in journalism, which I liked. The brand new apartment on the Rue de la Tour would be easy to care for and was near the school the children would be ready to start soon.

Jim was going through changes himself. He'd separated from the girl who looked like me, he'd moved from a furnished flat to the Hôtel Baltimore and then to a luxurious Left Bank apartment he shared with a man named Peter. Then he bought an apartment for himself which he started to furnish from what we'd collected on the Rue du Docteur Blanche. I assured him that I didn't mind what he took as there was more than enough for both of us but his selection became intriguing to note. Everything he wanted seemed to be Italian in origin, from the multi-colored marble-topped cocktail table to a trio of porcelain lamps he'd brought back from Italy, plus paintings of Venice an Italian artist had painted. It seemed that everything Italian in the house was being loaded into a van to be taken to his new abode.

It wasn't long before the inspiration for his Italian period was known. Jim had a new lady in his life who was moving from Rome to Paris to live with him in his Italian decor. She was a beautiful Italian model named Isabella who charmed everyone she met, I was told by several friends. I wasn't at all jealous as I'd decided that the happier Jim was the easier life would be for us all.

Talking myself into the advantages of moving into a new, modern apartment on the Rue de la Tour in place of the *petit pavillon* on the Rue du Docteur Blanche was one thing; actually leaving our home was something else. No need to go into the boring details of packing up and moving out of the only home I'd ever loved and the only one Cathy and Janne had ever known. I kept putting it in the back of my brain. Fortunately the children were installed in Trouville with Catina for the summer and their new home would be ready for their return. Then they'd begin their first school days at the nearby Cours Victor Hugo, discovered for me by Joyce and Jules Buck, who were interested in schools for their daughter, Joan Juliet Buck to attend. (The little girl who grew up to be the editor of the French *Vogue*.)

Surrounded by boxes, barrels, trunks and luggage piled higher than I was tall, never had I felt so alone. It was here that I started to write long letters to my sister in her cloistered convent. My sister could write to me only rarely and her letters could contain not much more than that she was praying for me and my children. I'd never given much thought about the power of prayers and didn't until later when prayers were all I had going for me.

Before moving into the apartment, I had another talk with Eric Hawkins at the Paris *Herald Tribune* and told him that I'd be willing to start my column before the summer was over if he was still interested. He beamed and assured me that it would be a fine thing for all of us. I mentioned again that I wasn't so sure I'd be the ideal one for "society" but he just laughed and said if I could only think of the word "society" as meaning "people" and not a list of names in a social register, I'd be okay. He repeated what he'd said at our first meeting. "Write about people you know." I asked if he'd like little snippets like Drue Mallory Heinz in Paris en route to the South of France to buy a villa; American-Parisian, Marquise de Piolenc, sponsoring an unknown Bulgarian-born pianist named Siegi Wiessenberg; and Cary Grant passing through Paris from Madrid after filming in Spain. "That's it, Maggi. That's what I want!"

My first column was delivered to Eric in the middle of July. It was written on my trusty portable typewriter plunked down on a full carton of household utensils in the empty living room of the new apartment. I perched on a kitchen chair hunched over my machine, pecking away with all my might as the moving men piled furniture all around me.

The days, weeks and months that added up to years at the Paris *Herald Tribune* started off like stepping on a giant merry-go-round, climbing on a wooden horse and starting to move slowly, "round and round" to music. Then going faster and faster until there was no getting off, no matter how dizzy you felt.

The first surprise facing me when I started to write twice-weekly reports of who

Champagne...

was doing what, was how many people read my columns. No matter where I went, someone had something to say. They were diplomats, business people, military folk assigned to Versailles and Fountainebleau, hoteliers, barmen and movie stars.

David Stein took me over to the Hôtel Raphael one day to meet William Holden. He jumped up to greet me like I was a long lost friend, saying when he was shooting *The Bridge on the River Kwai*, everybody ran to the airplane bringing supplies and newspapers and fought over the *Herald Tribune* to see what "Maggi Nolan says," and that all the actors got a big thrill out of being called "Mister" in my column. That was the first time my attention was called to the fact that other columnists didn't put "Mr." before people's names. I don't know why I did it but perhaps it was because I had so many dukes and princes and counts in my column, that the least I could do was call the other gentlemen "Mister."

Another time I mentioned in a column that it was so hot in the Ritz Bar that people could still have their tongues hanging out despite all they drank. (This was in pre-air-conditioning days.) No more than a day later, giant fans were installed in the ceilings but they were so strong that they blew the potato chips right out of their bowls. Charles Ritz was an avid reader of the "Trib," and once asked me if I could use my influence with the publishers to put back a certain cartoon ("Dr. Rex Morgan"), as he didn't feel like starting his day without it.

Some remarks from readers weren't very pleasant. One super snobbish American-Parisian lady I knew from the pre-*Herald Tribune* days cornered me at an American Embassy residence party and said, "Maggi, where DO you find those people you write about? I don't know ANY of them." At first I was going to say I didn't know them either but I just let it go. You couldn't win with Mary Hoyt Wiborg, known as "Hoytie" to her friends. I called her "Hoytie-Toytie" but never out loud and never in print.

The new job as a Paris columnist and my so-called expertise on celebrities offered me several other projects to do. First, I was asked to do an interview with Olivia de Havilland for a new English edition of the slick French magazine *Realities*; then International News Service (INS) wanted a weekly article to cable to the USA; then Jack Vietor, publisher of a magazine called *San Diego*, came through Paris and ordered a monthly round-up of celebrity events for his publication.

One of the smoothest-going projects was the *Realities* Fashion Award. Eve's husband, Alfred Max, turned over the plan to his new British executive editor, Garith Windsor, and he gave the job to me to find five or six outstanding American ladies in Paris to serve on a jury with outstanding French ladies. The group would be shown a parade of *haute couture* fashions which they would judge with points from one to ten, and the winning creations would be the ones gaining the most points.

Our first American jury consisted of the Duchess of Windsor, Mrs. Lauris Norstad, Gloria Swanson, Mrs. Charles Miller and Mrs. Charles Saint, with the French members, Mme. Jean Masurel, Mme. Claude Serreulles, the Countess of

Maudhoy, the Duchess of Mouchy and the Viscountess d'Harcourt. *Realities* took over the sumptuous salons above the restaurant/nightclub l'Orangerie, owned by Claude Terrail who also owned the Tour d'Argent (and still does, of course). Seven top dressmakers presented six models each and after the parade was over, the ladies lunched in splendour in another salon at a long gleaming table set with porcelain, crystal and silver from the Terrail collection. The menu was straight from the kitchens of the Tour d'Argent. This was the first Fashion Award, so successful that I was asked to do it again and again. Other juries included chic ladies like Olivia de Havilland; Ethel Woodward de Croisset; Mrs. William Patten; Marquise de Surian, who was Millie Cowgill of San Francisco; Mrs. George de Braux from Philadelphia; Alice O'Gormam, President of the American Women's Club of Paris; and Mrs. Sturgis Lee Riddle, the wife of the Dean of the American Cathedral on the Avenue George V.

Having signed columns in the *Herald Tribune* brought old friends to my door, like John Ringling North, the owner of Ringling Brothers and Barnum & Bailey Circus, who called me up at the office one day and invited me to dinner. We had met several times when I was married to Jim and had dined with John and his American actress friend, Dodie Heath. John came to Europe every year by luxurious ocean liner, always bringing his long, drawn-out Cadillac with him and his chauffeur, Jerry. I liked John. He was relaxed, funny and enjoyed the good life. He was very sweet on the telephone, saying he wondered what had become of me when Jim and I got divorced and then picked up the *Herald Tribune* and there I was. I accepted his dinner date and he told me that Jerry would pick me up at my home to bring me to the Ritz, where we'd have a drink before going to Maxim's for dinner.

When I stepped into John's Cadillac that night, I felt like I was entering a palace on wheels featuring a full stocked bar with crystal glasses plus a writing desk with all accessories. The car seemed to float along and I felt like a princess on the way to meet this king of the circus. John had a rather ostentatious suite in red brocade overlooking the Place Vendôme, but it seemed to suit the gentleman who had created the *Greatest Show On Earth*, including such marvels as Gargantua, the Gorilla, and ballet with original music by Igor Stravinsky.

We were served champagne and canapés by John's favorite floor waiter named Georges, and then off we went to Maxim's to be greeted by Monsieur Albert like we were stars. John was adored as a good-looking, well-dressed, amusing "big spender," who liked the best of everything.

After dinner John wanted to go to one of his favorite "boîtes" for the rest of the night; spots like Casanova or Sheherazade, where violins played until the wee hours. The first dinner date we had, I agreed to go nightclubbing with him, which he then wanted to follow with onion soup in his favorite spot in the Les Halles meat market, where you'd eat and drink next to the local butchers in their blood-stained aprons. I didn't like this at all; as much as I enjoyed John's company, it was too much. I told him a bit about my routine: up early with the children every a.m. no matter what time I'd gotten to bed; off to the office to get mail; accept invitations; write up whatever I'd gathered the night before; lunch where I could collect news; more hours in the office until my afternoon time with the children; then get all decked out for whatever invitations I'd accepted for the evening. It was only on weekends and Thursdays that I didn't go to the office, but I still got up at the same time every morning. If I wasn't at the breakfast table when Cathy and Janne arrived, they'd come bouncing into my room to see what was keeping me.

John looked bored by my monologue because he was a night person and wanted everyone else to have his happy habits. He stayed up all night and never got out of bed until noon or later. He was also a "people person" and that's where I came in. He loved to look at all the invitations I got in the mail and hear what was going on. You couldn't get him to go to a concert or the theater or any such "sit still" occasions unless it was the opening of a nightclub or the gala new show at the Lido on the Champs-Élysées, where there was as big a show in the audience as there was on stage. He especially loved parties where he could be my escort and meet a lot of amusing people. Of course, that was nice for me too, because everybody liked him; so he was *sortable*, which means suitable for going out. Besides, his chauffered car and good-humored driver, Jerry, was fine for flitting about from party to party.

One time when John arrived in town and went over my invitation cards, he saw that there was a gala evening at the Lido coming up and he definitely wanted to take me to that. I told him I'd already asked Prince Louis de Polignac to be my escort but John looked so disappointed, I promised I'd ask the organizer, Georges Cravenne, if I could come with two gentlemen instead of one. Georges was a darling and when he heard that I was planning to bring QUALITY as well as QUANTITY, he said it could be arranged.

The Lido night was unforgettable; there was a celebrity in every chair. The Lido in the fifties was tiny in comparison to its ballpark size today. Georges gave Louis, John and myself a table for three which was angled so we could see everyone there—Maurice Chevalier, the Duke and Duchess of Windsor, Michèle Morgan, Aly Khan, Jacqueline de Ribes, George de Cuevas, Jean Cocteau, Françoise Sagan, Elsa Schiaparelli, Yves Saint Laurent, Jean Gabin, Annabella, Roger Vadim, Maharanee of Baroda, Prince Alexander of Yugoslavia and Princess Maria Pia of Savoy.

When the show was over and everyone got up to leave, we were just about at the bottom of the staircase when we heard a loud, high-pitched voice calling "Maggi...Magggggeeee" and John and I turned around to see the Duchess of Windsor heading our way through the crowd with the former King of England following close behind. She reached us and said she wanted me to meet her husband and then turned to him and said, "David, this is the lady who writes those columns in the paper," and he said that he was glad to meet me and that my articles amused him a lot. He added that his wife read my columns to him in the morning while he was shaving and sometimes he laughed so much he almost cut himself.

John couldn't get over this meeting and told everyone we met what the Duchess had said to Maggi. I was pleased that they liked what I wrote, of course, but I didn't kid myself for one second that it was important. I tried to tell John that having the Duchess as an amused reader of my work came in handy when I asked her to do something like being a member of the Fashion Awards for *Realities*, but flattery for my silly chatter was something I didn't want to hear.

John and I were seen around Paris so much while he and his palace-on-wheels were in town that we were invited to some events like a couple. Ann and Art Buchwald invited us to a Thanksgiving feast where fellow American-Parisians showed up in droves. We had a fabulous evening with people like cover girl Dorian Leigh, Dorothy and David Schoenbrun and Marion and Irwin Shaw. Many there thought we were an "item" as the saying goes; the little darlings couldn't have guessed that although we liked each other, there was no way that either of us could fit into the other's routine. Who would have guessed that when we left the party, the chauffeur would drop me off at my apartment and John would have the rest of the night and early morning to find further entertainment on his own.

All the time he was in Paris, however, he never failed to check in with me in the afternoon (morning to him) and make plans for where we'd go and the time for his chauffeur to pick me up. One afternoon when I was taking care of the children at home, John called and asked me to come to the Place Vendôme because he wanted me to go across the square with him to Patek Philippe to pick out a watch as a gift from him. I told him I was touched but that I could not go there because I was with my children. "Well, then," he said, "I'll come over there." In about an hour, he was at my door with a bag of watches in cases. He set them up in a row on the dining room table and said, "Okay, Mag-pie, take your choice." When I hesitated he reminded me that I needed a good watch and, in addition, if I didn't take it I would hurt his feelings. I said I'd never accepted jewelry from a man and he got impatient, saying, "This isn't jewelry, dumb cluck, it's a goddam watch for your work."

The perfect "working watch" we picked out looked like a fat, gold bracelet, but it had a little secret panel you could flip up with your thumb to see the time. "John, it's not only gorgeous but no one will ever know when I'm clock-watching at parties." He gave me a big grin and looked like a kid having a good time when he scooped up all the watches to take back to the Place Vendôme. I asked him to stay for a drink but he said he wanted to return the "loot" as soon as possible and complete the purchase of our choice. That evening he fastened the watch on my wrist, saying he was happier now that I had the ideal watch for the kind of job I had to do.

A lot of people I wrote about pretended they didn't care whether or not they saw their names in the paper, but John came right out and said he thought it was great. He was easy to mention because he was always saying something interesting or funny. He told me about the huge fortunes he and his associates had lost in the circus business, how he had to streamline his gigantic, stupendous productions to make a success and how, finally, he was forced to abandon exciting circus tents for roofed, air-conditioned premises. The story l liked best was when he was facing the end of the circus altogether just when oil was found on some land he owned in Oklahoma. "Did you ever hear of feeding elephants from an oil well?" he laughed.

During one of John's visits to Paris, I threw a dinner party in his honor in a picturesque restaurant on the edge of Paris in the Bois de Boulogne. (The owners of this spot were pleased to offer an evening for me and guests after I'd written a few paragraphs about their lovely place.) John's night at the Pavillon d'Armenonville, former hunting lodge of the Kings of France, was unique. It happened on a starry night twinkling over the little lake outside the windows, a perfect dinner with John's choice of wines, the right kind of music by Aimé Barelli, and a guest list of some of John's favorite friends like Dorothy and David Schoenbrun, Charles Collingwood and his wife Louise Albritton, Jack Forrester, Verna Ostertag and Prince Louis de Polignac. When dessert time arrived everyone at the table seemed to gasp in surprise and pleasure. The pastry chef had created a cake replica of a three-ring circus, complete with sugar flags flying, a silver sugar bulb-studded ticket booth and a sawdust floor made with crushed almonds. "The greatest sugar show on earth," John said happily.

Jim wasn't a visitor to the Rue de la Tour very often those days but every time he came he seemed to be in a good mood, so I assumed that everything was going well with him. He'd bounce in, visit with the children in their room and then, if he found me in the salon, would have a chat on his way out. I was thankful for his easy-going mood and that I no longer had to remind him of what he owed for the children as it was now paid automatically into the bank. More than that, he asked me to meet him at the American Embassy one day four months after I'd started my new life in a new home, so we could sign a legal paper between us to guarantee a sum for myself and future rent payments for me and the children.

"This is great, Jim," I told him when I saw what he was volunteering toward my welfare and future. I was really touched and explained to myself that his new generosity must be because he was happy in his new life. (Little did I know then what I found out later: such a paper was necessary so that he could complete the sale of the house.)

Following what I considered Jim's remarkable thoughtfulness and generosity in November, came a shock from his selfishness in December when he refused to give up his skiing vacation schedule to help me bring Janne home from the hospital after an operation. She'd gotten sick all of a sudden, I'd called the baby doctor out of bed in the early morning hours and he'd arrived right away to announce she'd have to have her appendix removed without delay. I had no problem getting her to the Left Bank clinic he arranged, and Jim came to visit in the afternoons after her operation.

After Christmas, the day before Janne's birthday, the doctor said she could be discharged, but when I called Jim to help me bring her home he said, "I can't, I'm going skiing." No amount of pleading could get him to change his mind. I was hurt and furious at the same time as I ordered a taxi to take me to the clinic, wait for me and Janne and drive us home. It was quite a struggle, carrying a blanketed, almost five-year-old and trying to load the taxi with plants, toys and books that had collected during her stay. A nurse put everything on the sidewalk and went back into the clinic. The taxi driver stayed behind his wheel, saying he had a cold...("and the father went skiing," I wailed to myself). Anyway, we got home by ourselves and everything was all right again except little Janne never forgot her horrifying experience of being "maimed for life" and being fed horsemeat, which they said would build up her strength, which it might have done but she also broke out in big red blotches all over her body.

Jim bounced back into our lives in January as though nothing had happened; nothing had for him as he had merely followed his skiing routine of years, but I was looking at life in a different light since Janne's ordeal.

Christmas/New Year festivities would have been put aside if I hadn't had obligations to fill two columns per week. I found myself agonizing over Janne at the same time as I had to go through the motions of people-watching, reporting and making sure I spelt the names right. The stupidity of my journalistic endeavors came into my head over and over as I'd traipse from home to hospital to office and back to hospital before returning home to dress for a celebrity-stacked cocktail party, a VIP dinner, or a grand gala not to be missed. Sometimes I'd look at the fancy-dressed, bejeweled ladies all around me and wonder if they, too, were hiding their agonies behind their make-up. It was then I decided never to make up my mind on outward appearances. Taking the old Indian adage, "Never judge a man until you've walked a mile in his moccasins," I reworded it to suit myself: "Never judge a lady until you've danced all night in her sequined sandals."

Although our lives were comfortable and organized in those days, every once in a while when I'd least expect it, the pain of losing our little home jumped back in my mind to hurt again. During one of Jim's visits to our apartment, he stopped on the way out for a chat with me in the living room and didn't seem a bit upset when he announced he'd lost "a pile of money" investing in a German airline that folded before it even began. When he told me how much he'd lost, I got such a huge lump in my throat I couldn't talk. The amount of money he mentioned was the same sum he'd originally paid for our *petit pavillon*, the home I'd been pressured to leave because I was "sitting on a fortune." I stared at Jim but couldn't say a word. He rattled on, assuring me that there was nothing to worry about as it wouldn't affect his finances.

I think I was overly tired at the time because all I wanted to do was go to bed and cry myself to sleep. During the night I found myself dreaming about the little house, the garden, "my" tree, the children's swing and Jim's antique wooden

Champagne...

horses. When I woke up, for a few seconds, I actually thought I was still in the master bedroom on the Rue du Docteur Blanche. There was too much to do from morning to night for me to dwell on the subject, but it was clear that the loss of our home left a deep, still painful scar.

Chapter Fourteen

One fine day, Jim said he'd like to invite Cathy, Janne and Catina to his new apartment now that it was complete. When they came back from their visit, they were full of talk about "la belle Isabella," the lady they'd met at Jim's for tea. This was the first time they'd been presented to one of Jim's girlfriends. As soon as Catina put the children to bed, she filled me in on the details of "la belle Isabella." This lovely Italian lady was beautiful, liked children and seemed to be sensitive. Catina said she'd heard one snip of a conversation between them when Jim had said they should get married and take the children to Italy with them and Isabella had replied she'd love the idea if the children's mother agreed.

I was fascinated because she seemed ideal for him. Maybe her influence would induce him to spend more time being a father and less time trying to be the sexiest man in town.

After a few more visits to Jim's apartment and glowing reports about "la belle Isabella" and Catina going so far as to state that this beautiful Italian lady would make a fine stepmother, Isabella disappeared from Jim's life. That was not the only disappearance. Jim lost his job at TWA and top management announced on the business pages of newspapers that they were reorganizing and getting rid of "dead wood." I cried over that. No matter what had happened between us, I still had fond memories of when we were working as a team and having a happy time with TWA work and play. And I couldn't enjoy the bad luck of my children's father.

The next time Jim invited the children to his home, it was to meet a German artist and pose for their portrait sitting side by side on a couch. This young fellow from Germany seemed to be Jim's flatmate, though it wasn't clear whether he was paying his share or had been befriended by Jim, who was sponsoring his career in Paris. The subject was not one I cared, or dared, to bring up. When the portrait was finished it was around Christmas time, and Jim drew up a document he gave me as a Christmas present stating I had half-ownership of the children's portrait; the painting I never saw, nor do I know if it still exists somewhere in the world today.

Champagne...

As he did every year, Jim's father arrived in Paris for his usual round of receptions and ceremonies, never missing the pilgrimage to Picpus Cemetery in honor of General Lafayette. He didn't come to see his grandchildren, while I'd run into him at various receptions. Many times at a celebration at the American Embassy residence people would come up to me and announce that they had just spoken to my father in the garden or in one of the salons. After hearing "your father is here" a few times, I'd go and find him. He always looked elegant on these occasions in a conservative navy blue three-piece suit with the French decoration–a little rosette on his lapel. When I asked him if he was going to visit his grandchildren he always answered that he would when he had the time. I tried to get news of Grandma Nolan from him but he was vague, announcing that I should realize she was too old to travel anymore; however it was obvious that he didn't like my queries.

Even though I hadn't really known Grandma Nolan well or for any length of time, I missed not having her in my life. When I wrote thank-you notes to her for gifts she'd sent to the children through Jim, I didn't know how much she knew about our problems and hesitated to even put our return address on the envelope, because I didn't know whether Jim had told her he'd sold the house she'd paid for and said she liked so much. Often I wanted to call her but I knew she didn't answer the phone because of her deafness, and even if I did manage to get a call through to her it would be hard to have a conversation. Overseas calls were not like today. You had to wait for hours to get through; sometimes it was impossible to hear over noises that sounded like crashing waves and sometimes you'd hear the first and last words of a sentence and nothing in between. I thought about Grandma Nolan often as our new life carried on.

Home life in those days was easy and fun. We had a breezy, bright maid-of-all-work, Marienette, who was short, round and curly-haired and sang all day when the sun was shining, but was very moody in the rain. "She's from the South," Catina explained. Marienette was efficient, Catina content, the children making progress in school, and we now had a concierge downstairs to take care of anything that might go wrong so I could concentrate on my work during the week and spend weekends at home.

It was around this time that I started to try to teach English to Cathy and Janne with informal lessons right after Sunday breakfast, when we'd go back into my bedroom and they'd jump on my big double bed. Up to then we had always spoken French in the household and even when their father came to call, he spoke only French. Our unofficial classroom on the bed started by pretending we were on an airplane going to America. Of course it was an American airplane where American English was the only language allowed.

I'd start, "All right, you're hungry, so you have to tell the stewardess in English what you want to eat." Then, "Okay, what do you say if you have to go to the loo?" "Now, you want a blanket...a pillow...you want to take a nap..." and so on. When they'd tire of that, we'd try some nursery rhymes like "Mary had a little lamb" or sing some silly songs like "I'm a little teapot." When we wore out the airplane ride, we pretended we were in an American restaurant and then we were going shopping for shoes, coats, dresses and hats. Their little minds always amazed me, absorbing words and phrases that stayed with them until the next session.

Cathy and Janne were doing very well in school, marching off with Catina every morning with a bounce in their step and full of happy chatter. Once a week it was my turn to pick them up after class and we'd walk back together planning our excursions for the rest of the day. After the first few times I met them at the door, Cathy asked me, very politely, if I would mind not speaking to them before we crossed the Avenue Victor Hugo. "Ah-ha," I thought, they have now noticed that I speak French with a strong American accent. We'd spoken only French at home since they were born, but it seems that now they encountered other mothers who spoke properly and their mother was "different." I understood that, said "Okay," and kept my end of the bargain.

Often I'd see Tina Onassis at the door waiting for Christina. We had short, pleasant chats in English while we waited. I liked her and when her daughter came through the door they always had a happy, loving greeting for each other. Christina looked like such a contented little girl that I can never stop thinking of the contrast in her later life. (I knew Tina suffered in silence in those days because I could never forget the night at L'Éléphant Blanc when I saw her husband deliberately put the lighted end of his cigar to her bare shoulder as she got up to dance with André Dubonnet. I was right behind them and saw Tina flinch but go on as if nothing had happened.)

The first December Cathy was in the Cours Victor Hugo, she was invited to Christina's apartment on the Avenue Foch for her 6th birthday party and came back beaming over the good time she'd had with lots of children, games and fancy food. She gave me such a complete and animated report of the party that I printed a short paragraph about it in my next column, never dreaming at the time that little Cathy Nolan would become the Paris-based journalist for the magazine *People* when she grew up.

The first time Cathy came home with her medal gained for being the best student in her class, Catina beamed and I almost wept with pleasure. Of course, she was the star of the family for the next few days. When Jim came around to call, Cathy took his hand to go down the hall and show him what she had on the dresser. When Jim saw the medal, he said when he was her age he had a whole drawer full of medals like that. Cathy was crushed and afterwards it didn't seem like anything we said could cheer her up. A few weeks later, Cathy brought home her second medal. This time when Jim heard the news, he turned to Janne and asked her if she thought she'd ever get one of those or if she was going to be the "dumb blonde" of the family. I tried to talk to him in the hallway about his hurting remarks, but he wasn't in any mood to listen. Instead, he asked simply why I didn't want the children to know he'd gotten medals in school and what was wrong

Champagne...

with being a "dumb blonde," as there was one in every family.

I wonder if he ever thought of his remarks when Dr. Janne Nolan became a permanent fellow at Brookings Institution in Washington, D.C., and authored a book with the title *Guardians of the Arsenal–The Politics of Nuclear Strategy*.

People might giggle, scoff or even laugh out loud at this statement but it was tough going as a journalist in my kind of job. The lighter I wrote my copy, the harder it seemed to be. Eric Hawkins was always complimentary, saying things like, "This is the first time we've had the kind of column I've always wanted," but I needed more than pats on the back. The income was low and I had to battle for every extra *sou* to pay for expenses incurred going to cocktails, dinners and balls to find the stories to fill my twice-weekly space. Sometimes, when I stopped to figure out what it had cost to go to a grand "soirée" after paying for clothes cleaning, white gloves, hairdresser, transportation, etc., it seemed impossible to go on. I did a lot of writing at home in the mornings, at the desk I loved so much that had been such a beautiful part of the salon in the little house. But now it was installed in a corner of my bedroom and stayed open all the time, piled high with papers, cards, invitations, mail and a datebook reminding me of where I had to go, whom I had to call, which people I had to see. One of those "agendas" was over twelve inches high and handy for me to add the guest list of where I'd been, so I wouldn't forget to mention the most important names when the time came for me to write my articles.

Writing about people twice a week, one had to develop certain working habits to get it all together. One thing I did, since I never, ever, took a notebook with me, was to write out as many names as I could remember before I went to bed, while the scene was still fresh in my head. It's amazing what the brain can do. I would come home late after a dinner party or multiple receptions and put the scenes together again from the time I walked into a room; whom I saw, what they said, who was sitting where around a dinner table, and even recall names from table to table when I was at the Tour d'Argent or Maxim's for a special gala night. Conversations I could put right back together without worrying about misquoting someone.

Many hosts and hostesses, especially at diplomatic or business events, would present a guest list to me for my social reports. Some would even put a dot or check beside the names they hoped I'd mention. There were some very thoughtful hostesses who knew I'd be carrying a tiny evening bag, so they'd prepare a single-spaced list on the thinnest paper so it could be folded neatly away. Others might hand me something that looked like a manuscript and it would have to be checked like a coat. When a host shoved a sheaf of papers in my hand and realized it wouldn't do for me to carry it around all night, he'd offer to have it delivered the next day; but I'd never take that chance when deadlines for my articles seemed constantly at hand. Once I took a guest list that was several sheets long and went into the ladies' room, where I folded it flat and placed it neatly in my girdle for the rest of the night.

In these hectic days, I always appreciated friends I could count on to give me social/celebrity news fit to print.

One American-Parisian of the fifties , a good friend and valuable source, was J. Melville Forrester, known as Jack by all. He started life as a poor boy who danced in the streets to earn his meagre way, then became a song-and-dance man in vaudeville and played bit parts in films. Maurice Chevalier discovered him in New York and brought him to Paris for appearances at the Casino de Paris. In France and Spain after the war Jack discovered that he had financial talents far more important than singing and dancing. When he advised top film executives who had frozen assets in Europe on how to handle their problems, it paid off and he was on his way up in a new career.

Word got around to enough tycoons that Jack's business clout was worth paying for so they sought him out and Jack started his own company, World Commerce, on the Rue Royale, and made a fortune. His top client, of course, was his friend, J. Paul Getty, who did a lot toward making Jack a multi-millionaire. Jack Forrester liked to give lavish dinner parties, for business friends and associates, which I attended several times and sat near Paul, getting very bored by their heavy business talk all through the evening. At first I thought Paul was dull when he'd look at his plate a lot and not say much, but little by little, I'd catch a glimpse of him after someone made a funny remark, and see his eye twinkling and a glimmer of a smile. After a few dinners with Jack and his business cronies, which always included Paul, I began to get acquainted with this tall, quiet, unassuming man and he became more and more interesting.

One day I received a fascinating piece of news about Paul, but it didn't come from him or Jack. Ethel LeVane, the nervous little lady who'd come with Nate Cummings, Jack and Paul to the Rue du Docteur Blanche after the races so many Sundays ago, called me from the Ritz, telling me she knew of my whereabouts when she picked up the Paris *Herald Tribune* in the Palace Hotel in St. Moritz, Switzerland. I asked how the art book she was writing with Paul was coming along.

She answered, "Oh, that's over and done," and promised to send me a copy. Then she added, "But I'm not calling you about that. I'm calling you to tell you about Paul's ships." I hated to admit that I didn't know anything about any ships, even though I had dined with Jack Forrester and Paul Getty several times within the past weeks.

She explained to me that Paul had invited her to christen his very first super-tanker constructed in a French shipyard, and she was in Paris to pick out a hat to wear. She told me she'd already bought six hats from Madame Paulette but she couldn't decide which one to wear. I told her to "hang on to her hats" and I'd be right over to see if I could help her with this world-shaking decision. In

Champagne...

Ethel LeVane and J. Paul Getty at a Nate Cummings party on a Bateau Mouche. They were co-writing a book about art at the time. →

← Texas and California Americans in Paris. Top model Dorian Leigh with big businessman, Jack Forrester. They usually argued over politics.

the meantime, I couldn't believe that Jack hadn't told me about this project.

Until Ethel LeVane came back to town, I didn't realize that Paul was building supertankers in France and the first one out of the shipyards would be launched in a very short time. Jack insisted that I certainly DID know about the project as that's all they ever talked about. I must not have been listening. Business talk to me was worse than politics–and besides, I was out for social news and nothing else.

Over at the Ritz in Ethel's sun-drenched suite overlooking the Place Vendôme, she showed me the pile of headgear from which to choose. There were seven hats, not six. I couldn't help being concerned about a lady with an obvious "head problem" as well as hat. While I was ooohing and aaahing over the lot, she filled me in on the big event, which was costing her seven hats from Paulette to smash a bottle of champagne against a hunk of a hulk.

She said that the shipyard was in St. Nazaire and everyone would have to go down there in the morning, have the christening in the afternoon and then stay the night, coming back the following morning. That inspired me to point out to her that she needed to take three hats, not one, so her job was to pick a simple one for the train and a simple one to wear on the way back with most fabulous one saved for the big event. We eliminated a cartwheel as too big; in a harsh wind it would blow away with her in it. We pushed aside one that had sparklers on it as too "after dark" for the event, and so on until we got the right choice for every hour. She told me that I should come along as Paul would love to invite me, but I explained I had

a family to think of and too much work to do in Paris.

Ethel still insisted that Paul would like me to come as he'd told her already that he always read my columns. I laughed and reminded her that I wasn't on the financial pages.

"But you write about people doing things. Paul likes that," she said.

She seemed so much more relaxed that we were able to actually have a nice talk, during which she mentioned that Paul's decision to own his own supertanker fleet came after Aristotle Onassis and his brother-in-law, Stavros Niarchos, raised the prices of ship leasing so high that they made him furious. I thought of making a joke that they were trying to "hold him over a barrel–oil barrel, that is," but Ethel didn't seem to have much of a sense of humor, so I let it go.

Ethel came back from St. Nazaire jubilant and full of information about her big day. She handed me printed programs, gala menus and lists of the guests who attended. Proudly, she showed off the diamond bracelet presented to her after she christened the ship "George Franklin Getty" after Paul's father.

"Of course a gift wasn't necessary," she said, waving her arm in the air so sparkles shot out in all directions.

The item in my column about the ship launching with a picture of Ethel LeVane brought a few telephone calls to me at my office, namely Sam White of the *London Evening Standard*, whom I knew in passing as I often saw him at the Hôtel de Crillon, where he seemed to have a second office in a corner of the long bar by

Champagne...

a telephone. The gist of Sam's conversation was that I was completely out of my depth writing about ships when everyone in the world who knew anything at all was aware that no ship weighed 53,000 tons. Not sure of myself, as usual, I thanked him for his call and immediately called Jack Forrester to check on my facts. He was adorable, saying the story was great, everyone was very pleased and there was not one mistake from start to finish, though he guffawed over the part where Ethel said she didn't care whether or not she got a gift. "You should have seen her grab that bracelet and count the diamonds," he laughed. He added that as far as Sam White was concerned, I could tell him that there might not have been a supertanker that big LAST week, but there certainly was now.

The next important call I received in regard to my Getty report was from George Abell in the Paris bureau of *Time*. He said my story was very intriguing and he'd certainly like to meet Paul Getty. I told him to call the George V, where he had a permanent suite, but George called me right back and announced that the hotel said Mr. Getty didn't exist. Okay, back on the phone to Jack, I told him that *Time* couldn't get Paul at the hotel. "Tell him to ask for Monsieur Paul, and he'll be put through," Jack told me.

George Abell got through to Jean Paul Getty, alias Monsieur Paul, at the Hôtel George V and made an appointment to see him in his suite at the hotel a few days later. George called to thank me for the chance to meet this intriguing fellow and asked if I'd please come along with him to "break the ice." At first I told him I just

J. Paul Getty was just another American businessman in Paris when he stood on the balcony of his Hotel George V suite.

didn't have the time, but when Jack Forrester called me, he insisted. "You'd better be there, Maggi," he said. "You might even learn something." I agreed to go but I didn't think I'd listen enough to learn anything because I had a very short attention span when it came to business talk.

George and I arrived to be greeted by Jack Forrester at the door of the "Getty headquarters," which was a top-floor two-room suite of the Hôtel George V, with a balcony overlooking the avenue.

One entered a long hall that was piled with business manuals, books and papers past a bedroom door and into a large living room with an oversized couch and chairs of all sizes and shapes. In front of the couch was a long, low table covered with more books and manuals plus a giant box of chocolates with its top off to tempt anyone who cared. There was Coca-Cola and mineral water to drink with glasses already lined up on a side table. George and Paul got down to business talk right away after the introductions, and I sat in pretended attendance while I was longing for a glass of champagne and small talk that might make an item for my column. Nothing was forthcoming and I tried in vain to catch Jack's eye to tell him with raised eyebrows and a glance to the ceiling that I wanted out. Jack wouldn't look at me and I knew he'd heard this "oil talk" so many times he knew it by heart, but he followed every word.

I couldn't help but be impressed by the Getty mind. His head was a computer with facts, figures, past history of the oil business plus names, places, dates of discovery of deposits, amounts drilled, cost of production, profits made. George was scribbling away a mile-a-minute but if he'd look up as though he doubted one item, Jack would jump up and find the official records to prove Paul's point. It was really amazing; Paul got my full attention when he started talking about his youth, his parents, education, travel, interest in art. This was my kind of talk and he fascinated me. Between the lines, I could sense that Paul had an obsession about proving to his father that he was a financial wizard, though his father was long gone. Paul was very frank about his lifelong disappointment that "Papa," a very wealthy oilman from wildcat days, had left him so little in his will, proving that he had no faith in his son's capabilities. When he spoke of his mother, he gave her credit for his love of art, music and poetry. It was she who decided to call him Jean Paul Getty, after her favorite German poet, Jean Paul Richter. This kind of talk kept me in rapt student-like concentration, but they got back on big business boredom again and all I could think of was how much I'd adore a little bit of my favorite brew.

At long last, George and I were on our way downstairs in the elevator. He had tiny beads of sweat on his brow when he said, "Maggi, if this guy's telling the truth, he could be one of the richest men in the world." I said, "I don't think Paul is lying. Why should he?"

George was very excited about his tremendous scoop for the Paris bureau of *Time* and was completely aghast when the New York editors cabled Paris over and over again, questioning his facts and figures. First, he was on the phone to me like I was his mother-maggi. But I kept insisting that he just had to get back to Paul and Jack for whatever proof he needed because I was totally out of the picture. One thing I had learned, however, was that Paul respected *Time* and had been flattered and pleased with the attention he was getting; he'd obviously taken a liking to George, who was such an avid listener and intelligent questioner.

Cables regarding J. Paul Getty's meeting with George Abell on February 11, 1957, Paris-New York-Paris went on for weeks until *Time* printed George's first story in the business section entitled "The Unknown Giant." Paul was very pleased except for one sentence where George had his facts wrong. He wrote that Paul's long-sleeved sweater was worn out at the elbows. Paul assured me that all of Abell's business facts were correct but, "I haven't worn a long-sleeved sweater since I was in grammar school," he said flatly.

I don't think that the amiable George Abell ever got credit for "discovering" Jean Paul Getty for *Time*. His interest, his follow-up, his struggle to get the New York editors to print his first story went by the wayside when *Fortune* took over and dug into Paul's financial background, deep enough to decide that he was the richest American in the world, which they featured in their magazine seven or eight months later. Following that, *Time* published a cover story on J. Paul Getty in which the Paris bureau asked for my help, entitled "The Do-It-Yourself Tycoon" with a portrait of Paul on the cover and five pages of text inside. This was exactly one year and 13 days after George Abell had his first meeting with Paul.

After *Time*'s cover story on J. Paul Getty, Frank White of the *Time* office in Paris sent me a little note of thanks for my help and a check to go with it. My help didn't amount to much after putting George Abell in touch with this "unknown tycoon." George's tireless cable campaign with New York to recognize his story was the real work that mattered in the first place. But I loved getting a letter from *Time*'s Frank White and still have it after forty years.

A few months after the *Time* story I received a telegram from Richard Clurman of *Newsday*, asking if I would write a 1000-word feature on Jean Paul Getty. The idea scared me but the first thing I thought to do was to ask Paul. By then he was in London, installed at the Ritz Hotel where I got hold of him immediately and told him about the *Newsday* offer. He was very nice and pleased that I had the assignment. The way he looked at it, he said, now that the "cat was out of the bag" about his empire, he'd rather have people who knew him writing stories than people he'd never met. I thanked him but I still was too nervous to take on such a tremendous assignment, so I told *Newsday* I'd provide enough information for someone else to sign. Photos? That was easy because Paul told Jack to take me down into the cellar of the Hôtel George V to go through a trunk that was stored there and take my choice. Jack was cagey though: every time I picked out a photo of Paul having a good time in a nightclub, Jack took it out of my hand, saying "No, that won't do. You can't have that one." Oh well, I was grateful for what I got such as Paul going over maps with King Saud in Saudia Arabia plus Paul with Ethel "Bunny" LeVane; another of Penny Kitson and Paul with the Prime Minister of Kuwait plus one of Paul posing on the balcony of his Hôtel George V suite.

While I was collecting page after page of information for *Newsday*, I attended the christening of another Getty French-built supertanker in Dunkerque. Paul didn't attend because the sea between England and France was too agitated and he refused to take an airplane. Several people claimed that Paul was just too upset to be seen in public after the *Fortune* disclosures, but Jack confirmed what I knew instinctively. Paul loved the attention from such a prestigious publication and even said, "I wondered when that magazine would finally get around to me." Despite the absence of their host, countless friends and associates of Paul jumped on a plush, private train to lunch and launch the 4th Getty tanker of the year called the "Oklahoma-Getty." J. Melville Forrester was the official Jean Paul Getty representative of the day when about fifty of us descended the train to be met by 20 shiny sedans whisking everyone to the dock where there was a flower-and-flag decked grandstand for the ceremony. The godmother this time was Jean Pochna, the mink-wrapped wife of John Pochna, who was one of Getty's international lawyers. Jean received a diamond necklace for her effort of taking a little hatchet

The tallest lawyer in town, Charles Torem of Coudert Frères, aboard a J. Paul Getty supertanker built in France.

to cut the ribbon which let fly the bottle that christened the 54, 000-ton ship. After the ceremony, everyone got a stem-to-stern tour of the ship while the song "Oklahoma" blasted over loudspeakers attached to a high-fidelity record player in one of the cabins decorated by Penny Kitson. The tour was followed by a five-hour lunch in a casino at Bray-Dunes where Paul's American friends could get better acquainted with the French bigwigs of the "Chantiers de France," which built the tanker paid for by Americans, which would fly a Liberian flag. The Liberian Consul General, William Fernandez, was there with his wife; from Kuwait was Yatezzat Gaafar; Kanaan Al Khatib from Saudi Arabia; and Paul's friends from all over the world.

Lunch was over by 6 p.m. and everybody was loaded back on the train for Paris; some of them more loaded than others. I sat with a fascinating fellow named Paul-Louis Weiller, whom I had never heard of at the time but, afterwards, I never stopped hearing about. Paul-Louis Weiller was an interesting train companion, telling me stories about people he knew and places he'd been. He was also an enthusiastic reader of the Paris *Herald Tribune*, which I could tell by his specific references to people I'd been writing about. During our talk on the train, he told me how he'd influenced his son to learn English. "I gave him a nickel for every new word he learned," he said with a sly smile. And that's when I commented, "Money talks," and made him laugh. I liked him a lot and told Jack back in Paris about this splendid man I'd gotten acquainted with on the train. Jack told me I had pretty good taste in men: Paul-Louis Weiller was easily the richest man in France since he had sold his company, Air France, to the French government.

When I wrote my story about the launching, I was careful to mention the important Frenchmen in attendance, like the president of the Chantiers, Lucien Lefol, Count and Countess de Mohl and Paul-Louis Weiller, of course. At the end of the story, I added a line I hoped would make Paul-Louis laugh. "They drank a toast to the absent host which went like this: The Middle East is east and the Middle West is west and J. Paul Getty is making ends meet."

Paul was an eager partygoer after long hours of work. That's why it seemed so ludicrous after he hit the headlines that people who didn't know him described him as a lonely, frustrated recluse. I saw him everywhere at all the best parties in Paris. Among his friends were people like André Dubonnet, Sir Charles and Lady Mendl, Ludwig Bemelmans, John Ringling North and, of course, Paul-Louis Weiller, who was not only a friend and host; they also had business dealings together. Paul liked to surround himself with people he called "life-enhancing" men and women. Still, he was so discreet in public that he kept quiet in the background as long as he could after *Time* and *Fortune* had found him out. Once I tried to convince an *Associated Press* photographer to take a picture of Paul at a party but the fellow thought I just wanted to please a friend.

It was the all-night ball honoring Salvador Dali in the Left Bank apartment of the young, up and coming Raymundo de Larrain, protégé of George de Cuevas.

I spotted Paul at the buffet table and pointed him out to the photographer, saying he ought not to miss that tall man over there named J. Paul Getty. The name didn't mean a thing to him and he looked at me as if to say he wasn't about to waste his film on a stranger when he could get pictures of people like Elsa Schiaparelli, Jacqueline de Ribes, Pamela Churchill, Rosita Winston and Maxime de la Falaise. Later, when he saw me chatting with Paul, he came over and snapped a shot of us together, which I thought was dumb because he could never sell a photo of a celebrity next to a journalist. It turned out that the photo was taken as a favor to me and when he brought it in person the next day, he gave me the negative with the picture as well, saying "I thought you'd like a picture of yourself with your boyfriend." I didn't bother trying to explain to the young fellow that I had been trying to steer him toward a good photo for the A.P. files; I just thanked him profusely for his thoughtfulness and put the photo in my personal collection.

Naturally I wrote all about the "Dali Ball" in the Paris *Herald Tribune* and got a lot of mileage out of it over the years. Fleur Cowles quoted my report in her book *The Case of Salvador Dali* in 1959 and Dominick Dunne quoted Fleur's quotations from my column in his article for *Vanity Fair* about Raymundo de Larrain, followed by his book, *The Mansions of Limbo* in 1991. (I know that doesn't pay the rent, but it pleases me just the same.)

No matter where Paul traveled, Jack always kept me up to date on his news; where he was, what he was doing, what he thought about various things. More than once, Jack mentioned that fame was a two-edged sword. Poor Paul, since he had been declared the richest man in the world, was being pursued in every way, shape and form by damsels who were definitely after his dough, and he was getting very tired if not downright annoyed by the unwanted attention. This inspired me to write a "lament" for him which I gave to Jack to present to Paul if he thought he'd get a giggle out of it.

From the "pocketbook anthology," "NOT SO DEEP AS AN OILWELL"

LAMENT

She's looking for a man with lots of dollars
Whom she can squeeze until he hollers
Money, she says, is no key to life's charm
But neither can it do her very much harm
JP: (Oh, the pretty maid who calls me honey,
Is she sweet on me or stuck on money?)
She'd follow a rainbow until the end
To find herself a lot of gold to spend
Gold in the bag, in the bank or a pot
Is better to have than to have not

Champagne...

JP: (Oh, the pretty maid who asks me to tea
How can I be sure she's the cup-cake for me?)
Though it may be strange, it may sound funny
What she won't do for love she MAY do for money
Not for a mink or a block-long Cadillac
But for cold cash that she won't have to give back
JP: (Oh, the pretty maid who closes her eyes
Is she counting on money or paradise?)
She insists that money can't bring happiness
She's ready to bear all the sorrow and stress
She's decided in life she's better off by far
Drowning her tears with champagne and caviar
JP: (Oh, the pretty maid with eyes so bright
And sweet talk spouting both day and night
Do you think she'll finally get off my trail
If I get her an oil well————HOLE-sale?

Chapter Fifteen

If it's true that variety is the spice of life, I must have had the spiciest life in Paris when I started writing for the *Herald Tribune*. Invitations to all kinds of events started to arrive from the beginning and soon took up a lot of time being read, thought about, accepted or declined. I learned very fast that I could not accept invitations unless there would be something to write about. There just wasn't enough time to go to strictly "fun things" or even to see my favorite friends, for that matter.

Taking a look in my old datebooks or picking up a handful of my columns from the big box of yellowed clippings, one can see what a variety there was in one week: a dinner at the Japanese Embassy residence in honor of the brother of the Emperor (that's where I sat next to a young designer from Christian Dior, whose name was Yves Mathieu Saint Laurent before he dropped the Mathieu; an animated cocktail party upstairs at Maxim's where host Earl Blackwell from New York honored Shirley Booth (Bricktop flew up from Rome to sing at the party). Next, I was asked to participate in a television show featuring Jack Warner, which was shot in the Salons George V, owned by Claude Terrail (Jack Warner's son-in-law at the time), followed by a fabulous reception a few blocks away given by a little lady named Trixie, wife of French industrialist, Serge Landeau, in a magnificent, high-ceilinged apartment with Impressionist paintings on the walls and Hollywood stars in every room. That's where I first met Rita Hayworth and Merle Oberon and became acquainted with a handsome Air Force colonel named Godfrey McHugh. He became a general and was President Kennedy's pilot on Air Force One from the beginning of the presidency to the last flight from Dallas.

Some days at noontime, I had my ever faithful friend, Eve Max, in my life. She'd zoom-zoom up to the *Herald Tribune* and whisk me off to lunch at the Ritz where I could gather news and have a good time as well, a sort of work-and-play arrangement. After lunch we'd go on errands together. She had fittings at Dior and Balenciaga and I always had things to pick up for the children, the household or myself. Once we stayed at Balenciaga to see the latest fashion collection and I said

Champagne...

I just loved his new tunic dresses that buttoned all the way down the back. The next time we lunched, Eve wore a back-buttoned dress that I'd never seen before and I said, "Balenciaga?" and she answered, "No, Balmain backwards."

Often when Eve and I were together, we'd get the giggles over our fashion experiences. Her favorite misadventure was the time she was a guest at a stuffy dinner party with politicians, publishers and big business tycoons at Margaret Biddle's. Eve had just acquired a model dress from the latest Christian Dior collection. It was a pencil-slim, slick, floor-length silk dress that looked divine but as she sat at the dinner table, the dress split in two right down her back before she'd finished her *consommé*. The black-tied gentleman next to her removed his coat and put it over her shoulders until she could slip upstairs and be pinned up by Mrs. Biddle's maid, ready to face the rest of the evening.

My unusual adventure concerned a black satin, full-length gown which I bought on sale at Pierre Balmain for a really small price. It was skin-tight but completely lined and boned inside so that no undergarments were necessary. There was more satin gathered in a bow behind the knees, which gave a marvelous silhouette. Pierre Balmain called this creation "The Merry Widow," and I found it ideal to wear at a formal dinner at Maxim's. I had a big success on entering Maxim's and had no trouble at all sitting down to dinner but when I went upstairs to the ladies' room, I had a big surprise. There was no way that I could move that dress from where it was except by unzipping the outer layer to undo all the inner hooks and snaps and remove the entire gown from the top down. I laughed so much, standing there stark naked with the dress in a pile at my feet, that the other ladies outside my door must have thought I was a bit bonkers.

Now I knew why "The Merry Widow" hadn't sold and why I got it for such a tiny price.

You'd think one would have a problem dressing for every occasion when invitations were so numerous and varied, but clothes for every outing did not present a problem. I had made friends with enough dressmakers to borrow something simple-to-sensational to suit my every need. All I had to do was stay skinny enough to wear the models, take care that no harm came to the merchandise while it was on my back, and be certain to return everything the very next day.

Even before I'd become a working journalist, Ginette Spanier lent gala gowns to me from Pierre Balmain's collection because she knew that guests would ask me who designed some of the magnificently-embroidered creations I wore and that this might be good for future sales. One time, Pierre's young assistant, Erik Mortensen, saw me at the Travellers' Club Ball wearing one of his creations and was so pleased to see the success I was having with "his" dress that he asked Pierre to tell Ginette to let me keep it.

The house of Balenciaga had a reputation of never letting anyone borrow an outfit for an evening but my faithful saleslady, Madame Alice, made exceptions for me. She understood that I had to go among the same people often at Maxim's, the

Tour d'Argent, the Ritz and to grand galas. She knew that I'd promptly return whatever I'd taken and in good shape on my way to work the next day. Another important advantage of having Madame Alice in my life was that she could recognize certain dresses in each collection which would be just right for me to own when the models were through with them each season. She put aside classic shapes, neutral colors, creations without fussy details: never so outstanding that the top-paying clients would clamour around for first choice. Thanks to Madame Alice, I collected a classic wardrobe for next to nothing, clothes that could be worn today and still be in perfect taste, if I hadn't worn them out!

Once I borrowed an unusually outstanding purple, crushed velvet gown with matching coat from Madame Alice to attend a Maxim's dinner party given by a pint-sized hostess, Mafalda Davis for Princess Faiza, sister of King Farouk. (Mafalda was Egyptian-born, married to an American, and best known as a PR

Pierre Balmain called
this dress "Merry Widow"
and it gave me a big laugh
in the ladies' room at Maxim's.

lady for Salvador Dali, who paid her in jewels and art.) Jack Forrester was among the guests and raved so much about my outfit that I told him it was borrowed from Balenciaga and I'd have to give it back the next morning. At coffee time, Jack said he'd decided that, in appreciation for all the favors I'd done for him and Paul, he'd like to make a gift of the dress and coat to me. Mafalda overheard his remark and interrupted, "Don't you dare buy that dress," she said, and went on to explain that as much as she loved Cristobal Balenciaga and his clothes and as beautiful as that outfit happened to be, she would never approve of Maggi owning such a color in such a fabric. She was a dynamic creature and had more to say, pointing out that in Paris if I was seen a few times in that "purple thing," it would look like I didn't have anything else to wear. "And furthermore," she added, "do you know the price of that purple thing? You could buy a television set for the price of that."

Before the evening was over, Jack leaned over and asked if my children had a TV set. I shook my head. Those were the days when not very many families had television in their homes and I had not yet even thought about owning one. The next day, a huge black and white television set was delivered to my door, addressed to Miss Cathy and Miss Janne. Mafalda Davis' dinner at Maxim's was duly reported in my column but without mention of television, of course. In my head, I classified that dinner party as "the night a dress turned into a TV set."

Much of the social and celebrity news for my column was collected at David Stein's home. I often thought David should have been given some sort of prize for the number of celebrities he could collect in his mansion at any given time. At a little get-together honoring Bob Taplinger, who had just been named Vice-President of Warner Brothers, there was Jack Warner, Barbara and Claude Terrail, Maurice Chevalier, James Mason, Milton Berle, Gary Cooper, Rita Hayworth, lawyer Charles Torem, banker Serge Semenenko, and two lovely ladies who were seen at all the best parties in those days: Maxime de la Falaise and Pamela Churchill. It was at one of David's parties that I first got acquainted with Hilda and George Marton, who invited me to a small dinner party at their home in honor of their visiting friend, Paulette Goddard.

What fun I had at the Martons on the Avenue Paul Doumer near the Trocadéro. Hilda Marton was a nice lady from Hollywood, full of energy and good humor. (She was the mother of film writer, Peter Stone, who became famous for successes such as Cary Grant's *Charade*, and *Father Goose*, for which he got an Oscar.) George Marton was a Hungarian-born agent, producer, promoter and I don't know what else. I found myself seated at the dinner table right across from Paulette Goddard, the actress who'd been married to Charles Chaplin and starred in *Modern Times* and *The Great Dictator*. Paulette was a very amusing lady and seemed interested in talking about everything except movies. During dinner, when I happened to mention that I had seen the cellars at the Hôtel Ritz and was absolutely fascinated that they had a whole village down there, her eyes started to sparkle and she begged me to take her along on the next tour. I had to explain that there was no such thing as an organized tour; I had been taken there by Charles Ritz, son of César Ritz, who'd founded the hotel, after I had mentioned to him that the Ritz had the best potato chips I'd ever tasted. "We have our own machine downstairs," he told me, "and we have one man there who does nothing else all day." When Charles showed me the chip machine, I caught sight of other intriguing things like live trout in a stream and then a very strange contraption that looked like it was full of BB gun shot under water, which turned out to be a special device for polishing heavy Ritz silverware to a gleaming brilliance. One thing led to another until I'd had a full tour of the premises. The more I told Paulette about it, the more she insisted she had to see it for herself. When I began to think about it, I figured that Charles Ritz would be thrilled to entertain a guest like Paulette Goddard and it would give me something different to write about as well. So I promised Paulette that I'd make the date for us to visit the Ritz cellars. Alas, when I called the hotel the next day, I learned that my pal, Charles, had gone fishing. The manager, however, was very nice and said that one of his assistants would be happy to show me and my guest around anytime we wanted.

A few days later, Paulette Goddard and I met in the Ritz Bar for our tour of the Ritz "city below the street." We were joined by our young guide from Ritz management who led the way under the hotel. Paulette said on our way downstairs that she always liked to get to the bottom of things and I said that remark would probably end up in my column. Paulette looked as cute as a kitten in a bright red skiing suit as we started our tour of the kitchen, bakery, complete electrical plant, laundry, furniture restorer, on to huge hams floating in iced water, the potato chip machine, etc. When Paulette saw the strange silver-polishing method, she looked down into the water and said, "What's that, drowned caviar?" We accepted the invitation to take a look at the 100, 000 bottles of fine wines they had farther on and when we came to a narrow passageway, Paulette went ahead followed by the young man. I was right behind him and distinctly saw that young man give Paulette a pat on her shapely behind. Mortified and embarrassed I joined Paulette and asked her if she wanted to leave. "Of course not. This is interesting," she told me and we continued our tour. The keeper of the wine cellar took great pride in showing us all around. Paulette said she was surprised to see all the bottles so clean and shiny but he pointed out, with contempt for the housekeeping habits in other wine cellars, that dust on the bottle has nothing to do with the quality of content. When we finished our visit and went back upstairs, I was still furious with that fresh young fellow who had insulted a famous movie star and asked Paulette if she wanted me to tell Charles Ritz. "Oh forget it, Maggi. Don't be a fuddy-duddy," she said. She was grinning and insisted that he paid her a compliment and she found it hilarious that he didn't have a clue as to her identity. I wrote a story about our adventure "walking on wine on the Place Vendôme" and didn't mention the young man who dared touch the *derrière* of the former Mrs. Charles Chaplin, soon to be Mrs. Erich-Maria Remarque. Later I got a big laugh out of Paulette when I said she wasn't the only one at the Ritz who liked to get to the bottom of things.

It's been said that the more work you do the more work you CAN do. Just when I'd think I was busy to capacity, something would come my way I didn't want to refuse. I was asked by Stan Davis of CBS Radio in New York to do celebrity interviews on tape. They made it easy to do by sending a list of questions for each celebrity so I wouldn't have to rack my brains about what to ask or worry about whether my material would be interesting to listeners in the USA. There was another advantage I found: if the celebrities thought the questions I asked were silly, they knew they didn't come from me. Furthermore, if I kept my wits about me, the CBS interviews could give me material for my columns in Paris for the *Trib* and *INS* plus Jack Vietor's magazine in California.

The first CBS Radio interview I did was with the old Aga Khan at the Ritz. When I first called for an appointment, a man answered and I asked to speak to the secretary of the Aga Khan, giving my name. The gentleman said, "Wouldn't you rather speak to ME insofar as my secretary is not here right now." That was my introduction to the old fellow, who immediately accepted to see me and added that he liked to read my column in the paper and did I suppose that I'd have room to mention that he was going to have a birthday party for himself that week. What a hoot! We set up the taping date to be done in his private apartment at the Ritz and I contacted the CBS man to bring his equipment. For such a project in 1956 the technician had to show up with equipment that it took two to carry, with cables as fat as rattlesnakes all over the place. The old Aga Khan was in a jolly mood and seemed to look forward to this adventure. While the machinery was being set up, he asked me all sorts of questions and when I told him my birthplace was San Francisco, he told me he was there during the great earthquake and didn't know what to do or where to go so he stumbled into a drugstore and sat at the counter ordering the biggest, best ice cream sundae he'd ever eaten in his life. He was a giant hulk of a fellow, completely filling a huge armchair, easy to feel relaxed with, good humored and interested in everything.

The Aga had an amber cocker spaniel at his feet and a silver-gray parrot perched in a cage over his left shoulder. He sat still, chatting with me, while his wife, the Begum was flitting in and out. She was dressed in a cherry red hostess coat–an absolutely gorgeous six-foot creature who had been "Miss France," such a stately beauty as one seldom saw in Paris. But she seemed ill at ease, nervous per-haps, until her husband said, "Sit down." And she did, on the arm of his chair.

Before we started the questions and answers, the parrot started squawking so loudly that the Aga called a servant to put the bird in the bathroom next door. A bit later when the Begum started chattering away, the Aga told his wife to be still or he'd have to put her in with the bird. Before she quieted down however, she insisted on telling me that her husband did not tell the truth when he said he was 80 years old, as it was going to be his 79th birthday and not his 80th. He patiently explained to me that he was not lying; in his opinion a child was one year old already the day it was born, so if he was born 79 years before, he was really 80 years old. "Okay?" he asked and I answered, "Okay."

We went through our taped interview beautifully, without any rehearsal as he said if he didn't know in advance what the questions would be, his answers were sure to be more interesting. After we finished our work and the technician was collecting his equipment, the Aga insisted that we have some tea and, like magic, there seemed to be servants everywhere putting everything in front of him. His American secretary, Merioneth Whitaker, from Denver, Colorado, joined us and the old Aga held court, telling us all sorts of interesting things such as, contrary to popular belief, he was not given his weight in precious jewels every year. He'd had his weight matched three times in gold, diamonds and platinum. The money from these jubilee weighing ceremonies went to school scholarships, charities and worthy projects for his followers.

One of the questions in the interview was whether or not he thought diamonds were unlucky and he said, "Of course not, some of the owners of diamonds are unlucky and they are giving diamonds a bad name." After the tape he added, "Have you ever heard that expression 'diamonds are a girl's best friend?'" and then added, "well, you'd better believe it, my dears." Then it was the Aga himself who asked me if I'd like to have a photo of him with the Begum. I couldn't believe his enthusiasm over the possibility of getting his picture in the Paris *Herald Tribune*. When I told him I didn't have a photographer, he said his German maid, Frieda Meyer, took excellent pictures and he'd see to it that she took a photo of him and his wife before they went out to dinner that very evening. True to his word, the photograph was delivered to me as promised in time for my *Herald Tribune* story which appeared the day after his birthday dinner for fifty guests at Maxim's.

Before I left the Aga's suite, he told me a few simple truths about his son, Aly Khan. He said the title "Prince" belonged only to the Aga and Aly was not entitled to a title, no matter what he claimed. Then he explained that the word "Aga" means "leader" and no one in his family could use that in their name either. He said, quite frankly, that whenever newspaper people put a title on his son's name, he called them up and corrected the mistake so if I did that I shouldn't be surprised to hear from him. Just before I bid the Aga goodbye, I was standing in front of him and he beckoned me to lean over to hear what he wanted to say. He asked if I had met his son, Aly, and I said I saw him very often at social and celebrity functions. Then he went on to say that his son would certainly ask me to go out with him one day and for my own good, I should refuse. "Unfortunately," he sighed, "my son has no values and no taste—no taste at all—not even in his mouth." I was shocked that a father could speak like that of his own son and I never forgot it.

The only celebrity who refused to be interviewed for CBS Radio was Maurice Chevalier, but he made up for it by becoming a friend. When I called him for the interview he seemed to be in a very bad mood when he gave me his immediate three-word reply, "*Non–non–NON*." I said, "*Merci, Monsieur*" and hung up feeling truly let down. A few days later I received a lovely handwritten note explaining that he had an agreement with NBC Radio and feared conflict, which made me feel a lot better.

After that, down through the years, he greeted me warmly every time we met and had my name put on his list of guests for his performances and invited me backstage after his One Man Show to pose for souvenir photographs with him.

The last celebrity I interviewed for CBS Radio was Ingrid Bergman while she was living in Paris at the Hôtel Raphael with her husband, Roberto Rossellini, three children, Italian servants and a Siamese kitten. She greeted me at the door wearing slacks and oversized shirt, led me into a salon where we sat down together on a couch. She was immediately climbed on by her four-year-old twins, Isabella and Ingrid, who didn't look at all alike. Isabella had straight hair and a pixie grin while Ingrid had a mass of curls and a shy "love me" look. Ingrid said

After Maurice Chevalier refused my request for an interview, we became good friends. At Maxim's with Lady Coventry.

they differed in character as well as looks and she found them fascinating little people. Displayed in the salon were the latest works of art by her seven-year-old son, Robertino. She pointed them out to me, one by one, saying Robertino was very advanced for his age. His art featured butterflies but there was one composition showing a Surrealist cathedral blazing with color. Very impressive for a seven-year-old.

If I hadn't had my list of CBS questions in my hand I think we would have talked about nothing else except children, as it seemed to be our favorite subject but then I had to get down to business and talk about her career. She was in Paris rehearsing for her first appearance on the French stage, the production of Robert Anderson's *Tea and Sympathy*, opening shortly. In addition to this, her latest film for Anatole Litvak, *Anastasia*, was about to open in America. (We didn't know then that she'd win an Oscar.) Ingrid Bergman laughed a nice hearty laugh when one of the CBS Radio questions on the list asked how it felt to be making a comeback in films. "I've never been away from films," she said, adding, "I've been away from America, but not away from film making."

Chapter Sixteen

My people columns of the fifties I found tedious at times, though I never said so. Then one fine day at the Ritz I found myself confiding in two people I liked, Joyce and Ted Schulze.

Ted was the son of Margaret Biddle and I'd met him and Joyce several times at the beautiful Biddle home during luncheon or dinner parties but we hadn't really had a chance to get acquainted. I joined them at their table and we started our usual Paris chitchat of who's in town and what's going on. Finally, Ted looked me in the eye and asked confidentially, "Don't you get a little tired of having to list names all the time?" I confessed I certainly did, especially since I'd just been called into Eric's office because he'd gotten complaints from irate lady readers who said I'd called someone a Princess when she wasn't any such thing. I wondered what you were supposed to do when a lady, herself, said she had a title. Ted said that I shouldn't take anything too seriously and, if I wanted to have a little comic relief, I ought to stick a few invented names in my articles to amuse myself and get the best of the whole funny business.

"Oh, I couldn't do that," I told him, and I really meant it. He dropped the subject and, during our second glass of champagne, he asked me how come I never ever said anything in my column about Mrs. James Langdon Othomere. I said, "Who?" He said she was the former Lilla Clayton and she was always doing and saying very amusing things, like the other day while she was lunching at Maxim's she said, "I really don't like diamonds but without them I feel so drab." I thought that would make a nice little item and asked him if he thought she'd let me use it in my next column. "I'm sure you can get permission to quote her," said Ted, while Joyce was laughing so much that she had to put her drink down on the table so it wouldn't spill in her jiggling hand.

Ted and Joyce confessed that Mrs. Othomere existed only in their imagination and they'd love to see her name in print. The more I thought about it, the more I wanted to print their item just as they had told it to me. I did and it gave me the little lift I needed. After the short paragraph appeared, I received a dozen, long-stemmed pink roses in my office with a very expensive engraved card which read, "Mrs. James Langdon Othomere." This was such fun for me that I knew it was not the last time I would include that lady in my columns. A few days after that, a friend sent me a clipping of a column written by Sam White for the *London Evening Standard* and it had my Mrs. Othomere item reprinted word for word. I couldn't believe my eyes. The next time I ran into Sam at the Crillon, I told him my attention was drawn to his reprint of my paragraph and he straightened up in a huff, saying, "Come off it, Maggi, you're not the only one in Paris who knows that woman." I didn't dare tell him the truth as I knew he'd tell people I was putting phoney names in my column and it could jeopardize my job. So I went giggling homeward and couldn't wait to report the incident to Ted and Joyce.

Of course Ted gave me more items to fill my space and cheer my days. He told me that Mr. Donald Finger and five members of his family were coming to Paris to visit his cousin, *Monsieur Ferdinand Finger*, who was moving house, and the five American Fingers were going to lend him a hand. The Finger family joined Mrs. Othomere in my column much to my mirth.

I liked Joyce and Ted; they were relaxed and fun. Ted's sister was married to the tenor, Morton Downey (before he married Ann van Gerbig in Palm Beach), and they provided me with legitimate items about him for my column as well as more social ones on Mrs. Othomere, who decided that because all her friends were getting so old she was going to have her annual ball in the daytime and call it a "Tea Ball."

One noontime I was sitting with Norman Winston and Ted and Joyce Schulze in the small bar of the Ritz. Norman was complaining about the long, long lunches he had to attend where there was absolutely no table talk of interest. Soon we were talking about starting a club for people who liked small lunches with heavy talk instead of the usual Parisian heavy lunches with small talk.

We ordered club sandwiches and, of course, that's how our club got its name, "Club Sandwich Club." We began making up some rules that members would have to follow such as "our polo-playing member has to come down off his high horse;" "the secretary can't take more than an hour to read the minutes;" "the Eiffel Tower has to be called the Awful Tower;" "the Place de la Concorde will be known as Red Grape Square." I added "Club Sandwich Club" news to my column, then mentioned it often enough that people were asking how they could join. I asked Ted and Joyce what I should answer to that and Ted said, "Tell them to ask Mrs. James Langdon Othomere."

In the fifties the historic café on the Boulevard Saint Germain called Les Deux Magots was taken over by zoot-suiters who were known as *les zazous*. When my newsman friend, Joe Dynan of *Associated Press*, saw me lunching at Maxim's with Maggie Vaudable he started saying, "On the Left Bank we have 'Les Deux Magots' and on the Right Bank we have 'Les Deux Maggies.'" I liked to be with Maggie at her favorite corner banquette, having a light lunch and listening to her talk about

Champagne...

Paris, people and the projects she had in her head for Maxim's future. Often, when she had something special to tell me but I couldn't take the time for lunch, I'd have a teatime *coupe* of champagne in her luxuriously-furnished office on an upper floor above the restaurant and private salons. The restaurant business had been far from her mind when she met and fell in love with Louis, who'd inherited Maxim's from his father. Maggie had studied both law and music before becoming a journalist. She then decided her place was beside her husband, working for Maxim's. Both Louis and Maggie hated the spotlight, and stayed in the background while lunching and dining at Maxim's all the time to make certain that all went well.

It seemed that they were always on the premises though they owned a luxurious apartment at the Palais Royal on the picturesque Rue de Montpensier in the same building as Jean Cocteau and had a country home in Rambouillet. Maggie also had a hideaway on the top floor of Maxim's under the eaves, which she created as a little escape for herself.

While the Vaudables stayed behind the scenes, it was Maxim's imperious director, Monsieur Albert, who greeted and seated guests. He catered to the Old World characters with special attention to former Monarchs of no longer existing places and did not see eye to eye with Maggie, who wanted to concentrate on youth, beauty and projects to build the future. Louis was often like the mediator trying to keep peace between them.

Old Albert insisted that the past must prevail despite dwindling numbers of the high born on hand. He had strict seating arrangements in his head that he'd follow without fail. In the far left Royal Corner banquette, he'd place people like ex-King Farouk, the Aga Khan III, the Duke and Duchess of Windsor, or any Maharajah like Jaipur, Baroda or Rajpipla of Bombay. At surrounding tables were bearded tycoons and pigeon-breasted wives while the first banquette on the right was kept for the remnants of White Russian nobility, though they might be down to their last tiara and "forget" to pay their bills.

Certain other "kings" with names like Dubonnet or Lanson or Taittinger could count on royal treatment, but a mere top star of Hollywood might get seated in "Siberia," which was on the right on the way to the kitchen's swinging doors.

Maggie Vaudable was forever telling M. Albert that movie stars should be on display up front so as to be seen. "They may not be important to YOU but they are important to Maxim's," she said once and he straightened to full height and said, "Madame, I AM Maxim's." So Louis had to be called in once again.

Maxim's for lunches, dinners, suppers and private gala parties became such a steady part of my life that the Vaudables seemed almost like family to me, always there in the background to make certain all was well. I could see how Monsieur Albert could be difficult sometimes, but he was always nice to me.

Out on my own in Maxim's several times a week with people I was writing about, I could see by M. Albert's face whether he approved of my companions. One day I started to call him "Papa" and explained that he reminded me of a stern parent greeting a naughty child sometimes when I came into the restaurant with someone he didn't think was right. He was pleased at my remarks and told me that he would have been proud to have had a daughter like me. So it became our routine. On entering I would say *"Bonsoir, Papa,"* and he would answer, *"Bonsoir, ma fille."* One night, when I was with David Stein and Mr. and Mrs. Alan Ladd, Sue Carol Ladd and I went straight upstairs to the ladies' room as we came in, and M. Albert had already seated David and Alan when we came down to our table. Ye gads, we were in SIBERIA! This was a first for me, but I said nothing. It was my policy to sit still, shut up and mentally write my report for my next column. I had a marvelous time with the Ladds that night because they were funny and very bright. When we were first introduced Alan said he bet that I was surprised to see that he wasn't ten feet tall, as so many people were shocked when they saw how short he was. I said something like I didn't think the height of someone mattered very much in this world. And he said, "Oh, but it does when you're an actor and you have to make love to an actress who's taller than you are." Then he told me that when I saw him kissing a girl in a movie, I should always remember that he was standing on a box or she was standing in a hole. At the table, when he saw me looking at the rather ornate gold tie pin he was wearing, he showed me his giant gold cufflinks plus his huge all-gold watch, and gold rings on both hands. "You know what this is, Maggi," he said, "this is the manifestation of my insecurity." The next time I went to Maxim's I asked "Papa" Albert why he had placed an important American actor like Alan Ladd in "Siberia," and he said, "He was wearing too much jewelry."

Uppermost in Maggie's thoughts was the need to woo young French socialites to Maxim's so they'd be the *habitués* of tomorrow.

Maggie Vaudable hated to be photographed but she agreed to this one with me at Maurice Carèrre's restaurant in Montfort l'Amaury.

Champagne...

One of her first successful projects was the instigation of Tuesday night *soirées* featuring a special favorite recipe of an outstanding young man or lady from a top French family. The honored personality of the evening was given a table to entertain young friends, enjoy the unique menu and dance the night away. Maggie's idea had an instant success as the word got around in a hurry that Maxim's on Tuesday night was the place to be. I loved these events because there was a lot to write about and I could have a lovely evening at the same time. The best one of the series was the evening honoring the nineteen-year old Prince Jean Poniatowski, the youngest son in a family of princes about Paris, with old world ancestry from Poland. He selected the family chef's recipe of *filets de sole polonaise*, as special dish of the night. Jean was celebrating something pretty important in his life that not many people there knew about: in three days' time he was off to Morocco to start his three-year stint in the French Army. A few weeks after our fabulous feast at Maxim's he sent a postcard from his barracks telling me that he was assigned to sweeping the floor.

Around the main room at Maxim's on the night of the "*sole polonaise*" Prince Rainier and Princess Grace were in the Royal Corner. Grace was in her "heir-conditioned" dress as she was awaiting the birth of her second child in a few months' time, and her husband had grown a black beard which looked kind of scary to me.

There were outstanding people at Maxim's worth knowing like Maurice Carèrre, Maxim's organizer-decorator of fabulous gala occasions. He was known as a man of great taste when he ran the wining/dining/dancing club called l'Orangerie on the Rue Pierre Charron, where he signed up singers like Édith Piaf, Yves Montand, Juliette Gréco and Eddie Constantine, to sing for supper guests.

He also took over and redecorated an *auberge* in the village of Montfort l'Amaury which had been an 18th century flour mill. He turned it into an exquisite stopping-off place for lunch, dinner or staying the night. Maurice Carrère was a happy, round-faced fellow from Biarritz who had a flare for dreaming up the perfect decor for extra special evenings at Maxim's as well as the knack of gathering together really impressive people to guarantee success. One charity ball he created was an old-time 1900s cabaret scene in Maxim's with red-topped tables, gilt chairs, soft lighting and giant potted palms in every available spot. On a specially-built platform draped with burgundy velvet he put on a parade of Maxim's *fantômes*, who were members of Paris' young social set dressed in 1900s costume through the courtesy of the Comédie Française. Jean Marais presented a poetic introduction as each personality appeared reciting words written for the occasion by Jean Cocteau. After that, a pay-as-you-bid auction took place where the bidders paid every time they opened their mouths whether or not they won. It was amazing to see the money pile up from people like Aristotle Onassis, Paul-Louis Weiller, Guy de Rothschild, Arturo Lopez-Willshaw and Stavros Niarchos. The bidders were vying for an ensemble including a ballgown from Paris' newest couturier, Guy Laroche, a mink stole from Christian Dior, and a necklace with earrings from

Prince Poniatowski sat at the next table from me when he was the honored guest
at a formal Maxim's dinner just before going into the army where he was
assigned to sweep the floors.

Van Cleef & Arpels. The final winner of the goods was Mme. Jacques Fath, but
everyone paid dearly for the fun of bidding. On the scene that evening were
socialites, celebrities and sophisticates like Bob Hope, Ingrid Bergman, Charles
Boyer, Elsa Maxwell, Baron and Baroness de Cabrol, Lady Deterding, Countess
Albert de Mun and the Vaudables, of course, in a discreet corner watching that
everything measured up to their perfectionism.

Maggie Vaudable and I didn't always agree on everything. She could be
tough, stubborn and hard to convince that there might be another viewpoint
besides her own.

Once she told me that Elsa Maxwell was a great journalist and Dorothy

Champagne...

Princess Grace of Monaco (pregnant with Albert) wore an "heir-conditioned" dress and Prince Rainier wore a beard at Maxim's on Prince Poniatowski's big night.

Kilgallen was a witch. For those who weren't around in those days, Kilgallen did a syndicated column out of New York on "café society" and entertainment, while Maxwell did international "society" with lots of photographs. When I wouldn't let Maggie drop the subject of Maxwell-versus-Kilgallen, I finally got it out of her that Dorothy Kilgallen had written a line in her column years before that Maggie said insulted Maxim's. She couldn't quote the item but she never forgot the slight whereas Elsa Maxwell had always been complimentary to Maxim's. Of course, my opinions were just the opposite. Kilgallen had been good to me while Maxwell had been awful.

My friend, Jack Tirman, a press agent I'd met through Warner Brothers' Bob Taplinger, asked me to do a guest column from Paris for Dorothy Kilgallen in New York while she was on vacation. I rewrote some items in my latest columns about the best known celebrities in the U.S., like the Duchess of Windsor, Aly Khan, and wine and champagne personalities like Betty Lanson and Alexis Lichine, and sent it off. After it appeared I received nice notes but more than that, began to see my name in Kilgallen's column, sent to me by friends all over the map afterwards. I'd done the guest column for nothing and Miss Kilgallen seemed to be paying me back in nice items.

My upset with the inimitable Elsa Maxwell came during an all-night ball hosted by Norman and Rosita Winston in their palatial town house on the Rue Saint Dominique. In the middle of the festivities I was frightened that she was going to put me out because she bellowed, "No journalists are here tonight." I had been invited to this glorious affair by the host himself, at one of our "Club Sandwich Club" lunchtimes at the Ritz.

Norman was not the jewelry Winston. His wealth came from housing development and he was serving as High Commissioner and personal representative of the Mayor of New York at various international building and construction fairs throughout Europe. His wife, Rosita Greenway Winston, had coal black hair and ivory skin. She loved beautiful clothes, jewels, parties and international high life. Her husband said that's why she teamed up with Elsa in the first place. I asked Norman if he was certain it would be okay for me to come to the party but he assured me that he "damn well" could invite anyone he wanted as he was "picking up the tab for the whole shebang."

When I wrote up my "party report" about Elsa's birthday ball, everything I wrote was right, but I didn't tell ALL. While I was wandering through the salons, getting my bearings and trying to capture the whole scene I caught sight of Elizabeth Taylor standing in front of a floor-to-ceiling bookcase while her husband, Mike Todd, was chatting with the host a few feet away. She looked a dream in flowing yellow chiffon and you couldn't but notice that she was expecting a baby; she was radiant. I got closer to her, pretending to look at the bookshelves and when I looked over at her, she was looking at me. "Tennyson, anyone?" I said, glancing back at the books and she laughed a big, lusty laugh which I thought was great.

We started chatting and I felt like I'd known her all my life. When she admired the pale green silk taffeta ballgown I was wearing, I told her I had borrowed it from Pierre Balmain and had to return it in the morning; and I admitted that I sometimes found my job tiring, but I liked it anyway. When Mike Todd came over to join us, he looked down his nose at me and said something like, "And what is your TITLE, my dear?" But Elizabeth took his arm and said, "Hey, Mike, she's okay–she's American, she writes for the *Trib*, and she has to give that dress back in the morning." He changed immediately, gave me a big grin and then took us to a trio of gilt chairs saying, "Save a place for me while I go and get us some booze." A minute later he was back with three glasses and an opened bottle of champagne. He filled the glasses and plunked the bottle under his chair. It was plain that he didn't care much for this kind of party but he was in a better mood now that he was sitting next to his wife.

After a few minutes, Baron Philippe de Rothschild drew up a spindly chair to join us, shaking his head when Mike offered him some champagne, saying his doctor told him he mustn't drink. Minutes later, Elsa Maxwell sidled up to us and Philippe jumped up to give her his chair. She sat down next to me and asked me if we'd met at somebody's palazzo in Italy, and wasn't I the daughter of Princess So-and-So. Philippe corrected her, saying I was a journalist, which seemed to infuriate her but she still kept her hand on my knee while she sputtered that there were no journalists there that night. Mike leaned over at this point and said softly, "Elsa, will you take your grubby hand off her dress? She has to give it back to Balmain in the morning."

I was certain I was about to be put out the door but a tinkling piano a few feet away saved me. Hazel Scott had come into the room, sat at the piano and started to play. Elsa jumped up so fast that she upset the chair and went to join Hazel Scott on the piano bench. They sang and played for hours afterwards and I was free to roam the rooms before going home with my next column tucked neatly in my head.

My disagreement with Maggie Vaudable concerning Dorothy Kilgallen stayed in the back of my mind for future reference, though knowing Maggie, I didn't hold much hope of getting her to change her mind on anything. She was as stubborn as the proverbial mule. Then one day, I thought my chance had come. My New York friend, Jack Tirman, wrote that Dorothy Kilgallen would be coming to Paris and he hoped that I could make her feel welcome. I went straight to Maggie Vaudable and gave her all the reasons why I thought she should give a little party for her. Maggie had a cat fit! "Never!" she said. I went on and on about what a marvelous thing it would be for Maxim's. Dorothy was not only a syndicated columnist all over the USA, but she and her husband, Richard Kollmar, had an early morning radio program called "Dorothy and Dick."

I didn't let up. I went on about Dorothy writing every day of the year for all of America, not just twice a week; and if she was happy with Maxim's there would be no end to the times she'd mention it during the year, plus the fact that her husband was important and influential. He was a Broadway producer and owned a nightclub in New York called The Left Bank. I think I really clinched everything when I added that they had a daughter going to school in Switzerland and said, "Hey, that could mean something to Maxim's in the future, couldn't it?"

Maggie began to warm up to the idea of winning over Dorothy and Dick for Maxim's but she insisted that she'd stay entirely in the background if I held a cocktail party in my name. We did it! It was great! The reception was up one flight in the Imperial Salon of Maxim's starting from 6:30 and going on until way after 9:00. Maggie and Louis gave orders that "the sky's the limit" and every one of my favorite Maxim's fellows seemed to be on hand to see that everything was perfect. Guests included Gene Kelly; Mrs. Darryl Zanuck and her daughter, Susan Hakim; Drue Heinz, who wore one of the first Saint Laurent "trapeze" styles; the Marquis George de Cuevas; Anton "Pat" Dolin from the London Ballet; writer Marcel Achard; Prince Charles d'Arenberg; André Dubonnet with his daughter, Lorraine Bonnet; Mrs. Barney Balaban, wife of the president of Paramount Pictures; and Dorothy and David Schoenbrun. Kilgallen was thrilled

Elsa Maxwell, the society-journalist who almost put me out of a party, and Elizabeth Taylor at Maxim's.

with her party. Of course Maggie and Louis Vaudable showed up to take a look at the goings-on, but the guests didn't know they were paying for the party. My honored guest and her husband had fun. Dorothy Kilgallen did two stories about the party as her "highlight" in Paris, between trips to Brussels and London. It was a great satisfaction to me to give the clippings of the columns to Maggie for her Maxim's collection. Another good thing out of that party–Mrs. Barney Balaban told me she had such a good time that she was going to send me a little present. The gift: a gold pill box from Cartier.

That gold box played an important part in my life later.

Chapter Seventeen

April in Paris 1957 will be remembered by many as the time the young Queen Elizabeth II of England came to call. All of Paris was a-twitter and the gorgeous chestnut trees burst into such glorious bloom that they looked like popcorn trees. (That's how I thought of them: popcorn trees, until Paris pollution got so strong that it takes all their strength to barely bloom.) Everyone, of all ages, from all walks of life seemed to be chanting "the Queen is coming," but I still was surprised when little Cathy came into my room one evening and asked if she could have a word with me. We perched on the edge of my bed and I couldn't imagine why she had such a serious look on her face. "Can you take me to see the Queen?" she asked, looking solemnly into my face. She had heard about the Queen at school and during the news on television and I was faced with a challenge I never imagined would come my way. I started out telling her that there would be thousands of people wanting just that and I wasn't certain how it could be arranged. Then I remembered that Claude Terrail, owner of the Tour d'Argent, had invited me to a dinner party on the night that the Queen would be floating by on a royal barge down the Seine while Tour d'Argent guests would have a bird's-eye view of the procession from the sixth-floor, glassed-in restaurant overlooking all of Paris. At first I must admit, I hadn't been too enthusiastic over the idea of lapping up a lot of calories but it seemed like a lovely story if I could write that a little girl beside me watched the Queen go by. I promised Cathy that I'd try to arrange for her to see the Queen, but that I needed a little time. She seemed quite confident that I could take care of the whole thing and bounced happily off to bed.

Claude Terrail, a very nice fellow who likes children, thought I had a great idea and assured me that my daughter would be treated like a princess. So the big night found Cathy by my side dressed in her little girl gray skirt and sweater with half-socks and two-buckle shoes. The Tour d'Argent had the titled and entitled of Paris at every table and Claude had cooked up the same menu that the Queen had enjoyed there when she was a Princess in 1948. Cathy refused *filets de sole, poussins farcis, nids de pommes soufflées, asperges de Lauris* and *soufflé glacé.* "I'm not hungry," she said.

While waiting for the Seine parade, I pointed out to Cathy some of the personalities at tables around us: ambassadors from Luxembourg, Sweden, India and Brazil, as well as the Prince of Nepal, Princess Maria-Pia, Prince Alexandre, Count de Beauregard, and Count and Countess de La Fayette. "Where's the Queen?" Cathy asked. I could see that Cathy's patience in this heady atmosphere was on the wane and Claude Terrail's wife, Barbara, noticed it as well. She came over to where we were sitting by the window.

Mme. Terrail (the former Barbara Warner of California) suggested that Cathy would be happier one floor below in the private apartment of Americans, Mr. and Mrs. Bertrand Taylor, and so she was. After a cocktail of tonic water, Olive Taylor wrapped Cathy in a pastel mink jacket and a silk Hermès scarf and led her to a corner balcony of her own, just as the fairyland below came to life. The spectacle: Notre-Dame in all her illuminated glory, a pyramid of white-robed singers, the colorful Vert-Galant flower markets, Paris firemen's water fountains shooting into the sky and hundreds of balloons strung from the roof of the Tour d'Argent with flags and floodlights everywhere.

Suddenly the crowd's roar on the quay below announced the royal arrival. Cathy was speechless until the yacht passed before her eyes. "The Queen," she announced solemnly. At that moment the balloons were let free and took to the sky, the fireworks burst in all directions, and Cathy squealed "*Magnifique!*" with all her might. After the *fête* it took two hours to get home because more than a million Parisians had gathered for this memorable occasion, but it was well worth the trouble to prove that adage, "Cathy can look at a Queen."

All through the fifties Claude Terrail's Tour d'Argent was a top favorite restaurant in Paris from every point of view (and, indeed, it still is today while other favorites have dropped by the wayside). Claude put his heart and soul into the Tour d'Argent just as his father did before him. When I first met Claude, he was not only a hard-working restaurateur but he was also a fine polo player and what I called a "part-time playboy," who had a tremendous success with the ladies. His inconstant companions were always the most beautiful, the best dressed and often with names one knew well like Lorelle Hearst and Ava Gardner. But I always thought of him as a man with many facets. I'm certain he could have been a successful diplomat or politician or an actor or even a news commentator with his resonant voice, but I'm glad he decided to make an historical monument of the Tour d'Argent instead.

Newswise, the Tour d'Argent was one of the very best sources of celebrity information. Whether I went alone with a friend or to a dinner party, I always came away with a few items of interest. There were endless special occasions there as well. Like the Hat Wearing Night, for instance. Every Wednesday night dinner would be a time for every lady to show off her evening headgear. One of those evenings was nearly enough to fill my column when the distinguished

Champagne...

Duchess de Montesquiou-Fezensac (a beauty who always wore Balenciaga) showed up with her daughter, Victoire, and the polo-playing pal of Claude, Porfirio Rubirosa, brought his wife, Odile Robin. More there that night: the handsome hero of Anapurna, Maurice Herzog; Line Renaud; Prince Michel of Yugoslavia and Count Jean d'Ormesson. In those days everyone wore hats in the daytime and this after-dark hat habit caught on, especially with ladies who could hide lousy hairdos under hats and still look good. (I had flower-bow-veil creations I called "night caps" for these occasions.)

Another outstanding inspiration Claude had was to create a gastronomic museum on his premises for all the world to see. It contains unique, historic and well-preserved momentos from famous royal dining rooms, inns and eating places dating from the year 1582. He included priceless souvenirs such as the first fork of Henry III, Napoleon's plates, Czar Alexander's mouth rinsing bowl, chairs from Edward VII and table services belonging to fifteen different kings. One outstanding menu was lent to Claude by Philippe de Rothschild which includes such dishes as stuffed donkey's head, bear steak and kangaroo set before guests during the siege of Paris. At the official opening of the museum were such notables as the Duke and Duchess of Segovia, Count Stanislas de La Rochefoucauld, Mr. and Mrs. Bertrand Taylor, Col. Daniel Sickles, Count and Countess A. de La Rochefoucauld, M. Jean Sablon, the historian M. Heron de Villefosse and M. Paul-Louis Weiller.

I could add another facet to Claude's sparkling possibilities–he could have been a journalist, I'm certain. Once he wrote to me from the South of France about a memorable birthday party for his father-in-law, Jack Warner, at the Cap d'Antibes, that was so vivid that when I wrote it up for the paper friends swore that I'd been there, though it was when I was in Deauville with my children.

"Cap d'Antibes A-Glitter" was the headline for my next column. "Friday at Cap d'Antibes was an unforgettable star-spangled night on land, sea and in the sky for the birthday of Mr. Jack Warner, celebrated in fabulous fashion at the Villa d'Aujourd'hui. Every one of the 200 people there was a celebrity or social figure of note, except for the eight police guards hired to protect the billions in jewels worn by the lovely lady guests.

In a festive, flowered setting, candlelighted tables were scattered on three terraces leading down to the sea, a dancefloor covered the entire patio, and magical light effects came from giant underwater projectors playing on the rocks. Guests were entertained by two orchestras and a bevy of beautiful dancing girls called "Miss Baron's Ballet" from Juan-les-Pins. At the appearance of the birthday cake, Mr. Jack Benny picked up a handy violin and played "Happy Birthday to You." Careful candle counters insist that there were only 38 candles on the cake. With a twinkle in his eye, the host explained that he believes in "picking a good age and sticking to it."

Among the impressive guests: Miss Lily Pons, Mrs. Serge Semenenko, Mr. and

A rare photograph of Paris' two top restauranteurs together: Claude Terrail of the Tour d'Argent and Louis Vaudable of Maxim's.

Mrs. Henry Fonda, Mr. and Mrs. Tony Martin (Cyd Charisse), Mrs. Florence Gould, Mr. and Mrs. David Wayne, Mrs. Pamela Churchill, M. and Mme. Claude Terrail (the host's daughter and son-in-law), Mr. and Mrs. Stavros Niarchos, Mrs. Jessie Donahue, Mr. Ted Straeter, Mr. and Mrs. Billy Rose, Comte and Comtesse de Lamaize, Mr. and Mrs. John Pochna, the Maharanee of Baroda, M. André Dubonnet, Mrs. Elyse Hunt, Miss Arlene Dahl, Mrs. Lorelle Hearst, M. Gianni Agnelli, Sir Simon and Lady Marks, Jacqueline de Ribes, Mr. and Mrs. A.F. Martell, Duke and Duchess de Segovia, Mr. and Mrs. Gilbert Kahn, Lord and Lady Orr-Lewis, Mr. and Mrs. Basil Goulandris, and Mr. and Mrs. Nicholas Goulandris. A more impressive celebrity guest list of the fifties did not exist.

Claude Terrail's father, André, was quoted as saying that his favorite possession was the Tour d'Argent, but he owned huge chunks of Paris property with hotels, offices and restaurants. The Terrail family home was on the corner of the Avenue George V and the Rue Pierre Charron (where banks and apartment houses now stand). Papa Terrail's view from his front windows was a convent where the nuns coming in and out might look like penguins from where he sat. When the convent was closed he bought the land and built the Hôtel George V, which opened at the end of the twenties. The family divided their time between Paris, a family château and a hunting lodge. Claude's life wasn't all fun and games; his father instilled a sense of learning, working and accomplishment in him at an early age. He learned to be Paris' first restaurateur from the bottom up, literally. One of his first jobs was in a basement kitchen, perfecting the art of pastry making and cake decorating. (He said he spent a lot of time looking through the grilled windows watching all the pretty legs going by.)

After several years of basic training in every corner of the Tour d'Argent, Claude Terrail was named director in 1947. From that moment on, he's had Paris at his feet from his tower overlooking the church of Notre-Dame, Paris' 100

Champagne...

steeples, the flowing Seine River and the statue of Sainte Geneviève watching over all. It's no wonder that Claude is a "history nut" when you think that Paris is 2045 years old, Notre-Dame took 167 years to build before it was completed in the year 1330, and dear Geneviève turned away Attila and his hordes on horses decorated with human heads before the year 500.

Today Claude Terrail still rules at the top of the Tour d'Argent. He has a beautiful Finnish wife, Tarja, and a bright teenage son named André who is learning his father's and grandfather's profession from the top of the tower to the famous wine cellars far under the street.

In the fifties American-Parisians such as I felt that Paris was a "petit village" with family-run enterprises like the Vaudables at Maxim's; Mme César Ritz and her son, Charles, at the Ritz; François Dupré at the Plaza Athénée, George V and La Trémoille, often seen at the races where he owned thoroughbreds or at art galleries and antique dealers buying something elegant and outstanding to decorate his hotels. The family Jammet owned Le Bristol, where eight Jammets worked in every department on the premises. The only family-owned palace hotel in Paris today is the Hôtel de Crillon on the Place de la Concorde, owned by the Taittinger family of the champagne bearing the same name.

Times have changed but, happily, Claude Terrail has not.

Paul (Getty) and I
at the Dali Ball given by
Raymundo de Larrain
in 1957.

Right after my column about the star-studded night on the Côte d'Azur, I began a Deauville dateline where glamorous "names" were everywhere you looked.

The summer of 1957 started out as what seemed like perfection. I found a tiny house in Deauville just one block from the seashore and three blocks in another direction to the casino. Deauville in those days was eye-boggling with celebrities and fabulous activities going on day and night. The casino tables were surrounded by the big spenders like Sam Spiegel, Darryl Zanuck, Bella Darvi, Simone Simon, the Dolly Sisters plus polo players, the horsey set and beautiful ballet dancers. Deauville was ideal for me because I could spend an entire day *en famille* and then dress up to the eyebrows for an evening in and around the casino, where I'd get enough news to fill my newspaper space. I was bursting with pride that I was able to rent this funny little cottage all by myself without asking for Jim's help. There were enough bedrooms and an additional pull-out bed in the living room, so I assured Jim there was plenty of room for him whenever he wanted to come. I added that if he preferred to be there when I was not in residence, I'd tell him in advance when I was going to take the train back to Paris to deliver my articles, pick up the mail and tend to various errands every week. He wasn't pleased; he looked downright annoyed that I seemed to have organized a summer without having to beg for help. He gave me a cold look and announced that he had made "other plans" for the season. I stewed over his attitude for a while, wanting appreciation for working hard, doing right by all, and making it easy for him to spend time with his daughters.

When I mentioned Jim's reaction–which I found strange–to Dorothy and David Schoenbrun, David looked at me and shook his head, "Maggi-bird, Jim's crazy with jealousy at your success–can't you see that?" That seemed even stranger to me. "What success?" I asked myself. "Is having your name in the paper with a postage-sized photo next to your columns 'success'?"

My worries over Jim and his moodiness plus the possibility that he felt some sort of professional jealousy were all put aside when I saw how happy Cathy, Janne, Catina, Marienette and the Big Black Bird were in their sunny summer home. We had only one bathroom but even that didn't seem to matter when everyone spent most of the time on the beach. Marienette did all her chores with a song on her lips and found herself a sun-drenched corner in the tiny back garden where she could work on her suntan while the laundry dried on the lines above her in the warm breeze. As soon as the sun went down and everyone was ready for bed, I sashayed over to the other world. In those days, "Papa" Albert took charge of a miniature Maxim's across from the casino. Ciro's was the place to see endless "fugitives from Paris" in the cozy, relaxed downstairs grill or the fancy gourmet restaurant upstairs where *habitués* included people like Aly Khan, Arthur Rubinstein, the artist Von Dongen, Porfirio Rubirosa, and George de Cuevas whose ballet was scheduled for ten performances in the jewelbox-like theater in the casino. In those days, no one thought it odd or unusual in Deauville for a lady dressed in a full-length evening gown to be by herself in the casino bar and restaurant because so many escorts were "tied up" at the gaming tables. It was such a current sight to see gorgeous creatures dripping in jewels, sitting alone, that I wrote about one outstanding lady in the lime-light who showed up with several escorts at one time so she'd never be alone.

Ballet nights in Deauville were ablaze with bejeweled beauties like Jacqueline de Ribes in the audience and prima ballerinas like Rosella Hightower on the stage. The pocket-sized theater with its cane-backed seats had walls completely lined in *toile de Jouy* (that pastel, country-patterned material created in 1759 in the village of Jouy-en-Josas), lending romantic charm and warmth to the atmosphere. Seen there on so many nights were the very young Count and Countess Michel d'Ornano, long before he and then she became Mayors of Deauville.

An ideal evening in Deauville for me was one that would begin with "Papa" Albert and his news of the "who's who" at Ciro's, where I'd have a *coupe* and maybe a bit of smoked salmon with a dab of caviar on top. After that, I'd march through the casino and into the ballet, knowing I'd run into friends and pick up some news on the way. The ballet was like a dream to me. I adored it and always felt uplifted and maybe even "on my toes" when I went out. One night when I was leaving, Bob Taplinger, Warner Brothers' Vice-President, called to me and asked if I'd like to join him and Mr. and Mrs. Serge Semenenko to go to Brummel's. This pleased me very much because it was a place where I would never go by myself. Happily I joined them and discovered that Aly Khan and Bettina were also at the party. We settled at a ringside table and the champagne began to flow far into the night. Russian-born American Serge Semenenko was a very successful Boston banker and his wife, Virginia (called "Ginny") was an animated blonde who was very fond of parties, so the mood was mellow and there was no big business talk possible with the loud orchestra going full blast. Just about the time I thought I'd better hurry home before I turned into a pumpkin, someone announced that we were all going to go over to Aly's house for breakfast. Serge let out a large "hur-ray!" saying that Aly served the best breakfast in town. Aly seemed enthusiastic at the idea as we all trailed out, down the street, past the Hôtel Normandy and into the back door of Aly's villa. Instead of going into a salon, Aly led the way down the back stairs into a huge kitchen of hotel proportions with a lengthy table in the mid-dle. Aly said he wasn't about to get his servants out of bed at that hour so we'd all have to pitch in. He started to line up eggs and bacon; Bettina got out the bread.

I couldn't help staring at Bettina as she was leaning over a breadboard, cut-ting big chunks from *baguettes* for our impromptu way-after-midnight supper. A quiet young woman with shiny hair hanging straight to her shoulders, she was wearing a simply-cut cover-up gown of sky gray jersey and not one bit of make-up. Remembering her so clearly when she was a top model in the Givenchy and Jacques Fath fashion shows, always dressed in the sexiest outfits and wearing lip-stick so red and thick that it hit your eyes like a stoplight at a busy intersection,

(left to right)
School chums,
Karim Khan and
Prince Alexander
of Yugoslavia
at Longchamp race track
with Karim's father,
Aly Khan.

it was hard to believe that this was the same Bettina. She was smart because the new Bettina was exactly as Aly Khan wished her to be and she was the one he wanted to live with and keep by his side, despite his countless fly-by-night-and-day escapades.

Everybody was so busy doing something that they looked like bees in a hive and made just about as much noise buzzing around. Ginny was banging skillets from the wall to plunk on the huge stove while the gentlemen were emptying drawers and cupboards for the wherewithal to set the table. I felt rather useless until I saw Aly struggling to uncork a bottle of champagne. I'd found my night's duty. "Here," I said, "Let me do that" and he laughed heartily as he handed it to me, saying "You think you can do it?" He didn't know that Claude, the barman at the Ritz, had shown me the trick of opening champagne without a struggle, without a noise and without spilling a drop. Aly looked on in disbelief as I handed him the uncorked bottle almost as fast as he'd handed it to me. "Look," he announced to everyone, "The champion opener" and he gave me another bottle to see if I could perform again. "Well, it's nice to be a champion of SOMETHING" I laughed, as everyone looked impressed.

After that evening and early morning breakfast, I often saw Aly Khan in the daytime taking his little daughter, Yasmina, across the avenue to the riding ring where she'd ride the horses around and around for seemingly hours on end.

Sometimes he stayed near the stable and sometimes he'd go back to his villa

Champagne...

where he could observe her from the huge bay window. When I'd pass him and Yasmina while I was with Cathy and Janne, we would nod a neighborly greeting but not stop to talk. In the evening however, he would sometimes come over to me at the casino and say friendly things like, "Have you opened any good bottles lately?" and once he told me he thought my white brocade evening gown with its tulle stole strewn with forget-me-nots was "very stunning." When I thanked him and then added that I thought he'd seen this outfit at least three times that week he answered that he didn't care how many times he had seen it, "It's still stunning," he said. I liked him after that; he seemed like a regular guy to me.

My "regular guy" opinion of Aly Khan was not shared by my American-born friend, Countess Eugenia Gaetani di Laurenzana. Married to an Italian, she was born Jean Byfield in Chicago, the stepdaughter of film maker Mervyn LeRoy (of *Madame Curie, Mr. Roberts, Random Harvest* fame). When we first met at Maxim's she gave me her card with all of her names engraved on it. I gasped and said, "Wow, with all those names, what do people call you?" and she answered, "Mousie." I liked her. She was pretty and funny and we got along fine. She was decorating a new apartment in Paris at the time and had a little daughter, Katherina, about the same age as mine, so we spent some Sundays in each other's company. Then one day she confided in me that Aly Khan was calling her up and sending her masses of red roses but she didn't know whether she should accept his invitations. If she expected advice from me, I didn't say anything more than "Just do what you want to do, Mousie." (There was no way that I'd repeat what the old Aga Khan had said about his son.)

Well, she did accept his invitations and seemed to be taking him seriously until it became obvious to her that she was just one of his many dates while she wanted to be a one-and-only. Finally she dumped him and she also dumped his roses upside down in a wastebasket in the salon where all her friends could see what she thought of Aly. No matter how hard Aly tried after that, she wouldn't see him or even talk to him on the telephone. A few years later, her mother, Kitty LeRoy, told me that Aly Khan's name was "mud" in the whole family. He sold Mervyn LeRoy a thoroughbred racehorse with great credentials but when the horse was shipped to the United States the LeRoys discovered he was blind in one eye.

Chapter Eighteen

Paris, 1957/58 was star-gazing paradise. Columns were filled with news about celebrities in town every week like Errol Flynn, Eddie Albert, Trevor Howard and Juliette Gréco, who were filming *Roots of Heaven* in Paris studios under the direction of John Huston and the watchful eye of producer Darryl Zanuck (who'd bought a luxurious showplace apartment on the Rue de Bac). The Vaudables closed Maxim's to the public long enough for the film, *Gigi,* to be made on the premises where Leslie Caron, Maurice Chevalier, Louis Jourdan, Hermione Gingold and Eva Gabor were working hard by day, and seen on many a social scene when they were not filming. Sophia Loren came to town to be wined and dined, but her real reason was to find a fabulous gown to wear at London's gala opening of *The Key* in the presence of Princess Margaret. In and out of Paris all the time to take a penthouse suite at the Hôtel de Crillon was Gloria Swanson with daughter, Michelle, who looked like Jean Seberg with her short-cut hairdo. Lewis Bredin gave a party for Gloria in his new home where I saw Betty and Henri Lanson, Roger Dann and my loving friend, Dorothy de Piolenc.

Enjoying friends while star-gazing for my name-dropping reports was easy when I went to Marion and Irwin Shaw's parties. Irwin was selling his books such as *The Young Lions* to the movies by then and every time someone from Hollywood arrived in Paris, it was an excuse to have a celebration. It was at the Shaws that I first met Joan Fontaine, looking very blonde and slim, sitting on a lime green velvet couch. I gave her a big smile when we were introduced and said, "Hi, I'm a friend of your sister's." She snapped, "Oh, really," turning her back to me to talk to the gentleman seated beside her. (It was much later that I learned there was no love lost between Olivia de Havilland and Joan Fontaine.) Tyrone Power was at the Shaws but he didn't stay long because David Stein promised to set up a blind date for him with a local beauty at the Hôtel Lancaster. (David was an expert blind date maker; he fixed a date for Clark Gable once just for dinner and the date lasted for months.) It was at the Shaws that I got my first close-up look at Simone Simon, another of my teenage idols (never dreaming at the time what good friends we'd become, and that I would give the celebration lunch for her 80th birthday many years later); plus Annabella, former wife of Tyrone Power, and the gorgeous covergirl, Sophie, with her husband, Anatole Litvak. That night's guest list included old friends like Dorothy and David Schoenbrun and Ginette Spanier from Balmain, with her husband, Dr. Paul-Emile Seidmann. Ginette was wearing three shades of black including black mink, black wool and black satin. She told me she was writing a book about her wartime experiences as well as her life in the fashion world, called *It Isn't All Mink*. My sidekick Eve Max was there in a beautiful, long-sleeved, ivory silk dress. Before the evening was over, she had rolled up her sleeves and was tending the logs in the fireplace. It was an animated party. Sophie Litvak ended up playing cowboys and Indians with the Shaws' 10-year-old son, Adam.

For Otto Preminger's midnight supper party at Maxim's after the gala showing of his *Joan of Arc* film at the Paris Opéra, Mme. Alice lent a bugle-beaded white chiffon gown, from Balenciaga's current collection, which was so fragile that I didn't enjoy one second of that beautiful affair. Before dinner, every time I saw someone smoking a cigarette, I'd take flight in another direction. When we sat down at the table for a fabulous feast, I was so scared I'd spill something that I barely lifted a fork. But maybe it was all for the best because I could concentrate on my mental list of guests to go in my column. Never had I seen so many to remember: Bob Hope, Anita Ekberg, Olivia de Havilland, Paul Getty, Anthony Steele, Eddie Constantine, Ludwig Bemelmans, Jeanne Moreau, Raymundo de Larrain, Honeychile Wilder (who was now Princess Hohenlohe), Salvador Dali, Jean-Pierre Aumont, Maurice Chevalier, Graham Greene, Vincente Minnelli, Louise de Vilmorin and the Countess de Gaetani. This was actress Jean Seberg's introduction to the celebrity world of Otto Preminger. Before the evening was over I asked Otto if he'd be a guest speaker at the next American's Women's Club luncheon. He not only agreed but promised to bring his teenage star, Jean, with him. All during the evening I kept noticing a sinister-looking man who didn't take his eyes off the sexy Anita Ekberg. Otto laughed heartily when I asked him who that mysterious fellow might be. "He's a guard from Cartier," laughed Otto. "Anita borrowed that 300,000-dollar diamond thing she's got on her head."

Irwin Shaw hosted a big-time Maxim's gala of his own when his story *Lucy Crown* became a Paris theater piece starring Jean-Pierre Aumont. The first night had a brilliant audience and most of them showed up at Maxim's for a supper party afterwards, where I could gaze at a lady-in-red, Ingrid Bergman, escorted by Lars

Anita Ekberg wore a Cartier necklace on her head at Otto Preminger's Maxim's dinner after the showing of *Saint Joan* at the Paris Opéra.

Champagne...

Marlène Dietrich often went to Maxim's, but she really liked to make
pot-au-feu at home for her friends.

Schmidt (before anyone guessed they'd marry); newlyweds M. and Mme. Jean-Baptiste de Vilmorin; supposedly engaged couple Brigitte Bardot and Sacha Distel; singer Colette Mars; and of course, Jean-Pierre Aumont and his wife, Marisa Pavan, along with Marion and Irwin Shaw; and once again, Ginette Spanier and her husband, Dr. Paul-Émile Seidmann. They were always full of chatter every time we met and I heard items for my columns because they had so many celebrity friends. It was Ginette who told me that Claudette Colbert was planning on settling down in Paris and that Laurence Olivier and Vivien Leigh were "hiding out" at her house, but "please don't print that until they've gone back to London."

The Spanier-Siedmann story I liked best concerned their dear friend Marlene Dietrich, who loved to stay with them when the fans hanging around outside her Hôtel George V got too troublesome for her. Ginette and Paul-Émile had a luxurious apartment on the Avenue Marceau connected with his doctor's offices. Marlene loved to houseguest with them. She would kick off her shoes on arrival and hot-foot it to the kitchen to cook up something delicious, acting like the true "haus frau" she was. She stayed with them so often that she seemed part of the family. One evening she arrived at Ginette's to find that Noel Coward was occupying the only guest room. Marlene still wanted to stay so she settled herself in the doctor's office, insisting that she'd be perfectly happy on his couch. The next morning she handed Paul-Émile a list of messages with his breakfast, explaining that his telephone had rung several times; she'd answered and written down everything that was said. Little did those patients know that their doctor's assistant was Marlene Dietrich.

Sophie and Anatole Litvak gave a party in their private apartment to honor Deborah Kerr and Yul Brynner before they took off for Vienna with Tola Litvak to film *The Journey*. Sophie, a top flight model and cover girl before her marriage, appeared in an ice-blue satin sheath covered in black chantilly lace. It was breathtaking and several guests tried to guess which dressmaker had created it until Sophie confessed that she'd made it herself. That night Yul Brynner was with his wife of long date, actress Virginia Gilmore (it was soon after that he met a young dental assistant in Paris named Doris Kleiner, who swept him off his feet). Kay Kendall and her husband, Rex Harrison, were standing next to me cursing about journalists in general, with words so bad that I kept out of their way for the rest of the night. Jean-Pierre Aumont and his wife Marisa Pavan came over to me and congratulated me on my good guessing–I'd been so sure that they were going to have a baby boy when I'd seen them a few months before that I'd put it in writing for them and now they were proud parents of a brand new son, born in California a few weeks before.

Whenever I was invited to David Stein's town house for a dinner party, I knew

Champagne...

Yul Brynner dined at Maxim's next to *Coco Chanel's* star mannequin, Marie-Hélène Arnaud. Wine steward, Monsieur Palmier, poured.

it would be a night of star-gazing and I'd find plenty to write about. One night he hosted a birthday party to honor Audrey Wilder, the wife of film maker Billy Wilder, who was in Paris shooting *Love In The Afternoon* with Audrey Hepburn and Gary Cooper. They all showed up that night. Audrey Hepburn was in a Givenchy wasp-waisted black evening dress with lots of petticoats and wore immaculate white kid gloves that just barely covered her hands and were buttoned with one tiny pearl button at the wrist. I liked those little white gloves so much that I bought several pairs for myself and pushed the longer ones to the back of the drawer. (I wore those "shorties" with everything except strapless evening gowns that called for gloves so long they almost reached the shoulder.)

I loved Audrey Hepburn. She was sweet and funny. During the evening, when a gentleman guest tried to put his arm around her waist, she stepped away and said, "Hey, I'm a married lady," which said everything in a delicate way. Another guest at the party that night was the musician and composer, Matty Melnick, who was doing the music for *Love In The Afternoon*. He was teasing me and said that he'd write a song for me inspired by another composer's *Stella by Starlight,* but he'd call his *Maggi by Moonshine,* which inspired Audrey to quip, "Opening words can be...in the STILL of the night."

The celebration dinner as always *chez* Stein had a marvelous menu, starting with caviar and going through course after course of gourmet delights, right up to the cloud-light angel cake baked especially for Audrey Wilder's birthday. I was writing my report in my head all through the meal and was delighted at the angel cake because it was baked by the cook named Gabrielle. ("Angel Gabrielle," see?) The surprise of the evening was Gary Cooper, who sat in silence the whole night and refused all food except some red wine and Camembert cheese. I couldn't get over the difference between Gary and Cary. How could ANYONE get them mixed up?

David was a marvelous host but he could get a guest into trouble with the great amount of fine wines, champagnes, cognacs and liqueurs he poured out. He had one special after-dinner drink that could do you in if you didn't watch out. He'd soak fresh full peaches in brandy for heaven knows how long, plunk them into the bottom of giant snifters and pour iced champagne over that. This drink was glorious to taste but could knock you for a loop. The first time I tried it I went around with a head as heavy as the Eiffel Tower for days. Afterward, I named that drink "sneaky peach" and warned anyone around who might be worth saving.

When I wasn't star-gazing, luxurious parties in private homes were ideal places for people reports. The guests had known names, the clothes and jewels were dazzling, the chitchat often newsworthy and, of course, food and wine was divinely served by gloved servants who made careers of their art.

There were outstanding hosts and hostesses of various nationalities such as George de Cuevas, Chilean-born founder of the most exciting ballet appearing in Paris. Invitations to his private *soirées* in his Quai Voltaire home introduced a whole new international social scene.

Through an ancient archway, up massive stone stairs into a marble hall leading into high-ceilinged salons overlooking the Seine River, it was "old world" at its most impressive. Every antique table, chair, statue, painting, crystal chandelier and even the rug on which you stood was a work of art. Still one could feel right at home in this splendor because the warm, Chilean-Spanish host could make you feel like his priceless possessions were there to please the guests. (In those days I didn't ask, or even think about where the money came from to make all this possible. It wasn't until Dominick Dunne did his thorough investigative reporting for *Vanity Fair* that I learned of the Rockefeller connection–George's wife was a granddaughter of John D. Rockefeller.) It was at these parties that I met a dashing polo player, Juan Capurro, who had a diplomatic post in Paris for Uruguay, but didn't seem to have much time for duty when his days were spent on the polo grounds and his nights at Maxim's and L'Éléphant Blanc. George introduced me to Marie-Louise Bousquet, a fashionable hostess of note who had a "salon" for artists, writers and intellectuals (where I met one of her discoveries, Bernard Buffet). George presented his protégé, Marquis Raymundo de Larrain, whom he said was his nephew.

At George's parties, I was elbow to elbow with a vivacious black-eyed beauty Jacqueline de Ribes, whom I'd admired from afar for months before in Paris and

Champagne...

Deauville. The first time I saw her *chez* Cuevas she was wearing a chic, black velvet dress with white mink collar and cuffs, which I admired and learned from her that she had made it herself. It looked like perfect *haute couture* and I wasn't a bit surprised when she was named one of the best-dressed women in the world and when she started designing her own fashion collections professionally. Among the many seen on the Cuevas scene: Baroness Frederic de Cabrol, whom everyone called Daisy; Arturo Lopez, who married a lady named Patricia Willshaw and changed his name to Arturo Lopez-Willshaw; and more impressive titles than you could shake a swizzle stick at like Princess de Bourbon-Parme; Duchess di Sangro; and Infanta Pilar of Spain, granddaughter of King Alfonso; plus Princess Niloufer, granddaughter of the last Sultan of Turkey, who later married an American businessman named Edward Pope. The genial host, George de Cuevas, always had a special drink in his hand which he sipped throughout the evening, made with champagne and fresh raspberries. He called it his "French ice cream soda."

Those were beautifully enchanting evenings *chez* Cuevas, but in all the times I went to that exquisite Quai Voltaire party place, I never saw the host's wife, Margaret Strong de Cuevas or their two children, Elizabeth and John.

Since the death of the Marquis George de Cuevas, creator of the outstanding successful Ballet de Cuevas, a lot has been written about whether or not he was a Marquis and that the young Marquis Raymundo de Larrain was neither a marquis nor George's nephew. In the fifties however, nobody seemed terribly interested in that sort of thing as long as he was such a talented and friendly man with friends who truly adored him, like Jacqueline de Ribes, who did a great deal to boost him to the top, socially and professionally.

One of the most amusing gala nights at a private home during all these cocktails, dinners and balls I attended was the one André Dubonnet hosted with his daughters, Lorraine and France, in his showplace home in Neuilly. More than 200 black-tied and long-gowned guests arrived at his gate to enter his house and take the elevator up-up to the glassed-in terrace penthouse for an all-night dinner and dance overlooking a park across the boulevard which André had spotlighted for the event. Champagne flowed like the water fountains around town gifted to Paris by a do-gooder named Richard Wallace; a cha-cha orchestra played for dancing specially hired from the *Babar Blanc*; and there were countless celebrities everywhere you looked, like Tina Onassis and the Maharanee of Baroda. The eye-catching star attraction was Brigitte Bardot, dressed in miles and miles of black and white ruffles, who showed everyone how the cha-cha should be danced with Count Guy d'Arangues from Biarritz. Someone arrived with hula-hoops, which were just becoming a Left Bank craze; and Tina Onassis, all in white with blazing diamonds and emeralds, got up to show us all that she'd mastered the hula-hoop-hoopla, while B.B., not to be outdone, joined in the fun. At one high point of the party, I went to the luxuriously-furbished ladies' room in the penthouse where the loo was encased in glass that the user could see out of but the others powdering their noses

Lorraine Dubonnet and Gerard Bonnet came to my party for Dorothy Kilgallen. I wore the pink satin Balmain coat that got caught in a door a year later in London when I dashed to meet the Queen.

could not see into. I knew my way there but the trouble that night was that there were countless ladies lined up to use the facilities. When I came out disappointed, the host was nearby and I went to tell him that there were about a dozen ladies waiting in there. He beckoned for me to go downstairs, pointing to a door below and then putting his finger to his lips, saying, "Shhh." Happily I pranced downstairs, into a bedroom with its private bathroom and felt privileged, indeed! Alas, when I came out, there was André standing all alone in the room. "Ooo-la-la," I thought, "I'm in trouble." He stepped toward me while I was trying to figure out how I'd solve my problem, but it dissolved right then when his little gray poodle started howling and barking outside, flinging his furry little body and scratching his sharp little claws against the door. I started laughing so hard I was bent double and André did the same. He opened up to the excited creature who was so happy to see his master that he didn't think to bark at me or bother to bite. "I think Elyse Hunt told that dog to see that you behave yourself while she's gone," I giggled as we returned to the party upstairs.

I got acquainted with André's daughters, especially Lorraine, who married a broker named Gérard Bonnet and changed her name from Dubonnet to Bonnet. That made lines in my column: here's a lady who dropped the "du" in her name instead of adding a "du" or a "de" like a lot of them did. (*Lorraine has a darling daughter named Catherine Bonnet, who can be found in the PR department of Louis*

Champagne...

Vuitton at this writing.) The famous Dubonnet party place was sold to the King of Morocco and became the residence of the Moroccan Ambassador to France.

Gérard and Lorraine Bonnet had a lovely country home in Ville d'Avray where they did some delightful entertaining. One night their guests of honor were Porfirio Rubirosa and his bride, Odile Rodin, but they didn't arrive alone. Rubi brought a four-piece orchestra with him to play for the 20 guests all through the night. Showing up on that scene were Ruth Dubonnet, Mrs. Barney Balaban, David Stein, Ray Ventura, Willy Rizzo, Prince and Princess Albert Poniatowski and a New York composer named Jule Styne, who wrote songs like *It's Magic, Three Coins in the Fountain, I've Heard That Song Before* and *Saturday Night Is the Loneliest Night of the Week.* He was a delightful fellow, looking like an owl in his horn-rimmed glasses. When I asked him if people didn't get him mixed up with David's brother, Jules Stein, he told me that his name actually was the same but he had changed his spelling so there'd be a difference. Then he told me that once David's brother, Jules, had asked Jule to change his name to something like Dick Ford and led him over to a mirror on the wall and said, "Look, you're Dick Ford." Jule said he looked and looked and he sure didn't see anybody except Jule Styne, so that settled that. Before the night at the Bonnets was over, Jule was playing the piano, accompanied by the musicians the Rubirosas had brought, and it was Rubi himself leading the orchestra.

Private parties with Sir Charles Mendl were always sure to give me notable quotes and bits of banter to fill my space. He'd been a British diplomat around Europe and the USA for many years and loved to surround himself with amusing, interesting, important personalities. When I got acquainted with him, he was a widower (having been married to Elsie de Wolfe, an American interior decorator who collected fabulous furniture and art objects as well as outstanding people around her everywhere she went).

I considered Sir Charles Mendl a good friend of mine until he got to be of a certain age and stage of his life that people called "gaga." From friendly "hellos" that I once got from him, I became fortunate indeed if his eyes even focused in my direction. Never mind, I still had fond memories of happy luncheon parties in his apartment on the Avenue d'Iéna. Waiting in the marble entry for Sir Charles to greet you, you might hear whistling in the distance. When someone asked him why he whistled all the time, he answered because he couldn't sing. On his mantelpiece was a personally-inscribed photo from the Queen Mother. On an end table there was a pile of gold coins melted together to form a decorative paperweight which was engraved on the underside with the signatures of the Duke and Duchess of Windsor, with the message: "Your friendship is worth more than a pile of gold." Another photograph of the Queen Mother was taken with Lady Jebb and her daughters. "Look at all those beautiful English ladies," he'd say proudly.

Sometimes at the luncheon table Sir Charles would announce to guests that he was quite deaf and no one should mind if he didn't listen to the conversations going on but just go on as though he wasn't there. One time however, two of his gentlemen guests began gossiping about their mutual friend, Joan Fontaine. Sir Charles started tapping his fork against the glass saying, "Speak up! Speak up! You know I'm hard of hearing!"

Once at a lunch party in his apartment he was urging everyone to be sure and see the revival of the film *Notorious*, which was being shown on the Champs-Élysées. He pointed out that it was made in Hollywood when he lived there and he had a bit part in it, standing in magnificent sailing attire. He chuckled and said he got the handsome sum of 2,000 dollars just for looking elegant. By this time, Sir Charles was beginning to forget names and had to be reminded that the stars of that film he was in were Cary Grant and Ingrid Bergman. "Oh, yes, I remember them," he chuckled, "They were pretty good too!"

The last time I saw Sir Charles Mendl was at a Sunday luncheon in his honor given by Paul-Louis Weiller in one of his historic houses on the Rue de la Faisanderie, which the Duchess of Windsor attended. Next to me was a pretty girl with flashing blue eyes whose placecard read "Pamela Churchill." Of course I had seen her at countless parties, but had never gotten a chance to talk to her. During the lunch served at one large, oval-shaped table for about twenty guests, I said to Pamela that I hoped she did not mind having me on her left instead of a gentleman, but it looked like there weren't enough men to go around. She didn't say whether or not she minded but just looked at the Duchess of Windsor across the table and said, "It's her fault," explaining that since David didn't lunch with Wally but preferred to play golf instead, that's what a lot of men did these days.

When I wrote up the birthday luncheon honoring Sir Charles Mendl, I didn't mention that poor Charles was gaga by then. He turned in the middle of the meal and asked who that creature standing behind him was and what was she doing there. He had to be told that she was his long-time private nurse. I didn't mention the lack of gentlemen either, but I did go on and on about the fabulous food and the fine wines and what the Duchess was wearing. After this column, I got upset with the men on the newsdesk. This was the first and only time I ever complained to Eric Hawkins about someone changing my copy. I had carefully mentioned turkey with whole truffles accompanied by rare Château Clos Vougeot 1923. Someone on the newsdesk crossed out "accompanied by" and changed it to "washed down with." I was horrified, thinking that anyone who knew anything about fine dining would be shocked by such a vulgar phrase, and it would be humiliating for me to face my friends. Eric Hawkins agreed and said he'd make a rule that no one touch my copy unless he gave the order. I don't think that made me very popular with the "boys in the backroom."

Chapter Nineteen

It seemed like no time at all after starting my column for the Paris *Herald Tribune* that I began to have "pen pals" of the highest quality with ability to communicate very printable information. One of the first and finest was Princess Grace of Monaco. When Princess Caroline was only a few months old, journalists started reporting that another little Monégasque was on its way. I sat down and wrote a little note to the Princess in her palace asking if what I was reading was true. That sweet lady sat down herself and penned a lovely answer in her beautifully clear and distinctive handwriting, which I was able to print word for word under the heading "MOTHER KNOWS BEST: The newspapers always know more about these things than I do—However, these rumors are bound to be true sooner or later as we both would like more children. Princess Caroline is adorable and already has a special smile for her daddy. Kindest regards, *Grace de Monaco*."

After that, I received notes from her whenever anything was coming up in Monte Carlo which she thought would be of interest and I started to get printed information and engraved invitations from the palace Chief of Protocol, Count "Buddy" d'Aillieres. Happily for me, my name was added to the invitation list for Paris events where I met Prince Rainier's father, Prince Pierre of Monaco, at the next official celebration in Paris commemorating Monaco's national holiday. Funny me, it was the first time I realized that my chum, Prince Louis de Polignac, was Rainier's cousin. (He was godfather of newborn Prince Albert.) More "headline" news came from Princess Grace when she was named the best-hatted woman in the world by the American Millinery Institute. The prize wasn't a hat; she received a gold mesh pin from Van Cleef & Arpels.

The next precious piece of mail from Monaco was a photograph of Prince Rainier and little Caroline on the occasion of her first birthday party with the news that a Russian-born American composer, Dr. Avenir de Monfred, had written a symphony dedicated to Princess Caroline which would be played on her birthday over Radio Monte Carlo by an 80-piece orchestra.

After that I received loads of news from Monaco and felt sometimes that

Monte Carlo was almost a part of Paris. Once I received a very personal note from "Grace of Monaco" which is the only one I've kept all these years—but that came later.

My favorite "star pen pal" of the fifties was Olivia de Havilland. After writing my one-page report on her Paris life for *Realities* I was relaxed whenever we met and discovered she had a sharp wit and big brain under that curly head of hers. She didn't do much socializing in restaurants and I never saw her in a nightclub; she was more apt to be seen at the American Women's Club or an American church or on a committee for a charity affair. She'd also signed up with the American government as a "Dollar-a-Year-Girl," which meant that she'd visit any and all American military installations where she could visit with U.S. soldiers. When I heard about this, I asked her if she'd drop me a note about places she'd be visiting and projects she'd be undertaking and she gracefully agreed. After that, I received all sorts of news from her with amusing remarks like the time she figured she had only earned 18 cents of the dollar the government was going to pay her that year, so she had to get busy and make some more appearances before ringing in the new year. Once when she was appearing before a mixed group of French and American soldiers, she left the high-ranking officers all around her to march down to the mass of French boys and greeted one in particular named Francis, with a big *bonjour* and a hearty handshake. Francis was the hairdresser sent by M. Alexandre when Olivia was filming *The Ambassador's Daughter* in Paris with Myrna Loy, Edward Arnold and John Forsythe, and she'd not forgotten. He was so proud and happy, becoming an instant big shot in the mass of recruits.

Olivia sent many beautifully hand-written pages when she was on location making a film called *The Proud Rebel* with Alan Ladd and his son, David, in Utah, 6,500 feet above sea level. Between shooting, she explored a lot of the surrounding territory and conversed with a man coming out of a mine whom she thought was a local yokel, but he turned out to be a visiting psychiatrist. Farther on, she asked some sheepherders who had a giant-sized shotgun fastened to a horse's saddle if the gun was "for people" and one of her newfound friends said, "Now, Miss, don't go believing we're as bad as you're making us in your movie." It was before I ever had enough nerve to ask the darling Olivia about her love scenes with Alan Ladd. Did HE climb up on a box or was SHE standing in a hole? (On July 1st, 1993, when I celebrated Olivia de Havilland's birthday with her in Paris at the Club Interalliée, I finally asked her. She said the director, Mike Curtiz, shot love scenes on a hill with Alan Ladd standing a few steps above her. "Very uncomfortable!" she added.)

Artist, writer, humorist, bon vivant, Ludwig Bemelmans was a friend who became a truly newsworthy correspondent every time he left Paris to travel around Europe. He was a colorful Austrian-born American artist and writer who had a sparkle and gleam in his eye which he was able to put into words and illustrations for his Madeleine book series featuring a little girl living in France. When he heard that I had two daughters around the same age as his Madeleine (inspired by his own daughter, Barbara) he went right over to the Rue de Rivoli and bought two of his own books to inscribe to Cathy and Kiki, which they still have today. "Bemmy," as he was called, was an *habitué* of the Crazy Horse Saloon where he was greeted as the Prince of Bavaria and given a special corner "box" with plenty of elbow room while other guests perched on low stools so close together that it sometimes seemed to reach steam bath temperatures.

Whenever Bemmy went on trips around Europe, he'd send me short notes in his gigantic scrawl, a few words on each page. He always wrote about himself in the third person. Once I received a letter telling me about his pal, John Huston, wanting Bemelmans to act in a film.

He had agreed to play a part in a Huston film to be made in Japan but happened to read what the movie was about when he was en route. *Townsend Harris* was a wartime film of violence, starvation, disease and wild rats. He said he knew John well enough to know he was a realist to the bitter end and he didn't want a part of it. After sending me that little snippet he came back to Paris, went to Maxim's, drank a whole bottle of champagne, penned a note saying "NO JOHN NO" on the back of a menu, rolled it up, placed it inside the empty bottle and shipped it off to Huston.

Bemmy decided to stay in Paris and finish enough paintings for a show which was attended by ambassadors' wives, Mrs. David K.E. Bruce and Mrs. Amory Houghton, plus Anita Loos, Marie-Louise Bousquet, Charles de Beistegui, Princess Elisabeth of Liechtenstein and Dodo de Hambourg (his favorite Crazy Horse dancer).

Another time I got a card saying "Wait til you hear about Bemelmans' big escape." A few days later he was back in Paris to recount the horrible adventure he'd had in a private clinic in Switzerland, where he went to lose weight on the advice of our mutual friend, John Ringling North. "They starved me, Maggi," he wailed; "I was dying!" But he escaped from the clinic through the bottom of the garden in the middle of the night to find his way back to Paris and a good meal. Bemmy was brilliant. He sold the story of his mishaps to an American magazine for lots of money, much more than he'd paid to get into the clinic in the first place.

Soon after we met, he started calling me *suppenwurze*, explaining that where he came from there was a certain kind of flavoring you put in dishes to give them a special zest called *maggi suppenwurze*, and he decided that I was the special flavoring in the Paris *Herald*. I said, "Thanks for the compliment, I THINK!" and he assured me that it was.

As a little gift for me one time, he sent away for a copy of his book, *Father, Dear Father*, which he inscribed to "*suppenwurze*" with love. (Today Bemelman's paintings adorn the Carlyle Hotel Bar in New York.)

John Ringling North liked to stay up all night in Paris but I only tried
that once—at Sheherazade in 1956.

Dorian Leigh was an American-Parisian of the fifties who was lovely to look at
as a top "Cover Girl" but also delightful to know because she was witty and smart.
She came to Paris as a top model, famous for her "Fire & Ice" advertisements for
Revlon. Every *haute couture* season brought her to Paris to pose in the newest
French fashions. I think of these days as Dorian's "B.S. time," which means
"before Suzy," (before her baby sister, Suzy Parker, whom Dorian taught to model,
became famous). In the early days Dorian was the star of the family as the oldest
of four Texas beauties: Dorian, Florian, Georgibell and Suzy. I met Dorian for the
first time at the Buchwald home on Thanksgiving and discovered that she had a
sense of humor that made you laugh at everything she said but afterward, you
couldn't remember exactly what she said that was so funny. After several yearly
jaunts to Paris for the fashions she decided to stay. It was she who opened the first
modeling agency in Paris and later, another one in London. But the first night of
our meeting I found out something else about this glamorous creature. She had a
passionate interest in cooking and took more peeks into the kitchen to check out
the turkey and trimmings than she paid attention to the guests in the living room.
Years later it was no surprise to me when she opened her own restaurant on the

outskirts of Paris. Today she writes cookbooks and contributes impressive articles to magazines like *Gourmet*.

Dorian and I didn't have much more than a superficial, social friendship in the beginning of our acquaintance because of the lack of time and the difference in our careers, but we had the chance to know each other as years went on. The fifties were times when I knew her as a precious asset to a party; she showed up looking gorgeous and never failed to amuse and delight her fellow guests. Once she arrived at one of my formal dinners in a truly amazing gown that caught the eye of everyone. It was deep red taffeta, draped dramatically around her shapely frame and decorated with one gigantic brooch on her left shoulder. When I remarked at how outstanding her dress was, she told me it wasn't really a dress. She had wrapped ten yards of taffeta round and round herself just before coming to the party. I swear I don't know how she kept herself together that evening, but she did.

Another time, Dorian invited me to dinner at her favorite Italian restaurant. In the middle of the main course she screeched, called for the head waiter and announced, "There's a spider in my spaghetti," pointing to her plate. He bowed to her and whispered that the object she saw there was actually one of her false eyelashes which had fallen from her face. Dorian was such a good sport, she roared with laughter, plucked the eyelash out of the plate, pulled the other one off, wrapped them in a handkerchief, tucked them into her handbag and went merrily on through the night.

In all my days at the Paris *Herald* (sometimes I called them my "daze") I don't think I regretted one second of those overworked and underpaid moments. As Dorothy Schoenbrun wrote of our lives then, "Even the bad days were good." There were times, of course, when you couldn't be with close, longtime friends and would find yourself surrounded by acquaintances of the moment. Then again, there was the chance that acquaintances today could be longlasting friends of the future. In those hectic times I didn't have many moments alone with Dorothy and David. We were all "on the run" and I didn't entertain at home anymore. I did try to keep up with everything David was doing; I mentioned in print every time he had a book published or gave a speech somewhere. When his book, *As France Goes* came out, I was writing about it in the office when one of the wags on the newsdesk suggested that I rename it *France Has Gotta Go*. (I didn't print THAT.) The Schoenbruns were always giving glorious dinner parties with top flight politicians and diplomats but every time they invited me, I felt like a dumb-dumb trying to follow their high-level discussions and, worse yet, I'd come away with nothing to write about except to list the names of the guests around the dinner table. One time I was thrilled when David asked me if I would do a professional favor for him–sit with a famous woman lawyer, Maître Suzanne Blum, while she was being televised in her own home during a live overseas broadcast of "Small World" with Judge Welch and Ed Murrow in New York, and Lord Birkitt in London. I accepted and found myself in a fabulous Left Bank duplex so full of books that it looked like an annex to the National Library. She was a brilliant international lawyer, the legal representative of the Ministry of Foreign Affairs and a legal advisor for American film makers operating in France, as well as being an author of several books and the recipient of several citations and decorations. I couldn't see how she thought I could help her, but she admitted frankly that she was scared out of her brilliant bean of "freezing" in front of the television equipment and forgetting everything she ever knew how to say in English. She performed beautifully, even going so far as to correct Ed Murrow when he kept calling her "Madame," explaining that a woman lawyer in France is not addressed "Madame" but "Maître," please. She did alright; I didn't seem to be of any use. But afterward, she disagreed with me when I said she hadn't needed me at all. "Yes, I did," she insisted. She explained that just seeing me there, ready to help her if she faltered, gave her the confidence she needed. I liked her a lot and happily reported to David how well everything went. I never imagined that day how important she would become in my life in the not too distant future. Nor could anyone have predicted at the time that this brilliant lawyer would be the one to arrange the auction of the Duchess of Windsor's jewels to benefit the Pasteur Institute, now dedicated to cancer and AIDS research.

Often I went to have a cup of coffee with Dorothy Thorp de Piolenc, who had tired of hotel existence and taken a top floor-apartment at the Étoile on the Rue La Pérouse. There was always something going on at her place. All sorts of people were drawn to her–ex-nobility, embassy officials, doctors, ballet dancers, dressmakers, artists, and a smattering of the very famous like Gloria Swanson and Ginger Rogers. She had a beautiful Bechstein piano on which I first heard Siegi Wiessenberg (before he changed his name to Alexis and became an international concert pianist). It was at Dorothy's that I met Gweneth Dulles, an English lady who had been married to Harrison Dulles, cousin of John Foster Dulles. Gwen had a luxurious apartment overlooking the Avenue Foch, an apartment in London and a property in the center of France. (Dorothy told me I hadn't lived until I took a spin in Gwen's 1928 Rolls Royce, saying every time she got into it she felt like Queen Victoria.) It was at Dorothy's that I first met the most animated American lady in Paris, Elmore Caruthers Richmond from Memphis, Tennessee. She had the energy of a cheerleader and an infectious laugh that made every day seem like the 4th of July. It was Elmore who introduced me to Dr. Pierre Marois, who became the world renowned dentist of so many celebrities that his appointment book looked like a top star agent's client list, or David Stein's guestbook.

Dr. Marois had a combined office/home near the Opéra, decorated with glass brick walls, indirect lighting, abstract paintings, low-slung, brightly-colored, modern furniture; he installed high fidelity music which was new to Paris ears. Pierre spent time every year in California, bringing back the latest in stream-lined, modern material to perfect his professional as well as personal life. What a host! Thanks to Dorothy introducing me to Elmore, who introduced me to the

Champagne...

good Doctor, I had a treasure of tidbits for my column, completely different from the rest.

Dr. Marois' patients were mostly American-Parisians like Elmore and Mr. and Mrs. Clement Brown. But soon it seemed like every visiting celebrity beat a path to his door where you might run into Burt Lancaster, Deborah Kerr, Ingrid Bergman, Charles Boyer, Robert Stack and Edward Arnold; these were followed later by Brigitte Bardot, Romy Schneider and Jane Fonda, not to mention Jean-Paul Belmondo, a patient and friend for more than 30 years. The man with the perfect teeth, John Ringling North, went to Dr. Marois every year for what he called his "tooth shine" and then sent friends who sometimes wanted a completely new smile.

Roger Dann was in and out of Paris all the time, working on films or on the stage out of town, but always returning to home base. Every time I saw him, he was full of news and good cheer. One day I ran into him on the street as I was coming out of Dorothy de Piolenc's building. He was with a tall, handsome fellow and introduced me to Gayelord Hauser, the food and health guru who believed strongly in the fine qualities of blackstrap molasses. They had just visited their friend, Greta Garbo, and Mr. Hauser was now on his way to Sicily after opening a health food store in Paris. We talked about his work and I mentioned that I knew his expression "beauty is as beauty eats." He added more: "It's not only the army that travels on its stomach, it's the whole world. I'm dedicated to making that path a pleasant one."

I loved seeing my old friends and missed the old days when I could entertain them in my home but now, it seemed, my home was strictly for family and what

Burt Lancaster and celebrity-dentist Dr. Pierre Marois in 1956. Burt was in Paris filming Trapeze with Tony Curtis and Gina Lollobrigida. Dr. Marois' patient book read like a Who's Who in Paris from Hollywood.

entertaining I did in those heady *Herald Tribune* days was on the outside.

The owner of the Pavillon d'Armenonville, where I'd given my dinner party for John Ringling North, welcomed me and a table of friends any Friday night I pleased. It was "black tie night" with ladies showing up in droves wearing floor-sweeping ballgowns and the most elaborate jewels to dine and dance all night by candlelight to the music of Aimé Barelli.

One night I gave a dinner party for Millie Considine, the very vivacious wife of world renowned newsman, Bob Considine and another society columnist from California, Cobina Wright, Sr. At that party was Mischa Auer, plus Verna Ostertag, Alain de Lyrot, Roger Dann, George Abell and the Duke de Maille. In the middle of dinner, I asked Mischa Auer if it was okay with him if I said in my *Trib* report that he was the host of the evening. That tickled him and he said it would be an honor to take all the credit for this wonderful party. He was a very sweet man. The next day I received a tiny porcelain vase full of baby roses. (The Limoges vase from that funny fellow was in the shape of a bidet.) About a week after my column about our dinner appeared in the *Trib*, Mischa called me in a total tizzy. "Maggi, don't EVER do that again!" he pleaded. It seems that someone representing the income tax department of the United States Government had read my column and contacted Mischa immediately to say that if he could host fancy parties in France, how come he was in arrears with his taxes in the USA? One never knew who was reading my giddy social reports.

Although I often claimed that entire columns could be written while sitting in a corner of the Ritz, there were so many places to go where celebrities and socialites

Here I am with Eunice Grayson and Roger Dann, the actor-singer called "the French Cary Grant," who played in the Sound of Music on the London stage for seven years. The children were regularly replaced as they grew up, but Roger never changed.

Champagne...

Darryl Zanuck and Bella Darvi
were often seen together in Paris
but even more often in Deauville
at the Casino, elbow to elbow.

could be seen. Each time a new restaurant opened, the titled-entitled Parisians crowded in to check out the food, decor and of course, each other.

A new club opened on the Rue St. Florentin that had butterflies of all sizes, shapes and colors all over the place. The owner was a young socialite named Baron James Mallet, who brought his lifelong butterfly collection in from the country by the thousands. It was a good gimmick inspiring silly remarks like, "A Butterfly Bar? I didn't know butterflies drank."

One of the clubs where you'd always find celebrities and friends was the Élysées-Matignon, right off the Champs-Élysées. The street floor was a regular restaurant but the downstairs club was impossible to get into if you weren't known by the manager, Marc Doenitz.

If you weren't a shining star, producer, writer, photographer or assistant's assistant in stage, screen, radio and the new medium, television, you were wasting your time trying to go down the stairs. But if Marc let you in you'd see stars in their after-hours moods while dining, drinking, watching television, comparing notes and notices; plus producers and directors discussing what's new in the entertainment world. A typical night would find Michèle Morgan dressed all in white with a new feathery hairdo; Darryl Zanuck with Roman Gary, who'd just written *Roots of Heaven*; and Bella Darvi, who was often just an elbow away from Mr. Zanuck in Paris and at the gaming tables of Deauville. Here at the Élysées-Matignon you'd often find the theater/movie critic for the Paris *Trib*, Thomas Quinn Curtiss, the man declared to be a walking encyclopedia of the stage/film world.

Tom, or T.Q. as some of his friends call him, lived first at the Hôtel George V, then rented an apartment from "Hoytie-Toytie" Wiborg but, after a spat with that difficult lady, he took an apartment in the Tour d'Argent building where he still lives today after forty years.

One place near the Trocadéro that I just adored because it was so outrageous was Chez Anna. She was a Basque (or "Basquaise") and liked animals more than she liked people. Her place had sawdust on the floor and animals running around. There was an old hen named Charlotte and a brown poodle named Bill, who knew how to jump up and open the door when the fat lady dog or any of the nine cats wanted to go out. You had to learn early Chez Anna that the animals had the right to do anything they wanted, but the customers had to behave. If you complained that a cat was trying to paw at your spinach, Anna would explain that he liked spinach and what harm would it do for you to give him some. The fat old lady dog would put her wet nose all over your hand until you gave her a lump of sugar at coffee time, and the chicken would peck-peck around your feet. At Anna's you'd find people like Darryl Zanuck, his daughter Susan Hakim, and all the film-making Hakims; plus Irwin Shaw and Ludwig Bemelmans, who had all learned that the beasts came first and if you didn't like it you might be put out by Anna, followed by a fire of flaming insults. She explained, "I can always get new customers, but I can't replace my pets." The food was good, the wine strong and cheap and, despite the furred and feathered friends, Chez Anna was good clean fun.

Another unique eating place where you'd see familiar faces was around the corner from the Ritz, called La Quetsch, where a line of huge hams hung along with gorgeous crystal chandeliers. You'd sit at a black marble counter and order what you wanted from the window cases on both sides of the entry. From the time you stepped in the door your mouth would be watering in expectation of gobbling down all the goodies you'd been staring at. There was only one problem: the waiters were young fellows in oversized aprons who seemed more interested in talking among themselves than in coming anywhere near you to take your order. Eve Max sat in silence one time, speechless in her fury at being ignored, and then she looked up and stated, "To be or not to be served. That is La Quetsch."

Paris was full of Russian restaurants and clubs of all sizes with names like Palata, Dinazarde, Maisonette and one first named Drap d'Or, which Americans immediately nicknamed "Drop Dead," so the name was changed to Rasputine. Several restaurants charged only ten dollars for all the shashlik you could eat and all the vodka you could drink. There was a lot of dancing on tables, smashing glasses, weeping to gypsy ballads and cornering of fortune tellers to hear what the future might bring–besides heavy hangovers.

Champagne...

The elegant Russian restaurant, L'Auberge d'Armaillé, was the most successful of all, thanks to "Prince" Vladimir Rachevsky, who could be counted on to bring celebrities and socialites. Of course he was paid for his efforts as well as getting a cut on the champagne he was selling, but Vladimir's "*grand seigneur*" appearance and gracious manners allowed him to lord over all he did. He laughed when people called him a prince, saying just because his sister was married to the Grand Duke Boris that didn't "entitle" him. Every Russian New Year Vladimir arranged an all-night ball in his sister's private mansion, filling the house with gigantic urns of roses, lighting only with huge candelabra throughout, creating a parquet floored dance club in her salon where two orchestras alternated until dawn. Little round tables with gilt chairs were scattered everywhere with buffets a few steps away laden with Russian delicacies fit for a czar. Vladimir's sister brought out her crest-embroidered linens, priceless porcelain, crystal and silverware for the guests to enjoy once a year.

Vladimir invited his international list of friends to mingle with the remnants of White Russian nobility in Paris, with numbers dwindling as years went by. Elaborate ballgowns, impressive jewels and sparkling tiaras on well-coiffed heads of middle-aged *grandes dames* was quite a sight to behold.

Chapter Twenty

In the fifties everyone I knew in Paris had a favorite barman whom they'd swear was a genius and then go on and on, telling stories about how clever Georges or Paul or Rudolph or André or Louis or Bertin was. My "genius" was young Claude at the Ritz, who taught me how to open a champagne bottle; arranged platters and served buffets like a seasoned "*maître d'hôtel*;" knew secrets of Paris' top people and never opened his mouth; would take care of anything any Ritz guest asked for with charming discretion; AND was responsible for my encounter with "Papa" Hemingway.

When Claude was still a *chasseur* at the Ritz, Ernest Hemingway decided to take him on hunting trips and teach him everything that a Great White *Chasseur* ought to know. He became a lifelong friend of Hemingway's and has many memories and mementos of those days.

Those were the days when I kept seeing Ernest Hemingway at the Ritz. But it wasn't his face that was familiar, it was his back. His habit was to slink in and take up his favorite spot at the end of the bar with his back to everyone else. He was someone I had never really gotten excited over because I couldn't stand bloody sports like bullfighting or shooting whales in the head; nor had I ever gone in for the war stories that I associated with the big fellow standing there. Still I thought he might be interesting to meet and I mentioned that to Claude, but I did not say that I wanted to interview him because I wouldn't have had a clue as to how to begin. But that's what Claude thought I had in mind.

A few noontimes later, as I was walking toward the bar, the ladies' room attendant standing in the lobby said, "Good morning, Madame Nolan" and a giant of a man seemed to jump out from behind his newspaper and bellowed my name. I was startled when Hemingway came over to me, looking like a great grizzly bear with half-glasses perched on the end of his nose. He towered over me.

"SO, IT'S YOU. I UNDERSTAND YOU WANT TO INTERVIEW ME." ("Yes," I said.)

"AS MUCH AS I'D LIKE TO TALK TO YOU, I CAN'T. DO YOU

UNDERSTAND?" ("Yes," I said.)

"IF I GAVE YOU AN INTERVIEW THERE'D BE A WHOLE STRING OF PEOPLE WANTING INTERVIEWS, DO YOU REALIZE THAT?" ("Yes," I said.)

"ANYWAY, I HAVEN'T BEEN WELL LATELY. I GUESS YOU'VE HEARD THAT, HAVEN'T YOU?" ("Yes," I said.)

"I DON'T EVEN GO INTO THE BAR THE WAY I USED TO, EXCEPT FOR ORANGE JUICE, YOU UNDERSTAND?" ("Yes," I said.)

"WELL, THEN, YOU WON'T BE TOO UPSET WITH ME IF I DON'T GIVE YOU AN INTERVIEW?" ("No," I said.)

Then he half bowed and went back to his place on the couch behind his newspaper. When I went into the bar, the barmen crowded around me and asked if I'd gotten my interview with *"Monsieur "EM-INGUE-VEY."* "Yes–and no," I said.

Early in 1958 the creator of Celebrity Service, Inc., Earl Blackwell, came into my professional life. I'd known him socially since he first stepped into the garden on the Rue du Docteur Blanche with Zsa Zsa Gabor and Rubi Rubirosa, and saw him every time he came to Paris to host or attend gala events; however I knew little about his celebrity bulletins published in New York and Hollywood announcing arrivals and departures of stars and how to make contact with them. In England in 1952, Earl met an English lady who was a walking-talking dynamo, Jeannie Hoskins, who told him she'd start a Celebrity Service, Ltd. business in London.

She was married to a top-ranking Fleet Street journalist, Percy Hoskins, and they were known for their outstanding entertaining in their Park Lane apartment. Earl made an agreement with her in 1952 to allow her to use the Celebrity Service name in Britain. Jeannie had a going concern from the start and later sold it to American "celebrity watcher" Diane Oliver, who still owns it today.

In Paris in the same year, 1952, Earl opened a branch of his American company on the Champs-Élysées, where he put an American former U.S. Army officer in charge. Spring 1958, he called me up at the *Herald Tribune* and said he had something very important to discuss. We met at the Hôtel California across the street from the paper. It was the first time I had ever had the chance to sit down with him and have a *tête-à-tête* conversation. It was easy to talk to this elegant southern gentleman, born and brought up in Atlanta, Georgia, who oozed charm like honey. He got right to the point of the meeting: he was looking for someone to take over his Paris office and he thought I could do the job of collecting names and assuring that bulletins got to his Paris subscribers. My head started spinning at his question–"Would you like the job?" All the projects I already had, the countless hours it took to gather information for my articles, plus my family routine and obligations, made it impossible to take on more. I told him that I had to think it over and we agreed to meet in a few days' time. Meanwhile, that same afternoon, I had an appointment with Eric Hawkins in his front office for the sole purpose of asking him (once again) for a raise.

Poor Eric. Everyone was after him all the time to discuss the same subject, which brought him to an instant boiling point. He was always very kind to me but his answer remained, "There's nothing I can do. My job is to get the paper out every night. I don't hold the purse strings." When I mentioned that Blackwell had asked me to work for him but I didn't have the time at the rate I was going, Eric had a brainstorm–if he gave me an office upstairs in the *Trib* building, I could combine the two jobs which were somewhat alike. Eric said he had the power to give me an office and telephone of my own, but no more money. I got back to Earl Blackwell and told him of Eric's offer. Earl seemed hesitant to give up an address on the Champs-Élysées, but when I told him he'd have no rent to pay just around the corner, you'd think that I'd just announced that he won a lottery.

What Earl Blackwell offered to pay me at the time might have been taken as an insult, but I accepted readily because it was more than I had been begging Eric for as an increase at the paper and would go toward helping me to take care of my obligations. Another advantage which I didn't mention to anyone (and barely wanted to mention to myself) was the increasing discomfort I felt working in a big newsroom. There were "boys on the desk" as Eric called them, who never seemed to miss a chance to say something like, "What are the RICH doing this week?" or "How are the BIG SHOTS treating you, Maggi?" Worse yet, I could feel a strange, unfriendly attitude building up in Art Buchwald. It was more than my over-active imagination. Once, right after I had written my guest column for Dorothy Kilgallen in New York, Buchwald yelled over at me, "What gave you the idea to write for Kilgallen?" I would have grinned but he had a look on his face like he was accusing me of some dastardly deed, so I just shrugged and said, "It wasn't my idea. I was asked to do it and I did it." He turned his back, saying nothing more. It wasn't long after that Eric Hawkins called me into his front office and I said to myself, "Yegads, what have I done now?"

Eric closed his door and I awaited the "chewing out" about misspelling a name or giving a title to someone not entitled to one, but instead Eric gave me a sheepish smile and said he wanted me to be warned that the placement of my articles in the paper was going to be changed. He didn't seem to believe me when I told him that I hadn't even noticed that I had a specific placement in the paper. He unfolded one copy after another of the *Trib* where my articles were included and pointed out that (1) I was on the same page as Buchwald, and (2) sometimes my columns were above Artie's on a page. Before I confessed that I still didn't get his point, he announced that Buchwald was complaining about the situation. I just shook my head in disbelief and then assured Eric that I truly didn't care where I was on a page or what page, for that matter. Joking then, I added that he could print my stuff upside down if he wanted. Eric seemed relieved and appreciative of my "understanding and cooperation." I went away happy that Eric was happy but still perplexed by Artie's attitude, asking myself how such a small thing could be so important. (In later years an expert on the subject explained to me the importance of placement to a writer and how journalists measured their editor's esteem by where their material was placed on a page. Even the number of the page was important. Okay, but it still seemed silly to me.)

As soon as I told Eric Hawkins that Earl Blackwell was in favor of his idea, he outdid himself in kindness to me. He gave me a little penthouse office with an entrance that had room for visitors' chairs with a terrace overlooking Paris rooftops and chimney pots with a bird's-eye view of the Sacré-Coeur on bright days. It was ideal. Eric promised that workmen in the building would furnish the office without delay. Like angels performing miracles, the scene was changed magically overnight with desks, chairs, tables, end tables, and even a magazine rack and easy chairs in the guest space. (Lord knows who was missing what in the building that week!) At the same time deliveries of file boxes and papers plus a funny old stencil machine came from the Champs-Élysées office. (The stencil had to be turned by hand like the organ grinder's music boxes on the street.) Another surprise "inheritance" from the office around the corner was an adorable dark-haired secretary/assistant named Françoise Serre, who was bright and seemed thrilled with her new "bureau." Earl left Paris for Rome and Venice while Françoise and I got down to serious work together. My capacity seemed endless now that I had an ivory tower of my own and the challenge of a new enterprise combined with the good-humored, bilingual efforts of a very smart girl. We were well installed and operating when Earl returned and he was both pleased and impressed. He decided to invite some people up to see the penthouse and take a look at Paris from our little terrace. He amused me because he never looked up at the Sacré-Coeur; he'd take visitors out there and point downward to the Rue de Berri saying, "That's where Elsa Schiaparelli lives."

As soon as Françoise and I began working together in the new penthouse on the Rue de Berri, I realized that Celebrity Service, Inc., had to have more Paris subscribers to survive. Getting the information to fill the pages was easy, I had celebrity names coming out of my ears every day, but the actual number of subscribers didn't cover the cost of stencils, ink, paper, envelopes and stamps. What a joke! I sat down with Françoise and announced that if we wanted to be winners we'd have to get out a mailing. She was a brilliant, bilingual brunette, but she was perplexed at my statement and said, "We have to get out a WHAT?" I explained to her what it meant and took the client list to show her where we might find potential subscribers. If we had one French journalist, there were more possibilities out there; if we had one dressmaker—ditto. And even some celebrities might sign up to see when other celebrities were going to be in Paris. See? She saw.

We wrote a half-French, half-English memo on a plain piece of paper and mailed it out even before our new letterheads were printed. The list I drew up for

Maurice Chevalier, Olivia de Havilland, and Earl Blackwell in my penthouse office
at the *Herald Tribune*, 21 Rue de Berri.

Françoise to type envelopes from made her raise her eyebrows. Funny, we'd just started working together and I understood a lot of her feelings before she opened her mouth. I pointed out to her that she might think it a dumb idea to send our little memo to duchesses, princesses, countesses and the like, but they were people I was seeing all the time, and some of them might be interested in getting our "who's who" in Paris celebrity bulletins. She still had one eyebrow raised but she was dutiful as well as beautiful and followed through without comment.

We sent out the notes telling of what we did, enclosing a sample of our latest bulletin which had names like Cary Grant, Marlene Dietrich, Gene Kelly and Yul Brynner. We received subscriptions from British Paris correspondents for the *Daily Express*, *Daily Mail* and the *Mirror*. A week or so after our little mailing project, Françoise was ecstatic when I came into the office one morning. She handed me a note and a check from the Duchess of Windsor for a subscription. I tried to be matter-of-fact when I explained to Françoise that it was completely logical that the Duchess would want to subscribe. She thrived on knowing what was going on in Paris and didn't want to miss a thing. Also, she probably knew a lot of the names we mentioned and might want to know exactly when they'd be in Paris and where they'd be staying. "You can bet," I added, "if she finds friends on our list who are amusing, and know how to play bridge, she'll invite them to her parties." Then I looked at the check and got a jolt. It came from Buckingham Palace. What a surprise! I couldn't figure out what kind of arrangement the Duchess had for paying her bills. Too bad there was no such thing as a photocopy machine in those days and too bad we were in such a hurry to bank all checks that I didn't have the time or money to have a photographer come in and take a picture of the check. "Buck House" paying for Paris Celebrity Service in 1958 would have been an amusing souvenir.

Another subscription that came in later was from Princess Grace of Monaco, but hers was paid for with a check in her own beautiful handwriting from her personal account in a Paris branch of an American bank. This subscription wasn't a result of our mailing; it came directly from her own initiative. (Years later in 1987 James Spada wrote in his biography, *Grace*, that the Princess liked to have visits from her old friends and used the Celebrity Bulletins to keep track of movie stars arriving in France.)

Miracles were happening. In a matter of weeks, we were doing so well that Françoise needed an assistant AND we had money to pay for one! We had two phones, one for Celebrity Service and the other came from the switchboard of the *Herald Tribune*. They rang from morning to night. It was hectic but it was interesting. When the girls got annoyed with the ringing phones, and callers asking endless questions, it gave me a chance to deliver my speech: "Don't forget, when people ASK you something, they're also TELLING you something!"–and they began to enjoy getting "scoops." When someone called saying he'd just seen Marlon Brando at Fouquet's on the Champs-Élysées and wanted to know where he was staying, Françoise answered politely that she didn't know and then hung up to announce jubilantly, "Brando's in town!" When we got tips such as these it was no problem tracking down where people were staying because they stayed in a few top hotels and had favorites year after year. Brando for instance–if he wasn't at the Raphael around the corner from David Stein's, he might be in David's upstairs suite which was his special hideaway. One knew darned well not to print that or even tell anyone. David's houseguests were TOP secret.

As busy as days were in early 1958, I had a late afternoon and early evening routine with Cathy and Janne, sitting in the living room visiting before they went in to the dinner table and I went to my room to prepare for yet another people-watching event. Our time together was great. I could relax in an armchair, put my feet up and enjoy the sight of two little girls growing up in front of my eyes. They'd tell me their news from school, ask me endless questions about all sorts of things and have chats between themselves which always fascinated me. Jim came to see them from time to time, usually before I got home from the Rue de Berri. He now owned his own public relations company on the Rue de Stockholm but never talked to me about it so I didn't know what clients he had or how successful his business was.

One evening Jim was still there when I returned from the office and he announced that he'd like to speak to me. He sent the children away and stood in the middle of the room, shaking his head when I asked him to sit down. Pacing the floor, he announced, self-consciously I thought, that he was planning to get married. Then he went on to say that she was a French lady from a fine family, she lived in Switzerland and, he added, she was an excellent skier. He stood in front of me after his speech as though he awaited my reaction with impatience. I said the first thing that came into my head–it was a big surprise but if he was going to be happy, everyone else would be happy, too.

The first chance I got to talk to Catina by herself, I told her what Jim had told me. She had the same reaction as I had; if he's found someone who's right for him, it was certainly good news for all. Then, I brought up the subject of what we might plan for the children's vacation. Deauville was out of the question for me now that I had a full-time office and staff to consider and we decided that perhaps a country cottage not far from Paris would be nice for a change. By then our "maid of all work," Marienette had left us to get married to her longtime beau from the South of France. We had a barrel shaped cook/housekeeper named Odette. I told Catina I'd start a search for a country place close to Paris which would be easy for me to get to by a direct train line. When we told the very plump Odette of our plans, she was delighted. She confessed that she was worried that we'd planned to return to Deauville and didn't think much of the idea. "Can you imagine me in a bathing suit?" she sighed.

Jim was full of surprises. I had barely absorbed the news of his upcoming marriage when he announced that it had already taken place. He said that it was now his plan to divide his time between his apartment in Paris and her apartment in Zurich, adding that he was thinking about buying something in Klosters where "the skiing is great." When he told Cathy and Janne, their reaction was upsetting. The first question out of Cathy's mouth, "What's going to happen to us?," needed reassurance from their father but the only thing he found to say was, "You'll get used to it," which wasn't an answer. Janne had a different reaction–she asked what he needed another wife for when he had a perfectly good one already. Jim gave me a black look as though what he was hearing was my fault. He announced that he was taking Cathy, Janne and Catina to lunch on Saturday to meet his new wife. It was okay with me. Frankly I was curious to know what the lady was like and whether she resembled me, in focus or not.

When the children came home after their first visit, Cathy was totally silent and went straight to her room. Janne came into my room and sat down on my bed. When I sat beside her, she half climbed onto my lap and whispered, "*Maman, elle est méchante.*" When I whispered back, "Why is she not nice?," she started to tell me what had happened at her father's house. When they arrived, the wife presented them with toys, dolls and a doll carriage. Janne assured me that they'd been very polite and thanked her but when they got ready to come home she took everything away from them and said they could only play with them when they came to see her. (God, I thought, this poor woman didn't know how to treat kids. Why didn't she tell them that the toys were there for their visits

Champagne...

BEFORE they thought they were theirs to take?) I dined at home that night and found Cathy still silent, far removed from her usual talkative mood at mealtime. Later, when I asked Catina what the new wife was like, she didn't want to discuss it. She said, "This person is no Isabella," reminding me of how much Cathy, Janne and Catina had liked the Italian lady "*la belle Isabella*," who'd been a part of Jim's life just a short time before.

The next morning was Sunday and when Cathy and Janne jumped onto my bed for their imaginary air trip to America, Cathy handed me a note she wanted me to send to their father. I put it aside and we had our usual English speaking-and-singing session. When they went to their room, I unfolded the paper and read (in French, of course) the sentiments she had been holding inside since returning home the day before:

"Dear 'I've Had Enough' and 'Banana Skin': You can keep your toys. We don't want them. We have toys of our own."

I didn't send it. I asked Catina if she knew that Cathy was calling the new wife *peau de banane* and she told me that's what Cathy and Janne were calling her in chats with each other. Why? Catina didn't know but suggested perhaps it was because she had long blonde hair. What was even more worrying was that Cathy called her father by the nickname she'd given him years before when he lost his temper in the nursery on the Rue du Docteur Blanche. I thought it had been long forgotten.

Jim invited them back the following week for another lunch. My instincts told me that I'd better try to smooth the way so I asked Cathy and Janne to promise to be good and polite and not to make anyone mad at them.

They took this very well and seemed to understand what I meant. Both promised to be "very good." When they came back the second time, they made no secret of their feelings. First, they assured me that they'd been good as promised, but they did not want to go back. They both referred to their father and his wife by the made-up names and when I looked over to Catina, she shrugged her shoulders in silence.

It didn't take long for Cathy and Janne to fill in details of their second visit which gave me more indication that this lady had trouble knowing how to make friends with little people. The children told me that she had pinched Cathy's arm at the lunch table, told her she was too fat and announced that she'd put her on a diet as soon as she was in charge of her. During the visit she had blown smoke in Cathy's face and laughed when she coughed. As soon as I could have a private word with Catina she verified everything I'd heard and added something else. The new wife was talking about arranging a tonsil operation for both of them as soon as they got to Switzerland. "Wait a minute," I said to Catina, "there's never been any conversation about Cathy and Janne going to Switzerland." Catina said perhaps there wasn't any talk of it *chez nous* but there certainly was *chez le père*.

Chapter Twenty-One

Planning our summer this year I found a comfortable furnished cottage to rent from an American girl in Vaucresson. It was pure country village life, very near Paris on a picturesque road. The house, surrounded by trees, had a luscious garden full of greenery and flowers and there was plenty of room for everyone. I mentioned it to Jim when I saw him but his attitude told me there was something amiss. I soon found out what it was when I got my next bank statements and saw that nothing had been deposited in my account and my balance was disturbingly low. Checking the bank, they assured me that nothing had been received. When I called Jim, I said there must be a mistake.

"There's no mistake," he announced. "I've withdrawn the arrangement." In shock, I asked him to come over to discuss it as it really was a big problem. He seemed calm and sure of himself as he told me we'd talk it over that evening when he came to visit the children.

Late that afternoon, Jim arrived when we were all in the salon. He had a briefcase under his arm, the air of a visiting diplomat as he ordered Catina to take the children away as he wished to speak to me privately. Catina led Cathy and Janne away after no more than a hello and goodbye from their father. My heart was beating fast because this fellow in front of me didn't look like anyone I knew. "I've decided to take the children to Switzerland this summer," he announced. I told him as calmly as I could that it was too soon as they were not yet accustomed to his new life and not acquainted with his new wife, but that would certainly come in time if we went slowly and understood their feelings. I saw his fury building up but pretended not to notice when I started to talk about the shock I'd had when it was brought to my attention that the payments we counted on to live were being held up. I had been thinking about it since I had the news and told him what was on my mind, pointing out that if he wanted a new agreement between us, I'd have been happy to discuss it, he didn't have to cut us off without warning.

Trying to convince him that I was making headway and would soon be in a position to ease his burden, I outlined, off the top of my head, all the progress I had made in my work from the *Trib* to *Realities* to CBS to Celebrity Service and all the rest but it just made him mad. (I should have remembered what David Schoenbrun had said about Jim's jealousy of my "success" but I didn't.) When I totalled all my earnings, it was still like nickels and dimes in comparison to family and professional expenses. Jim lost his temper when I was adding up everything I'd paid for without having to ask for help.

He stopped me, saying he'd come over to discuss the children's vacation in Switzerland, not finances, and as soon as I'd agree on that point we could go on to other matters. "You can't be serious about this, Jim," I said, "you mean you'll only give me what you owe if I agree to let the children go away to a house of a stranger in another country?" He said that summed it up and if I didn't agree I'd be "damned sorry." When I told him it was out of the question he turned his back and left, slamming the apartment door with all his strength.

I sensed that I was in trouble but I didn't know how much.

Making the social rounds for my column, I tried to keep a smile on my face while I was worried sick about my family situation and the fact that the father of my children had become a stranger. Once again, I saw Jim's father, my children's grandfather, at a diplomatic reception and asked him why he didn't visit Cathy and Janne and why I didn't hear from Grandma Nolan anymore. He seemed reluctant to speak to me but said that he had every intention of seeing the children and that Grandma Nolan was "just the same." A few days later, I came home to the news that Grandpa Nolan had indeed paid a visit but Odette informed me he spent more time "looking into everything" than he did with the children. I knew what Odette meant when I went into my room. It was obvious that my desk had been gone through by strange hands. I was accustomed to finding little drawings or notes in my daily diary by Cathy, which delighted me or an occasional comment by my old pal, Eve. (Once I was talking too long on the phone to suit Eve when she was waiting to go to lunch, so she wrote in big letters, "Your hat is on fire!") But this "invasion" by Grandpa was a shock. What he was looking for was beyond my understanding. I had no secrets.

That night I confided in John Ringling North that I was having trouble with Jim now that he had a new wife and that Jim's strange behavior was haunting my existence. He let me finish my sad tale and then just shook his head at me saying, "Mag-pie, you amaze me. You know ZERO about men," and went on to say that it was obvious that the new wife was "calling the shots" and was behind everything Jim was saying and doing, adding, "Don't you know that the woman who tells the guy what to do is the woman he's got his pecker in?"

Almost automatically, without thinking, I said, "Is that what you call 'pecker order'?" John guffawed. I didn't think it was funny.

The next time Jim came to the apartment, it was to tell the children of his plans for their summer in Switzerland. Both Cathy and Janne told him they didn't want to go. He stayed on in the apartment until I came in to tell me that it was obvious to him that I had turned the children against him. He was ready to leave after this angry accusation but I stopped him in the hallway, swearing I'd said nothing and trying to convince him to "go easy, go slowly" and look at the situation realistically. We already had the house in the country, I'd already had their big doll house, chairs and a load of toys sent there for the summer. There was everything there for a lovely holiday and he was free to have the house. I added that it wasn't fair to spring this change on Catina as she was much in favor of Vaucresson. Ah, but I was wrong; he had no intention of taking Catina to Switzerland, he said adding, "My wife doesn't want a SPY in the house."

A spy? What a strange word to use for Catina who'd given constant care to Cathy and Janne since birth. I was pleading and repeating all of the above when he lost his temper and announced that he was well aware of his rights. The words "spy" and "rights" frightened me.

That was the last I saw of Jim for weeks. Strangers began coming to the door with registered envelopes containing pale blue, lightweight paper on which was printed all sorts of declarations and accusations in legal language that I could barely understand, but I got the message. Jim was accusing me of not letting him have "access" to his children. Jim was taking action to prevent me from standing in the way of his "exercising rights" as a father. The accusations were sickening. But there was more in store for me. Blue papers in registered envelopes came to me from the owners of the apartment to inform me that my right to live there would expire on the first of July. I couldn't believe it. When Jim found the apartment for us so he could sell the house and paid the rent for two years in advance, I thought that we could stay as long as the rent was paid. Further, when he took me to the American Embassy so that we could sign a paper which would "guarantee your security," he specified that he would give me a dollar income every month plus pay the rent either for the Rue de la Tour or its equivalent. The rug was now out from under me as of the first of July.

Very early in my people-watching time at the Paris *Herald Tribune*, I learned to listen a lot everywhere I went and never waste time talking about myself. If I talked too much, I'd get back to my desk with nothing to write. But now everywhere I went, people were talking about my personal life whether or not I liked it and asking questions and expecting replies.

One evening at a very fashionable reception celebrating a Franco-American wedding, a distinguished French gentleman, General Édouard de Souzy, took me aside to have a word. He asked me if I knew the present wife of my former husband. I shook my head and he started to talk about her in outspoken detail. He was related to her he said, and she had shocked everyone when she left her husband and four children to run away to Switzerland with a young man. He said she was a nervous, capricious woman and one never knew what she'd be up to next. I told the General of my husband's intention to take my children to her home in Switzerland. He snorted, saying that she didn't even LIKE children and I'd better

Champagne...

be careful of her. From a relative, this was pretty scary.

It wasn't only the new wife I heard gossip about; a lot concerned me. I could tell the minute someone started to talk to me about "the situation," that they'd been listening to Jim, who could be very convincing when he turned on his charm. People would ask me why I thought it right to keep the children from their father. One French Catholic friend of many years asked me bluntly if I didn't think all my troubles had started when I refused to keep my promise regarding religion. And one very elegant lady who knew me only by sight went so far as to ask me if I didn't think it was better for my children that they live with their father and his wife who was not a "career girl."

My fears for what was in store for us grew and felt heavy in my head. One evening I was invited to a formal dinner party in the luxurious home of Mr. and Mrs. Clement Brown whom I knew from earlier days when Clem was with Pan American Airways and Jim was with TWA. (Clem became a tycoon for a pharmaceutical business and a leading citizen in the American-Parisian community.) The Brown mansion on the Square du Bois de Boulogne off the Avenue Foch was a showplace where old world entertaining of interesting guests took place and a lovely time was guaranteed. That night, however, the talk around the table of ten guests went straight to the recent marriage of my former husband. I tried to pass it off as fast as I could by saying that I was sure Jim would be happy now that he had a wife who could ski. Guffaws and snorts were heard around the table with the voice of Irwin Shaw raised above the noise. "She–ski–that's a hot one," he said, inciting more laughter. He began to report in detail what a rotten skier she was and about the time she threw up red wine all over the snow, making a mess you could spot for miles. Others joined in the report on the new Mrs. Nolan, suggesting she resembled a black widow spider as she descended the ski slopes. It was obvious that the Klosters contingent at dinner that night did not hold this person in high esteem. Worse yet, before the evening was over I was told that she had a violent temper and had hit someone over the head with a bottle in a Klosters nightclub.

There was too much at once for me: no payments from Jim coming in, no apartment in view, a prospect of being homeless and Jim pressuring to take the children away without Catina. The only person I thought I could turn to was David Schoenbrun. He listened to my sorry story and summed it up fast, "You need a lawyer, Maggi-bird," and he called up a friend of his who, he said, was one lawyer he knew who wouldn't ask for much money. The fellow was a war refugee who had recently started to practice in France. Right away I knew he was sensitive because I saw the look in his eyes when I told him my sad story from the beginning. I gave him all the blue papers that had come my way and told him to do whatever he had to do to protect my children. He was nice but it turned out to take much more than that to prepare for the legal confrontation that Jim was preparing.

One step he was convinced was a good one to take was to get a report on just who this woman was Jim had married so he suggested that he have one of his legal associates (private detective, I called him) go to Bordeaux to check out her background. Before we were called to court for a preliminary hearing, the legal associate had returned from Bordeaux with a confidential report and a copy of her divorce papers. When he handed it to me, he warned that it didn't make for very pleasant reading.

Jim's new wife was from Bordeaux, the daughter of a horse trainer, who married in June, 1939. She had four children but the husband got total custody. The divorce judgment stated that *Madame* was "violent," subject to "*crises*" and that her husband had lost his respect for her completely. No mention of visiting rights to the children for her and no mention of alimony. After the divorce she left Bordeaux and went to live in Zurich, Switzerland.

In addition to the official papers brought back, there were reports from neighbors who said that she left in the company of a very young skiing instructor. Everyone was well aware that she went out a great deal with other men and lived in a world that was not to the taste of her husband. Neighbors claimed that although *Monsieur* was held in high regard in the community (he manufactured industrial alcohol) his wife left only *mauvais souvenirs* (bad memories).

I stared at the paper with fear at what was happening and shock that Jim was acting so horribly to his family since this woman came into his life. The lawyer tried to assure me that we were bound to succeed in convincing the courts that Jim's demands were not acceptable. There was nearly a month before the first hearing, during which time the lawyer said he had prepared a very adequate dossier.

The day that I was summoned to the first hearing of Jim's case against me was Friday, the 13th of June, 1958. This was a preliminary audience before going in front of judges in a courtroom. Nervous before entering, I was shocked to dizziness when I saw the scene across the room. Jim was sitting with his new wife on one side and his father on the other; all three with their heads very near in serious discussion. The scene sickened me. Neither Jim nor his father looked my way, but every time I looked over there, the woman with stringy blonde hair and sharp features, wearing a yellow sweater, checked skirt and two-toned spectator pumps, glared at me with a look that made me feel that daggers were heading my way.

The lawyers presented their cases in language I didn't understand but I knew what I was being accused of was untrue. They said I refused the father his right to see his children. They said I was jealous of the new wife. They said this American former wife was trying to turn the children against the new French wife, suggesting that nationality entered into the situation. They said my unreasonable attitude on all matters was forcing the father to seek legal assistance. My reply was that I never refused the father his rights; that I offered a country house with them for the vacation; that I opposed the idea of a vacation out of France until the children were accustomed to the new situation. The response to this was that they took a dim view of my trying to force vacation plans on them as they were perfectly able to make their own plans, which included Switzerland, without the children's nurse who was unwanted as well as unnecessary. After this first encounter, I saw Grandpa Nolan, dressed in his best suit with the French decoration "rosette" in his lapel, walk brazenly into the private office behind us and announce in a loud voice, "I am a member of the Bar of Pennsylvania."

The next court appearance I had to make was in front of three judges in an overcrowded courtroom full of other people and their lawyers presenting cases such as mine. The new wife on Jim's arm had gone through a transformation. She was in an expensive looking metal-gray dress draped across the bodice and her hairdo was obviously done by a hairdresser. Our case was presented without inter-ruption despite one of the three judges falling asleep before our eyes. The words went on and on in what seemed like a Surrealist film. When it was all over, I was told that the judges would hand down their decision in a week. I walked away in a daze, followed by my lawyer who tried to reassure me that I couldn't lose because my side was so fair and honest and sincere.

When I went home and told Catina what I'd been through and what might be in store, she sighed and said that if Switzerland was decided upon, I should-n't worry because she'd do everything to see that the children got the best of care. When I told her that *Monsieur* was definitely not including her, she looked like she'd been slapped in the face. She turned white and whispered, "How can he do this?"

In that awful time sweating out what the French court would decide, I was invited to have tea with the Marquise Dorothy de Piolenc. She sent a car and chauffeur over for me and the children to have a *goûter* with her. Dorothy loved little ones; she'd never had children of her own and treated those of friends as though they were partly hers. As soon as we arrived she gave goodies to Cathy and Janne and some games to play on the floor. Among the guests there that day was Dorothy's British friend, Gweneth Dulles who waited until Cathy and Janne were absorbed in a game and beckoned for me to come into the next room. She said she'd heard from Dorothy about the trouble I was having with my children's father and she wanted to warn me about something of vital importance. "You'll lose your children in French courts," she announced. I thought she was exagger-ating and being dramatic but she went on to tell me she'd faced a similar prob-lem with her American husband in France who wanted to take her sons to Switzerland. She insisted that laws in France were made for men and the interests of women and children were not considered. She insisted that French law gave children to the man after they were seven years old if the man had remarried and the woman had not.

I kept shaking my head, saying my case was certainly different but she got very impatient, insisting that a man could marry any old thing he picked up in the street and the fact that he had a *foyer* with a wife would give him the right to take chil-dren away from a working mother. "Mark my words," she announced like a British statesman, "You'll lose your children in a French Court."

I was shaken but still not convinced. She didn't give up. She told me that if she hadn't taken her British-American children born in France straight to England to make them Wards of Court, she would have lost them. "In England the laws are in the interests of the children, not fathers-versus-mothers," she said. With that we rejoined the festive people in the salon until it was time for the chauffeur to take us back to the Rue de la Tour.

What could I do about all these dangers Gweneth Dulles pointed out? Nothing. What could I do with all the frightening things I'd heard about the new Mrs. Nolan? Nothing. When the judgment was handed down, Jim was granted everything he asked for and I was instructed to go to the American Embassy to get passports for the children and take them off mine, where they'd been since birth. The paper stated that no appeal of this decision was possible until after the summer holidays were over. The next day was Saturday when embassies were closed but this had to be faced on Monday, without fail. I still had a hope that I could speak to Jim personally but his wife answered the phone when I called and forbade me calling again.

The night after the frightening judgment, I was expected at a formal dinner party at Leonora Corbett's stable house setting for her "horsey" party and afterward at the Travellers' Club Ball, which was the gem of the season. I felt wretched but I was obliged to go if I wanted material to fill my next column. I was so disturbed that morning that I decided to go to the American Embassy to see if there was someone who'd talk to me. I knew that official offices were closed on Saturdays but there was always someone on duty for emergencies and to help American tourists in distress. I was far from being a tourist, but I was an American in trouble and took a chance on finding a friendly soul.

Those were the days when Americans could go in and out of the Embassy building like it belonged to them, before the situation made security measures necessary that could rival Fort Knox. As soon as I set foot in the door I ran into a fellow I knew from all sorts of social, cultural, and charity events, Joseph Verner Reed. We exchanged friendly greetings and I lost no time telling him that I was in trouble and needed someone to give me some information. He assured me that if he couldn't be of help, he certainly could indicate someone who could. "Why don't you come to the office and tell me what's on your mind?" he said.

He was a tall, slender, smart and witty fellow who always looked as busy as a bee, but I could never figure out exactly what his official job was at the Embassy. He seemed to be a "man of means" with a lovely house where he and his wife entertained a great deal. She was an attractive lady named Permelia Pryor Reed, but I always called her Mrs. Joseph Verner Reed in my column for fear of misspelling her first name. Joe's job at the Embassy always involved cultural and social affairs like a cultural attaché, but there was already one of those when he arrived with Ambassador Amory Houghton. He was more like a personal assistant and friend of the Ambassador, and he assisted His Excellency whenever and wherever he was needed. Anyway, he was there and kind and willing to help me if he could.

When I told him my "horror story," his mouth opened in disbelief at the French court's order to an American mother who had full custody of her children, to take them off her passport to leave the country. "It's true," I assured him and held up the envelope full of official papers I had in my hand.

Joe Reed was so concerned with the story I told and the papers I had with me that he seemed outraged against "the French." He wasn't a diplomat and blasted out at the "obscene" adventure I'd had in French courtrooms those last weeks. I found I had to calm his fury to continue our talk. I repeated that I was searching for a way to solve this problem without hurting anyone and without going up against French rules and regulations. After all, "the French" didn't ask me to live in France and as long as I did, I knew I had to respect their laws. Poor Joe was so upset that he sounded like he was ready to make a Franco-American incident out of it, but we finally agreed that he'd talk to some of the top attachés in the Embassy who would be acquainted with situations such as mine, to find a solution.

After my Saturday visit to the closed American Embassy and the painful experience of having to tell my most intimate troubles to a comparative stranger, I had to transform myself into "the glamorous Maggi Nolan" to keep my formal dinner engagement with the horsey set in the home of Leonora Corbett. This outstanding British stage actress held her memorable racing dinner in her usual apartment on the Avenue de Wagram which had once been a stable and was turned into a luxurious, long, drawn-out apartment in a trellis and vine covered courtyard. For Leonora's party she had decorators create a southern scene, *à la* Scarlett O'Hara, and featured the racing colors of her horse-owning friends at each table. Here one was elbow to elbow with Baron and Baroness Édouard Rothschild; the Duke de Cadaval; Simone Simon; Gertrude Widener from Philadelphia; Count and Countess François de Ganay; Mme. François Dupré (her husband was attending the horse owners' dinner at Maxim's at the same time); Lady Doverdale; Thomas Quinn Curtiss (hardly a horsey sort, T.Q. knew Leonora as the "*Blithe Spirit*" in Noel Coward's Broadway production); Johnny Galliher; Princess Amedée de Broglie; Mr. and Mrs. George Wildenstein; Liz Miller; Charles Clore from London; Mme. Suzy Volterra, whose outstanding racehorses earned her the title "Queen of the Turf;" and Aileen Plunkett, who'd just become Mrs. Valerian Rybar. Most guests at Leonora's dinner turned up at the all-night Travellers' Ball afterward, as did the hostess after her last guest had departed.

Sunday at home and in the park with my family was always relaxed but this Sunday, awaiting Monday's problems, I could feel my nerves jumping and sweat beads forming on my scalp. Both children sensed something different about me. Cathy said, "*Ça va, Maman?*" and Janne took my hand as we walked and didn't seem to want to let go.

I was up early and off to the Embassy on Monday morning where I found that dear fellow, Joseph Verner Reed already there, though he had a reputation throughout the building of never showing up until noon. He gave me names of key people I ought to see and patted me on the shoulder saying, "*courage*" with the French pronunciation. And so started my day on a merry-go-round of meetings and lengthy talks with various people who knew about such things that filled the big envelope that I took with me everywhere I went. The people I talked to were already among my acquaintances through American-Parisian organizations and Franco-American social activities. Everyone told me that our talks were "off the record" because of their diplomatic positions. No one showed the outrage that Joe had manifested but I understood the delicate position. All, without exception, warned me that once I took the children off my passport, no one could assure me that they'd be returned to me.

After my talks with top Embassy officials, I was walking toward the exit when I saw Joseph Verner Reed in the hallway. He walked with me to the door, still interested in my problem. When I repeated everything that everyone had told me, he got a sparkle in his eye, took my arm and announced that he had an idea: what I ought to do is take the children to Switzerland myself and pick them up when their vacation was over.

That dear man had a good idea but I was still afraid that I'd have to have Jim's okay so I wouldn't be accused of defying a court order. I went back to the office of a number one man at the Embassy and told him of the idea, but also confided that Jim's wife wouldn't let me talk to him on the telephone. He was very understanding, winked and picked up the phone to talk to Jim himself. He said Jim sounded annoyed but would come to the Embassy to talk it over. When Jim was advised by this VIP to accept the proposal he agreed.

Joe was still interested in the outcome. He gave me key names of American diplomats in Geneva and Bern to write to informing them of the situation and asking their cooperation to see that the children did not leave Switzerland during the vacation. I was grateful to him and followed his advice immediately. One answer came back by return post stating that such an assurance was impossible to give. Nevertheless, the new plan went forward. I was to come to Zurich on the following Sunday with the children and Jim would pick them up at my hotel after lunch. I sat down with Catina to outline the official plan and then added a plan of my own. She should go with us, I said, as I was certain that when Jim saw her there and knew the children wouldn't hesitate to go with him if Catina was along, he'd soften up and agree. She thought it was a good idea, saying that she had a good relationship with *Monsieur* for so long and that he'd told her countless times that she was part of our family. (She even had a little framed photo in her room of herself with Cathy, Janne and Jim's housekeeper, Madame Passiti, taken by Jim in his apartment during the days when Jim's artist friend was painting the children's portrait.)

She began to prepare the children's clothes and necessities for the trip and I told her I didn't think it was a good idea to arrive with her own luggage as well,

Champagne...

because that would vex him. It was better that the idea come from him. Then I added that if she'd prepare her luggage in advance and leave it at home, I'd send it to her the minute I returned to Paris. She agreed with that as well and everything was ready for the trip.

I still couldn't stop worrying about the children so I sat down at my desk and prepared a three-part request for Jim to sign before he took the children:

1. Promise not to put the children on diets while they are in Switzerland.

2. Promise not to have their tonsils removed in Switzerland.

3. Promise not to leave Zurich while the children are in Switzerland.

Chapter Twenty-Two

It was painful knowing that this was an ordeal that we had to go through. I decided to do it in comfort by going to Zurich the night before and staying in a top hotel. I bought airline tickets for the Saturday before my Sunday meeting with Jim at the Baur au Lac, so I could spend my last night with my family at that famous place. Our adventure began with a joyful airplane ride and a royal welcome as we checked into a hotel suite with flowering balconies at every window. The children were happily intrigued by their surroundings, going from room to room exploring what comprised luxurious hotel living. This was before TVs and mini bars in hotel rooms. They were thrilled by other things. Cathy was fascinated by the king-size, flat-topped desk in the salon with its endless interesting objects like an elegant leather folder bursting with postcards, envelopes and writing paper plus a letter opener, an ink pot and pens. "Shall we write to someone?" she asked. Janne was intrigued by the selection of miniature soaps, delicious smelling lotions and shower caps for everyone in the bathroom. She came out smelling of Chanel number 5.

We went for walks around the beautiful gardens and in the town. There were flowers blooming everywhere and the children were bouncing joyously around all the sights. When it was time to order dinner they pleaded for spaghetti, which they never had at home. I exchanged a look with Catina and saw that she wouldn't mind so I said, "Okay, spaghetti it is." Everyone slept well in the crisp, fresh atmosphere, raring to go out again in the morning. This time, Catina took them out while I went over my notes and prepared for Jim's arrival.

When the phone rang announcing that Jim was on his way up, I asked Cathy and Janne to wait in a bedroom with Catina while I had a talk with their father and off they went, leaving me alone in the salon when Jim came in. He seemed very nervous at first, not asking where the children were, so I told him as I handed him my paper with its three promises and motioned him to sit at the desk. He read very slowly and then said, "No diets, okay. No operations, okay." He took up a pen from the desk set and signed items one and two, handing the paper back to me.

Champagne...

When I tried to give the paper back to him telling him that point three was very important to me, he refused to take it, reaching for the checkbook in his pocket instead and spreading in on the desk in front of him. Without looking up he said, "How much do you want?" I was having trouble with my nerves and couldn't keep my voice from quivering when I asked him what he meant. "You know–alimony–maintenance–whatever you call it," he said.

Still shaking, I told him he knew very well what he hadn't paid since springtime and we were now in the first week of July so I didn't see why he wanted to dramatize the sorry situation. He seemed to be enjoying this interlude while holding his pen above his opened checkbook. When he saw he wasn't getting any reply from me, he wrote out a check with a flourish, waved it in the air and handed it to me, announcing that this ought to "hold you" for the summer. The check was for a sum less than he was supposed to pay for one month. I slowly tore it up and put it back on the desk in front of him.

He stood up, announcing our meeting was at an end and telling me to call the children as his wife was waiting.

When he saw Catina coming through the door with them, he asked what she was doing there. Cathy said Catina always went on vacations with them and he said, "Not this time, and I wonder where she got the idea that she was invited," looking at me accusingly. Both Cathy and Janne started talking at once, telling him they didn't want to go without her. He was getting into a fury, this time accusing me outright of making it impossible to "exercise rights." By this time I had calmed down a bit and asked him as quietly as I could to please take Catina as it made all the difference between a peaceful start of the vacation and upsets.

"If there are any upsets," he said, "you're the one causing them." Our entire conversation had been in English and when Jim tried to take Cathy's arm she pulled back and took a place standing behind me. I said "Jim, all this can be avoided if you just take Catina," but he was furious and picked up luggage by the door which had Cathy and Janne's names on it, ordering the children to follow him. They didn't budge.

"What about me?" Catina finally asked, the first time she'd said a word. He said, "You stay with Madame, I'm taking the children." She began to cry. It was the first time in all the years that she'd been in our lives that I had seen her cry and it hurt like knives cutting into me. The children went to her side, anguished by her tears. It all seemed like a nightmare. I begged Jim to find another way to proceed as this would not work. He put the children's luggage on the floor and folded his arms in silence for what seemed like a long time, but was probably a minute. Then he announced that he would take their belongings on ahead and that I should follow with the children in a taxi. He added that he would figure out the total amount of money that had not been paid to me and have a check ready on my arrival at the house. "What about Catina?" I asked and he said to leave her behind at the hotel because she was causing too much trouble. He left, lugging the bags. I told Catina exactly what he had told me to do. Cathy came straight over to me. I can never forget how little she was; she could have stood under my outstretched arm. She was crying, her forehead wet with perspiration. "*Maman, tu ne peux pas faire ça à nous,*" she said looking into my eyes. No, I could NOT do that to my children. I knew what I had to do and a small child had shown me the way. We gathered our coats, went downstairs, paid the bill. got into a taxi and went straight to the airport to fly back to Paris together, just as we had arrived, minus the children's luggage.

Back in Paris after the ordeal, I told Catina I'd arrange for a car and driver to take her and the children to Vaucresson the first thing in the morning to have a complete change in the country. I had to stay in Paris to report the Zurich incident immediately to the lawyer and give him proof that we had been to Switzerland as promised.

Very early the next morning just after we had had breakfast and Catina had gone down the long hallway with the children to get ready for the trip to the country, the doorbell rang and Odette opened it to find Jim standing there with his briefcase. I heard him ask to see me urgently so I went out to join him in the salon. A look of hate and fury was on his face.

"I could have you arrested for what you did," he announced as he started to take some papers out of his case and put them on the couch. He was wasting his time with papers by now. The trust I had had in him was now turned to total fear.

"Look, Jim," I said, trying to be calm, "I took the children to Switzerland. What happened is not my fault." I was so nervous I felt sick but was determined not to show it. He started what seemed like a well-prepared speech, saying that because I had "denied access" I was guilty of "*non-présentation des enfants*" as well as being in "contempt of court" and that he was in a position to put me in jail.

"However," he added, with an explanation that all I had to do was sign the papers he had and my problems would be over. I refused to look at the documents he put under my chin. When he saw my defiance, his hate and fury came to the fore. His tirade started again and he added how happy everyone would be to see me in jail. That word "everyone" set me off and, despite my vow to stay calm, I remember raising my voice, saying I knew exactly whom he meant by "everyone."

After all these years it shames me to think about those horrible moments when I said, "Everyone–everyone–you mean the woman who provokes bad memories in Bordeaux, the woman who left her children, the woman who ran away with a skiing instructor." Going on, I reminded him that no decent father would take children away from their mother to turn them over to an unstable. violent, capricious stranger.

Jim gave me a push with all his strength, sending me to the floor on my back with my head hitting a leg of the couch. Hurt and in shock, I got to my feet but not before Odette had come to the doorway after hearing us to ask if she should call the police. Jim was mumbling that I'd lose my children FOREVER now. I'd asked for it and I was going to get it. I picked up a tiny bronze bust of sculptor, Jo Davidson, and threw it in Jim's direction as he went out the door. It missed him but made a black mark on the wall.

The noise brought Catina and the children into the front hall as Odette announced that she had called the police, and Jim slammed the front door and was gone. As it happened, no policeman showed up. A routine call came soon after telling Odette to tell *Madame* that she must appear in person to make a complaint. "Thanks a lot," I thought, "what if my back was broken?"

When everyone left for the country (including the bird) I dressed to face my day with the lawyer first before going to the office. I gathered all receipts I had for airplane tickets and the hotel so he could see that we had been to Zurich.

After I gave him the papers and told him the sad story, I was amazed to see that he was disappointed that the case had not ended. Feeling helpless, I nevertheless knew, instinctively, that he must file a report as soon as possible to show that I had followed orders, but it was the children who wouldn't go with their father. Before I left the lawyer did promise to work on the problem but I was frightened by his lack of enthusiasm and worried that maybe he didn't even know how to proceed.

Leaving the lawyer's office, I went straight to the Rue de Berri to finish my next column, sift through all the mail and invitations, and give celebrity names to the girls for future bulletins. When I called to check on the family at Vaucresson, I found that all was fine. The girls were in the dollhouse big enough to house two kid-sized chairs, and the big black bird was having a fine time flying around in one of the bathrooms while talking a blue streak.

I assured Catina that right after work I'd go to the Rue de la Tour, change clothes, and make an early train to the country.

No complaint against Jim was filed at the police station. I was too ashamed.

I arrived at the end of the day to an empty apartment, exhausted but still determined to join my family. I had barely closed the door when the bell rang.

When I opened the door I had the shock of seeing Jim with a strange man holding official-looking papers in his hand. He announced that they were there to "take possession of *les enfants*" and their papers proved that they had the right. I tried to explain what had happened but I had no papers to prove the events over the weekend. When I told them that the children were not there, the French official requested and got from me the address where the children were, and I even showed him the rental agreement for the country house. When they left I realized that Jim had never looked in my direction, nor had he uttered one word in my presence. His henchman had done it all.

I couldn't get my lawyer on the telephone at that hour so I went as fast as I could to the country house to warn Catina of what was surely going to happen the next day. We were informed the following morning by the local police that there would be an official visit that afternoon. I told Catina and Odette that I'd take a walk around the neighborhood at the time set for the visit because I didn't think that I should be there, but I did have a friend, who had a house in the neighborhood who might be with them. My friend who lived nearby, Bea Mazarrini, agreed to come over. She was a distinguished, white-haired, American grandmother who loved little children and had knitted sweaters for Cathy and Janne when we lived on the Rue du Docteur Blanche.

It was hell walking up and down the roads that afternoon. When I thought it was time to return, I saw a strange brunette woman in dark glasses sitting in the passenger seat of a shiny car at the end of our road, and knew instinctively that the ordeal was still going on. I made another tour and the next time around when I saw that the car was gone, I made my way back to the house.

My American friend was at the door when I came in. She put her arms around me and whispered, "It was horrible," but I saw Cathy and Janne at the dining room table in the distance and thought, "Thank God, they weren't taken away." Before I could hear what had actually happened, a knock on the door brought back a local officer who had accompanied Jim and the two bailiffs. He had brush-cut hair, wore a heavy tweed jacket and shoes with the thickest soles I'd ever seen. I'll never forget those shoes because I stared more at the floor than anywhere in my misery and shame at this situation. He stated his conviction that Monsieur Nolan was *pas normal*. This man in the big shoes was sensitive. He said that in all his professional years he had never encountered such a strange man as the father of the children who was set on taking children away when it was so obvious that they didn't want to go. Then he confided that the only reason that the children weren't taken by force that day was because when Jim handed him the formal order to act, he noticed that it was a carbon copy and not the original, which gave the officer the right to refuse a request of force. "He'll be back tomorrow. And he'll have the original. It will be better if the children are not here," he said, shaking hands all around, smiling at Cathy and Janne and clomp-clomping across the wooden floor out the door.

Little by little, I learned the rest of the story. Janne had clung to Catina's skirts and Cathy had hidden in an upstairs closet, screaming when Jim tried to pull her out. The policeman was right; a father doing this to his children was not normal.

Like fugitives, we were on the run again back to Paris. We left Odette to take care of the house and Noirice. We slept in our own beds that night but I was frightened of who might pound on the door next. In the morning, when I called Dorothy de Piolenc, she insisted that Cathy, Janne and Catina come over to her until the nightmare was over. I accepted the invitation right away, knowing they'd be alright with the merry Marquise who loved my little ones, while I ran around to the lawyer, and then to my office. After all of my errands, I went over to Dorothy's to try to figure out what to do next and found that tall British beauty, Gweneth Dulles, on the scene again. She was a lady who didn't stoop to saying,

Champagne...

"I told you so." Instead she had a sheet of paper she handed to me as soon as I came in the door.

"Here's the address of my apartment in London," she said. "Plus the name of the solicitor who took care of me several years ago. He's a darling and knows what to do." Then she added that her teenage sons and a very good housekeeper were on the premises in London and would be happy to see us. I thanked this lovely person but told her I wouldn't leave France. There was surely another way to solve our problem. She shook her head saying no more after asking me to promise that I would not lose the piece of paper she had just put in my hand.

Dorothy de Piolenc sat close to me on the couch with Catina in a chair close by who awaited my translation of everything Dorothy said. Dorothy wanted us to go to Deauville and said that her chauffeur was ready and willing to drive us anytime we wanted and added, "Preferably, right now!" Catina and I were confused as we pondered the fact that Cathy and Janne's clothes were scattered from Paris to Zurich to Vaucresson.

Finally I said that I'd go back to the apartment and pack bathing suits, sun sandals and dresses to take until we could get properly organized. Dorothy was happy that her chauffeur could drive us out of danger; Cathy and Janne heard the Deauville news with delight at a new adventure. Off I went to the Rue de la Tour to see what I could pack for the beach. I asked the driver to wait on the Avenue while I went around the corner to the apartment, but when I turned into the Rue de la Tour I saw a strange-looking crowd in front of my building. There was Jim and the same dark-haired woman in black sunglasses I'd seen in the shiny car in Vaucresson. There were policemen standing around with curious neighbors and passers-by; a police car was parked at the curb. I absorbed the whole scene in seconds and ran back to the chauffered car, crouched low in the back seat and asked to be taken as fast as possible back to the Marquise.

Dorothy insisted and I agreed that I should leave with the children for Deauville right away. Catina said she'd go back to the apartment and meet us in Deauville the next day with the necessities we'd talked about. Not knowing where we'd be staying, I promised to call her as soon as we were installed. Dorothy offered to advance money for the trip but I'd been to the bank that day so off I went with my two little daughters, who didn't seem to notice that they hadn't changed clothes all day.

Within a few hours we arrived in Deauville and found a place to stay. No roomy cottage this time, no fancy suite in a top hotel. We found a little walk-up family hotel on a backstreet. It was sweet though, with lovely people running it, a beautiful garden in the back and the beach only short blocks away. When I called Catina and told her the name of the place, her voice sounded strange when she said I didn't have to give her the address as she knew it and would join us in the morning. When she arrived the next day with beachwear, the children had had their baths in a fat-legged tub in a bathroom down the hall from our room and were wrapped in giant towels. We got them into their bathing suits and sandals and as soon as Catina was installed in her room we headed for the beach.

Before the day was over, Catina explained to me how she came to know the place where we were. It had been one of her hideaways when she was with the Jewish family during the war. I got a tingling sensation on the back of my neck when she told me her story. During our conversation I asked her if she felt like she was "at war" again. She answered in a small voice, "Now is worse."

Hiding away in Deauville, I had to do some hard thinking. There was no way I could know what Jim was planning if his use of police force to take the children succeeded. Grandpa might be arranging to put them in a convent which he said so many times was the "right" thing to do. Lord knows what the woman Jim married had in her head. Jim's motives were obvious–get rid of a former wife who was a burden. Turning the children over to his father would cancel that responsibility as well. Whatever the plots behind the scene, I was frightened for Cathy and Janne who had no one to defend them if I let them go.

One look at the telephone system in our little family hotel in Deauville told me that it wouldn't do for my needs. There was an ancient wall telephone in our rooms but it only connected to a rickety switchboard at the reception desk. It was a mere intercom to inform you when you had a call which you had to go downstairs to receive. In those days there was no such thing as a direct telephone line, not even in the most luxurious hotels. Leaving everyone at the beach, I went to one of the top hotels where I'd seen such fabulous times, hoping I wouldn't run into anyone I knew because I was far from 'glamorous' with my quivering voice and hands that shook when I picked up my pen, to say nothing of the tired clothes on my back.

Finding the telephone operator in her little cubbyhole on the ground floor and tipping her in advance, I started my verbal marathon on the phone. Odette in Vaucresson sounded happy to hear from me, reporting in a voice that sounded like she was gasping for breath that the officials and "the father" had indeed returned early the next morning after we had left. After she finished telling me this I told her to try to rest, relax and enjoy the countryside for the moment and I'd keep her posted as to our plans. Next I called my office and found Françoise hard at work and wondering what had become of me. I promised to get back as soon as possible, saying I was "with friends" and asked her to report to Eric Hawkins that I had no column to deliver that day. That was the first time I'd missed a deadline. Then she reminded me that I had a lunch date with Drue Mallory Heinz at the Lancaster Hotel. Yegads, I'd forgotten everything except my problems! Drue was a lady I truly liked and whose company I enjoyed. There were endless messages but missing my visit with Drue meant the most to me.

Françoise assured me that the Celebrity Bulletin would get out on time with plenty of names on it so I mustn't worry about that. She was marvelous. We had only worked together for about four months but she had a brain like a blotter

Champagne...

absorbing everything I told her plus handling every detail in the office on her own with her assistant. (One day I got special satisfaction when I heard her explaining to the new girl what a "mailing" was and how important it could be for business.) I told Françoise I'd be back in Paris the next day so "not to worry."

My call to Drue was lengthy. She knew both Jim and me from the early TWA days before she married Jack (whom I called "the world's most glamorous grocery man" in my column) and she asked endless questions as to how we could get to such a sad state of affairs. In answer to her query as to what I was going to do next, I told her I didn't know. I mentioned that Gweneth Dulles had suggested that I go to England, though it was really out of the question. I had all my arguments for not leaving France on the tip of my tongue. I'd been a Parisian for twelve years, Cathy and Janne were born there, they were going to school there. Besides that, I had jobs in Paris that were going better every day. Drue was very sweet and sympathetic, asking me to be sure to keep in touch with her and let her know if there was anything that she could do. After my uplifting talk with her, I felt I had the strength to call the lawyer to find out what had transpired. He sounded warm and enthusiastic. Official reports came in from Vaucresson verifying everything I'd told him and he assured me that he was working hard on my predicament. I learned that the man with the thick-soled shoes in Vaucresson who'd warned me that Jim would be coming back with his order to use force was the local *commissaire*, the police commissioner himself, from Versailles. He was a fine human being I thought, deciding that the man with the thick soles had a good soul as well.

After my telephone marathon from Deauville all morning, I went down to the beach to join my family. Cathy and Janne were busy building a sandcastle a few yards away from Catina's parasol where I knelt down and told her I'd have to go back to Paris for a few days to attend to our affairs and try to do some work in the office. She was visibly upset at the prospect and begged me not to return to the Rue de la Tour as she'd heard the miserable details of what had gone on straight from the concierge, who hadn't missed a thing from beginning to end. Catina was afraid that I'd be arrested if I went back. Although I assured her that it hadn't come to that, she was so overwrought that I promised her I wouldn't stay in the apartment but I did have to run in and out to get whatever I needed. But *where* to stay? Dorothy de Piolenc's door was open to me I knew, but she had so many people coming and going that I wouldn't be able to concentrate. Then, like a flash, I thought of David Stein's five-floor town house around the corner from Dorothy at the Étoile, just a few blocks from my office.

When I called David's number I learned from his maid, Simone, that he was in Monte Carlo *en vacances*. Simone was a dear person from Sologne in the Loire Valley, where all the big hunting estates were and gave the impression that she was a lady who always had her feet on the ground. She was a perfectionist in her work and although she was pure French, she reminded me of a proper English lady.

I'd gotten to know Simone pretty well after becoming an *habituée* of David's fancy parties and Simone had become the top personage in David's household after he let Gabrielle go. (Apparently Gabrielle was no angel after all.) I told Simone enough of my problem so that she assured me that *Monsieur* would certainly let me stay upstairs and she'd call him right away to make sure. When I called back later Simone said that *Monsieur* was indeed *d'accord* and she'd be at the door to greet me, show me around and give me a key. Catina was relieved about my arrangement and I took the next train to Paris.

Chapter Twenty-Three

The atmosphere of David Stein's empty five-story town house was strange. I was accustomed to parties with gorgeous creatures in fabulous *haute couture* gowns and glittering jewels in animated chatter with elegant gentlemen *en smoking*, clinking glasses while smooth music from hidden speakers floated through the air. Except for our simple foursome dinners with Cary Grant, it was always a heady formal affair at David's. Now it was so quiet you could hear the ticking of a clock. David's house was a typical old-style French mansion with the kitchen located underneath the street floor. You entered through his street door into a marble foyer with his office and a butler's pantry on the left. Further on was a reception salon and a vine-covered, glassed-in terrace before you came to the heavily-carpeted open staircase leading up to a formal salon and dining room where a huge grand piano had a place of honor. On the first landing of the staircase there was a birdcage-like elevator to take you to the upper floors if you didn't feel like climbing. The whole house was jammed with antiques plus oil paintings that were hanging one above the other right up to the high ceiling. I adored David and I loved his parties but I must confess that I felt awful in his empty house. It gave me the creeps like I'd been abandoned in an ancient tomb of some long-gone monarch. Simone was a darling to me however, asking me what I wanted or needed, showing her willingness to be of service to me during my stay. I told her I'd need nothing but a bed and a bathroom; I planned to be out early in the morning and back at bedtime.

Chez Stein thus began my houseguesting in the same hideaway suite in Paris favored by Marlon Brando. I truly appreciated David's hospitality. Still, I sort of shuddered to think of how many people had been in "Marlon's bed" before me.

Momentarily installed in David's mansion practically in the shadow of the Arc de Triomphe, I walked back to work down the Champs-Élysées to the Rue de Berri. Back at my desk I was amazed at the pile of mail and messages that had accumulated in the short time I'd been away. On top of the heap I found a handwritten envelope from Drue Mallory Heinz who'd left Paris for the South of France.

Her letter, beautifully written, was so touching that it brought tears to my eyes. She ended her sentiments saying that if I decided to take the children to England, her London Mews house was mine to use, adding the address, telephone number and the name of her housekeeper who was on duty at all times. What a lovely lady Drue was, beautiful on the outside and inside as well.

(Over the years I heard a mass of mean gossip about Drue and never accepted a word of it. Women jealous of beauty, brains and success made a habit of verbally attacking other women and you didn't need glasses to see through them. One woman writer wrote a whole book about ladies who'd married rich men as though that had been their only goal in life. When the book was given to me with a request to give it a "plug" in my column, I saw that Drue was included therein and immediately tossed it aside. Drue was an angel in my life when I needed angels desperately.)

There were lots of newsworthy notes from people like Princess Grace, ballet master George de Cuevas and my favorite writer-painter-friend Ludwig Bemelmans. Then I came to one from the "Sugar King of Cuba," Julio Lobo postmarked New York, New York. It was a thank-you note for something I barely remembered doing for him. One Friday evening at dinner in the Plaza Athénée dining room with Jack Forrester and friends, he told me that he was supposed to be in New York on business and had discovered that his visa had expired after the U.S. Embassy closed for the day, and wouldn't reopen until Monday morning. He was desperate. It was like fate when I noticed a top American Embassy official and his wife sitting at a table with a group of friends across the room. I didn't want to intrude on his party but when I saw that they were getting up to leave, I excused myself from my table and went out to greet the American diplomat in front of the *vestiaire*. I'd known him and his wife for some time in Paris so I didn't hesitate to tell him of the plight of the "Sugar King of Cuba." He'd heard of Julio Lobo and gave me his diplomatic calling card to give to Julio, assuring me that he'd be at the Embassy personally the next morning at ten a.m. sharp and would "do the necessary." Happily I handed the card to Julio, telling him that his troubles were over. Now I was even happier that this polite Cuban gentleman had gotten his visa, arrived in New York, and was nice enough to put his appreciation in writing.

Despite my troubled mind, I tried to face my professional situation to see how I could get up-to-date and perhaps, even ahead, before my next meeting with the lawyer concerning my personal catastrophe. The "people-watching" picture changed in the summertime. Like David Stein, a lot of people of means were drawn to Monte Carlo now that the glamorous Grace Kelly had become Her Serene Highness Princess Grace, in a pink palace with the handsome Prince Rainier. The Paris scene starting on the first of July was different from all the other months. All the Parisians I knew closed the shutters of their home all July and August, disappearing to country estates or seaside villas all around Deauville and scattered the length of the Côte d'Azur, while others sailed away on palatial yachts for exotic cruises.

Champagne...

At the same time, Paris became jammed with celebrities and personalities from movie and social worlds. It was a good time for filming movies in Paris with permission easy to come by in summer and it was also time for an influx of world renowned socialites with names like Ford, Firestone and Rockefeller. Familiar names and faces arrived loaded down with luggage to stay in many-starred hotels. They stayed weeks, even months, in those days bringing trunks full of many-petticoated dresses with matching shoes, handbags and accessories for each outfit, plus hatboxes piled higher than they were. At the Ritz you could always tell when Rosemary Kanzler, of the Grosse Pointe Ford family, arrived by the line-up of Louis Vuitton trunks in the hallway outside her suite; while John Ringling North's presence was known by the long, drawn-out Cadillac parked outside with the smiling Jerry at the wheel.

In the Rue de Berri penthouse office, I worked right around the clock starting with "the staff" during my business hours and then continuing with my correspondence and column writing after they'd gone for the day. I had three piles of invitations on my desk labeled past, present and future to go through, one by one, studying whether or not I could write an item on each. Calling hostesses AFTER their parties were over, I told them how sorry I was not to have been there, assuring them that nevertheless readers of the *Trib* would surely be interested in what had gone on. It was amazing how fast guest lists and menus and handwritten notes appeared at the door, delivered by butlers, maids, chauffeurs and, sometimes by the hostesses personally. Present invitations on my desk I answered by telephone, regretting a previous engagement but assuring the ladies that I was counting on them to help me do a little story for the paper anyway. Invitations to future charitable events were good to use as announcements. The hard-working organizers behind the scenes were always pleased with an advance paragraph and *Trib* readers interested in what was going on responded to items such as those, so everybody was happy.

This method of producing my columns was new to me and far from my favorite way of proceeding. I liked to see and hear things for myself and bring events to life for readers, but I was caught in a situation where I had to find a way to work and take care of my personal problems at the same time. This is when I coined a little phrase for myself: "necessity is somebody's mother," which made my old pal Eve laugh heartily. Unfortunately Eve and I weren't laughing together these days. She had come into my office one day, dressed in her best and raring to rush off to the Ritz, but I was hunched over my desk and had to refuse. She was furious, having gotten decked out and zoom-zoomed all the way into town from her home in the country, only to be greeted by my troubled face. She stood around insisting that I must change my mind and then gave up, flouncing out with a last remark that I was a "fat bore." That really hurt! Our friendship went on hold for awhile after that.

At the end of the week, I had an appointment to see my lawyer for a serious discussion of what had been accomplished and what had to be done next. I was very nervous on my way to him, but not half as nervous as I was when he told me his conclusions. He started his talk sympathizing with everything I'd been through but announced that he saw no other solution than to agree to deliver the children once again to Zurich.

I turned hot and cold, telling him that I could never, ever put my children through an ordeal such as that again. How could he think such a thing? Prefacing his next remark with a few more kind words, he then added that it seemed a very practical move on my part because that way, I'd be able to collect the money Jim had not paid since April, solving that problem without litigation. "I can't do that," I insisted, "I CANNOT do that." Our meeting was just before the long 14th of July weekend. When I got up to leave, he advised that I think it over during the national holiday weekend and we'd meet on the following Tuesday. As I went out the door he was saying, "There's really no other solution."

In Deauville on the 14th of July, I tried to hide my anguish. Cathy and Janne were sleek and sun-tanned. Catina looked well rested and calm, but I'd find her glancing my way as though she wanted to guess what had gone on in Paris. I couldn't talk about it. Not only did I try not to discuss anything serious in front of the children but I didn't think I had the strength to put anything into words. I was a worn-out wreck and Eve's words, "fat bore" were haunting me. There was no doubt that I'd become a bore but at least I wasn't fat. I could tell because when I fastened the inner workings of my wasp-waisted dresses, I could manage without a struggle. (That was very important to me because if I gained mere ounces I had trouble with the inner architecture of my clothes, and if I gained pounds I had nothing to wear.)

Installed on the beach under a parasol again, with Cathy and Janne busy building another sand castle, I thought I might be able to tell Catina what happened. The girls had little wooden figures bought in a toy shop to add to their *tableau* and a tiny French flag to fly from the tower when it was finished. I confided my woe to Catina, ending with the conclusion of the lawyer. "*Quelle horreur,*" she whispered adding, "*Madame ne peut pas faire ça,*" repeating Cathy's words to me in Zurich just a week before. I assured her that I agreed with her; I could not follow what the lawyer said was the only way. I told Catina that the best thing to do was go to England. She turned white under her suntan but nodded agreement. I pointed out to her that I'd have to go back to Paris after the holiday to scrape up money for the trip but she shook her head, "*Non, non,*" asking me if I had my passport with me. I assured her that my passport hadn't left my handbag since our Switzerland trip. In addition, I still had the slip of paper Gweneth Dulles had told me to keep plus the letter just received from Drue Heinz.

Catina reached into her oversized beachbag and brought out a small zipper-closed purse which looked like a make-up kit. She held it out for me to take. I unzipped the top just enough to see that there was folding money in there, much more than you'd ever imagine a children's nurse would be toting around on the beach. I tried to hand it back, saying I couldn't permit myself to take her money, but she made a "tsk-tsk" sound and said softly, "*Madame* MUST take it," adding that she had enough to live on until I could pay her back and reminding me that she had been in the Nolan household for more than seven years and had spent "hardly a *sou.*" Both of us had tears in our eyes when I thanked her and stuffed the kit into my purse. Our solemn moment was broken when Cathy and Janne called us to admire their completed sandcastle, flying its tiny French flag on the top.

The only person I informed about my decision was Simone at David Stein's home. I had a key to the big front door that I was sending back with Catina. Telling Simone my sad story made me realize that it really WAS happening.

Catina and I discussed a plan for her to go back to the Rue de la Tour and await my call from London. She must tell Odette to stay in the country for the rest of the summer. (I had a flash vision of all the toys, big and small, we had left behind and felt a lump in my throat.) Catina said she'd come to England to join us as soon as I said the word. "You'd do THAT?" I asked and she said, matter of factly that it was normal because she had to take care of the children so I could do my work.

The sooner I got to England the better, but I was afraid to fly from Deauville. Now that Jim knew I wasn't in Paris or Vaucresson, he could easily assume I'd taken the children to either Deauville or Trouville. I visualized, with a shudder, being arrested, having the children taken from me by force. Having no one to confide in, no one to advise or help me, I decided to take a taxi to Le Touquet and fly to England with the children from there.

To this day, I don't know how much of this Cathy or Janne understood. We never spoke of it. The only thing of which I was certain was that they were in favor of everything I suggested and treated it all like an adventure. When I hired a taxi to drive us all the way to Le Touquet to get a short flight across the channel, they jumped into the car with confidence that Catina would soon be joining us and waved goodbye to her out the back window until she was out of sight. (My heart ached.) We had only one piece of luggage between us, stuffed with cotton dresses and nighties and all the necessities. It seemed an endless junket, taxi arriving in Le Trouquet, spending one night there and taking the first little plane out in the morning.

During our plane ride, Cathy and Janne whispered together and then both said "good morning" in English, enjoying taking an airplane where only English was being spoken. It was their Sunday English lesson game now a reality. In the taxi on the way from the airport into London their eyes were wide to everything they saw and the first question Janne asked was why people drove on the "wrong" side of the road. The trip seemed to last an eternity from Deauville to the doorway of Mrs. Harrison Dulles in Kensington Court. We were greeted by the housekeeper and two lanky British-American teenagers who stared at us like we'd just dropped from the sky, which we had. The housekeeper was clucking all around us, saying she'd make some tea and suggesting that I call Mrs. Dulles in Paris to tell her we'd arrived. I sat on the big master bed *chez* Gweneth and called her number at the Avenue Foch. "My God, where are you?" she said in her British statesman's voice, when she heard my feeble "hello." I announced that I was sitting on her bed in Kensington Court while her housekeeper was brewing tea and her sons were showing my daughters how to play a card game called "Snap."

The three of us stayed the first night in London sleeping sideways in Gweneth's big bed. I didn't sleep the proverbial "wink" and ached all over. The girls treated it all like a game and giggled when my ankles and toes dangled over the side of the bed. We moved to Drue's the next night where there was plenty of room in her jewel-like Mews home, but I felt like an intruder, hesitating even to pick up the telephone to make calls, so I knew I'd have to find something of our own. The following day, we checked into an old-fashioned bed-and-breakfast hotel just off Sloane Square. We had a gigantic room with three brass beds in it plus a marble fireplace with a shilling-fed heater. The bathroom had a huge tub with room enough for two.

We went out exploring the neighborhood and stopped in front of the first supermarket we'd ever seen. Cathy and Janne were spellbound at the sight, so far removed from the Paris method of buying each item in a separate shop. Reminded that I'd better buy food for our evening meal, I took them into the store and watched ladies wheeling carts away from the entrance and into the store before we took one of our own. Cathy and Janne put all kinds of packages into the cart which I promptly put back, sticking to basics like milk, ham, cheese, bread, celery and plums. I couldn't pry them away from the "sweets counter." They'd never seen such a mass of colorfully-wrapped candy in their lives. Finally we settled for a package of multi-colored, variously sized "All Sorts," more because of the intriguing packaging than the licorice candy which we'd never tasted.

Back at the hotel, a wave of depression came over me as I spread a bath towel over a low coffee table in front of the fireplace and started to arrange our purchases. I was thinking of the stark, sad contrast between gourmet meals on the Rue du Docteur Blanche and this hodge-podge I was setting in front of my two daughters. How could I sink to this? When it was ready, we sat on the floor around the table. Janne beamed and announced, "*Un pique-nique! C'est magnifique!*" which raised my spirits up from the depths. Afterwards Cathy told me it was the best picnic she had ever eaten.

In the morning when a tray was brought to us we witnessed another sight we had never seen–a British breakfast. We were accustomed to eating a simple croissant or roll with their chocolate and my coffee to drink. Before us was enough food for days with milk, tea, eggs, toast, cereal, bacon, several kinds of meat we didn't even know the name of, plus a plump red apple for each. "Look," said Cathy, "They've brought us lunch for breakfast."

On the day set for my first appointment to see Gweneth's lawyer, I dressed the girls in matching cotton dresses and took them with me to the office of the law firm which had a long, lofty title–HERBERT OPPENHEIMER, NATHAN & VAN DYK, Charles Henry Connett, Solicitor–and was located in "the City" of London. With Cathy on one side and Janne on the other, I entered an office that looked like a stage setting from a Victorian play with dark brown panelling, floor-to-ceiling bookshelves, oversized desks piled high with papers, huge chairs and the distinct smell of leather and floor polish in the air. The lawyer who greeted us looked more like someone's country uncle in heavy wool with round, steel-rimmed glasses and cheeks like pink roses in full bloom.

The solicitor–I shall refer to him as CHC because those initials appeared on countless documents and letters from that day on–was a kindly fellow, showing Cathy and Janne a long bench to sit on by the bookshelves and giving them each a magazine to read. He motioned me to take a seat while he faced me across his desk to hear my sad story. He let me finish my miserable tale without saying a word, then he looked at his watch and announced that it was teatime, asking if my daughters would like milk and a biscuit. At that precise moment, I heard squeaky wheels rolling down the hallway outside. The door opened and a smiling freckle-faced, red-haired young lady wheeled the noisy tea trolley into the room. Cathy and Janne looked intrigued and the purpose of my visit seemed to be forgotten. In all my travels I'd been to many offices in numerous countries but I'd never seen anything like this. Tea was a relaxed and happy "ritual" during which the lawyer leaned back in his chair, chatted about such things as the weather and seemed all the more like a country uncle. When cups and crumbs were cleared away, he was back to business. Cathy and Janne behaved beautifully all through this and took up their magazines again, pretending to read the English text. I was so proud of them that it hurt.

Our "country uncle" leaned forward now, telling me he'd listened to every word I said and assured me that we would have no problem putting the children under the jurisdiction of the English court under the very worrying circumstance of the father resorting to force. Then he asked me to present a report of the children's "financial status." When he realized that I didn't know what he was talking about, he told me that it was his experience in cases such as this that there was a financial problem causing the situation. I said I'd explained all that when I told him about the French court judgment and the agreement made at the American Embassy. I could see that this calm and friendly man was getting impatient with me. "Mrs. Nolan," he announced, "Don't these children have 'holdings' in the United States? The actions of the grandfather and the father indicate this." When I told him that I didn't know and hadn't even thought about it, I noticed his pink cheeks turning red. He gave me a lecture about the responsibility of a mother who has the care of children, saying, "It is your duty to know these things."

CHC then outlined steps that must be taken immediately to make the children Wards of Court and what I had to do to comply with all the rules but after that, he returned to the "holdings in the USA" question. Now the "country uncle" was like a furious bulldog with a bone between his teeth and he wasn't going to let go. I gave him the name of Jim's bank in Reading, Pa., which was also the bank of Grandpa Nolan and his father before him. "Don't concern yourself with this," he said. "Official requests for information are made through the court."

We finished our long, drawn-out, first encounter with his assurance that everything would be under way immediately and he was certain that there was nothing to worry about as matters such as these were acted upon despite summer holidays. And I gave him my promise to take care of the personal part of our lives.

Before leaving his office he told me something I didn't know about my stately British friend, Gweneth Dulles. She'd been through a lot more than custody problems in France.

Living in Grenoble at the time of the German Occupation, she was interned in the nearby mountains of Vercors. An outspoken lady, she never stopped complaining about the unfairness of the "enforced residence" while her American husband was living it up with his mistress back in Grenoble. One night a German soldier burst into her quarters, ordered her outside at gunpoint and marched her toward a shed where others had been shot in cold blood. She held her little boy, Billy, in her arms and little Billy looked up into a sky brilliant with stars and said, "Look, God has all his little lights on tonight." The soldier turned and left the scene without saying a word. She never saw him again.

After our first trip to the City and the lengthy visit with the London lawyer, we went back to the supermarket to choose our next *pique-nique* and returned to our bed-and-breakfast headquarters. It was then that I had indications that Cathy and Janne were pondering our situation and not taking everything as calmly as they seemed.

One of them asked me, "Why did Daddy divorce us?" I tried to explain that a father never divorced his children; they would keep the same father and mother all of their lives. Sometimes fathers and mothers had differences between themselves but that could never mean that fathers or mothers would divorce their children.

My next concern was to find an inexpensive, furnished apartment conveniently located. Weeding through advertisements, I took the first one with room for us, plus Catina, located in Adam and Eve Mews, a dead end off Kensington High Street. The entrance was awful, up a flight of stairs to a flat above a garage, but it was charming inside. There was a terrace the length of the apartment at the back overlooking the private courtyard of a vine-covered church surrounded by small trees. The view on the right was over walled gardens of a private property where we could see arbors laden with grapes. (Later I learned that it was the studio/home of the painter, John Spencer Churchill.) This Mews place had everything we needed until I got our lives in order.

The first evening in our new home, I was fumbling around a bit. First, when shopping for groceries for ingredients to make a summer salad, I bought what I thought was a cucumber to go with the lettuce, tomatoes and herbs. The cucumber turned out to be a long, green, marrow squash which I skinned, cut into cubes and threw into the bowl. The result was a crunchy, delicious salad eaten with gusto. (Was this another "necessity is somebody's mother" invention?) Doing the dishes, I cut my finger on a sharp knife and little Janne took charge like she was head of the household. She told me to keep my finger under running water while she got something to bandage my wound. She came back trailing a roll of paper from the bathroom in streamers and insisted on wrapping my tiny cut.

After Cathy and Janne were tucked into bed, I stepped out on the terrace to breathe a few deep breaths of the night air. Standing there alone, feeling tired and lost, looking up at the dimming light in a moment of utter silence I was wondering if I'd have the courage to get through the trouble I was in and find the way to carry on. In moods like this, I always thought of that sturdy tree in the garden of the Rue du Docteur Blanche which always seemed to give me strength when I touched its powerful trunk and revealed my innermost thoughts. "But there's no tree now," I was telling myself when I heard organ music from a distance. The sounds were coming from the church across the narrow courtyard; someone practicing for Sunday no doubt. Then I felt a tingling in the back of my neck when I heard the strains of an old hymn I had known far back in the days when I lived on Seward Park Avenue in Seattle, Washington. I hadn't heard that music for more years than I could remember, when as a little girl I used to take off on a Sunday morning and go to "big people's church" all by myself. The words of the hymn came back to me as I listened. "Love lifted me, love lifted me, when nothing else could help, love lifted me." I couldn't recall all of it, but a feeling of strength and well-being came and I wondered if this is what people call a "religious experience."

The London lawyer told me that we had no reason to hide as the kind of fearful happenings in France could never occur in England. Pointing out the importance of an English tutor for the children, he gave me the name of a lady named Mrs. Parr who became an immediate part of our Mews life, giving daily lessons in English around the kitchen table. She spoke excellent French, was gentle as a lamb and she made jokes that made the girls laugh in two languages. After a few days she told me that I could be very proud of my daughters who were "excellent" students and would surely be ready for real school very soon.

I called Catina, telling her that all was well and she could come over whenever she wanted. She assured me that she WAS ready and asked if there was anything I wanted her to bring. I gave her a definite "nothing" as an answer. When she arrived, Cathy and Janne were jumping with joy, especially as they greeted favorite toys tumbling out of Catina's luggage, with skirts, shirts and sweaters. Catina reached into her own suitcase and brought out my favorite black Balenciaga cocktail dress, explaining that I might need it when I received invitations to go out. Touched, I hadn't finished thanking her when she dug deeper into the case and pulled out a shoe box from under her clothes. She handed it to me and I found it crammed with my most elaborate costume jewelry featuring long, sparkling earrings. She casually explained that perhaps I could "dress up" the black gown with different jewelry and people might not notice that I was wearing the same thing. I felt like laughing and crying at the same time but Cathy changed the pace when she came over and asked me in English, "May we take Catina to Kensington Gardens?" When I nodded approval, she turned to Catina and told her, in French, that she was about to be shown some fine London sights that were very near to our apartment and then in the future, we'd take her to a park farther away where we'd feed the deer.

Cathy and Janne were like Catina's tour guides. I was impressed that they'd absorbed so much around them so quickly. Within days, Mrs. Parr had charmed Catina with her good French and gentle manner. I was hoping that Catina would accept English lessons with Cathy and Janne but she was definitely nettled when I made the suggestion. ("Okay, okay," I thought, "I'm not about to insist." Everything was going so well that I didn't want to push.)

Chapter Twenty-Four

Soon I was able to get out on my own and contact people in my "other life." I'd kept in touch with Eric Hawkins and my office by telephone but that was all until I thought the time had come when I could actually pay visits to people in London like Jeannie Hoskins, owner of Celebrity Service, Ltd. We had always exchanged Paris-London Bulletins by mail but I had never met her or even talked to her on the phone. When I called her and told her that I was in London, the first thing she said was that I should hurry right over as she wanted very much to meet me and, "Come on over to the office, Maggi. I've got champagne on ice," she said. "Ah-hah," I thought, "now there's a lady I know I'll like."

In the fifties, Jeannie Hoskins' Celebrity Service, Ltd. was located on Arlington Street. On my way there, I almost bumped into an old acquaintance Fleur Cowles, who was scurrying out of the Caprice Restaurant as I walked by, looking for Jeannie's street number. Fleur was a joy to see–an attractive and brilliant American who'd owned her own New York advertising agency when she was very young, and started a unique, extraordinary magazine called *Flair*, which had all sorts of innovations like peephole covers, cut-ups, fold-outs and heaven knows what else. (There was a funny journalist I knew who said he had an article published in *Flair*, but it fell out.)

Fleur was looking gorgeous and she told me that she was married to an Englishman, lived at The Albany, and her name was now Fleur Cowles Meyer, which she pronounced "Meer." Further news, she was painting and would soon have enough creations for her own exhibition. I was thrilled to see her and hear all her news. We made a promise to see each other soon.

In the Celebrity Service, Ltd. office across the street from the Caprice I found that fabulous lady Jeannie Hoskins who captivated me without trying. She was bright, cheerful and full to the brim of her jaunty felt hat with interesting information about people we both knew and featured in our Celebrity Bulletins. You could tell her office was a happy, going concern. Paris presented a happy atmosphere, but business was piddling in comparison to London. Jeannie gave me a copy of her latest edition to take with me while she complimented me on Paris progress, showing we were bound for success. Jeannie made me feel great even before she opened the bottle of vintage French champagne which was like nectar of the gods after all the tea breaks I'd been having. We had a lovely visit and made a date for lunch across the street for the following week. That first Caprice lunch with Jeannie was the start of countless lunches in that fascinating place.

It had seemed like forever but only two weeks went by before the High Court of Justice, Chancery Division, declared the children to be Wards of Court. This meant that matters concerning them would have to have the approval of English Court judges. I was no longer alone in protecting the interests of Cathy and Janne. Official papers were sent to Jim at addresses in Paris and Zurich, in which he was asked to reply to the court within two weeks. Before that, however, a lengthy letter was received by my solicitor from Jim's London solicitor, asking him if he was aware that his client (me, of course) was in contempt of French Court, facing criminal charges which could result in a jail sentence. My anguish at these words brought CHC's right hand in the air like a stop signal, and he reminded me that we were here to discuss the welfare of two little girls in England, not legal entanglement in France.

He answered Jim's lawyer along those lines and at the same time took the occasion to request that "the father" return his children's clothing left in Switzerland as soon as possible. Another letter came by return mail stating that "the father" had said insofar as they'd gotten along without their belongings this long they could wait a little longer.

"This is a very unfortunate remark," said CHC, adding a slight "tsk-tsk" and a shake of his head, as we turned back to our task of completing a detailed statement from me on what had transpired which forced me to come to England with my children. It was painful to recall and record everything for an official legal document but I knew it was the only way; CHC's cool-headed help saw me through the ordeal.

My next trip to the City showed me another side of CHC when I walked into his office. That usually sedate, soft-spoken solicitor was standing up and handed me a letter, saying, "He's a bounder." When he saw my questioning look, he added, "A bounder is a cad." I sat down at the side of his desk while I read yet another letter instigated by Jim. It was full of accusations of hiding the children, being insanely jealous of a new wife and adding that no one knew what to expect from someone like HER who was pregnant when she married him.

I was so upset my hand couldn't hold the paper and I think I started babbling as I admitted that I WAS pregnant on my wedding day but I didn't know it at the time as it was only a matter of three or four weeks but we were in love and trying to get married in France and then England and finally in Vienna. But was he suggesting that he HAD to marry me or that I had tricked him into marrying me or that he was not the father of our first child? When I finally took a breath, CHC had already been holding up his "stop" sign hand, and took the chance to tell me it wasn't important.

But it was important to me and I was sickened by the obscenity of it all. Calmed down now, I still wanted to point out that I could confirm everything I said through the Paris doctor. Then I remembered our old passports which I still had. They showed our entry/departure dates when we made our Paris-London-Paris trip in January, then our entry/departure dates in February when we got married. The first baby born at the end of October didn't need a mathematician to prove a point.

Patient, understanding CHC kept reminding me that I was not on trial and our only concern was the welfare of two little girls who were now Wards of Court. Important to him was his official request to the USA bank for full information on the "Nolan *enfants*" financial situation. He explained how vital this was in preparing our sworn statements for English courts. As uncomfortable as I was discussing and delving into what I called "Nolan money matters," I knew CHC was right.

Leaving his office later, I felt sick again over Jim's cheap tactics...a dirty fighter hitting below the belt.

Cathy and Janne were thriving in their new environment despite all the changes in their lives of late. Sometimes I just stared in wonderment when I saw their little heads together and heard them joking in English or French and laughing merrily. Catina, with Mrs. Parr, had everything well in hand when I took my first flight back to France after our "escape." I'd been in daily contact with my office and checked up on Odette in the country, telling her to sit tight and enjoy her holiday. From time to time, I'd given Eric Hawkins a call to tell him he'd be seeing me soon.

During one of my calls I mentioned that there was so much "celebrity stuff" going on in London that I wondered if he'd be interested in items with London datelines. He sounded pleased, reminding me that my job was to write about interesting people and there was no stipulation about where these people were. Then he repeated his favorite phrase about names selling newspapers: "so let's have names, names, and more names."

After that remark, I started collecting items every day but I had no typewriter or desk so I had to write in longhand, seated at the kitchen table after the children had gone to bed. Soon I had long sheets of scratch paper full of readable items about known people, which added up to a London column that had only to be typed before I turned it in to Eric. (Another "necessity is somebody's mother" endeavor, I told myself.)

My first dateline had loads of celebrity names and interesting events, starting with a reception hosted by American Ambassador John Hay "Jock" Whitney; Danny Kaye appearing at a gala opening of his film called *The Colonel*, directed by Peter Glenville; Rex Harrison singing for a charity event on the same program with Noel Coward (who introduced an original ditty of his called "What's Going To Happen To The Tots?"); Barbara Hutton checking into the royal suite at Claridge's at the same time that Rita Hayworth was arriving with her new husband, James Hill, at the Savoy. I even had room to mention the future plans of Roger Dann to star in the London production of *The Sound of Music*, at the same time that Van Johnson was scheduled to be in *The Music Man*. This was only the beginning as I had material for future columns as well. When I called Fleur Cowles Meyer to ask her if I could announce her showing of paintings, she said it was too soon but perhaps I'd like to attend her party for Olivia de Havilland, expected in London from Paris. And she told me our mutual friend, John Ringling North, was arriving in his riverside suite at the Savoy for his annual visit.

It was obvious that London was enjoying a celebrity whirl not unlike Paris, making it easy for me to write a London datelined column which I had in my purse when I flew back to France.

Before flying off, I gave Catina and Mrs. Parr a list of names, addresses and telephone numbers to tack on the kitchen wall. On top of the list was CHC in the City, who showed such care and interest in Cathy and Janne. He had two lady assistants with good hearts as well as big brains so their names were on the list as well.

I told Catina that I had made a decision NOT to stay in our abandoned Paris apartment even though we'd been granted more time to vacate when the owners were reminded that the apartment hadn't been ready to live in when the rental began two years before. (It was thanks to Françoise in my office that this letter from me had been written as I never could have written that kind of French on my own.). Catina seemed relieved that I wouldn't go back to the Rue de la Tour, but turned totally skeptical when I said I'd move into the Ritz. I was determined to ask for the cheapest rate of the smallest room they had because I knew I'd feel safe and secure in surroundings where I felt "at home," knowing everyone from Charles Ritz to the teenage *chasseurs* who knew me by name.

It was a strange sensation, stepping back into "my" city which wasn't mine anymore. The first stop had to be at our former apartment on the Rue de la Tour, but I felt queasy as the taxi drove up in front of the scene of my nightmare-come-true. The concierge was right in the entry and seemed to pounce on me as soon as I stepped inside the door, spilling her version of what she had seen and heard on that horrible day. I tried to be patient but couldn't help being brusque as I hurried into the elevator. I just couldn't take another word on the subject of "the day the police came for you."

Upstairs in the apartment, I went straight to my bedroom, not daring the emotion of seeing any more of our former home than I had to. I packed all my legal papers first, including the box of divorce evidence collected against Jim but never used in France. I called the container holding all documents, letters, photos, etc., my "misery box," though it was an elegant satin-covered *coffret* which had once held expensive *bonbons*. Then I packed bags with day and evening outfits like I was going on a long journey and was ready to leave when I felt remorse over my treatment of the concierge.

Returning downstairs with a giant heavy silver serving tray that Jim and I had found in the flea market during happy days gone by, I gave it to the concierge, telling her it was a gift in thanks for all she had done for us and in appreciation of her interest and sympathy. She looked dumbfounded as she called her husband to come and see what "*Madame* is giving us."

"It's nothing," I said, putting it in her arms. "It's REALLY nothing." And I left the apartment on the Rue de la Tour for the last time.

This was the day I began my new adventure as a very special resident of the Hôtel Ritz, Place Vendôme, Paris. In the fifties, there were two kinds of guests staying there: people of means inhabiting luxurious suites or spacious rooms below; and then their servants who traveled with them, who stayed in tiny, single rooms high atop the hotel under the eaves. The entire top floor was reserved for personal maids, valets, chauffeurs, governesses and then ME. Charles Ritz told the director, Claude Auzello, that I had his permission to rent a top-floor room for one dollar per night. I practically curtsied when I heard the news.

Actually this "cheapo" room was quite nice, spotlessly clean, with a big brass bed, white enamel furniture, a sink with fluffy towels of all sizes hanging at the side, a roomy, built-in closet and an absolutely beautiful view of the Place Vendôme out an oval-shaped window. I loved that little room and slept like I was inside a cozy, safe cocoon. It was here that I discovered the thoughtfulness of the Ritz management. When I received my first dollar-a-night bill, my room was classified as a *chambre de journaliste* and not the usual category of "maid's room." "How kind, how elegant, how very Ritzy," I thought.

My Paris-London commuting began and my *Herald Tribune* columns full of items from both places were routine. Flying back and forth was made easier on my pocket through the kindness of a gentleman named M. de la Brosse at Air France, who offered journalists' rates for airplane tickets.

During those hectic commuting days between Paris and London, every time I stepped into the penthouse office on the Rue de Berri I found stacks of mail and messages on my desk. Now, at my request Françoise opened all the mail (even those marked personal) because everything I received seemed to have names and news for celebrity bulletins as well as my columns. Information was coming from many worthwhile sources. The very first stack I found on my return to Paris had tidbits concerning the "April in Paris" ball activities of the Duchess of Windsor with Claude Philipe and Maurice Carrère; upcoming projects of Curd Jurgens; an announcement that Bette Davis was in Paris en route to Madrid; an upcoming wedding of a part-American princess and so on. What I loved best was a photo of Olivia de Havilland's baby daughter, Gisèle, getting her first haircut from M. Alexandre, whose salon was becoming famous as Alexandre de Paris. Happily, I took that photograph to top my next column from Paris.

An amazing amount of material from outside of Paris was coming my way. In addition to society acquaintances in Deauville, Biarritz, on the Côte d'Azur and in Monte Carlo, I found interesting tidbits coming from friends traveling in Spain, Belgium, Switzerland, Italy and Greece; and even some written on expensive stationery engraved with "written aboard the...," with the name of the yacht the writer was on. After a few paragraphs in my columns under a heading "notes from near and far," Eric asked me where I was getting this "good stuff." I told him that it came directly from the very VIPs mentioned and that I'd started a reference file upstairs if he was interested in seeing it. He was pleased and joked that I had some pretty fancy "stringers" working for me. I laughed with him and said it was not only a godsend but "the price is right as well."

One morning the mail on my penthouse desk in Paris included a letter to me from Grandpa Nolan in Reading, PA. It was the one and only letter I ever received from Jim's father, an air letter *aérogramme*, needing no envelope (which Françoise didn't open when she saw the Nolan return address). When I spread it out in front of me, I couldn't help but be shocked at the typewritten message which began "Dear Madam." Further, Cathy and Janne's grandfather referred to them as "the wards." The letter was to inform "Madam" that he was attorney for the trusts of "the wards" and would instruct the bank to forward deeds as per my request insofar as "you have presently the care of the wards."

This letter looked like it was written for the benefit of others as well as an insult to me, the mother of his grandchildren. He knew I hadn't requested anything as it was now out of my hands. What was being done was in the name of the High Court of England, not little Maggi on the Rue de Berri.

When I next saw CHC in the City, I had the letter from Grandpa Nolan in my purse while CHC had copies of trust deeds on his desk confirming his original opinion that the children had holdings in America which were instigating Nolan actions to take possession of the children. The trusts, established by Grandma and Grandpa Nolan in 1952, stated that interest would be sent to Maggi and Jim Nolan every three months to pay for the children's needs. When I assured CHC that I wasn't aware of the trusts and certainly had never received any interest payments, he was determined to dig deeper to find where those payments had been made. "Especially since December 1955, when the mother had full custody and care of the children," he added. This money business made me uncomfortable and CHC knew that well by now.

"Don't concern yourself with this problem. It will be taken care of from here," he reminded me as we said goodbye.

Not long after this meeting, CHC received the information he wanted from the bank which showed cancelled checks all made out to me and Jim. On the backs someone had forged my name and even spelled Maggi with an "e" on the end. What's more, the false endorsement was scrawled across the middle of the back in the French way, rather than the American way in the upper left-hand corner. After pointing that out, I was in for a real shock when I saw that some checks had been deposited in a Swiss bank account in the name of Jim's wife. My hand was shaking when I picked them up and handed them to CHC, saying "That was the name of Jim's wife before they married."

CHC gathered all the papers to put back in a huge folder on his desk, stating quite calmly as he did so, that in all of his years of experience he had never encountered such behavior.

"These amounts taken must be repaid," CHC announced. "And payments must arrive in England to be paid to you for the children." That was welcome news indeed, but he was not yet aware of the workings of this Reading bank founded by Jim's grandfather, in which Jim's father held a powerful position. Later some checks arrived by mail to the City of London; some were in Grandpa Nolan's pocket when he arrived in England and they stayed in Grandpa's pocket when he left.

Soon after the trust deeds revelations, I discovered that Grandpa Nolan was still up to no good in my regard. A few weeks after his "Dear Madam" letter to me, a friend in Reading sent me a clipping from the local newspaper with information that only J. Bennett Nolan could have provided, stating that Margaret Nolan had ordered safe deposit boxes of James Nolan to be locked, blocked, confiscated or whatever people do when there are financial problems between two parties. I didn't order anything of the kind. I didn't even know that Jim HAD safe deposit boxes, but I did know that such a story put me in a very bad light in Jim's hometown.

What worried me most was the pain it must be causing Grandma Nolan and I couldn't get that lovely lady out of my mind. I wondered how much she knew of what was going on and if she was hearing all the lies being told about me. When I told the solicitor what a lovely person she was and how I feared that she had been turned against me, he looked at me quizzically and asked, "Didn't you know she died?," looking into his folder of papers and bringing out a letter from the Reading bank which referred to "the late E. May Nolan." I stared at the word "late" in silence while he was still going through his American correspondence and brought out another letter with the same saddening words, "the late E. May Nolan."

I was crushed, thinking what a shame it was that she missed knowing her grandchildren and what a pity that Cathy and Janne hadn't had the chance to know her. I felt pangs of guilt, as though somehow I could have prevented all this but all I could say was, "I didn't know. No one told me."

Chapter Twenty-Five

The London merry-go-round of celebrity reporting got into motion easily and fast because of two people in my life, Jeannie Hoskins of Celebrity Service, Ltd. and John Ringling North, staying royally as a circus king in his suite at the Savoy. Jeannie gave me copies of her twice-weekly bulletins, telling who was in town, where, why and how to contact them. What's more, she often treated me to celebrity-watching lunches at the Caprice where I got to know owner-director, Mario Gallati, who gave us top people treatment. Jeannie always impressed me with her friendly, easy-going, dynamic personality as she seemed to know someone sitting at every table and had a "my pal" relationship with the waiters as well. She was always bubbling with news of movie and theater people, big shots in business and journalism plus a smattering of socialites.

Jeannie was always planning some sort of entertainment in her office for journalists and subscribers to her bulletins or at home in her apartment on Park Lane, where she and her *Daily Express* journalist-husband, Percy, held court with their talking budgie named Charlie. It was at one of her parties that I ran into an old acquaintance from *Stars & Stripes*, Bill Richardson, who was now editor of a gentlemen's magazine in London called *Lilliput*. While we yacked about old times standing in Jeannie's happy mob scene, he gave me his card saying he wanted me to write some celebrity stories for his magazine, asking me to get in touch with him at his office. I took the card automatically, little knowing that I'd soon be the one responsible for a seven-page cover story in *Lilliput*, a magazine I'd never heard of until that moment. And neither had Paul Getty, but he agreed to do the article with me.

Another whirl, another world opened up for me when John Ringling North arrived in London, checking into his Savoy suite featuring a fabulous view of the Thames. His sitting room full of sofas and easy chairs looked as big as a ballroom with floor-to-ceiling windows the full width of the room. Here every evening before he went out on the town, he'd have cocktail-laden meetings with circus impressarios or worldwide assistants he hired to search out outstanding acts for Ringling Brothers Barnum & Bailey Circus, USA; this gave him the reputation of having "the greatest show on earth." The minute his business meetings were over, John was ready to tour his favorite restaurants and clubs. One of the first he took me to was the exclusive Park Lane club, Les Ambassadeurs.

The first time I stepped into the marble hall, past the statesman-like director, John Mills, and entered the elegant, luxuriously-furnished dining room, I felt like I was in Paris, sighting people I knew seated on the plush banquettes. On my right, the sugar king of Cuba, Julio Lobo, who stood up part way in welcome as we passed by his table.

John knew Julio Lobo from several ocean crossings, and during dinner the sugar king sent over his card inviting us to a cocktail party he was hosting at Claridge's in honor of Bette Davis.

At the table next to us sat Nicole Milinaire, a pert blonde television producer from Paris, who leaned over her dinner partner to tell me she was in London making a TV series called *Dick and the Duchess*. (Little did she know then that she'd become a duchess herself, when she married the Duke of Bedford.) It didn't take the owner of the club long to come over, stand in front of our table and have a chat. An old friend of John's, he had sent caviar to our table with his compliments as soon as we sat down, and now he was charming me with compliments about my *Herald Tribune* column, which he was pleased to see now included London news. Pointing out that his club was a top spot to gather celebrity items, he invited me to come anytime I wished as his guest. Further, he added that lunchtime was just as newsworthy as dinnertime.

"He's his own best press agent," John laughed, when Mr. Mills went away to charm other tables with his *grand seigneur* manner. That evening at Les Ambassadeurs, called "Lays-Aye" by *habitués*, was a first among countless others with many other hosts besides John plus some lunches, dinners and parties, which I hosted myself. But soon after the first evening, again invited by John, I was stunned with fear at what I heard a very handsome but also very drunk TWA executive saying at the next table to ours. Bragging in a loud voice of his great feat of successfully kidnapping the son of French actress, Michèle Morgan, in a London park, he raised his arm in a TWA take-off motion, laughing, "and we flew that little kid right to his dad in the USA."

I didn't have any way of knowing whether or not he was telling the truth; all I knew was that I wanted to go home. John talked me out of my fears, for the moment, but I still shuddered at the horrible thought that he might be telling the truth and had a nightmare about it soon after.

John Ringling North introduced me to another place in London which became my "home away from home" on many occasions. It was Siegi's Club on Charles Street, owned and run by a Polish-born Englishman named Siegi Sessler. The Club was small and friendly; most of the *habitués* were film folk like Sam Spiegel, Darryl Zanuck, William Holden, Gregory Ratoff, Carl Foreman, Bob Goldstein, Anthony Quinn, Stanley Baker and Gregory Peck. Then there were

J. Paul Getty &
John Ringling North
were guests at my
champagne party
in the penthouse of
London's Carlton-Tower

airline people like Fred Tupper from Pan American Airways and journalists like Louis Sobol, Earl Wilson, Rex North and Donald Zec. There was a cozy bar on the street floor and a gourmet restaurant one flight up where the pianist, Tommy Nicol, knew everybody's favorite song. I think I made an instant hit with Siegi when I admired the "mascot" of his club, a magnificently-coiffed giant poodle named Buster, who wore a solid gold chain collar more exquisite than you'd see around the neck of a wealthy dowager.

John and I didn't stay more than a few minutes at Siegi's on my first visit but it wasn't long before I felt at ease there among friends. There were two barmen, Sidney and Patrick, who had mastered the art of making guests feel at home. Once I made a list of everything they had behind the bar to please customers (besides booze) and counted seventeen items of value to those in need: aspirin, hand cream, hairpins, string, hand mirror, pencil, pen, elastic bands, straight pins, safety pins, drawing pins, needles, thread, buttons, glue, adhesive tape and money if you wanted to cash a check. To tease them, I asked to see what color thread they had and when I saw only black and white I said, "Ha-ha, I wanted pale pink." Naturally, the next time I went there to have my champagne, they placed a spool of pale pink cotton beside my glass.

The necessary London-Paris-London routine of my life was hardly ideal but the fact that I could keep my job under such circumstances gave me a bit of satisfaction. You never knew, however, what would happen next.

One noontime during a stay in Paris, I received a hysterical call from Odette in the country shouting into the phone that Noirice had flown out of the window and disappeared toward the forest of Vaucresson. When she stopped shouting, I tried to stay calm as I told her to go straight to the police and report him missing. "What?" she screeched, "You want me to go to the police about a black bird flying away?" I repeated my request but she began to argue that such a thing wasn't done. A bird flying away wasn't a missing person and besides, they'd think she'd gone crazy at the police station and what would happen to her next? My repeated request now became a command when I told her that she HAD to do this for me and do it NOW, reminding her that Noirice was more than just a bird; he was a TALKING bird and the beloved pet of two little girls. I could tell she was unhappy over my command but she agreed to go to the police right away. (I think by then Odette was acquainted with me well enough to know that I was easy-going when everything was fine, but I could be tough in a crisis.)

Odette reported Noirice's "escape" to the police but they didn't hold out much hope as heavy rains had begun to fall and continued for two days and two nights afterwards. On the third morning, the sun came out and so did Noirice...flying right into a garden where children were playing. When their mother saw this strange black bird and heard him say, "*Cathy...Kiki...Catina*," and then whistle like he was calling a dog, she brought some rice out for him to eat. He stayed by the children while the mother found a bird cage, put more rice in it and Noirice jumped right in to finish his meal.

The lady who found Noirice in the garden was an American who lived all the year in Vaucresson not far from where we'd rented our house for the summer. I'm not certain what other people would do if they found a talking black bird in the garden with their children, but this American lady went straight to the police to report her find. The police, aware of the "missing bird" drama, were happy to give the news to Odette. When I was given the bird finder's number, I called her immediately and she seemed very pleased to hear from me because she read my column and knew a lot of people I was writing about. I told her that when the bird episode was over with its happy ending, I'd like to write about *her* in my column and she sounded like she'd be pleased. I discovered that she was the daughter of the great Russian singer, Chaliapin, married to a Russian-American, Peter Schouvaloff, had four children, two dogs and several birds of her own. She delivered Noirice to Odette who delivered the bird to me and I wrote a report in my column under the heading, "The bird that got out of hand." With Noirice in his cage on my desk, I tried to get him to talk but he wouldn't say anything. I called the British Embassy and asked a diplomat, Edward Tomkins, how I could get Noirice a "passport" for London. He said it was easy as long as the bird possessed a health certificate from a pet doctor. So it was settled that Noirice would fly away, in an airplane this time, with me on my next flight.

On the plane to London, with Noirice in his cage on my lap, people around me seemed quite interested in this sleek, shiny, black bird who perched in one place and seemed quite bored with the world around him. When the man next to me asked why I was taking so much trouble flying a black bird to London when I could probably buy black birds over there, I explained that this was a special *talk-ing* bird. "No kidding," the man said, "How come he's not saying anything?" It was true; Noirice had not said one word since he arrived in my office or on the trip to the vet or when I fed him and taxied to the airport with him on my lap. Not a word! Noirice was silent in the London cab all the way to the Mews as well. When I opened the downstairs door to the apartment and started up, I heard Cathy and Janne chattering away and so did Noirice. Before we were at the top of the stair-case he was saying, "*Cathy...Kiki...Catina. Ça va, ça va, ça va,*" and he was flitting around like he was jumping for joy. After everyone had crowded happily around his cage he didn't shut up until nightfall, only to begin again calling his family at the first light of day.

The day came when I could not postpone facing the facts in Paris. The rent on the country house was up. Odette would be moving back to the Rue de la Tour where the extension given us to stay was nearing an end. When I called Odette in Vaucresson from my penthouse office in Paris and asked her to close the country house and return, the first thing she asked was, "But what about the doll-house...and all the toys?" I told her that I'd already thought about that. André Dubonnet 's daughter, Lorraine Bonnet, lived close by in Ville d'Avray and had a little daughter named Catherine. She said she'd be very happy to have what we'd left behind and would pick up everything before Odette went back to Paris.

With my rough Paris-London schedule, deadlines facing me twice a week, countless requests to appear in the City and all the London household details to tend to, I had no choice but to ask Odette to take charge of the Rue de la Tour and pack everything we owned to be picked up by vans and put in storage until further notice. She worked faithfully, letting me know of progress every day and then, one day, came by my Paris office to tell me everything was ready BUT...she was taking a job as a concierge and would need to furnish her street floor "cubbyhole" which would be her home from now on. She wondered if she could have the furniture in her backstairs maid's room. She handed the inventory to me: bed, chairs, dresser, table, lamps, radio, clock, flower vase, etc. I said, "Okay," knowing how important these simple things were to her when they meant so little to me.

She tried to thank me, profusely, and I found myself repeating what I'd said a short while ago to another concierge, "It's nothing, really nothing." Before Odette left, I told her there was only one thing I wanted to take with me before everything was put in storage and that was my portrait which she promised to have delivered to the office before the storage vans arrived at the Rue de la Tour. After seeing Odette, I had to rush back to London and the next time I stepped into the Paris office Françoise said moving men had delivered "your paintings" and they were stacked against the back wall, out of the way.

It might have been the moving men's error or Odette's that every painting I had was delivered, not just the portrait. There was my so-called Hubert Robert from the flea market, the pair of Zao Wou-ki lithographs, a Tuileries carrousel painted by a young man named Cohen (Earl Blackwell said he'd publicize him if he'd change his name to NEHOC, but the artist said "NO"), plus a few "works of art" with frames worth more than the pictures in them. I had to laugh at the stack against the wall and then decided to hang the decorative works in the office and take the paintings, one by one, with me on the plane to London.

No matter how crazy the pace was in Paris, every evening before leaving the office around six o'clock, I'd call London to check up on my family. I cherished those moments exchanging chitchat with Cathy and Janne, getting updates on what they'd seen in the park, what they'd learned from Mrs. Parr and even what the weather was like in London. One evening I called our London number and got no answer. Waiting a bit, I called again, and again, and again.

I was wild with worry, wondering what possibly could have happened, imagining the worst. Checking, I was assured that the line was in order so I tried and tried without success. It was too late to call the City and I didn't have Mrs. Parr's number and realized with horror that I didn't know her first name or initials. It was hell trying to think what to do.

Ready to drop everything and take the first plane to London, I suddenly thought of Olivia de Havilland who had arrived at the Savoy for the grand gala of her latest film in the presence of royalty that night. Never, ever, had I asked a personal favor from a celebrity. But there I was, telephoning the Savoy in London to try to get a top Oscar-winning Hollywood movie star on her royal gala night to check up on my chidren. I was crazy with worry and she was my only hope. All I wanted her to do was to find someone–anyone–who'd go to Adam and Eve Mews as soon as possible and report to me on my family. Olivia listened to my story and assured me that she would go to my children right away. Through tears, I told her that she couldn't do that, she'd be late for her big night. I didn't expect her to take the time, all I wanted was to find someone to go and check on my children. She let me finish and then told me very calmly that her young son, Benjamin, was with her and they'd take a taxi ride to my place and call me as soon as they got there. I was still crying that I didn't want her to be late for her gala, but she laughed, saying, "Stars are expected to be late. And besides, I'm a mother *first* and a star afterward." It seemed like forever, but it wasn't very long before she was on the phone to me saying that she was sitting in my flat with two darling little girls in their pajamas and everything was fine and dandy.

The evening's experience was so shattering that I felt ill back in my top-floor room at the Ritz. There was no way that I could go through with the night's invitation to a dress-up ball. The elaborate gown and matching coat I'd borrowed from Jacques Heim was spread out across the bed with its matching veil-and-sequined mask that Philippe Heim, son of Jacques, had found for me to wear. How ridiculous it all seemed! How long could I go on living like this? I cleared off my bed and climbed into it, staying almost motionless all night long until it was time to get back on the merry-go-round again. I whispered words of thanks to that angel, Olivia, to whom I would be forever grateful.

It wasn't long after the misery of the unanswered telephone that the mystery was solved. One afternoon in Paris, the dinner party I'd accepted was cancelled and my datebook was free. Work was cleared off my desk and articles delivered so I decided to take a plane to London that evening rather than the next morning. Bouncing in the door and up the stairs, I passed Catina and the children having dinner in the kitchen and noticed immediately that the telephone was not in its place on the hall table. It took seconds to trace the long cord down the hall to Catina's room, where the phone was covered with fat pillows on her bed.

I didn't touch the telephone but hurried to join everybody in the kitchen, opening the refrigerator for some chilled white wine as I explained my reasons for hurrying back a day sooner than usual, "We'll have all day tomorrow to go to Richmond Park and feed the deer," I said, taking a big sip of wine to calm my nerves. Catina left the kitchen for a few moments and came back to accept a glass of wine. We continued the evening as usual, though it wasn't. In the hallway, the telephone was back in place. Maybe I should have had a confrontation with her but I couldn't. I knew now she had a BIG problem, which was my problem as well.

From the beginning I knew that Catina didn't like London and didn't want to try to speak English. She never stopped her criticism, belittling everything about the British way of doing things. But this was more. I sensed that she resented my weekly trips to France and she was probably fed up with my nightly calls to chat, more and more in English, with Cathy and Janne. But did she have any idea of how necessary it was for me to live like this just now, and how cruel it had been to make me go through the agony of wondering if my children were all right?

One morning in Paris, after a four-day stay in London, the elevator man on the ride up to my top-floor office greeted me with a long face, unlike his usual jovial self. "Madame Nolan," he said gravely, "there was a strange person here riding up and down the elevator, telling everyone that she is the REAL Mrs. Nolan and you are the false Mrs. Nolan." At first I was intrigued, asking what the lady was like and he said, "In the first place she was NOT a lady," adding that she had a sharp face, blonde hair and was noticeably pregnant. He went on, saying that she didn't seem to be there to see me but merely to ride up and down in the elevator, making a nuisance of herself and annoying everyone. He stated that his elevator did not have enough room for such disturbances and if she returned he would be obliged to report her. This person sounded like Jim's new wife. It was a strange way for me to learn that my daughters were going to have a half-brother or half-sister in the near future.

The elevator operators at the *Trib* were very friendly; we'd had so many ups and downs together that we were like family. They got together regarding the strange woman and decided not to allow her back. They called her "*la folle*" and assured me that "the crazy one" would not ride with them again.

A few weeks later, there were indications that "*la folle*" was up to mischief again but I could never prove it, nor did I have time for such petty matters.

It was a Friday evening when I was taking the Paris-London plane I often took. When it seemed that we were about ready to land at the airport an announcement was made that we were making an emergency landing. We arrived in an open field and were requested to file out as fast as possible. As I stood, mystified, in tall grass with the rest of the frightened passengers we were told that there had been a bomb alert and the plane was being searched. No bomb was found and aside from being later than usual getting back to my children for the weekend, all was well.

On my flight back to Paris one of the stewards, who knew me by now confided that our bomb scare was no more than "some dame" who called up and said that the Paris-London flight would be blown up. Air France officials didn't believe it but they couldn't take chances. I wondered if the "some dame" mentioned was "*la folle*" of the Rue de Berri elevator, as it was so easy for anyone to find out what plane I'd be taking to London. But I was too busy to give it much thought.

There wasn't time to think about the strange "real Mrs. Nolan." I was faced with more pressing problems. In addition to an ever-increasing work schedule I was in debt for the first time in my life. I owed money left and right. My earnings from various projects were never enough and I'd reached the bottom of my piggy bank. The time had come to call a *commissaire-priseur* to take everything out of storage and put it up for auction to pay my debts. The gentleman put in charge of this ordeal seemed calmly accustomed to such happenings. He reminded me of a funeral director speaking to someone who'd just lost a loved one. He was kind, assuring me that everything in storage that came under the category of children's belongings, personal affairs, plus household goods like linen and blankets would be shipped to me in London. I felt sick but knew I'd have to turn my back on this drama, face work and take care of my family. Everything was carted away, but it was hard to forget what I'd never see again; I kept picturing all those funny objects we'd so lovingly collected. A parade of "things" were marching through my brain until I couldn't stand it. I had to straighten up and force such thoughts out of my mind. "Let go," I'd say to myself, "REALLY let go." By then I knew that "things" didn't matter when the time came to let go. Still, for a long time afterward, I couldn't look into antique store windows or second-hand shops without feeling a special sort of pain.

From the time I began to be a London-Paris commuter, Paris friends had various attitudes toward my new situation. When Maggie Vaudable first heard that I was dividing my time between Paris and London, she was not pleased. She told me that she was disappointed in me as though I was being unfaithful to France. Although CHC had warned me many times that I must not talk about my legal affairs, after Maggie made a few hurtful remarks I thought I ought to tell her why

I had to divide my time and asked her if we could have a private talk.

After our conversation, she changed completely and became like a sister who couldn't do enough to make my life easier and more cheerful. More than that, she invited me to countless celebrity-studded evenings at Maxim's where there were no other journalists in attendance. One day when I got back to my little room at the Ritz after a hard day, Maggie called to invite me to a secret dinner party she was planning for Maria Callas.

"I didn't even know Maria Callas was in Paris," I said. Maggie explained that she wasn't but that she'd be passing through Paris, changing her plane from Rome to another heading for Chicago and the Maxim's dinner would be held before Maxim's was opened for the evening. I found that a marvelous way for La Callas to pass the time between airplanes and was pleased to be included among the guests.

It was truly a unique Maxim's dinner party served at teatime in honor of the lady Parisians called La Callas.

This had to be the fastest banquet served during the shortest visit ever made to Paris. The Maxim's scene was set for a glorious feast at a long table covered in linen, draped down to the floor. The table was decorated *à la Tosca* with towering silver candelabra, gleaming flatware, sparkling crystal and silver bowls of pink roses. Maria Callas came in with her husband and about a dozen Pathé-Marconi executives just as her own recordings began to play in the background. The star's special Maxim's menu included miniature oysters, roast white fish with raisins, saddle of lamb with tender tips of asparagus, iced soufflé and magnums of outstanding vintage champagne (Perrier-Jouet, 1952).

The ornate, dramatic table decor for La Callas was the creation of Maurice Carèrre, while it was Maggie Vaudable's idea to invite friends for an early dinner at other tables on this unique occasion to give life and warmth to surroundings in the otherwise empty Maxim's. In inviting, Maggie said quite frankly, "Please come, help me with the atmosphere, no one should be expected to dine at Maxim's with nothing but empty tables to look at." Guests were delighted to comply. Among Maggie's friends that evening were Countess "Mapie" de Toulouse-Lautrec; her brother, Henri de Vilmorin; the Comédie Française actress, Mony Dalmes; Baron and Baroness de Cabrol; Count Guy d'Arangues from Biarritz; and Mme. George Auric, a painter whose husband wrote the music for the film, *Moulin Rouge*. I was seated on a banquette enjoying the same menu as the one served at the Callas table. We were having a wonderful time when one of the record executives came over to me, asking if I'd like to join Maria Callas for coffee.

Pleased with the invitation, I got up without an idea of what I'd say to her. Never mind, she was in such a mellow mood that she did all the talking. All I had to do was keep my ears open. She started out sweetly, saying that she was touched to tears over all the trouble Parisians had taken to plan this unforgettable French reception and dinner. And then she said that she was sorry she had never sung in

Champagne...

Maria Callas and
Ari Onassis in Paris.
Ari bought 50 tickets
for Maria's first
Paris Opéra appearance
in 1958.

Paris, but she was sure it would happen. She told me that she wanted to appear at the Paris Opéra as soon as she could be certain of the high quality of her supporting singers and musicians. That brought her to the subject of criticism pouring down on her for walking out of *Norma* in Milan. "They accuse me of temperament," she said. "But I was sick, sick, sick." Not long after this short, lovely interlude Maria Callas was back in Paris to sing at a grand gala at the Paris Opéra, followed by formal dining in the opera halls at elaborate *à la Tosca* set tables like the one Maurice Carrère had created for her at Maxim's.

(That was the memorable night when "Ari" Onassis did all he could to get into the spotlight. He bought fifty tickets for the concert and formal dinner and seemed to be in every photo with Maria and her husband. Gossiping about the "new Callas-Onassis romance" became the rage of Paris. All I could think of was that I hoped he'd never put his lighted cigar on her bare back, as I'd seen him do to Tina.)

Despite my lawyer's advice, I confided in another lady after my private talk with Maggie Vaudable. The next one was Princess Grace of Monaco. It came about when I lost control of my emotions, sat down at my office typewriter after everyone had gone and poured my heart out all over the page. It upsets me to this day to remember my letter to her but still touches me deeply when I reread her answer to me.

My outburst to her was written after I had seen the playboy/PR man, Johnny Meyer, strutting out of the Hôtel George V in the company of two buxom blondes. He gave me a loud "hello" and said he found it really funny that he should run into me just when he was on his way to dine with my former husband. I tried to be calm when he rattled on about his plans to take off for Monte Carlo the next day with Jim. He called Jim "your ex" and assured me with a wink that they intended to have "a hell-of-a-lot of fun."

I walked away seething. "So," I thought, "Jim will go to Monte Carlo and charm the former Grace Kelly, fellow Irish-American, formerly of Philadelphia and thus a fellow Pennsylvanian. And a Catholic." My imagination ran away with me. After a fretful night and a hard day's work, I decided to write to Princess Grace at her palace, telling her if she met Jim Nolan she shouldn't fall for his "Irish blarney" because he was the man responsible for my forced move to London in the interests of our children.

The minute I mailed my letter I felt I'd gone too far and never should have written it. Then I started hoping that she got so much mail that she might not even read it. Time passed before I heard from her but when the day came that I was holding her handwritten reply to me in my hand, I got that strange tingling sensation on the back of my neck, realizing that my feeling about Princess Grace was true. She cared enough to take her pen in hand and write words that helped.

I never kept a copy of the letter I wrote to Princess Grace, but I never let go of the one she wrote to me.

Miss Maggi Nolan
Herald Tribune
21 Rue de Berri
Paris VIII

Dear Miss Nolan —

    I have
waited to answer your
letter to see if there
were any incidents
concerning Mr. Nolan
to tell you about —

    The Prince
and I have not met
him here this summer
or anywhere for that
matter but I do appreci-
ate very much your
writing to me and

you have my deepest
sympathy in your
situation which must
be very difficult —
I do hope things
work out better in
future and that you
are able to raise
your children in peace.
For - a woman alone-
raising children. under
the best conditions -
is never easy —

All good wishes

Grace de Monaco

Wednesday

Chapter Twenty-Six

Not everyone I knew was sympathetic to my situation. My friend, Jack Forrester, never had much patience with me in my determination to stay cool and collected in public and refusing to discuss my personal problems with anyone. Once, at a Maxim's party, he took me aside to bawl me out after hearing a loud-talking guest say to me that she couldn't understand why I was going to so much trouble to keep a father from his children just because I was jealous of his new wife. Jack asked me why I didn't give that woman a few facts of life to mull over.

I'd never told my troubles to Jack; I didn't have to. He'd been a bachelor about town for so many years and seen for himself how Jim had behaved dating all sorts of women in restaurants and nightclubs when he was supposedly happily married. He'd lost respect for Jim when he'd show up at Franco-American parties with a strange woman while I was home on the Rue du Docteur Blanche. Now, Jack was annoyed with me that I wouldn't defend myself and accused me of still being in love "with that SOB."

After Jack had his say, I assured him that I was no longer in love but, after all, Jim was the father of my children, the only father they'd ever have and, besides, to answer everyone who thought they knew my business would take precious energy which I needed for more important matters. Jack just shook his head, saying he didn't know whether I was naive or just plain stupid and then added, "Women–women–I'll never understand women."

When Jack wasn't upbraiding me for not defending myself or accusing me of still being in love with "that lousy bastard," he talked about interesting people like his business associate, Jean Paul Getty, who was now a Londoner. Jack spoke to Paul every day and said that Paul had mentioned that he wouldn't mind if I gave him a call during one of my London stays. Paul was a permanent resident of London then, staying in a suite at the Ritz. "He likes you, Maggi," Jack said, adding that Paul liked the newspaper columns I wrote because I was "often funny and never rude." I liked that sum-up. (Many people had told me that they thought it quite nice that I never said anything bad about anyone and I had a stock answer for that. I'd say I didn't write bad things because I wasn't that kind of girl..."And besides, Eric won't let me.")

Jack told me about another fellow who was now a friend of mine, Julio Lobo, the Sugar King of Cuba. The details of this gentleman's life were both amazing and hair-raising. That sixty-year old business tycoon had a lot of enemies. He'd been gunned down and left for dead on a Havana street but became even more powerful despite the bullets he still carried around in his body. Another of Lobo's claims to fame: he owned the largest collection of Napoleon's personal belongings and one of his latest acquisitions was Napoleon's false teeth. Then Jack told me Lobo owned a fine collection of Rubens and Renoir paintings; that took my mind off my unhappy thoughts. The private side of Julio Lobo was full of remorse because Lobo had divorced his wife of many years to marry another woman who had "done him wrong" and he regretted his mistake ever since.

Knowing this about Mr. Lobo's private life made me understand his very kind and unusual generosity to my children, though he'd never met them. First, when he learned we'd moved to London he sent Harrods book tokens for them so they could start an English library. When Jack told him I'd left our television behind in France, a new one arrived at our London address with a card from Mr. Lobo saying that he thought this would help my daughters to learn English. When I tried to thank him in person, he seemed so uncomfortable that he looked annoyed; so Cathy and Janne wrote him thank-you notes which I mailed to Claridge's after every gift.

During the first few months of my London-Paris commuting I went to many meetings with CHC in the City to finalize our original statement to the High Court regarding the future of the children. It was many pages long, with details of our living conditions, marital troubles, divorce and problems leading up to the day that I flew away from France. It was a painful document to prepare but CHC insisted that every word was necessary including those of his own that reported all the monies Jim owed to the children and me plus the fact that Jim had not yet returned the children's suitcases.

The upcoming court hearing in front of learned judges would be to decide the children's future and my specific wish was that they remain in England as Wards of Court, in my care but with free access to the father in England and only on English soil until a better relationship was established. A copy of this document was sent to Jim's lawyers before it was officially sworn to and filed. The next time I walked into CHC's office, I could tell that he'd heard from Jim's lawyers. By now I'd had so many meetings with my City solicitor that I could detect his feelings by the way his cheeks got flushed or his jaw looked as hard as a rock.

CHC had received no acceptance or rejection or even an opinion of the paper he had sent. Instead, he was told that Jim would pay me every cent he owed if I would get separate passports for the children so he could take them to Switzerland.

Champagne...

"We're back to square one," I said. "He's asking me to sell my children."

I don't remember whether CHC answered this horrendous letter. We proceeded with my original statement, not changing a word. It was sworn to, signed, sealed and filed in October, 1958. Nothing was heard from Jim until November when he passed by the Adam and Eve Mews apartment to drop off the children's suitcases one afternoon when I was not there. This was the first time he had seen Cathy and Janne since that unhappy day in Vaucresson. Catina said he seemed very nervous and ill-humored, staying less than an hour but telling them he'd be back in December.

There was no reply to my October statement from Jim until about two weeks before Christmas when his lawyers filed an official statement of their own. In it, Jim denied every paragraph in my statement except for the vital statistics of names, birthplaces and dates. He swore he had never gone out with other women during our marriage. He swore that I would not let him see the children. He then devoted three pages to his new wife, whom he swore was "above reproach."

Jim's version of what happened in Zurich was nothing like mine. He claimed I tried to force him to sign a paper assuring continuation of our US Embassy agreement. Immediately that reminded me of the paper I'd actually asked him to sign assuring the welfare of Cathy and Janne while they were in his care and I told CHC about his refusal to sign the part about leaving Switzerland. Yes, I still had that paper which showed that my worry was the welfare of the children and not money.

After eight pages of remarkably imaginative claims and accusations, Jim got around to his proposals for the children's future which didn't go further than his taking them to Switzerland on their own passports to be issued immediately. He presented a paper showing that their hotel reservations in Klosters had already been made by his wife. I read all of this with more fear than fury, wondering if this sworn document full of lies was as obvious to others as it was to me. If Jim had his way the children would leave England and never come back.

CHC stated flatly that this "hostile paper" must be answered immediately and in detail. Dropping everything else in my life at that moment, I went back to my "misery box," collecting proof of Jim's girlfriends long before our divorce; his frequent trips away during holiday times; the confidential reports on the new wife supposedly "beyond reproach;" the paper Jim refused to sign in Zurich. Time was flying and Jim's last-minute Christmas request seemed calculated to make it impossible for me to reply.

In my agitated state, I filled a giant business envelope with the contents of my candy box and returned to CHC in the City. Emptying the envelope on his desk, CHC started to examine the material like a soldier checking his ammunition. He listed everything in front of him that seemed significant which must be included in our statement to be sworn to and filed without delay. He had a few facts to add of his own: although the father claimed it was inconvenient to come to London, it was known that he'd been to see his City lawyers at least four times in three months without visiting his children. Further, the interest payments from the children's trusts had been taken by Jim (and his new wife) in Switzerland and had not been repaid.

The remarkable CHC got everything together in record time and I found myself, once again, at another office in the City raising my hand while swearing to the truth of my statements. Among the documents included this time was proof of adultery long before our divorce; his cancelled passport showing countless trips to England and Switzerland during holidays, year after year, during our marriage; recent photos of him with his children in his Paris apartment when their portrait was being painted by his German friend; and happy-looking photos of his housekeeper, Catina, Cathy and Janne in Jim's apartment.

In record time my paper was filed officially. If Jim thought that my full schedule of Paris-London activities would prevent me from defending the interests of my children just before the Christmas holidays, he must have gotten a big jolt when he saw that it did not. No number of air flights, social events, people-watching and name-collecting activities, meeting newspaper deadlines or preparations of bulletins could keep me from my concern over Cathy and Janne. I was like a tigress protecting her cubs.

The matter of two little girls' Christmas plans was treated with urgency by the High Court of Justice, Chancery Division. Jim's request to take the children out of England was denied. He was asked to come to England to see his children and ordered to pay all costs of these court procedures.

Exhaustion, depression and downright disgust over this low-level fighting would have flattened me if I hadn't felt uplifted by the Court's decision which came through just before the Christmas holidays. I had two days to rush back to Paris to catch up at the office and be back in London just two days before Christmas. I felt renewed despite everything I'd gone through, knowing now that the children would have their first Christmas in England, safely without disruption, totally unaware of all the horrors that had gone on around them. And what joy to see the obvious progress they were making every day in their new environment. It was a joy that gave me a feeling of strength I didn't know I possessed.

Back in Paris in the penthouse office on the Rue de Berri and in my little room under the eaves at the Ritz, I was able to accomplish a lot bringing all of my work up-to-date, making countless contacts, preparing post-holiday bulletins, answering endless messages with calls or handwritten notes, working right around the clock. In between my cool, collected moments, if I'd start to get nervous, I'd take time out to think of little Cathy and Janne, our latest discoveries and adventures. I'd remember our first visit to the London Zoo, first photos with the pigeons on Trafalgar Square, first double-decker bus ride to Richmond Park, first meal in a new Chinese restaurant, and the first time we went to the circus when they had their picture taken with a clown.

Most outstanding in my memory was the Sunday we had our first experience attending an English church service. We often heard the organ music and singing coming across the courtyard to our Mews apartment when I asked the family if they'd like to go around the corner one Sunday to see what the church was like inside where we'd actually be able to see the people who were singing.

Cathy and Janne agreed; Catina said she'd get them ready but she'd rather stay behind. The next Sunday we arrived in time to take seats in a central pew while the church filled up all around us. It was a colorful scene with lots of middle-aged, plump ladies in flowered dresses. (I couldn't help thinking that they looked like walking tea cozies.) It was a warm, friendly atmosphere and the singing was so enthusiastic that I was inspired to sing right along, much to the wide-eyed amazement of my daughters on either side of me.

The end of 1958–the nightmare year–I felt happiness despite the knowledge that our first Christmas in England was going to be far from an elaborate event. Before I flew off for Paris, I told the children we'd have time to get our Christmas tree and do our shopping on the high street before Christmas (and then I remembered that all our fancy tree decorations had gone off to storage and then heaven knows where). This year I couldn't surprise Catina with piles of expensive do-dads as in other years, but I found an antique gold, flower-shaped pin in my jewel box which she'd never seen me wear. I put it in a fancy jewelers' case and hoped she'd be happy with that.

When I flew from Paris to London, I was loaded down with silly little surprises for little girls chosen from an inexpensive novelty shop on a side street near the Ritz plus a magnificent gift that Maggie Vaudable sent to the Ritz with a card saying "Merry Christmas to you and your daughters." It was shaped like a giant hatbox and filled with Maxim's' goodies from champagne, pâté, and *foie gras* to cheeses, chocolates and *petits fours*. For Catina, I rewrapped perfumes and a silk Hermès scarf I'd received at the office from gracious, grateful people I'd written about in my columns.

Despite all my contributions to our Christmas festivities at Adam and Eve Mews, they were nothing in comparison to the big surprise that Catina, Cathy and Janne had prepared for me. As I entered the apartment, laden down as never before, Cathy and Janne met me at the top of the stairs chanting "come and see our Christmas tree." Dumping everything in the hallway, I went with them to our living room (called our *salon* in Paris and now known as our lounge in London).

Perched on a little table in front of the fireplace was a gorgeous, fat-branched Christmas tree about three feet high, decorated from top to bottom with every one of my glittering, sparkling, shining, drooping, over-elaborate earrings. It was so dazzling that it didn't even need a string of lights as the crystals and rhinestones caught light from lamps in the room and shot sparkles out from every angle. I stood there staring at the most beautiful Christmas tree I'd ever seen in my life. I couldn't decide whether to laugh or cry so I did both, saying to Cathy and Janne that my earrings looked better on the tree than they had ever looked on me.

Between Christmas and the New Year in London, there was enough social and celebrity news to fill another London datelined column. This time I mailed my carefully hand-written material to Françoise in the penthouse after she offered to retype it for me and leave it on Eric's desk downstairs so I would have an unbroken holiday with my family. Françoise and her assistant were wonderful to work with and anxious to make my strange working conditions easier for me when possible. They enjoyed their work and were obviously pleased with the perks that went with it. When I left just before Christmas, I insisted that they take all gifts that came our way during my absence. They were delighted at the windfall of wine, chocolates, perfumes and floral bouquets they took home for the Christmas/New Year holiday.

Meantime in London, Cathy and Janne gave me endless satisfaction every moment. They often presented me with their drawings, cut-outs and little notes in English showing me the progress they were making; Cathy actually wrote her first many-paged story in English with illustrations about a little girl in England taking a little French friend to Kensington Gardens.

One night I was invited to Jeannie Hoskin's Park Lane apartment for a festive holiday get-together and when I came back to the Mews, everyone had gone to bed. In my room I saw a strange lump on my pillow under my bedspread which I found to be made by two little dolls, with a note pinned to each. In sketchy English and scratchy writing, both Cathy and Janne said, "Dear Mamy, please take care of my child for the night." I cherished these words and still have the notes.

As happy as I was with the children's progress, another worry wouldn't leave my head. Catina's discontent with living in London weighed heavily on my mind. Still using the old-fashioned French manner of speaking to me in third person, a day couldn't go by without grumpy *réflexions* on how awful life was in London, from the weather on. Noting that she'd always get into a better frame of mind when I'd suggest a family restaurant meal I spent a lot of time and money on these outings. Even then this gave Catina another opportunity to give her opinions of British fare, especially the places we fell upon where no wine was served, which she found totally "barbaric."

During the holidays, I led everyone to a downstairs restaurant on the high street which looked inviting. Catina grumbled at every step that *Madame* had surely picked another uncivilized eating place. At the bottom of the stairs, I asked the head waiter if they served wine and was pleased when he nodded yes, showing us to a table. Seated with menus in front of us, I asked for the wine list but he said they didn't have one. Then I asked him what kind of wines they had and he answered "All kinds. Red, white and pink." Another time, I promised Catina I'd treat her to a bottle of champagne at a nice place. When I saw their wine list mentioning only *"demi-sec"* champagne which is too sweet for my taste, I asked the waiter if they had a super-dry I liked called *"brut."* He looked down his nose at me and said, "Madam, in England we do not care for brutes." (We settled for Chablis.)

All during these days, Mrs. Parr was our angel tutoring the girls, helping Catina by ordering or picking up necessities during my absence and even doing her bit to get Catina in a good mood with French conversation beyond the school-room variety. And then it was Mrs. Parr who helped me to find a proper place to live. She gave me addresses of empty flats to rent which were near the day school where I wanted to enroll the children. In no time we found an apartment within walking distance of Glendower School. The timing was right; our *commissaire - priseur* in Paris had just written to ask for the address where he could ship our personal belongings.

Back in Paris after the holidays, ready to jump on a social/celebrity carrousel once again, I learned very soon that Jim had been busy in France. Deep in work in my office one day, a *huissier* came to the door to serve a summons for me to appear before the French police. With criminal proceedings this time, Jim was accusing me of *"non-présentation des enfants."* If I was found guilty this would mean a jail sentence.

Now, once again, I was in need of legal help but I didn't know where to turn. I knew I'd never go back to that lawyer who'd advised me to give up the children in exchange for the money owed me, nor did I ever want to see that expensive society lawyer who'd handled the divorce.

I telephoned Maître Suzanne Blum, one of the most important lawyers in France, not knowing if she'd remember me but wanting desperately for her to give me the name of a suitable *"Maître"* who could help me with my problem. When I announced my name she came to the phone immediately. When I told her the purpose of my call, she said she didn't understand why I hadn't called her long before. I told her I thought she had more important clients than I'd ever be. She bristled, saying that it was SHE who would decide what was important, adding that if I was suggesting that she only handled "big money" projects I was underestimating her as a Maître. After a lengthy conversation, I promised to deliver the French Police paper to her right away plus the official notice that the children were Wards of Court in England. She said she'd handle it "as a friend." Maître Blum went with me to the police who, when faced with copies of police reports from Vaucresson and the document from London showing that the children were "Wards of Court," decided with Maître Blum that this was neither a police case nor a legal one in France. I didn't understand their wordage. All I knew was that Jim's efforts to get me into trouble with the French police were harassing me and making me lose time, energy and money I needed for the children and my work.

After the ordeal with the police, Maître Blum and I stopped for coffee at a tacky little corner *tabac* where we sat in a haze of blue smoke and she volunteered to write a letter to my London solicitor, apprising him of the facts and assuring him that everything was in order in France. I felt like kissing her in thanks but she was so formidable a personage that I kept my distance. Reaching into my handbag, I brought out a red Cartier case holding the gold pillbox that Tillie Balaban had given me after my party at Maxim's. When I handed it to Maître Blum she took it with obvious curiosity, opening it, taking out the gold box and turning it over and over in her hand. She gave me a wry smile saying, "It's for headache pills, isn't it? A perfect gift for a busy Maître." When we parted, it was she who leaned over and gave me a quick peck on both cheeks, repeating that it was a pity that I hadn't come to her with my problems in the first place.

Returning to London, I found good news awaiting.

The hard-working CHC in the City had success in getting payments from the USA for the children from the trust funds. They came to the solicitor and not to me. All the income for Cathy and Janne was in CHC's hands thereafter, and I was asked to submit an itemized report on every expenditure in order to be reimbursed. I resented this time-consuming business of having to keep track of every pound, shilling and penny. But I did it faithfully, telling myself that it was a small price to pay for the children's welfare.

This new book-keeping system brought about another upsetting experience with Art Buchwald. In one of his "humorous" articles in the *Herald Tribune* he wrote first about actor Edward G. Robinson having to sell off his treasured art collection to pay off his divorced wife. Then he went on about a certain divorced lady in London buying all her children's clothes at Harrods , suggesting that she should, at least, buy all their underclothes at cheaper shops as no one saw children's underwear and thus she'd be saving money for the poor divorced father who had to pay

Suzanne Blum, France's great woman lawyer and my precious friend, lunched with me at Maxim's at Maggie Vaudable's invitation.

the bills of his extravagant ex-wife.

I read and reread than unfunny article, knowing that Jim had shown him my expenditure reports on the children's tutor, nanny, school, excursions, hairdresser, pharmacy and, yes, all their clothes from Harrods. But the real reason for going to Harrods in the first place was necessity. When I arrived in London, I had no money but I did have my client's charge card from the Aux Trois Quartiers department store, which was the closest thing to Harrods in Paris. This card was the only charge card I ever owned and I used it, with Jim's blessing, for everything we needed on the Rue du Docteur Blanche for children's clothes, toys, gifts, servants' uniforms, pots, pans, household linen, electric appliances–everything they had from the top floor to the basement.

Desperate in London and needing so many things, I had marched right into Harrods with Cathy and Janne on either side of me and presented myself to the credit department. I showed them my Aux Trois Quartiers card, explained we were moving to London and asked if we could have the same kind of arrangement with Harrods as we'd had with the store in Paris. I don't know how they handle such requests today, but I was treated like a Very Important Person and, after a short wait, received my Harrods charge card. This was a godsend before Jim had returned the children's luggage from Zurich, before Catina arrived and before personal belongings had been shipped to us by the *commissaire-priseur*.

Too bad Art didn't talk to me beforehand about his article because he might have written a more amusing one about "ladies in distress" going to top places when they were flat broke. I could have told him about my super sophisticated acquaintance who was between rich husband number two and three. She was momentarily broke, so she had to buy her entire wardrobe at Balenciaga because it was the only place where she was known and had credit. Then there was the lady who awaited the arrival of her super rich Sugar Daddy at the Ritz and had to hire a chauffeured limousine because she didn't have enough cash for taxis. Another lady, robbed of all her money and papers in London, went straight to Claridge's where she sat until her new passport was issued. The *maître d'hoôel* knew her as a client and when he heard her sad story he brought tea and cucumber sandwiches without presenting a bill. (Could this have happened at the corner pub?)

I was very hurt by Buchwald's "humor" at my expense. Then I began to notice that he based a lot of his columns on supposedly funny things about women and children. To me he wasn't funny anymore. I began to wonder whether his own children laughed or cried when he made remarks about them. Once he wrote that his home folk were expected to come up with a couple of column ideas each week or "out they go." I can't see how his adopted children could find that at all amusing.

My Paris-London-Paris schedule involving three days in Paris and then four in London every week (sometimes the other way around) was sometimes so exhausting that in the plane over the channel I might forget for a few seconds what the day's destination was. And yet the strength I needed seemed to be there for me when it mattered like I had angels hovering about with miracles on call. At the same time, it seemed that devils had taken over Jim's activities.

After Jim lost his last-minute bid to take the children out of England and he had not succeeded in getting police action against me in France, he instigated a French civil action at the Palais de Justice. In this paper he was using his accusation of "*non-présentation des enfants*" as justification to ask the French courts to cancel payments for the children's care and to declare null and void the financial arrangement Jim had made with me at the American Embassy.

Maître Suzanne Blum was intensely interested in my case by now and in steady contact with CHC in The City. She had the British Court documents on hand by that time including one Wards of Court order for Jim to honor his obligations to his children granted by the French divorce papers so she was not only ready but anxious to place her reports, documents, declarations and what-have-you before the French Court.

For me, once again, my stay in Paris meant another upsetting, energy-sapping appearance in court. It was a dismal, gray afternoon when the time came for me to climb the impressive, even frightening, stone staircase at the Palais de Justice to meet Maître Blum for our appearance before a judge in his chambers. Standing in the long marble hallway, looking confident, Maître Blum tried to ease my strain. "Don't worry, don't worry," she kept saying, tapping the folder of papers in her arms. I was at a low ebb, tired and fed up with the battle that never ended and couldn't get my mind off all that went before. How could Jim and Maggi have come to this? Jim and Maggi who'd been good working together, playing, starting a family, building a home with everything going for a great life.

Before I realized it, Jim was standing next to us, smiling at Suzanne while pouring on the charm. He might as well have tried to seduce a marble statue in the Louvre. The Maître was having none of it, keeping a fixed expression on her face.

Jim was without his lawyer as he started to explain to Suzanne that he had been thinking things over and was ready to withdraw all actions in France if only Maggi would agree to cancel all of his financial obligations. He was talking like he was exchanging chitchat at a cocktail party. I couldn't look at him. I fixed my eyes on the Maître who said, very coldly, that if she understood him correctly, he started all of this trouble to get out of paying money he owed for the upkeep of his children and their mother. Then, like she was speaking to a child, she spoke very slowly and precisely saying that he surely didn't mean to suggest that a father should be excused from his responsibilities to his children.

Jim wavered, nervous in the way the conversation was going, saying naturally he'd pay something for the children, though he thought he ought to have a reduction in the amount. Then he asked about money "to her." The "her" meaning me, of course. Suzanne looked at her watch, saying we weren't here to have private discussions in a hall but to appear before a judge. Just then we were called to chambers where Jim started to ooze his charm on the judge saying he'd decided to withdraw his French action and go to England to resolve our problems.

The hearing was over without being heard and Jim swept out without another word. Maître Blum still stood talking to the judge while I waited for her at the door. After her short conversation, she joined me and we marched down the marble hall, heels clicking and echoing as we walked. "What did it all mean?" I asked her, and she said it meant that Jim had backed out because he knew his action against me would fail. "Your former husband didn't have a leg to stand on," she said. Her contempt for him was even more outspoken when she called him *lâche*, which could mean anything from slack, loose, mean-spirited, shameful or dastardly.

Out on the street, Suzanne offered a ride back to the Ritz with her car and driver but I needed air and wanted to walk, even though there was a slight drizzle. It was a dark March night when we parted and my head was heavy with thought. What next? Today's withdrawal in Paris didn't mean a thing. Jim would go on and on and I was fearful of what his next step might be. Oh, I might win and win and win, but would I have enough strength to do my work and take care of the children?

Chapter Twenty-Seven

B ack in London when I called CHC to report that Jim had withdrawn his civil action in Paris, I was asked to come to the City as soon as possible. Jim had filed yet another sworn statement in English Court calling for an immediate reply. Here was proof that my fears were not unfounded. Jim had been in London to file his paper on the morning of the same day he'd been in Paris. This statement was even stronger than all others claiming that I was guilty of turning the children against him and that Cathy and Janne were under "the complete control" of a French woman who kept them from other children. Repeating again that it was too inconvenient for him to come to England he asked to take them to Switzerland for a holiday with him to be paid for from the children's trust funds. Oh, and in light of the foregoing "facts," the court should cancel all of his financial obligations to me.

This wasn't everything in Jim's latest "hostile paper," as CHC called it. He repeated his versions of what had happened in Zurich and Vaucresson, adding that my Paris lawyer had promised I'd return to Zurich to deliver the children a second time. Then he brought up the fact that I had been married four times and was really a career girl and not a mother. I took a lot of CHC's patience with my reaction to this shock, going into detail of my "non-marriages" which Jim and I had never discussed beyond that very first night in front of the Sacré-Coeur and I knew more about his former marriages than he did of mine. "Ah-hah," CHC straightened up with interest and took up his pen to scribble on a note pad that Jim, too, had been married four times.

The process of being obligated to answer and refute Jim's latest paper would have been too much for me in my present state of chronique fatigue, but CHC tackled the task with easy calm. "Bring Mrs. Parr's receipts for her tutoring; bring me that church program where the children's names are mentioned as singing in the choir; bring me the children's notebooks with their English lessons." He did not look up from his desk. Then, looking up and in my eyes, "How can a father know what his children are doing if he never goes to see them?"

Champagne...

When a Ward of Court judge was faced with the latest statement presented by Jim and my reply, he had to wade through a lot of slush before he got to the main points. Page after page from both sides only added up to Jim wanting the children out of England without delay and me wanting them to remain Wards of Court until the father established a good relationship with his children in England.

The judge decided that it was in the interests of the children to remain in England while the father made a sincere effort to get to know them better, underlining once more that he was free to visit them on a day's notice during times that would not interfere with their schooling. But Jim didn't come around after this for many months. One excuse could have been because his wife had just had a baby.

When the news came to CHC through Jim's London lawyers that a baby daughter had been born to Jacqueline and James Nolan on Friday the 13th of March 1959, I looked at the message in disbelief. I remembered another Friday the 13th of June, 1958, when Jim, his wife and his father were lined up against me across a French courtroom. It was just nine months to the day that their baby was born. Incredible. If you read that in a novel you'd think it too contrived but there it was, a true fact of life. After I pushed that thought out of my mind all I could do was feel sorry for that little baby and wonder what her life would be like.

In the Paris of 1958/1959 there were changes–changes everywhere. My own personal and professional life was so hectic that I might have barely noticed if it hadn't been for evenings like those at Dorothy and David Schoenbrun's home. Gone were the days of sitting around with family and friends talking about old times; and no more did I discuss my private life now that Maître Blum had taken charge. Since David's tremendous CBS Television success plus the important books he wrote, I was invited to formal dinners in their luxurious apartment on the Avenue Bosquet where I'd be seated next to a world renowned diplomat on one side and a political personality on the other. Table talk was so high and mighty that it went over my head every time.

One evening during dinner, when I'd just answered someone's question with "I don't know," David leaned across the table, looked me in the eye and accused me of neglecting to read the front pages of my own newspaper. I just sighed and said he was right. Stories of the French upheaval were splattered all over the papers and on television which absorbed David's whole being and he couldn't believe that anyone was able to ignore political "*crises.*" I read headlines, of course, and any fool could tell that France was in big trouble. I heard the experts around the table saying the country was "on her knees" and the Fourth Republic was going "down the drain," but I was too preoccupied with my family problems plus making my next column's deadline and not missing my plane to London, to ponder politics.

With the exception of the Schoenbrun gatherings, everywhere I went no one else seemed to care about what was being reported on front pages either. Receptions, cocktail and dinner parties, galas, celebrity-studded charity events were going on all around me despite the present *crise.*

David was right. I turned quickly away from uprisings and demonstrations and the latest declarations of General de Gaulle. I had problems of my own that I was fighting to solve while the front page of the *Trib* was bad news I could do nothing about. I was paid to amuse, entertain and flatter readers on the pages and that's what I tried to do.

Not long after David's dinner table remark, one of my social/celebrity reports was a good example of the state of society/celebrity affairs when the "star" of my column was Salvador Dali. Although I never cared for him personally, and his behavior made me very nervous, I knew he was considered "good copy" by Eric Hawkins, so he was often mentioned in my articles, making dramatic entrances and exits at the Hôtel Meurice, attending parties, twirling his cane or his mustache with gusto.

This night, he made a sensational entrance at the Théâtre de l'Étoile marching all the way down the aisle right up to the stage during an evening organized by a group called "International Center of Esthetic Studies." The black-tied, long-gowned, dazzling audience didn't know in advance that he was going to appear as his name was not on the program, but the organizers of the event obviously did because they left the stage as Dali took over and began his lecture.

His theme, in very strong Spanish-accented French, focused on how wheat, seashells and rhinoceros horns inspired him to create his masterpieces. He added that the rhino-horn topping his walking stick also had the power to make him sexy when he sniffed it. Furthermore, if you took a rhino-horn, ground it down to powder and made perfume of it, the smell would make you feel sexy, too. The speech was rather befuddling, but so was the whole evening. On the stage there was a massive loaf of freshly-baked bread, longer than the stage was wide, baked by white-capped bakers who were lined up behind the loaf sharing the platform with Salvador Dali, ballet star Serge Lifar, and French painter, Georges Mathieu. In the audience for this unusual event were people formally attired like Raymundo de Larrain, Jacqueline de Ribes, Susan Zanuck Hakim, Barbara Warner Terrail and Elsa Schiaparelli.

My next column, of course, featured Salvador Dali and that intriguing "International Center of Esthetic Studies" with special attention to the celebrated names in the audience and a few descriptions of what some ladies were wearing. Outside the theater door that night the Fourth Republic was disintegrating but nobody paid any attention.

The Fourth Republic fell and France had a new President between December 1958, and January 1959. The news filled every page of the paper and could even be found in my columns. René Coty, the outgoing President, attended his last gala social event in December 1958, and the new President, Charles de Gaulle, attended his first big night in January 1959.

Champagne...

Many years after the fall of the Fourth, when a man named Charles L. Robertson wrote a book about the Herald Tribune *called* The First Hundred Years, *he had unkind words to print about my "dreadfully sophisticated" columns written while the Fourth Republic was "crumbling." That's right; reporting what people were doing in Paris was exactly what I was UNDERpaid to do and that's what I did. I couldn't help wondering why he didn't pick on the sportswriters writing about sports events or the fellows who gave us "funnies" to look at while the Fourth Republic was falling. At first I was hurt by Mr. Robertson's words, but then I remembered what Cary Grant had told me. When people attack you unjustly, that's their problem, not yours. Cary also taught me to look at the positive side and when I did I realized that I was lucky to be included in the history of the* Trib's *100 years when I wrote "dreadfully sophisticated" columns for such a comparatively short time.*

The December 1958 event was a glorious night at the Paris Opéra where Maria Meneghini-Callas, known as La Callas, sang for the first time in France, at the *Légion d' Honneur* gala, bringing out glittering titled and entitled personalities in fabulously formal attire. With La Callas the star of the evening, it looked like guests were there more to see her than do honor to the Legion or outgoing President René Coty, and not a word was heard about the fall of the Fourth Republic. Then, in January 1959, the towering Charles de Gaulle attended his first gala as President of the Fifth Republic of France. The formal dinner and ball benefitted St. Cyr, the West Point of France, and was a rare appearance of de Gaulle who avoided social affairs. The event attracted more than 1,000 guests from high military, diplomatic and social circles to the ornate Napoleon III Ballroom and Empire Suites of the 100-year old Hôtel Continental.

And so I went around the whirl. Little by little, however, I cut down on social affairs that took more time and energy than I could afford to give, spend or waste. Refusing invitations made me uneasy because I didn't want to disappoint hostesses but it became a necessity if I wanted to survive.

However, there WERE charity events that I felt compelled to attend no matter how tired I was or what upsetting thoughts might be whirling around in my head. One was the *"Bal d'Hiver"* which was the winter ball-of-all to benefit children's charities and brought out the *crème de la crème* of Paris socialites and celebrities. The organization was headed by a beautiful lady everyone called Daisy, the Baroness Alfred de Cabrol, who'd asked me to make advance mentions in my column to help sell tickets. Of course, I was glad to do it as she held a series of society teas before the ball coming under my heading of social events.

When Daisy sent me an invitation to thank me for my help, I knew I couldn't refuse. The ball was to be held in a stately home on the Place des Vosges, which was the birthplace of the Marquise de Sévigné, the 17th century letter writer of royal court circles, who chronicled Paris social life from the year 1669 to 1695.

The big night came and I felt so exhausted when I went "home" to the Ritz to get dressed that I almost changed my mind until my conscience got the better of me and I was on my way in the best of my Balenciagas, determined to stay just long enough to absorb the scene, put guests' names in my head and leave as quickly and quietly as possible.

The evening was unforgettable in the candlelighted 1600s setting. After being greeted graciously by Daisy, I saw familiar faces everywhere I looked, plus one ever-present society photographer, André Ostier, buzzing around like a bee in a flower garden. With names like Tina and Ari Onassis, Wally and David Windsor, Count and Countess de Ganay, the Marquise de Bremond d'Ars plus Daisy and Fred de Cabrol in my head, I was ready to leave. Descending the grand marble staircase to get my cape and escape, just before I got to the foyer, I heard a familiar cry from above, "Maggi–Maaageee!" and there was the Duchess of Windsor at the top, looking down. She stayed where she was, preferring to screech in her grating voice that I must tell her where I was going. I said home with an imitation of a sleeping mime, but she insisted that she knew I had something fascinating to do and it wasn't fair keeping secrets because she wanted to go where I was going. People around me at the bottom of the stairs began to laugh and make fun of "poor Wally" and her fear of missing out on something. I repeated my tilted-head-on-hands act, turned my back, got my cape and left, feeling sorry for the Wallys of this world who had nothing more to think about than entertaining themselves.

On the plane the next morning after the *Bal d'Hiver*, I couldn't get my strange and tiring Paris-London schedule off my mind. Was this way of life I'd found for myself really necessary? Of course I knew it was as long as my work was in the penthouse on the Rue de Berri.

As soon as I got back to London I felt better. Cathy and Janne gave me endless satisfaction with their smiles, enthusiasm for everything, their progress and just being in their company no matter what we did. The London celebrity chasing possibilities were growing every day as well as I found items for my columns easy to come by, like Dorian Leigh, former model and cover girl, opening a London agency; American producer Albert "Cubby" Broccoli, beginning James Bond films in London. He introduced me to unknown Swiss actress, Ursula Andress, and the Scottish heartthrob, Sean Connery, whom he was signing up for his first Bond film called "*Dr. No.*" Another American-Londoner, film executive Mike Frankovitch, introduced me to his actress-wife, Binnie Barnes, who grew prize-winning orchids. My list of London "people news" items got longer every week.

The beginning of the end of my Paris days came when a fancy friend took me aside at a party and whispered that there was a rumor going around that I was going to be arrested by the French police. When I called Maître Blum she assured me that it was not possible. I had a pretty good idea who was spreading the "news" but there was nothing I could do about it. That ugly rumor had its effect on me, however, as I seemed to withdraw even more from the Paris social circuit.

Immediately off the plane I'd check into the office to type columns, prepare bulletins, address material to various outlets, follow up on invitations, thank-you notes, mail clippings to people mentioned in my articles and finish the business at hand before hurrying to the hotel to dress for evening activities I felt I shouldn't miss. But time after time the festivities gave me a certain sensation that felt like fear, especially when there were too many people I didn't know.

Among people who were supposed to be my friends, I'd find myself looking at each face, wondering if they were looking at me differently or what they had heard and how much they believed and what their feelings toward me might really be. At many receptions I hardly spoke to anyone, like I was a recluse in a crowd. Worse yet, out on the street I'd find myself shaking in fear and anguish when I heard the "pin-pon-pin-pon" of a police car blocks away from where I stood.

It became clearer and clearer to me that life like this could not go on. A few sleepless nights of tossing and turning gave me my answer. It was time to say good-bye to France and concentrate all my energy in England. It was "let go" time again.

As soon as the decision was made it felt like a heavy weight was off my shoulders. After so many of my Paris friends had been prodding me to "move back home," now I could tell them that "home" was not here anymore, but in London where my children were secure and happy. There were a few friends I thought I really ought to see and talk to before I finally left France, but in trying to contact them the truth of many changes taking place became very clear.

Dorothy and David Schoenbrun were seldom in Paris as David was constantly called to New York or Washington, D.C. by CBS Television, or he was on another promotion tour for a book or traipsing to far-off places where there were "trouble spots" to cover. Dorothy went everywhere with him, even to war zones. There was no chance or time to see them alone for heart-to-heart talks like we had in the past.

When I ran into Jack Forrester on the Rue Royale, I did not have a chance to speak because he was so excited, maybe even agitated, about what was happening in the oil world in the Middle East, where he was now spending a great deal of his time. He went on and on about how strange the people were with no idea of money, filing cabinets stuffed with dollar bills and the corners of their offices stacked high with gold bricks. "And their offices, Maggi," he emphasized, "are nothing but shacks in the sand." Jack was very emotional, insisting that "oil money" was changing the economy of the world.

My old neighbors, Harriet and Pierre Boudet, I gave up trying to find. Pierre's chewing gum business had expanded to imported chocolate nut bars, canned peanuts, and I don't know what else. The Boudets could never be found at their Boulevard Suchet address. Now, in addition to Paris, they had a house in New York, a farm in Normandy, a country home in Grasse, and they were negotiating to buy a duplex in Monte Carlo. (Pierre would never get a medal for bringing chewing gum to France, but he made a lot of money.)

When I confided in David Stein that I was planning to give up Paris, he looked at me in disbelief. Telling me I was "crazy," he sounded off about the great career I was throwing away when fame and fortune were just around the corner, using every Hollywood agent's cliché and ending with, "I thought you liked what you are doing." I nodded in agreement, adding that I loved my work but, "I love my children even more."

I truly wanted to see Eric Hawkins in person before I left but the *Herald Tribune* was going through changes and it seemed impossible to contact him. Either he was not on the Rue de Berri or he was "at a conference" lasting hours, or simply "gone for the day," which just could not have been in the past; but now John Hay "Jock" Whitney had bought the paper and was planning international expansion. Eric Hawkins had been with the Paris *Herald Tribune* for 40 years when I started to work there and it was obvious that he was on his way out.

On my way to meeting Gloria Swanson one day at the Hôtel de Crillon, across the street from the American Embassy, I practically collided with the scurrying diplomat, Joseph Verner Reed, one noontime. We stood on the Place de la Concorde for a few minutes and I confided in him that I would be an American-Parisian no more. He got that very special, undiplomatic, indignant expression on his face again and put the blame on "The French," looking like he wanted to turn it into an international incident. He insisted that I should stay, that I should be rewarded for my contributions and not chased away. I was touched by his sentiments and impressed by his sense of drama, but as he talked I couldn't help thinking about what my friend Eve would say–"Don't kid yourself, nobody gives a rat's ass!" Of course, I couldn't say that to a gentleman like Joe.

Never in my life had I felt so alone when I faced leaving Paris and not being an American-Parisian anymore. It hurt when I sat by myself in the penthouse office arranged especially for me. When I stepped out on the little terrace and looked in the distance to see the sugar white Sacré-Coeur Basilica against a darkening sky, it brought too many memories back for me to endure. I stepped back trying to lock out the pain when I shut the French windows. I took last looks at the office I'd decked out with pictures on the walls, lamps, plants, celebrity photos, radio, clock, right down to the porcelain cups and saucers and a pint-sized typewriter perfect for typing fresh information on our file cards. "You're leaving this business and this place a lot better than they were when you took them," I said to myself to try to cheer my last goodbye.

In the little room at the Ritz I packed everything I had there except for the tall pile of hatboxes stacked in a cupboard. All my fancy Paris headgear just didn't seem right for London life so I decided to give them to the maid who'd admired them so much, who might like owning them as much as I had. I spent my last night writing letter after letter. The shortest one was to Eric on elegant pale blue Ritz stationery, telling him how much I had enjoyed working with him but, because of personal reasons, I could no longer be a columnist for the Paris *Herald*

Champagne...

Tribune. The longest letter was written on rough scrap paper from the office, page after page to my sister spilling out everything that was on my mind.

From the time my sister had written to me that she was entering a cloistered convent, I 'd written my heart out to her every time my life's road took a dramatic turn. Sometimes I'd spend the whole night writing about problems, ideas, dilemmas, but not forgetting to bring her up to date on her niece's progress, funny things they did and said, places they liked to go, how they were doing in school. My sister's answers weren't more than assurances that she was praying for me and reminders that angels were ON my side and AT my side in need.

My sister and I didn't know it at the time but we were both writing poems. Hers were long and serious while mine were short, light and sometimes tongue-in-cheeky. Neither of us dreamed that the day would come when we'd publish a little book with her religious poems and my verses together. We called it *Angels' Advocates* from one of my poems:

I am possessed
by angels' presence
everywhere I go
and yet you look at me askance
when I insist it's so
still to me
it ever seems
that angels light
my waking dreams
sit still
let's have a chat
of that
and I will be
the angels'
advocate..

Chapter Twenty-Eight

C all it angels, call it luck. England was good to us and good for us. Cathy and Janne thrived at their little girls' day school and I found journalist jobs with the short-lived *London-American* and then the *London Evening News*, after freelance copywriting for an Anglo-American advertising agency.

Our new apartment in Drayton Gardens was furnished bit by bit on my trusty charge card. Then when the money came from the Paris auction there was enough for everything and everybody. First, Catina got back her precious savings she'd advanced us plus her salary up-to-date. Then, one Saturday morning Catina, Cathy, Janne and I went over to Harrods together with a long list of what was missing from our home. We spent the day there, choosing everything, and even found a big wire birdcage on wheels for Noirice in the pets' department.

Comfortably installed now, Cathy and Janne were enrolled at Glendower School, not far away in Queens Gate. Every morning they donned their snappy purple uniforms with matching berets and off we'd go to school together. I walked with them right up to the hedge in front of the school and went on to work; Catina met them every afternoon after class.

They liked school, the teachers and fellow students of many nationalities right away and seemed to fit right in. I was ecstatic watching their progress and often would sing, "Oh, what a beautiful morning–oh, what a wonderful day–I've got the funniest feeling–everything's going my way" as we walked along until they'd clap their hands over their ears in mock fury at my singing. Sometimes I'd just walk along listening to what they had to say to each other. One day they decided that the little drizzle of mist that often fell in London was "dishonest rain" and another time, when there was genuine rain falling, I heard Janne giggling while Cathy sang, "Rain, rain, go away–come again on Mother's Day."

At school, it was something else: SERIOUS. They learned fast, they got good grades; the headmistress said she was proud to have little American girls who spoke perfect French; the name of Catherine Elizabeth Nolan is engraved on one of the silver cups honoring top students at their school.

Champagne...

We had a cozy relationship, yet they kept me on my toes. Once I'd been invited to appear on an early evening television talk show with a young, up-and-coming British singer, Petula Clark, and the best-selling American author, William Saroyan. I thought I'd done alright and was quite pleased until breakfast the next morning. Cathy announced, "We saw you on television last night. Why did you keep your mouth open all the time?" Janne added, "and you kept twisting your beads."

Another late afternoon, I was going out the door on my way to see Judy Garland at the Dorchester. I thought I looked chic in my black fur hat and matching collar on a slim black suit, but Janne pulled at my sleeve and whispered, "Mother, do you really have to go out in those scary clothes? "

It wasn't long before all of our trunks, suitcases, barrels, bags, cartons and packages arrived from Paris with our belongings. After we opened the children's trunks Catina was going through their clothes, lamenting on the obvious fact that they'd grown so much in such a short time and Cathy and Janne were sorting toys and games into two piles (what was "baby stuff" they'd outgrown and what still gave them delight). At the bottom of their trunk were all the cuddly animals they'd left behind which they grabbed, hugged and kissed like long-lost friends. Cathy favored a little lion that Catina had given her while Janne sought out a funny-looking pale green rabbit with floppy ears. The lion and bunny were placed on their beds and the menagerie lined up on a window sill.

A "miracle" came later when I opened our largest trunk plunked down in the middle of the lounge. It was packed to bursting with linen, draperies, sheets, pillow cases and the lovely embroidered tablecloths and matching napkins that Grandma had given us. When I got down to the blankets I came upon our silver, everything from the Jensen tableware to coffee and tea set to serving bowls, ashtrays, baby cups and spoons. Odette had carefully packed every piece between the blankets, surely to protect them, never dreaming the outcome of her efforts. I couldn't believe my eyes as I started to pile everything on the floor and I couldn't help crying as I brought out every piece. Here on my knees I thought of the day that I had had to "let go," never imagining that I'd ever touch these things again. What a gift! So much of this had come from Grandma Nolan that it was as though she was with us.

Janne peeked into the room from the hallway and came in when she saw tears streaming down my face. When she asked me why I was crying, I had to answer, "because I'm happy."

Despite the Wards of Court judge's advice (or was it an order?) that Jim visit his children in London to get acquainted with them nothing was heard from him for months. CHC had told me to expect a request from the father to spend part of the summer holidays but nothing was forthcoming. We had plenty to keep us busy with Cathy and Janne's school, outside activities and family excursions and my work polka-dotted with freelance assignments.

In the summer when I received pay for my first story in *Lilliput* I told CHC we'd waited long enough for the father to do something about summer holidays, so I'd plan something myself. Choosing a spot in England for a visit, I just spread the map out on a table and put my finger on what looked like the southernmost spot where there'd be the most sunshine. A close look told me my finger pointed to St. Catherine's Point, Isle of Wight. I laughed and said to myself, "Cathy–Catina–St. Catherine's Point–serendipity." We had our first short and sunny stay on that unique island which we liked so much that we returned again and again.

Finally in the fall CHC was on the telephone telling me that the father was making plans to spend a weekend with the children at a friend's country house and had agreed that they be accompanied by the nurse. Of course I was frightened that this might be his great kidnap caper, but there was nothing I could do about it but accept his plan. I arranged to get a car and driver (at a friendly rate) to deliver Cathy, Janne and Catina to a place called Odiham on the first Saturday afternoon of November, and call for them on Sunday afternoon. I went along with them, right to the door of this strange house, wondering what it would be like for two little girls who hadn't seen their father since he returned their suitcases just a year before.

I stayed in a hot-cold sweat after making arrangements, delivering the children and waiting until it was time to pick them up. Jim spent two half days and one night in that country house with Cathy, Janne, Catina, his wife, his seven-and-a-half-month-old baby and his host and hostess. When I arrived on Sunday as planned, Catina and the children were standing in front of the cottage waiting for me, smiling broadly but seeming a bit anxious, as though they thought I might not show up to take them home. But I wasn't a minute late. On the drive back to London I asked as casually as I could if they'd had a good time and they said they had. Cathy mentioned they'd roasted some kind of sausage on big long forks and Janne told me there was a little baby there that Dad said was his. Then they seemed more interested in what they were seeing along the roads as we drove by so I didn't ask for more details of their visit, though I was keenly interested to know what they did and how they felt.

When the girls were at school Catina began to fill me in about the weekend tension and *Monsieur*'s bossy, pretentious wife, while admitting that the baby was *mignon*. Then she began a tirade about the "barbaric" way these people entertained the children. "They burned a man in a bonfire in the garden," she said accusingly. I tried to explain that it was an English 300-year-old tradition on Guy Fawkes Day, celebrating the conspirator who tried to blow up the House of Parliament so long ago, and it was really only an excuse for children to light firecrackers and play with fire. Nothing could make her change her mind; the British were barbaric and that was that.

Champagne...

⤿ ⤾

After countless freelance assignments writing advertising copy for an agency owned by Anglo-American Charles Lytle and unsigned articles for British magazines like *Lilliput*, Mr. Lytle applied for a British work permit for me so he could make me a member of his staff. I was truly appreciative but, before it came through, I was invited to an elegant London town house with a group of fellow journalists to discuss an upcoming weekly newspaper to be called the *London-American*. There that day were William Caldwell, American editor from *Time Magazine;*;Barbara Taylor, British beauty and fashion writer; and Lawrence Copely Thaw, an American art, theater and movie critic (whose New York socialite family I'd met in Paris). When I was asked if I could fill a double spread of celebrity/social news each week in the upcoming publication, I felt like I was dreaming. Then and there, I became a part of the team.

Completing my latest Charles Lytle assignment, I delivered it with the news of my decision to go with the new newspaper. Mr. Lytle listened to me politely before announcing that my work permit had just been issued and he had it on his desk. I winced and could feel my face grow hot when he handed an envelope to me with the card in it. He was a gentleman and true professional, saying, "Not to worry; they will add the newspaper's address as your present place of employment." He not only wished me luck in the new publication but promised to steer some of his accounts toward buying advertising in the *London-American*.

Before very long I was cozily installed in Piccadilly offices, helping to prepare a pre-publication issue of the new weekly for distribution among potential subscribers and advertisers. My double page, called "Maggi Nolan's Celebrity Circuit–The All-American Whirl," featured first, news of my old tried and true standbys like J. Paul Getty, Dorian Leigh, Olivia de Havilland and John Ringling North, plus my new party-giving friend, Gloria Lewis, announcing her latest charity event. The first article was easy to put together with something new to say about each person plus some photos from my own collection to decorate the pages. I didn't forget Charles Lytle and his kindness, mentioning him from the beginning every chance I got.

Just about a month before the first edition of the *London-American* came out for sale the publisher, Richard Boult, asked me to host a promotional celebrity-studded party at John Mill's Milroy Club above Les Ambassadeurs on Park Lane. All the people whom I asked to attend the event were enthusiastic. John Mills offered the use of the club, hired the orchestra, overseered the elaborate buffet and filled every table and corner with giant bouquets of flowers. Justerini & Brooks stocked the bar as only J&B could. Barbara Taylor and Bill Caldwell invited top London journalists while I collected a celebrity list for the big event. The party was set just before Valentine's Day, so I bought hearts of all sizes to scatter around and pinned a row of them on a Balmain ballgown to wear on the big night.

There must have been about 200 formally-dressed and very happy-looking guests there that night like J. Paul Getty; Robina Lund; John Spencer Churchill and his bride, Lullan; Bruce Cabot and his date, Jane Whiting (whom he called Lady Jane); Charles Clore; Dorian Leigh; Trevor Howard; Nicole Milinaire; Captain Michael Parker; and Henry Ringling North, John's brother, who arrived from Rome with his Italian-French bride, Gloria. Henry "Buddy" North said he'd talked to his brother John, who was in the middle of the Atlantic on a ship headed for Manhattan and furious that he was missing the festivities.

The *London-American* promotional party received a fine send-off with the British press reporting the upcoming event in glowing terms. Spirits were high in the Piccadilly offices as everyone worked hard toward the success of the new publication due out on the newsstands on March 17, Saint Patrick's Day. The London office of TWA flew a load of shamrocks in from Shannon as a good luck offering on the big day.

Life for me in home and office was more than satisfactory while, behind the scenes, the Nolan-versus-Nolan battle went on.

Soon after Jim's short stay with his daughters, he was in and out of London again, but not to see his children. Ahead of us was a High Court case to determine Cathy and Janne's future which would be in the presence of Jim and myself with our solicitors and counsels before a Wards of Court judge, who would have the last word.

Jim filed statement after statement, each of which had to be answered in official replies by me. CHC took to calling Jim's efforts "another hostile paper" because they were all attacks on me to try and prove that I was a money-hungry career girl, hiding children from a loving father who was now married to a woman above reproach. Specific accusations I had to refute: he said despite the money he gave me, it was he who paid for Paris schooling, doctors, etc. But I had the bills and my check stubs. When he blamed me for not allowing the children to come with him in Vaucresson, it gave CHC a chance to present the official police reports from there, all properly translated and filed with British courts. His glowing report of his ideal wife made it necessary for CHC to produce her divorce papers. This unsavory mess was not only sickening but costly in time, energy and patience, as well as money.

With Jim's countless words presented to British Court under oath, the only plan he ever put forth for the future of his children was to take them to Switzerland on their own passports.

The most important day of my life came at the end of March, the day of an official hearing in High Court to decide the future of two little American girls, born in France and living in England. My appearance was scheduled on a day when many other things were demanding my attention. In the *London-American* office Richard Boult had called a staff meeting; there was a parent-teacher gathering at

Champagne...

J. Paul Getty loved parties. Here he is with me at the Mirabelle in London, watching my guests coming down the stairs. Behind us are Penelope Kitson, his friend and interior decorator, and Robina Lund, one of his lawyers.

Glendower I couldn't miss; I'd promised Erwin Schleyen I'd come to the Mirabelle at the end of the day to discuss the guest list for an upcoming party there; and, that evening, I'd accepted an invitation to a Royal Performance Gala night at the Leicester Square Theatre, which the Queen would be attending.

Getting dressed early that morning, I had to wear something that would be appropriate all day until changing to formal clothes for the Queen. I chose my usual "uniform" of black suit, high-necked black blouse and single strand of pearls. At the last minute I added a tiny lace handkerchief in a top suit pocket with just a bit of lace peeking out to lighten the black-on-black that day.

Stepping into that high-ceilinged courtroom with CHC by my side, a horrible sweep of fear came over me, though CHC kept telling me to be calm. I was nervous–very nervous–in this strange atmosphere looking like history come to life. I'd seen English court scenes in movies but this was real life Nolan-versus-Nolan. Black-robed gentlemen, wearing gray, curled wigs on their heads and crisp white "doilies" around their necks, moved about the high-ceilinged room making me shake inside before the hearing began. Then, when I tried to follow the legal language in clipped British accents, it almost seemed that they spoke a foreign tongue I'd never heard.

As soon as I began to settle down, taking deep breaths instead of short intakes that had been robbing me of air, the gray-wigged, black-robed gentlemen pleading Jim's case turned toward me, pointing a finger. "Look at her," he demanded, and then turned to his table to pick up a page from a tabloid newspaper which he waved in my direction as he spoke. He was saying that this demure-looking person sitting in the courtroom was really THIS person in the paper giving champagne parties on Park Lane.

The newspaper page he was waving from a Sunday tabloid had been written in advance of the *London-American* party at the Milroy and hadn't even been among the clippings saved in the office because there was no mention of our weekly newspaper. The photo of me was one Jim had taken himself, years ago, in the privacy of our salon at home. Jim had given it to our journalist friend, Noel Barber, editor of the *Continental Daily Mail*, when he was doing a story about life in Paris. Noel published another one of me and left this one on file. My hair was around my shoulders and I had a provocative expression on my face, turning toward the cameraman, my husband, in the days when we were busy getting newspaper mentions for TWA everywhere we could.

I felt faint when this article by a silly-sounding journalist I'd never met was bandied about the courtroom. It claimed I was an international hostess paying for champagne-flowing, celebrity/society celebrations and now in London to set the town on fire. While everyone got a good look at Maggi-with-her-hair-down, I stared at my clenched fists in my lap, shook inside, and couldn't believe that my children's father could do this to me. It's impossible for me to remember who said what to whom after that. In shock, I was saying that I never went out in public with my hair down; that it was Jim who took that photo; how it got into the newspaper file in the first place; I'd never met the man who wrote the story; the party was not mine; the way I dressed today was exactly the way I dressed every day as far back as when I worked with Jim on the Paris *Herald Tribune*.

After all these years have passed, that's the only incident I can recall during the High Court of Justice proceedings behind closed doors in camera that day. After it was all over I felt sick, leaving with CHC who kept repeating that everything was alright, that everything would turn out as it should. I didn't believe it; I felt weak and beaten down. All I wanted to do was go home, go to bed and hide under the covers.

That was impossible. I had places to go and things to do.

At Glendower School I should have been uplifted to the skies while hearing how well Cathy and Janne were doing in all subjects and how happy the headmistress was with "our American additions who speak perfect French." But my mind kept going back to the courtroom nightmare and my fears that the judge might let Jim take the children out of England.

At the end of the day, I was in no state to keep my appointment at the Mirabelle, but I went anyway. I couldn't let Mr. Schleyen down after he had offered his private room and a full cocktail-buffet party at his expense for our new Anglo-American paper I would make the invitation list and host the affair while he stayed in the background seeing that everything went smoothly.

When I stepped into the restaurant foyer, I was told that Mr. Schleyen was waiting for me in the downstairs reception room with Mrs. Vaudable from Paris. "Oh, my Lord," I thought, as I almost ran down the thick carpeted staircase; I'd completely forgotten that Maggie had told me weeks ago on the telephone that she was coming to London. Until now, I'd always gotten Jeannie Hoskins to report her arrival and arrange something during her stay. And it was Maggie herself, who'd introduced me to Erwin Schleyen, the man behind the inimitable Mirabelle Restaurant. How could I forget?

Maggie Vaudable stared at me with her extra icy look as I was greeted by "the best soupmaker in the world;" when I turned to her, she stepped back from my embrace and said in her chilliest tone, "Isn't it nice that you are so successful in London that you forget your Paris friends." That was just about more than I could take on this day.

"Maggie, please forgive me. I've been through hell and it's not over by a long way." My voice cracked as I tried to explain while she didn't seem to be listening, busy picking up papers on the table and folding them into her handbag. Meanwhile, Mr. Schleyen was looking at both of us, shaking his head. When I stopped talking he turned to us and said that he was introduced to one Maggi by another Maggie and he needed both of us in his life and couldn't stand it if we didn't love each other.

My emotions got the best of me and I didn't care anymore that CHC kept reminding me never to speak of my legal affairs to anyone. I took Maggie's arm and begged her to listen to the fight I had and where I'd been that day, even to the dramatic waving of a newspaper in my face and the horror of the possibility that the children might be taken out of England. At the beginning of my outburst Mr. Schleyen had left the room but now he was back with a waiter carrying an elegant tray with silver ice bucket, champagne, and tulip-shaped glasses.

Maggie looked at the tray while I was wiping the tears from my face. She smiled at me, then at our genial host and came over to take my hanky-free hand in hers as she said to Mr. Schleyen, "*Cher ami*, you've only brought two glasses. Please get another one for yourself and let's get down to business." We sat down at one end of the long banquet table and clicked our crystal glasses before sipping vintage champagne.

Maggie Vaudable was in London to discuss a very special night in Paris which would introduce an English week at Maxim's, presented by the Mirabelle, featuring English chefs and decor. British tycoon, Charles Clore, had promised to send treasured pieces from his English silver collection to be showcased in Maxim's' foyer, while theater and movie moguls would lend framed posters of their star-studded fare to decorate the entry walls. Maggie wanted me to invite London and Paris personalities for the opening night of Mirabelle-at-Maxim's week, and entertain a table of at least ten guests.

I shook my head at this but Maggie reminded me it wasn't going to happen until the month of November and "everything will be fine by then," she insisted. When Mr. Schleyen saw my hesitation over Paris, he changed the subject to his upcoming cocktail-buffet to be held in that very room. I handed him my suggested guest list which you could see was very pleasing for him to read. He handed it to Maggie to look at, smiling and saying, "Not bad, eh?" But Maggie just

A trio of tycoons at the London American launching in the Milroy Club: J. Paul Getty, Charles Clore, and Henry "Buddy" Ringling North.

shrugged and told him he should have seen the guests at our Maxim's' party for Dorothy Kilgallen.

When we finished our talk and the champagne, I looked at my watch and gave a big gasp. "Oh Lord, I won't make it to the theater tonight," I sighed. Maggie insisted on knowing exactly where I was supposed to go and when I told her about the Queen attending a Royal Command Gala, she gave me a speech about my "professional obligation" to go, that I must not miss seeing the Queen of England, and the importance of reporting such events for people who'd never have a chance like that.

Then her suggestion, which was more like a command, that I take the car and driver she'd hired for three days which was waiting right outside the door with nothing to do, seemed impossible to refuse. "Don't argue, just GO," she ordered as she gave me a goodbye kiss on each cheek. Upstairs I was ushered into the largest, longest Rolls Royce I'd ever seen in my life. It was a deep bottle-green and the chauffeur was wearing a matching uniform. Maggie instructed him to take me home, then to the theater and home again, not to return to her at the Savoy until the next day.

On the way to Drayton Gardens, I pushed a button to lower the separating glass and explained my problem to the driver: must hurry home to change, must arrive at the theater before the Queen, must come right home after the performance. He nodded knowingly, probably accustomed to such routine and pointed out politely that I'd have to be ready to leave my home very, very fast.

It was the children's bedtime by then but I managed to tell them some of the lovely compliments about them I'd heard at school and say, "Sweet dreams," before peeling off the clothes I'd worn since early breakfast that morning over an awful lot of territory. There was no time for a proper bath so I sponged around, scrubbed my face and slap-dashed mascara and lipstick before all the hooking and zipping it took for my wasp-waisted pink satin Balmain evening gown. Stepping into matching pink satin pumps, I clasped crystal chandelier earrings on my ears, before wrapping a pink satin evening coat around me and grabbing the huge invitation from the top of the pile on my desk, and a tiny evening bag with white gloves and a lace handkerchief already inside.

I was almost outside the door when Catina, standing in the hallway, handed me the keys I would have forgotten. I said, "Oh, thank you," but I could tell by her stern look that she disapproved of my getting home so late and going right out again. I didn't have time to explain.

It should have been relaxing to ride in a luxurious Rolls Royce which was like a magic carpet taking me to see the Queen, but when I took my white kid gloves out of my evening bag to put on, I realized that I had left without any make-up and without any money. My bag held keys and a handkerchief, nothing else. Worse, I realized that it was the end of the month and I was broke except for the little bit of cash left in my daytime purse. I had planned to borrow again on my gold bracelet watch, but hadn't done it on this drama-filled day. Tomorrow, April Fools' Day, I could do it but tonight I was having a mini nightmare in the back of a luxurious bottle-green Rolls.

At the theatre, it was plain to see that I was late; the Queen had arrived and they were closing the doors. I'm certain that whoever was in charge of the doors saw the magnificent car, the uniformed chauffeur and the pink satin damsel in distress, because I was allowed to sneak in a half-opened door which closed so fast some of the satin of my coat caught for a few seconds. I was shown the way up the stairs behind the guests standing at velvet ropes separating them from the royal party. At the top of the stairs, a bit out of breath, I saw a place where I could stand and see the Queen climbing slowly, very slowly, to the top.

The Queen of England looked like something straight out of a dream, dressed in a shimmering, glittering white gown with a dazzling diamond tiara on her head that seemed to shoot sparks in every direction. As she neared the top of the stairs, I was fascinated to see how white her face was as though her powder was made of icing sugar. At the top, I was amazed to see what a tiny person she was; her photographs always made her seem so tall. Then I noticed what a huge handbag she carried for such a little lady. She had been smiling graciously all the way on the stairs but now I saw her eyes twinkle, and almost a wink directed to a man standing next to me. I looked and saw Douglas Fairbanks, Jr. at my elbow, an impressive reminder that my job here was to people-watch for my next column.

It was a great night with names, names and more names everywhere I looked. The seat I'd been given was perfect for my work, thanks to Columbia Pictures' Mike Frankovitch, American-Londoner. From where I sat a few rows behind the

Queen, I could see enough celebrities to fill my report and even got a few more peeks at the royal handbag, wondering what in the world the Queen carried in it. I knew what was in mine...nothing.

If I had to tell you what the gala film shown that night was all about, I couldn't. I didn't even remember who starred in it, though I knew the title because it was written on my datebook: *Once More, With Feeling.*

After the film showing, I wrapped my pink coat around me and waited outside for "my car." Standing next to me was Charles Clore, waiting for his steel-gray Rolls with the C.C. license plate. He was very nice, telling me that everyone was talking about the great *London-American* party I'd hosted at the Milroy and thanking me for the photo I'd sent, taken that evening of him with Paul Getty and Buddy Ringling North.

Then, when my green Rolls Royce rolled up, he asked me if I was going over to the Milroy right now where "everyone but the Queen will be." He did not believe me when I said I was going right home, and half-whispered when we shook hands, "sneaky lady, you've got something going and you're not going to tell me."

Chapter Twenty-Nine

The next morning after breakfast I asked Catina to please take the children to school today, but didn't tell her I was broke and heading to the fancy "hock shop" as soon as it opened to get a loan on my watch once again. She stood at the doorway of my room, saying nothing but looking down at my pink satin dress and coat draped over a chair. Her look was saying, "*Madame* goes out in fancy clothes but can't take her children to school." But she said, "As *Madame* wishes," and turned back down the hall. As they were leaving for school, she stopped at my door again where I was now seated at my cluttered desk. She announced, "*Madame* forgot to order the Dubonnet."

It was true, I'd forgotten her favorite aperitif after she'd mentioned that the bottle was empty. Maybe I should have told her to get her own as she had more money than I had but, of course, I said nothing. Instead, that evening I brought the Dubonnet plus a bottle of champagne for a weekend treat.

In the newspaper office the morning after my court appearance everyone was talking about yesterday's staff meeting where we learned that we'd be moving from Piccadilly to Cavendish Place. I was still so upset about the personal, private part of my life that I just listened to the office chitchat without comment, until later when I ran into Laurence Copely Thaw on the stairs and asked if the move would be for the better or for the worse. And Larry answered, "It's cheaper."

During the day, although I was probably making a nuisance of myself, I picked up the telephone when no one was within earshot and called CHC in The City. He was patient, as usual, repeating his positive assurances and insisting that my worries over Jim's tactics to discredit me were unnecessary. "Don't worry...relax...rest." Those words meant nothing to me, though I was going to try over the weekend, and planned a picnic in Richmond Park with Cathy, Janne, Catina and the deer.

In the middle of the following week a letter from CHC arrived. It was two pages and single-spaced, but the short second paragraph meant the most to me:

In answer to the points raised by you, the Judge confirmed the Order that the children remain Wards of Court and that their care and control be entrusted to you. As Wards of Court, the children cannot be taken out of the country without leave of the Court.

The letter went on that it was quite apparent to the Judge that the children did not know their father sufficiently well that they should be taken out of the country into his home in Switzerland in a strange atmosphere with strange people, and that he, Mr. Nolan, should make every endeavour to get to know his children by seeing them as often as possible in England. And the Judge suggested that the father should make arrangements to spend a two-week holiday with them in England in the upcoming summer.

After the Wards of Court judgment, Jim submitted plans for a two-week seaside vacation at a beach a few hours out of London. I gave my agreement without comment although I knew that Cathy and Janne had already been talking about a return to the Isle of Wight. I told CHC that I'd arrange to take them there after the vacation with their father. This time, Jim was accepting the presence of Catina and making arrangements to arrive with his wife and baby daughter.

After that horrendous experience in court it seemed I might be able to forget the nightmare Nolan-versus-Nolan and the shock of seeing my "hair down" newspaper photo waved around the courtroom, but I'm certain that my experience that day led me to cut off my long hair. I went to a flamboyant Mayfair hairdresser, sat down and said, "Cut it off–cut it ALL off." This fellow's name was Monsieur Raymond. He had been nagging me, with cards, letters and calls, to come to his salon for free hairstyling, cutting, shampoos, beauty treatments–the works–if only I'd mention him in my columns once in a while along with his celebrity clients.

Monsieur Alexandre de Paris he was not! Nevertheless, the next time Mister Raymond tapped or pounded on my door, I agreed to let him see what he could do with my head of hair which would have reached below my waist if I'd let it. In his salon as I saw my long hair making impressive piles on the floor, I did get a bit of a jolt but sighed and thought if I didn't like it I could just grow my hair back again.

A very light-headed Maggi Nolan greeted the world that day, surprising no one too much except my daughters who said I looked too young. It didn't take long to realize that my short cut meant many trips for trims, curlers and comb-outs, whereas long hair I could manage myself. So I was trapped, whether or not I liked it, and had to grin and bear this fellow in addition to mentioning celebrities I saw in his salon to keep him happy.

The day I heard that he was going to be sued by that darling Tiger Bay singer, Shirley Bassey, for something dastardly he'd done (I think he burned her hair, which forced her to wear a wig) I decided to let my hair grow out and never went back again.

Soon after my royal evening in the regal Rolls Royce, I received a call in the *London-American* office from a gentleman who told me he was the owner of the luxury car hire agency that had supplied the Rolls Royce and driver for my gala evening. He said his name was Paddy Barthropp and he'd like to talk to me about future plans. Immediately I thought he was trying to sell his services to me so I suggested that he must speak to our editor or publisher as I had no right to hire limousines.

"No, no," he tut-tutted, "you don't understand. I want to offer my cars when you need them." I kept watching for the catch as he spoke but he went on explaining that he knew my articles from the *Herald Tribune* and now *the London-American* and, since he was new in his field, he was interested in getting his service known in the *London-American* celebrity community. During our chat he told me he had been in the Royal Air Force with a close friend, Tony Bartley, who'd been married to actress Deborah Kerr. After getting out of the RAF, he bought a couple of second-hand Rolls Royces from the royal family garage to start his unique service.

"The one you rode in belonged to the Queen Mother," he said. "It's driven by a man named Rochester," he added. While Paddy was chatting away, my brain was at work. I remembered that John Ringling North had told me he wasn't bringing his Cadillac on his next trip to London, and Paddy's cars would be perfect for a King of the circus.

When I suggested this to Paddy, he sounded really pleased, saying he knew I'd be the right person to put him on the map. Then he gave me a few details of what his cars had to offer besides the comfort and drivers in spiffy uniforms that matched the cars. Television, stocked cocktail bars, writing desks, refrigerators, for instance.

"Say no more," I laughed, "if your cars are like the one I rode in and the drivers as nice as Rochester, I can't wait to tell the world about Paddy Barthropp, the R.A.F.'s gift to glorious ground transport."

From that day on, Paddy Barthropp was my hero every time I had to go out on an important social assignment. When I called his agency, he always came to the phone to ask exactly where I was going. It wasn't only because he loved to hear advance gossip of what was going on but he tried to match the car with the occasion. When it was a grand ball, a royal performance or a stately home, he'd send the long drawn-out Rolls Royces, but private parties on narrow streets to a Mews house or studio were something else.

"There's no room for a Rolls," he'd say. "You'll have to take a Bentley."

The moments of inner peace I'd felt after the dreadful court ordeal which ended happily didn't last very long. While Jim was going ahead with vacation plans in England he'd also been busy in France. Word came from Maître Suzanne Blum that Jim had opened up his French civil case against me in the Palais de Justice and his criminal charges against me at the Préfecture de Police. It seems that the matters had been shelved but not cancelled. "This is madness," I thought, as there seemed no way that he could possibly win either case. It looked like he had nothing else to do but harass me and poison my existence.

When I received letters from Maître Suzanne Blum in French and CHC in English, I stood in the middle of my room, shaking as I read and reread what both had to say about the French actions, which they were convinced he could not win. But what about me? It seemed that Jim was trying to wear me down so I couldn't take proper care of the children and do my work while having to defend myself in two countries. Or perhaps he thought I'd ignore the French procedures now that we were established in England and he could win in France by default.

Days later I received a short note from Maître Blum stating the criminal case was set for a hearing and she'd be in touch with me and CHC with details. I didn't wait. As soon as Catina had left the apartment to meet the girls at school I telephoned to Paris, probably sounding a bit hysterical when I got Suzanne on the line and blurted out all that I'd held inside. By now I was convinced that Jim and the "real Mrs. Nolan" were only interested in getting me back to Paris. What if something terrible happened to me while I was there? What did Jim and that "violent, capricious woman" have in mind? If something happened to me who would take care of Cathy and Janne? Then I announced in my shaky voice that I would NEVER, EVER set foot in France again and I didn't care what happened in French criminal court.

That wonderful lady lawyer let me rant until I had it all out of my system and then announced, in her calm, cool, collected manner, that there was no need for me to appear. All I had to do, she reassured me, was have CHC prepare an official statement for me which she would have translated to present in French Court.

No words can describe my appreciation of CHC in the City. On my next visit to his office, he had already prepared my statement which would be translated into French for Maître Blum to present to the French Police. He had gone through so much with me already and had such a collection of documents that he didn't need me snivelling across his desk anymore. As a matter of fact, he insisted that we make quick work of this so I could get back to family and my job.

Champagne...

In addition to the "errors" to be pin-pointed in Jim's claim, for instance that I had refused to present the children (ignoring the official reports from Vaucresson police that they had indeed been "presented"), CHC included a London statement by Jim saying he didn't object to his daughters remaining Wards of Court, plus proof of his access and actual visit. What's more, CHC had a letter from Jim's solicitor saying that Jim was now a legal resident of Switzerland. "So," stated CHC, "it seems inappropriate that an American mother residing in England should be criminally charged in France by an American father who is a resident of Switzerland, concerning children who are Wards of English Court."

My fury and frustration at Jim's maneuvering in France while at the same time scheduling a holiday in England with his children had to be hidden from everyone. I vowed to say nothing that might interfere with Cathy and Janne's vacation with their father.

When the family came back from their two-week, seaside holiday Cathy and Janne looked healthy and tanned; they didn't have much to say about their first vacation with their father and his new family but dug into their books, games and toys. Trying to be casual I asked if they'd had a good time but when one said "Okay," and the other said, "it was alright," I sensed I shouldn't insist on details. Who can tell what little girls are thinking; maybe they'd had a terrific time but thought my feelings would be hurt if they said so.

After their bedtime when I was alone with Catina, she wanted to talk about Jim's wife and started with remarks like, "It's plain to see who wears the pants in THAT family," adding that Jim's wife not only made all plans for every day's activities, but always took the wheel of their pale blue convertible they'd brought with them and decided whether the top would be up or down, ordering Jim to follow her demands. This scene was hard for me to picture and I wasn't really interested in trying. What was important to me was that my family was back and we were heading for the Isle of Wight.

The next morning Cathy and Janne had maps and booklets spread all over the kitchen table, planning to explore the island from top to bottom. Janne pointed to where Queen Victoria spent her holidays and said she wanted to see "the Queen's house." Cathy favored the pirates' caves and the Roman ruins. Looking over their heads, I picked the home of Alfred, Lord Tennyson, as a place we shouldn't miss, noting now that it was a guest house with dining indoors or in the garden. We made plans for every day of our stay and off we went by train and ferry boat, laughing merrily all the way.

In the middle of our vacation, CHC called me in our demi-pension, telling me he'd just heard from Maître Blum in Paris. He said she'd written to me in London as well and the letter awaited my return but, in the meantime he thought I'd be happy to know that Mr. Nolan's criminal charge against me had been rejected and that Jim had been ordered to pay all legal costs for me as well as his own.

Of course I was relieved to hear of another battle won but nothing could wipe out the fear I had of Jim. I knew so well his anger and temper when he didn't get his way. (The vision of him as a little boy trampling sandcastles that others had made kept coming back to me when I walked along the beach with Cathy and Janne.)

When we returned to London and the pile of mail that had accumulated, I found Maître Blum's letter to read first. In French, confirming what CHC had told me in English, she said that I had been *relaxée* while Jim was *condamné* to pay my legal costs. (At last, I sighed to myself, Maître Blum would surely send him a bill for all the work he'd caused her.)

Back in the *London-American* office there were urgent messages to call Maggie Vaudable at Maxim's in Paris, plus another from Erwin Schleyen at the Mirabelle, which I knew in advance had to do with their Mirabelle-at-Maxim's week to be held in two months' time. While waiting for Maggie to come on the line, I remembered her words a few months ago when she said my troubles would be over by November. They weren't of course, though British Courts had decided that the children remain in England in my care and the French police were not on my trail; so thankfulness was in order.

When I got Maggie in her Maxim's office, she barely let me say a word the minute she heard my voice. Rattling on and on about the big plans, she said everything had been arranged for me and I had nothing to worry about from the time that her car and driver would meet me at the airport. He'd whisk me right to Maxim's where I would stay in her guest suite upstairs. She would arrange for a hairdresser from Alexandre de Paris to come to me on the gala night to comb my hair; there was a *femme de chambre* on the premises to press my clothes and bring me anything I wanted to eat, drink or read; and my own private telephone to call anyone I wished. In the morning I'd be served *café au lait au lit* and Maggie's chauffeur would deliver me to the airport at the hour of my choice.

She was incredible! After that lengthy report of all she'd planned for me, to cinch her deal, she said if I wanted to see Maître Blum before going back to London I should invite her to lunch at Maxim's and, of course, there would be no bill. After assuring Maggie that I'd be there and do my best to help make it a successful evening, I called Erwin Schleyen for an appointment to make up the guest list and finalize plans.

On the top of my list of guests to have at my Maxim's dinner table from London was Charles Clore, whom I thought should be our honored guest; but Mr. Schleyen shook his head saying he didn't think Mr. Clore would agree to be at a table hosted by a journalist. I smiled, saying I thought he would accept; he knew I wasn't one to ask personal, political or big business questions and also knew I could throw a good party. ("What's more," I thought to myself with a smile, "did he know another journalist who rode around in a royal Rolls Royce?")

We were in Mr. Schleyen's office and I asked him if I could pick up a phone and call Mr. Clore right there. He nodded, still looking dubious but when the tycoon got on the line right away and said he'd be delighted to be my guest at

Champagne...

Maxim's, Mr. Schleyen beamed at the news and we went on from there. When I asked him if he'd be sitting at our table, he looked shocked at the question, reminding me that he was a soup-maker, first and foremost, and planning to sit discreetly on a *banquette* with the Vaudables.

After agreeing to pay the way and expenses for Dezo Hoffman, my photographer, he asked me what my fee would be and how I would like to be paid. When I told him I wouldn't think of charging anything in the light of all that he and Maggie had done for me, he shrugged and good-naturedly accused me of being a "lousy businesswoman." I agreed that he was right, adding that he wasn't the first person who'd told me that.

It was early in the morning when I took that memorable flight to Paris to host a table for ten on the big Mirabelle-Maxim's gala night. I was wrapped in a plain raincoat over skirt and sweater, but in my suitcase was my most ravishing white satin, small-waisted, big-skirted Balenciaga dinner dress with matching satin pumps, beaded evening bag, white kid gloves and a couple of lacy handkerchiefs to say nothing of my strapless lace waist-pinching foundation and lace-topped stockings that no one but I would see. As an afterthought, I packed my mink shoulder cape to wear on my way down from the top floor of Maxim's to check with Paulette at the *vestiaire* before going into the dining room.

Maggie's car and driver met me at Orly Airport as planned and another Maxim's faithful was at the restaurant's main door to take my bag and show me the way to Maggie's secret hideaway. I followed the leader up the carpeted stairs past the Imperial Salon, up more flights past offices and up some more to "my" door. When I stepped into the room it was like being in another world. Maggie had decorated everything in Empire style with an oversized, cradle-shaped bed, ornate porcelain lamps and vases on golden pedestals, elaborate oil paintings in heavy gilt frames. I stared in awe at the scene, taking in everything including the huge gold-and-black cradle telephone with its heavy base and circular dial that I found needed the strongest fingers to turn.

Maggie's bathroom was another sight to behold. It was as roomy as a small salon featuring gilt mirrors, a regal tub, fluffy Porthault towels of all sizes, each embroidered with Maggie's initials. A wall of shelves held soaps, bathsalts, oil, powder and perfume in beautiful, gilt-edged, crystal containers and even the water-glass looked fit for an empress.

Out the little windows of the room one could see the Rue Royale below with the Place de la Concorde to the right and the Madeleine Church to the left. While I was unpacking the *femme de chambre* arrived at the door with a fabulous golden basket full of all kinds of fruit so beautifully pyramided that it looked like a still life oil painting, blending perfectly with the decor and reminding me of how well the French can do the finer things in life. The maid looked carefully at my evening dress to see if it needed pressing. It didn't because the countless layers of half petticoats had protected the white satin from wrinkles.

The giant telephone tinkled politely just then and, afterward, didn't seem to stop. The first call was John Spencer Churchill to say he and Lullan had arrived on the Quai Anatole France and he wanted to confirm our dinner and give me his telephone number, which wasn't in the book. Then Alexandre de Paris fixed the hour that Martine would arrive to comb my hair and then added that M. Alexandre was sorry he couldn't come himself, but he had to be with the Duchess of Windsor. Maître Blum's office called to confirm tomorrow's lunch date and the doorman downstairs called to announce that flowers were delivered and on the way up. Of course Maggie called to make sure that everything was to my liking.

"Maggie, my God, what can I say! Everything's incredible!" I told her, feasting my eyes on the magical setting. (Never mind that my favorite French decor was Louis XVI. Tonight I'd be an empress on the Rue Royale.)

In the meantime, there were details to follow up. When the phone was not ringing I had to call Paris guests (and be careful not to break my fingernails on the dial) to make sure they remembered the hour of arrival and the formal attire. Dorian Leigh was bubbling with enthusiasm; Countess Eugenia "Mousie" Gaetani wanted me to assure her that Aly Khan would not show up; (all I was sure of was that he wouldn't be at OUR table); Jack Forrester said he'd be there "with bells on" and said Paul Getty was stuck in Baden-Baden and sorry to be missing the fun. When "Prince" Vladimir Rachevsky was called, he was his usual jovial self, saying how pleased he was to be invited by me because he loved to see me and besides he knew he wouldn't be seated "in Siberia" tonight.

Lunching in my room on smoked salmon, champagne and fruit, I finished the telephone calls, sent my final list of guests' names down to the office and stretched out on the cradle-bed with my feet resting on fat pillows, to await Martine from Alexandre de Paris to see what she'd do with my head. Never in all the countless times that I had to prepare for a gala evening did I have so much time to devote to myself, without even a worry about transport back and forth. And never did I remember having such fabulous surroundings. The stuff of dreams.

When Martine arrived she sat me down in a straight chair in the middle of the room and began to brush my not short, not long, messy head of hair, asking me what kind of hairdo I had in mind for this evening. "Do it YOUR way," I told her, not even caring that I didn't have a mirror in front of me to watch her progress. When I went into the bathroom to survey her headwork, looking at my semi-bouffant style from all angles, I was amazed with what she had done. It looked and felt just right. When I tried to pay her for her efforts she refused, telling me that Madame Vaudable had taken care of everything and she could not possibly accept another *sou*.

Preparing a bubble bath in that glorious bathroom with just the side lamps burning, I had an inspiration. There was more champagne in the half bottle brought up for my lunch, so I poured it into a gilt edged, crystal drinking glass and placed it on the edge of the tub for me to sip while I soaked. What a sensation! How easy it would be to get accustomed to this way of life! Stepping out of the tub into reality, I turned on a spotlighted, magnifying, make-up mirror over the sink to apply close-up powder, mascara and lipstick just the way it should be done. No slap-dash job this time. Remembering what Dorian Leigh had said once that most women thought they were made up when they'd only half finished the job, I went over everything with a bit more mascara, a brush-up of eyebrows and a stronger, smoother lipline. I could see what she meant.

The white lace, strapless waist-pincher with tiny hooks all the way up the back was easy to get into tonight, which told me I'd lost a few ounces these last few days, but I didn't care as it made dressing easier than ever when fastening the elaborate under "architecture" of a Balenciaga design. Ready to go, in white from head to toe, I added pearl drop earrings, necklace, and then a few strands of pearls around my wrist for good measure. I descended the many stairs down to the restaurant earlier than anyone except Monsieur Roger, the young director who'd replaced Monsieur Albert when "Papa" retired.

M. Roger gave me a big smile with sparkling eyes and tucked a big notebook under his arm as we shook hands. He was busy making the night's seating arrangements in the main dining room, a ritual he called the *mise en scène* because it was like setting a stage for the evening's drama.

In his book were formal placecards he'd ordered for me with each guest's name written in beautiful script. He handed them to me so I could do my own seating at an oblong table in the middle of the room. The scene was glorious throughout with gleaming white linen, crystal and silver on each table plus tiny pink-shaded lamps and silver bowls of pink rosebuds glowing against the rich burgundy red banquettes. Walls were covered with gilded mirrors and paintings of pretty pink Belle Époque ladies; the ceiling was stained glass in muted colors, subtly lighted behind the panels.

All was set for the gala opening of the *Semaine Anglaise* at Maxim's, featuring a very British bill of fare prepared by Mirabelle chefs installed in Maxim's' kitchens below the street level. Still with my mink stole on my shoulders, I went to my table to decide who would sit where, putting Charles Clore across from me with young, vivacious ladies (one American, one French) on each side of him. John Spencer Churchill, I thought ought to go on my right with Countess Gaetani on his right; then Vladimir Rachevsky next to her as "Mousie" was an interesting conversationalist in several languages. I did not forget to place Dorian Leigh next to Jack Forrester as they always had animated table talk with lots of laughs. As I was going around the table, I greeted several familiar faces among the waiters who were busy making glasses sparkle all the more throughout the room. Then when I went to check my mink stole for the evening, Madame Paulette came down from her perch in the *vestiaire* to give me the continental peck on both cheeks, saying how much I'd been missed and making me feel that I was part of the Maxim's "family."

Suddenly, it was like a curtain going up when formally-dressed guests started pouring through the door. Charles Clore was among the first. He was flushed and in his glory as he stood by the majestic showcases filled with silver treasures from his precious collection. When he noticed that the silver was under lock and key behind glass doors, he insisted that Louis Vaudable open up so guests could touch or handle the Gregorian and Victorian pieces if they wished, saying "Things of beauty are meant to be touched as well as admired–and never, ever locked up." Louis did as he was asked during the time we greeted guests in the foyer but when we went into the main dining room, Louis locked the case once more and dropped the key in his pocket for safe-keeping.

"Doesn't Monsieur Clore realize his silver is worth a lot of gold?" Louis commented later.

A tiny dinner menu, in the same lovely script as the place cards, was set before each guest but I managed to tell everyone that if there was anything they'd rather have, all they had to do was ask; but everyone seemed delighted as we began a dinner with fine wines which went on for hours getting more animated by the minute. Happily, I looked around the room, seeing celebrities and friends in every direction. In a corner was Aristotle Onassis with the Maharanee of Baroda, not far from Mr. and Mrs. Lowell Guinness, while farther down on the banquette was Captain Peter Townsend with his Belgian bride, Marie-Luce, who looked so much like Princess Margaret that all heads were turned to their table.

A few elbows away was Charles Sweeney's brother, Bob, a golf champion, with his bride. Farther on, the American-born Lady Beatty with her mother, in Paris from Ardmore, Oklahoma. It was amazing to see that the more I looked around, the more familiar faces I found. Over in a far corner was a top fashion model, Ivy Nicholson, who'd been the very first model to pose for Ann McGarry Associates. She was in a party with a lady named Sue Cardoza, who was doing social columns for the *Herald Tribune* (before she married a titled Frenchman and became a relative of President Valéry Giscard d'Estaing). In the opposite corner was my old Place Vendôme *antiquaire*, Maurice Chalom, not far from Princess de Bourbon-Parme and the Duchesse de Mouchy. ("Heavens," I thought," all I have to do is reconstruct this room in my head and my next article is done.)

At coffee and cognac time at my table, all was going strong. The young American seated next to Charles Clore, in Paris studying opera, decided to sing a Russian song along with the violins, bringing tears to the eyes of Vladimir Rachevsky, which meant he was having a wonderful time. Dorian and Jack were in heated discussion about who would be America's next president, with Dorian insisting that it would be Jack Kennedy because he was running with a Texan and nobody ever loses with a Texan by his side. John Spencer Churchill had latched on to Maxim's famed wine steward, M. Palmier, and was telling him all about his "vineyard" in Adam and Eve Mews while, across from me, Charles Clore was whispering to the French beauty on his right while she blushed, smiled and ever-so-lightly nodded her head.

Champagne...

Dinner was over but people stayed and stayed for dancing and champagne as the lights were dimmed. I didn't mind how long the guests stayed. All I had to do was make my way up the stairs when the evening was through. When at last my duties were over and my cheeks had been kissed so many times I thought they might be dented, Paulette put my cape on my shoulders just as Mr. Schleyen was leaving with a group of people by the door. He came to my side to say how pleased he was with the evening and that I must now come with him and his friends to hear some gypsy violins. I shook my head as he tried to insist until he saw I wasn't going to change my mind.

"No, thank you–thank you, really, but no." I kept murmuring, shaking his hand and then turning to the staircase. Everything had been perfect and I didn't want to push my luck.

Chapter Thirty

My Maxim's lunch date with Maître Blum was a subdued tête-à-tête on the burgundy red plush banquette with Suzanne summing up my legal situation in France which now had Jim's civil suit pending. I didn't want to tell her that I was too tired and fed up with Jim's shenanigans to listen, as she went on, point after point, until I felt my head swimming.

"Complicated, my dear, very complicated," she was saying, "nullifying an agreement by two Americans at the U.S. Embassy nearly a year after a French divorce. Must prove court incompetent," and so on, pointing out the importance of winning this matter so I could bring my family back to France. I told her, finally, that there was no reason to come back to France because the children were doing so well and looking forward to finding out what it was like to live in America.

Her look told me she understood completely but she still underlined the fact that this French civil case had to be fought until it was won and she was determined to see it through. When Maître Blum had to leave, I joined Maggie Vaudable at her usual lunch table in the Omnibus section of Maxim's near the entrance. Over more coffee, she said everyone was very pleased with last night's success and I should be very happy, adding, "When are you moving back?"

I found myself repeating to Maggie what I'd said to Suzanne. She let me finish and then asked, "But what about your career?" making me smile as I told her the only career I had was Cathy and Janne. And, so far, we'd had "miracles" happen to find work wherever I was to pay our way. Maggie nodded in silent understanding, just as Suzanne had done. As formidable as my two French career women friends were, they didn't argue with my stand.

Maggie's driver whisked me away from Maxim's to Orly airport and soon I was airborne for London, making it all seem like a dream. Amazing, I thought, I hadn't set foot outside the door of Maxim's but I'd seen enough friends and celebrities to fill two pages of the new weekly and give me pleasant memories for life.

Back at home in London the children greeted me like I'd been away for a long time rather than just one night. When I told them I couldn't bring back anything except a little box of Maxim's *petits fours*, they didn't seem to mind. Cathy was more interested in pulling me into my room to show me what she'd done while I was gone. I found my usual messy desk straightened up with the mail that had arrived in my absence neatly piled in the middle and my datebook opened to today's pages. What's more, she had been answering the telephone and writing messages on my agenda pages. As I complimented her, profusely, she handed me another "document." On a pale blue piece of paper written in deep blue ink, was a listing of everything she'd done in my absence and beside each chore she marked a few pence with the total on the bottom. Topping the page in capital letters were the words "THE WILLIAM."

"That's THE BILL for all the jobs I did," she explained. "*Tiens, tiens,*" I thought, smiling, "she likes to work and she likes to get paid for the work she's done–just like her mother."

I paid.

This unique weekly newspaper that I loved, the *London-American*, had a short life; in less than two years it was closing down. Luckily for me I was offered another job as a celebrity/society columnist for a daily newspaper. The job offer came during an elegant lunch with newspaper friends at the Mirabelle and my chance to become a Fleet Street journalist came before I even knew the way to that legendary area of London.

It was an unforgettable first time visit to Fleet Street to meet the editors of the *London Evening News & Star*. I got out of the taxi and stood staring at the gigantic building. As sophisticated as I was supposed to be, I felt like a country bumpkin. Somehow I found my way into a horrendously noisy newsroom with telephones clanging, people running in all directions, and typewriters clacking out deafening, weird music you'd never hear on the Hit Parade. This place seemed like Army Headquarters in wartime.

One of my lunch friends arrived at my side to take me into a glassed-in office before I was too unnerved by the scene so unlike the Paris *Herald Tribune* or the *London-American*, where I'd felt at home. Behind the glass partitions was a charming gentleman who made me feel at ease immediately. He seemed to understand what was on my mind, even before I had asked, "Am I expected to write my articles here?"

He said insofar as my kind of journalism depended on my personal contacts and entailed entertaining and attending social events, there was no need to come to the office as I could write from home, give my copy to a taxi driver and they'd pay the fare on his arrival at the paper. He told me he'd seen my articles in both London and Paris and my material was what they wanted with one exception: he wanted me to write in the first person. I made a meek remark that I'd never done that and didn't think much of the "I did this and I did that" method of reporting but he insisted that it was the best way. When he mentioned what the newspaper was ready to pay for each column I stopped arguing, nodded my acceptance and we shook hands in friendly agreement. Thus I became a weekly contributor to that gigantic newspaper, filling a back page every Friday with social/celebrity goings-on which I gathered in a whirl of my own. Sometimes I attended several parties a night, thanks to the limousine Paddy Barthropp sent whenever I wished.

The editors headlined the Friday page with "MY WEEK" with a byline that got bigger and bigger until I thought they were going too far when I measured one with my desk ruler and found it to be five inches long and two inches high. Trying to be funny once when I had the Feature Editor on the telephone, I asked him why he didn't make my signature a bit bigger. Quite seriously, he answered, "Sorry, Maggi, that's the largest type we've got."

I've heard that journalists get big heads to fit the space they've been allotted and the size of their bylines. That didn't happen to me. Too many times I saw my "big name" sticking out of wire trash baskets on Saturdays when I went shopping on Fulham Road and many times I noticed that Catina wrapped garbage in the Friday edition of the *London Evening News & Star*. There I was among apple cores, banana skins and chicken bones. That wasn't as shattering to any ego I might have had as the time I saw my likeness smiling up from the floor of our black bird's cage.

Pages to be filled every week with exclusive, first-hand material about well-known socialites and celebrities of all nationalities kept me on my toes all the time and made me thankful for personal invitations from Paul Getty to come to Sutton Place, as there were always interesting things going on, amusing things being said and fascinating faces around the table. What's more, the paper just never seemed to get enough to read about the "richest man in the world" in his stately home.

Paul was wary of journalists but considered my kind of writing harmless and, he said, "very amusing." Lunching at his lengthy, gleaming, authentic Henry VIII table with him when John Ringling North was there, Paul always sat at the end of the table and would motion me to be at his right in the most gentlemanly fashion. I'd shake my head, insisting that John sit next to him as they had so much to talk about. I loved to listen and I'd always come away from Guildford with paragraphs for my next column filling my head.

Those were the days before endless stories appeared about all the women who were supposed to be in his love life. The only lady I ever saw in residence was Mary Tessier, the Russian-French friend Paul had brought to lunch at Les Ambassadeurs when we were doing the feature for *Lilliput*. Mary was a vivacious, attractive woman who spoke several languages and said exactly what she thought in all of them. She loved showing me around Sutton Place through the Grand Hall, the ballroom and each of the 14 bedrooms, including Paul's pale green and yellow suite overlooking an expanse of beautiful gardens resembling an Impressionist painting. Paul had an amber marble bathroom with gold lion head water spouts, a setting fit for a king's throne room.

In Paul's exquisitely-furnished bedroom I stared at three different telephones beside his bed and Mary told me one was for all-night incoming calls from his associates all over the world; one was for his outgoing calls and the third was a hotline directly to the police. (Later, when Jack quipped "Getty doesn't go to bed with girls, he sleeps with three telephones," I knew what he was talking about.)

The Sutton Place bedroom that intrigued me the most was a burgundy red satin-walled room with a giant four-poster bed. Called the "South Room," it was supposed to be haunted by the ghost of Anne Boleyn but she was known as a nice ghost, never door-slamming but merely opening and closing them gently all through the night. Downstairs at the entry in a powder room, I saw the now famous pay telephone but noticed something no one ever mentioned: a big bowl of coins beside the phone for anyone to use, proving that Paul's motive for installing the phone was not penny-pinching but keeping his houselines clear.

Mary confided that she was "damn glad" to have that pay phone because she could call anyone she wanted and say what she pleased without being overheard. She nagged Paul unmercifully, I thought, while she was still good company and

J. Paul Getty with Mary Tessier.

remarkably learned on many subjects in several languages. However, she did get tiresome when she'd repeat her fury that Paul wouldn't let her have a horse; "He'll bring those damn lions all the way from California yet he won't let me have a horse," she whined.

Paul, the animal lover, liked to show off his watchdogs, Rex, Rusty, Odin and Sean, after lunch, marching his guests through a huge, ultra-modern, pale blue kitchen and out a backdoor to the kennels. Sean and Rusty were his favorites and looked ferocious but always wagged their tails when I approached. Once when Paul saw Sean licking my hand through the wire fence he asked me to please not tell anybody because he wanted everyone to believe the dogs were frightfully dangerous.

Sutton Place was often lent to charity groups for special events in the lower salons and gardens. It turned out to be a fine place for fundraising as so many people would pay a fat price to see the stately home and maybe get a peek at Paul. One sunny afternoon more than 1,000 guests showed up for a Christian Dior fashion parade to benefit the Royal College of Nursing. Mary, Duchess of Roxburghe, organizer of the event, reported with pink-cheeked pleasure that they'd never had such a success. Paul was a winner as well because when he let his home to good causes he paid less taxes at the end of the year. As for me, I gained a lot of good column material announcing the social/charity events in advance to help sell tickets, riding out in a Rolls Royce to cover them and writing articles afterwards. Once when I was worried that I mentioned the master of Sutton Place too often, the Features Editor assured me, "Getty's good copy. Keep it coming..."

Time flew by so fast that I barely realized we had not heard from Jim for months, even though I'd forwarded copies of school report cards to CHC to send on. In late Spring, CHC called me to say that he had contacted Jim's London solicitors in regard to summer plans but they had replied they had no instructions from their client so CHC advised me to go ahead with summer vacation arrangements. Back we went to the Isle of Wight but not before I'd delivered one article and written one in advance that I'd mail to the paper from wherever we were on the island because I was paid per article and I couldn't afford to lose the income.

Spring, Summer and Fall went by with still no word from the children's father, making me think—when I thought about it at all—that he'd probably wait until just before Christmas to make the same demands he'd made before. Cathy's birthday, Christmas and Janne's birthday went by and still no word. The idea that something might have happened to him was not possible because he was still active in France with his civil suit and those "opinion" papers kept arriving to CHC from Maître Blum.

In the early part of 1962, one morning I answered the telephone and heard Jim's voice on the line. It was the first time in years that we'd spoken and I was taken by surprise. He sounded overly friendly saying he was in London and wondered if he could drop around to see the children that afternoon. Without thinking, perhaps in shock, I agreed but as soon as I hung up I began to worry that I

Champagne...

Getting into Getty's drawers
at Sutton Place during
one of the many charity events held
there which gave him tax benefits.

hadn't followed court orders concerning his visits so I called CHC to ask if I'd done the wrong thing. He said it was alright but I must make certain that he didn't leave the apartment with the children and that I must be sure to have Catina remain on the premises during his visit.

Although I was far from thrilled to have Jim in my home, I told Catina to expect his visit and that I would stay away until he left. She accepted the news in silence and when I walked to school with the children I didn't go back to the apartment until I was certain Cathy and Janne would be at the dinner table. Alas, when I returned Jim was still there, standing at the kitchen door while the girls ate their dinner and Catina, who usually sat with them at the table, was leaning against the kitchen sink.

Jim was in one of his over-expansive moods when he turned to me with his full faced smile which I had once thought so attractive but which now frightened me because I couldn't guess what he was hiding behind it. He said he was in town for a few days and thought he ought to "check in" and see how we were doing and how things were going. No explanation of why he hadn't seen his daughters in such a long time but he did give the impression that he wanted to chat. Excusing myself I crossed the hall to my room and closed the door while my heart was beating like I'd run up a few flights of stairs. "What's he up to now?" was all I could ask myself as I stood there trying to calm down. Then I started to give myself a silent lecture, remembering how many times I'd said I wanted my children to have a father and for Jim to realize what interesting little people they were and not objects to throw around.

Many times I'd vowed to myself that I'd never show my disdain for Jim in front of Cathy and Janne and now, I had to prove it. As I sat on the edge of my bed, thinking hard, I decided that if Jim was really ready to get to know our children I'd better be big about it–for them.

A few days after the surprise visit, Jim's reason for being in London became quite clear. He had filed another statement with his lawyers full of more surprises. Jim had been in Germany on a new job with an American-based international public relations agency and he'd also obtained a divorce. He used his new job to explain why he hadn't been to England to see his daughters but did not try to explain his lack of communication. The point of his latest statement was a request to take Cathy and Janne to Switzerland for the upcoming vacations to his "luxurious chalet" which he described in detail as having two salons, six bedrooms and a large garden. His reason for not wanting to vacation in England was that it was "too inconvenient" and "too expensive." He repeated the "necessity" of getting separate passports for the children and conceded that "the nurse" could accompany the children on their voyage.

My head was whirling and my heart hurting as I wondered what was true in the paper I was reading. It looked like lies, lies, lies to me. Up until now I was able to argue or refute all other statements but I knew nothing of the actual situation in Switzerland or what Cathy and Janne would find when they got there. There was nothing I could do while endless questions whirled around in my head and vacation time was drawing near. As usual, CHC said "not to worry" but it didn't do any good; I worried anyway.

The Wards of Court judge made a decision that was like the others before him: the father must endeavour to spend time with his children in England and get to know them better. After this outcome, instead of disappearing as he had in the past, Jim began to spend more time in England and his visits to our home increased. Patience and determination not to show my feelings was difficult at first as I often found him still in the apartment when I arrived late afternoon or early evening. My shattered nerves were mending and I found I could cope.

But Catina couldn't cope. She hid her contempt from Jim while he was visiting but when we were alone she took her fury out on me, using her usual third person manner of speaking. One day she told me that *Monsieur* had seen the bottle of Dubonnet on the counter, asked for some and she had to pour it for him. Then, through her teeth, she said, "*Madame* will be asking me to serve his dinner to him next, *n'est-ce pas?*"

My attempts to placate her were useless as there was much more to her discontent than *Monsieur*. She never stopped hating England. She hated it even more now that she was feeling less and less needed by her charges.

Catina's constant nagging and endless demands weighed heavily on my shoulders and, no matter how badly I was in need of rest, it was hard to come by. Workdays followed by social evenings to collect material, figuring daily schedules so I wouldn't miss school events or meetings plus finding time for necessary shopping for food, clothes, etc. took full-time and careful planning with weekends filled with errands and excursions.

No use trying to sleep or even rest on Sundays. If I stayed in bed a moment more than usual, I'd hear a tap on the door and see a little face in front of me while a soft voice reminded me that I'd promised Catina I'd take everyone to Bushy Park or Hampton Court or Richmond Park or some place we'd never gone before. So I'd drag myself up and out once again feeling that I just couldn't shirk my mother/father duties no matter how tired I felt.

Our general weekend plans changed when I rented a little country cottage on the road between Sunningdale and Ascot on the way to Windsor where we'd go part of a Saturday or Sunday so we could get our feet on the ground. It was only barely furnished and didn't even have a refrigerator but it was such a tiny rent for such a lovely location in beautiful English countryside. Cathy and Janne loved the "camping out" atmosphere and tramping around the vicinity, discovering intriguing sites and seeing their first baby birds in a nest, cows in fields and even a garter snake or two. When we passed stables on our road and saw children riding horses around the grounds, there was no way I could hold them back.

We signed up for riding lessons which they looked forward to so much that often I'd find a reminder in my daily diary in big block letters "RIDING–3 p.m. " entered for Saturday by Cathy during the week while she also answered the telephone and took messages for me when I was out.

When I decided on the country cottage Catina called it a "folly" renting a second place before she even saw it. I reminded her that she was the one who gave me the idea, constantly reminding me every chance she got that big city life on pavements was far from ideal for growing girls and how much they loved country surroundings. Catina took to calling the cottage a "baraque" which I thought meant like army barracks but when I looked the word up in a French dictionary I saw it meant hut, shanty, shed or hovel. That hurt a bit but didn't change my mind about our little cottage which had yet another advantage that I didn't discuss. The tiny rental plus transportation to get there and back was nothing in comparison to our never-ending expensive excursions and fancy restaurants every weekend planned for Catina's pleasure.

Jim seemed to have become a part-time resident of England, though the only address we ever had for him was his lawyer. Once he mentioned that he was "staying with friends" but he never said where or with whom. No word would come from him for several weeks, sometimes, and then he'd bounce right back at our door as though he'd never been away, ready to play games with Cathy and Janne in their room or take them with Catina to the park or just sit around and talk, talk, talk.

By now I had trained myself to listen, only, without comment and without questioning; though sometimes it took more force than I thought I had. He talked freely as though I was some sort of relative or friend, telling me things that I thought shocking while he seemed quite pleased with himself. He said Jacqueline had met this much older, much richer man and so he and she had decided to get a "quickie" divorce so she could marry "this guy" and when he "kicked off" they'd remarry and go on like before. Listening to this trashy talk made me think that Jim's brain was warped beyond repair. As to their future plans, I wanted to say "in a pig's eye," but I bit my tongue so the words wouldn't come out of my mouth.

It seemed strange that he never mentioned his three-year-old daughter while he chatted away. It wasn't because he thought it might upset me as he was totally insensitive to my feelings as though I was someone else; anyone but the former Mrs. Nolan on the Rue du Docteur Blanche. The day he told me that he'd sold his "luxurious chalet" to his ex-wife's new husband, he said he let it go at half the price he'd paid for it because "after all, it was half Jacqueline's property." As my scalp tingled, he said this as nonchalantly as if he was telling me what he had for lunch.

It took everything I had to keep quiet while my thoughts raced. I was certain she'd never left that chalet in the first place and she would have been at the door if Cathy and Janne had gone to Switzerland. Their scheming was disgusting and now he had no chalet to talk about but he still seemed to accept and admire that capricious woman.

As Jim's visits became more frequent and he seemed to wait for me to appear to talk, talk, talk about himself, I devised my own way of shutting him up by telling him all of the latest news about his daughters' progress. When he bragged about big shots he was seeing, I told him that Cathy was top of her class and would have her name engraved on a silver cup. When he talked about the cruise he was planning to take, I told him about Janne winning a prize for her essay. When he said he was weekending in a stately home, I gave him an invitation to come and hear the girls singing in the Chelsea choir. Then I had Girl Guides, report cards and Janne joining the children's Committee of the League of Pity, (asking if he'd seen the pin she wore with the bluebirds on it) to talk about.

No matter how much time I took to give him news about his daughters, he'd go right back to talking about himself. He didn't like his work; as a matter of fact he didn't like working at all. He said he was never going to work again as soon as "the old man" died as he'd have enough money to devote his time to collecting antique golf clubs, playing golf, learning book binding and maybe he'd even buy a boathouse or boat.

I found I wasn't contemptuous of him but felt sorry for someone who didn't know the joy of working and the pleasurable feeling of a job well done. Cathy and Janne seemed to understand those joys and pleasures already and for that I was thankful. Despite my good intentions in regard to my children's father, sometimes

Champagne...

Jim got on my nerves when he didn't seem anxious to leave the apartment and I had to tap my foot and tell him it was getting late and I had to change for the evening. My nerves turned to out-and-out anger on the days I'd hear from CHC in the City about the state of Jim's civil case in France and then come home to find him sitting with Cathy and Janne watching television.

Chapter Thirty-One

While the big, wide wonderful whirl went on to fill the back page of every Friday's *Evening News & Star*, too many happenings behind the scenes were disturbing my inner peace, adding to the long-standing civil case in France. Not long before the lease was up on the Drayton Gardens apartment, I was informed that the renewal was possible only if I accepted a gigantic increase in rent. It seemed outrageous. I didn't know whether it reflected the real estate situation or the fact that my high lifestyle hob-nobbing with socialites and celebrities in the best places was there for everyone to read in the paper, inspiring the owner to take advantage of us. One thing I did know was that I didn't have the money to pay.

At the same time, more annoyances, inconveniences and expenses came my way when Paddy Barthropp's cars for special occasions were not so easy to come by. It was ironical; they were too busy now for Paddy to come to the phone and there were no cars available at the moment, but they'd always promise to see what they could do. I had to smile at this, knowing Paddy was grateful to me for my help in the beginning but he could no longer speed a limousine to me now that he was so successful. I just stopped calling him and decided to use those big, black, impeccable London taxis that were so comfortable and easy on billowing skirts and high hairdos. The drivers were nice, too, and often openly pleased and impressed when I'd tell them to take me to a fancy ball or celebrity event.

Another situation concerned conscientious, hard-working, talented photographer, Dezo Hoffman. At first he followed me around faithfully, taking pictures everywhere I went of people I pointed out, not having a clue as to who they were but counting on me to tell him. Those days, he'd bring around copies of every photo as souvenirs for me or to send to the people in them. From getting a copy of everything and then only getting those I was in, now I was getting nothing at all. Of course I wasn't paying his expenses anymore but merely getting him into the social/celebrity events I was attending. Once in the door he went his own way, not needing me to direct him to the "Who's Who" of the evening. He had learned which pictures to take and which newspapers paid the most on publication.

Ah, but I had a bigger problem–clothes. My wardrobe situation grew more critical every week. Every Paris *haute couture* dress I owned had gone through something: remodeling, repairing, shortening, lengthening and sometimes color-changing. In London there was no Madame Alice of Balenciaga, no Ginette and Erik of Balmain, no Philippe Heim of Jacques Heim; no one I could run to for help. And the gowns I wore, though architectural works of art they might be, were never intended for the wear and tear I'd been giving them and had now been worn for years.

To replace my wardrobe of cocktail, dinner and ball attire seemed impossibly expensive, taking money from everyday necessities of life and ever-increasing costs of collecting column material. With all my money problems filling my head, I had a brainstorm: ask the *Evening News* for more pay. When I got the Features Editor on the telephone, trying to explain my dilemma, he seemed to think that was the funniest thing he'd heard all day. "More money, Maggi? " he said. "Out of the question," adding that it wouldn't even be considered insofar as I was already the highest paid journalist on Fleet Street. I was crushed by his words; instead of getting an invitation to come down and talk it over I was told to "forget it." But surely he knew what I did for the paper was nothing like that of a Fleet Street journalist, nor was my work anything like a 9-to-5 desk job. But I knew a "NO" when I heard it and didn't insist.

Housing problems, transportation difficulties, wardrobe headaches seemed to fill my head all at once to add to the constant nagging of Catina, making it harder for me to play my "laugh-clown-laugh" role for the *London Evening News & Star.* Yet, I couldn't quite believe it was happening when I woke up one morning, got out of bed, and fell kerplunk in a faint on the floor. For the first time in my life, I was sick and didn't know what to do about it.

When the family saw the state I was in, Catina took the children to school while I faced facts. I had a deadline to make that very day and more than enough information to fill my page, but I had to somehow get it together and into the hands of a taxi driver. "No article, no pay" was impossible to accept, so I floundered around in my notes and found the name of a society doctor I'd met recently who was only a few streets away. He came around immediately, told me I was suffering from flu and fatigue which only rest would cure. When I blurted out my deadline dilemma, he said he'd give me an injection to provide quick force and stamina if I'd promise to go right to bed and stay there as soon as my writing was done.

In the state I was in, I'd promise anything, though I couldn't see how a little needle could help me as horrible and weak as I felt. As he was patting my arm with cotton, he told me actors had found this injection successful when they were ill but had to finish a performance in a "show-must-go-on" situation. "But be careful," he added, "this is not a cure and you must rest until you're well." I don't know what he gave me but it worked. The article finished, the taxi driver on his way to Fleet

Street, a few words to Catina and I was flat on my back, covered to my eyelids with blankets and sweating while shivering, finding out first-hand what it meant to be sick, really sick.

How many days it took to get back on my feet I don't remember but I'll never forget that it was a very concerned little Janne who brought tea to me in the morning and soup in the afternoon while Cathy took charge of the telephone and piles of mail that came through a slit in the front door. Catina took over the whole household but stayed far away from me; I didn't even see her when I'd stagger across the hall to the bathroom. I could hear her talking to our black bird. She didn't talk to me.

Never mind, I had plenty of talking to do to myself as the hours went by. I stayed awake longer and felt stronger every day thinking how horrible it would be if I lost my health and the strength to take care of Cathy and Janne.

When I was barely on my feet after winning the war with the flu and fatigue, a big packet of legal papers was stuffed through the skinny slot in our door and I found some more "opinions" in French and English concerning the French Civil Court proceedings,plus a letter from CHC telling me to telephone him when I had time for a talk. I called him immediately to tell him I wanted him to contact Jim's lawyers and offer to cancel our U.S. Embassy agreement right away if he'd pay

Bought on a sale, my Dior tunic dress prompted Jack Benny to say he couldn't tell the back-Dior from the front-Dior.

Dress & coat borrowed from Jacques Heim. Lace-topped stockings bought from Jacques Fath

what he owed me to this date and let me alone. CHC said, once again, that I was being too hasty and, furthermore, he had something important to tell me regarding trusts in the USA. He said he'd been in contact with various people in America and was now certain that there were other sums supposedly in trust for the children but controlled by their grandfather, with interest payments going to their father with the children "not seeing a penny" of it.

I listened to CHC patiently but then literally begged him to drop everything on one condition: that the father guarantee his children's complete education. That's all that really mattered. Then I insisted that he follow my wishes as to settling with Jim for only what was owed to this date and cancel our agreement, once and for all.

CHC gave his usual speech about "giving up" but realized I truly meant it and wouldn't change my mind this time. I heard a few sighs over the phone but CHC promised to follow through. This time, there were no counter requests to take the children out of England on their own passports. The reply was that Jim was in accord with my offer and the amount due was forthcoming. As soon as I realized that I would receive a lump sum of money larger than I'd ever gotten together in my life, it worried me more than making me feel light-hearted and well-off. Would I spend money on the much-needed glamour clothes for my job? Would I pay an outrageous rent increase to save the trouble of moving? How much of the amount I would be receiving would have to be paid for legal fees? I didn't have long to wait for the answer to that question as an updated bill arrived from the prestigious London Wall firm of Herbert Oppenheimer, Nathan & Van Dyk for a staggering sum due for all the work CHC had been doing plus Counsel's fees, court fees, commissioner's fees, filing fees, translation charges, airmail postage and "sundry incidental expenses." It was all there, reported day-to-day, with no mistakes. Following this came a bill from Paris. Although Maître Blum had never submitted a bill for herself, I promised to take care of legal charges, services, translations, telephone calls and postage.

And so what seemed like a large sum of money to be deposited in my account was dwindling right before my very eyes before it had been received. When CHC accepted payment for me from Jim's lawyers for what was supposed to be the total amount due to me he saw right away that Jim had "forgotten" to take into account what was owed for rent from the time we'd left the Rue de la Tour; so CHC was back in his bulldog-with-bone mood again. But I asked to please forget it because we'd gotten his agreement to pay for the children's college and that mattered much, much more to me than quibbling over the past, risking Jim's fury and future consequences.

After receiving monies due to me and paying the hefty legal bills plus everything else I owed, I had some serious thinking to do about my next step. After a sleepless night, the pondering was over. I decided to quit my job and move to the country cottage with Cathy, Janne, Catina and our talking bird.

The morning after the big decision made on a sleepless night, I felt stronger than I had in a long time, bouncing down the street on the way to school with Cathy and Janne. They seemed really pleased to see me out and about, which made me feel even better. When I asked them casually what they'd think of moving to our little country cottage, going to school in Windsor and getting better acquainted with the horses they liked so much, there was a little walking without a word.

"I'd rather go to America," announced Cathy. And immediately Janne added, "Me, too." After I assured them that they'd be in America for high school and college, they started to chat together about everything they could do in the country that they couldn't do now like having a big swing on their own tree, picnics in the garden and maybe even a barbecue pit. But then Janne said she'd changed her mind about the country because I'd be gone all the time and they'd never see me. I assured her I'd quit my job, stay home and only do freelance writing and she half skipped the rest of the way to school. Meantime Cathy was silent and thoughtful by my side, letting me know there was something on her mind.

"Does Catina know?" she finally asked, and I answered that I'd tell her after dinner tonight.

During the day I had a meeting with CHC, signing papers and giving him my usual expense report before telling him of my plan to move to the country, making sure I included all the good words I'd heard about the girls' school in Windsor. He listened intently and said he thought the idea was excellent and, indeed, in the children's interest but also in mine insofar as living expenses were concerned. Listing the advantages of country living, he asked me if I realized that this five-bedroom country house I had found with several acres of land cost only one fourth of what I was paying for a three-bedroom apartment in Drayton Gardens. (He didn't know the worst: our apartment had only two real bedrooms and my "bedroom" was made from the dining room connected by two glass doors to the lounge which I'd closed and covered with heavy drapes.)

Back home that evening I realized once more how amazingly understanding and discreet children can be. They had sensed that speaking to Catina about country living before I'd discussed it with her was a delicate matter not to be brought up and it was clear that they hadn't said a word about our talk on the way to school. They were chattering away in French with her while going through their usual routine. When Catina came to the kitchen at her aperitif time, I joined her and poured a little Dubonnet for myself but it tasted an awful lot like medicine. As I stood there I was reminded of what André Dubonnet used to say about his family's drink. He warned his friends that it was made from dregs and should never be swallowed before lacing it with a shot of vodka. We had no vodka in the house so I took my medicine as I told Catina that I had something to discuss after the children went to bed.

Later, when she heard my decision to quit my job and move to the country, prefaced by the fact that CHC approved of the plan which was in the interest of the children, she knew there was nothing to discuss. Instead, she took the chance to spurt out all her fury bottled up about life in London and everything she had against England, all of which I'd heard many times before. But now she had something new to add, "Can *Madame* really expect me to live in that *baraque?*" she asked. I assured her it would be very nice, fully furnished and fixed up; and then went into detail about the school in Windsor, its fine reputation, the swimming, while knowing full well I was wasting my time if I dared expect her approval.

Before we moved permanently to the beautiful countryside, we spent two Saturdays there and I made friends with a handyman who lived across the road who said he was anxious to have more work and would help us with gardening, repairing, painting, cleaning or whatever we asked for in exchange for a few shillings a week and no more. His first project, which stood him in good stead with Cathy and Janne, was to find a sturdy, thick-roped swing for the fattest branch on the biggest tree. One Saturday we asked for the swing and the next Saturday it was there looking like it belonged exactly where it was.

While Cathy and Janne took their riding lessons, I went through the house, room after room, imagining how the furniture we had would fit and making a list of what had to be done and what might be missing. Most of the time, Catina stood by a window staring out but when we came to the room that was to be hers, across the hall from Cathy's room, Catina came to the door to point out that her room was too far away from the bathroom and there wasn't even a place to wash her hands. I promised that she'd have a wash basin with hot and cold running water installed in a little alcove in her room which could make an ideal mini-dressing room.

Our country life in that funny 300-year-old cottage surrounded by rose bushes with wisteria hanging over the door was full of adventures every day. The lady who owned the stables down the road picked up Cathy and Janne in her car to take them to their riding lessons. They wore twill jodhpurs, turtle-necked sweaters, riding boots and chocolate-brown, velvet, riding hats–all from Harrods' horsey department in those pre-blue jeans days. They always looked tired but happy when they were dropped off at the gate, very dusty and smelling of hay.

Before school started, we went to a small department store in Windsor selling proper Upton House School blue wool jackets and skirts, blue and white cotton dresses, and everything else required including blue tank suits for the swimming pool. The headmistress was friendly, warm and even seemed pleased to have us, thanks to excellent past report cards and some kind words from the headmistress at Glendower in Queens Gate.

When school started, a rickety little school bus would stop at our gate and the driver would toot-toot if Cathy and Janne weren't already there. Off they'd go for a ride with fellow students through Windsor Park right to the school door and be brought back home the same way every afternoon. They seemed to fit right in, totally relaxed in their new environment as though they knew their way already while I felt like I was walking around in some sort of happy dream.

Waking up very early every morning was a joy, going into the kitchen to get breakfast and throw crumbs out the back door for the birds, then standing at the sink to watch the countless birds of all colors flitting about their business. The earliest birds were always blue jays, easy to recognize but most were mysteries to me as I watched them dive down, scoop up bits of bread and fly, up, up and away back toward Windsor Forest. Sometimes when we heard shots being fired from across the creek, colorful pheasants would land in the overgrown brush on our back property until the shooting stopped; some even pecked around the back garden near the house like chickens making themselves at home, sure they were safe with us.

We had more than birds coming to see us. Butcher, laundry man, repairmen of all sizes for many reasons, meter readers, the handyman in and out every day, grocery delivery boy and, of course, the Windsor plumber who installed pipes and an attractive Victorian-style porcelain sink with matching mirror and shelves above it in Catina's room. Was she pleased? She didn't say, while it was no secret what she thought of English country life. I'd remind her, in her own words, of the times she had lectured me about the importance of country living for growing children versus dangers of big city dwelling and how she had objected to my dress-up life running around in limousines.

As soon as I received stationery with our new address from Harrods engraving department, I wrote to countless friends and acquaintances telling them where I was and why but, once again, it was Jeannie Hoskins and her staff who told callers where I'd "disappeared."

We hadn't been in the country very long when Catina told me she had to go to Paris for a week and asked me to get her a plane ticket which I did right away, always feeling guilty that she never took a vacation or had any kind of life of her own. In the back of my mind was the thought that she was probably looking for another job and might not be back, but I said nothing when I gave her a round-trip ticket, wondering if she'd use the second half.

When Catina was in Paris, I received a letter from CHC advising me that my expense reports for the children could no longer include "the nanny" insofar as I was not working and "the nanny" no longer would be considered necessary. I stared at his words for a long time wondering how I was going to handle this. Of all the tough problems I'd had on my plate this was the toughest to digest. I found myself secretly hoping that Catina had found some terrific job and wouldn't want to come back. But she did, with a shapely Parisian haircut; yet she was as grumpy and unhappy as before. While the girls were at school, I told her straight out what CHC had written and that I couldn't pay her a salary anymore but wanted her to stay *en famille* with us for the rest of her life. She listened in silence, got up from the breakfast table to put her cup in the kitchen and went upstairs to her room, closed the door and stayed there.

I could hear her radio playing and the water running through the pipes to her room but not a peep out of her while I did the household chores: counting laundry, greeting the butcher, telephoning for groceries, and then feeding Noirice when it looked like Catina wasn't coming down to perform that daily necessity. When I left to walk to the fruit and vegetable outlet not far away, I told her through her door where I was going and when I'd be back, hoping she'd at least come downstairs to get something to eat while I was gone. God, this hurt. I didn't mind a minute of all the mundane things that made up my life, but the weight of Catina's unhappiness was heavy on my mind. As determined as I was to take care of her forever and even manage somehow to have her come to America with us when the time came, there was no way that I could make her happy, no matter what I did.

When Cathy and Janne came home, changed their clothes and went out in the garden to play while I prepared dinner, Catina remained in her room but she came downstairs after we were already seated and took her usual place. The girls had been chattering away in English about their school and friends but fell to silence when she came in because they knew she hated to hear anything but French around the dinner table.

"Cathy needs a haircut," announced Catina finally, back to her old self, at last. So we talked about where and when the haircut would take place and why not get Janne's hair cut at the same time. After that, Catina made a speech about not putting elbows on tables for Janne's benefit and passed a remark to me that the meals I was preparing for the children were not balanced. In the lightest tone of voice I could manage, I said it would help a lot if she'd say that BEFORE I prepared the meals instead of at the table; but while I spoke I knew I was wasting my breath. From that day onward, Catina had decided to do nothing but exist, never missing her meals and always managing to find something to complain about. She made the children's beds, laundered their underwear and took care of our French-speaking bird but that was all, preferring to stay in her room when Cathy and Janne were riding or at school.

At the same time as I suffered this kind of treatment, I think I understood...she'd never forgive me for not returning to France.

A country cottage on a winding dirt road might seem remote but ours was by way of Sunningdale through Ascot and on to Windsor which turned out to be easy to find for friends like John Ringling North, who rolled up in a Rolls Royce one day to try to talk me into going to Ascot with him. It took his chauffeur awhile to maneuver the car off the road and through the gate and I was standing in the doorway when John got out of the car. He was visibly shocked to see me in a cotton housedress with my hair pulled back by a rubber band. As he stepped into the cottage, I offered him a cup of tea but the idea seemed to horrify him as he stared at the flowery patterned oil cloth covering the dining room table. He stared at the children, who stared right back. He stood in the foyer with a few more words and then "goodbye." As his limousine turned back onto the road, I stood in the doorway asking myself, "He was expecting, maybe, Sutton Place?" (*At the time I had the feeling that I'd never see that entertaining, original circus king again, little knowing that we'd meet ten years from then to wine and dine in Paris as before, in the very best places.*)

Another Rolls Royce came to call, bringing a bubbling, friendly blonde Texas "tycooness," Frances Moody Newman, one day. Her car was full of fluttering, feather-hatted ladies, so I didn't have to worry that she'd try to talk me into coming along to Ascot. She was a dear lady, bouncing about, making a fuss over my "adorable" children and my "darling" little cottage while her chauffeur handed me a package which was obviously champagne.

"It's Dom Pérignon, dear," announced Frances, adding that she hoped I liked it. I assured her I LOVED it and gave her a big hug before she returned to her fancy friends to go off to the races.

The first overnight guest we had was Gweneth Dulles, who didn't mind a climb to the top of the house to the only extra bedroom and seemed to enjoy every minute of her visit which was so far removed from the luxuries of the Avenue Foch in Paris and the ultra comforts of London's Kensington Court. At first I thought Catina would be pleased to have a French-speaking guest in the house but it had the opposite effect. She refused to converse at all. And after our houseguest was gone, Catina came to the doorway of my office where I was pounding away on my rattling mechanical typewriter and announced that she wished to return to Paris and would appreciate it if "*Madame* can make the arrangements as soon as possible."

No words could make her change her mind. I had no choice but to do as she asked.

Chapter Thirty-Two

In Ascot, one lovely late fall afternoon when Cathy, Janne and I were taking turns on the swing, a funny-looking car drove noisily through our opened gate and crunched through the gravel right up to our door. It was Jim, in a junk-heap car, who bounced out wearing his ear-to-ear smile as he came toward us. As Cathy and Janne greeted him, I was amazed to notice that he looked like his father had the very first time I'd seen him in Paris. He wore sneakers, baggy pants and a rumpled nondescript jacket that didn't seem to fit. He did wear a tie but it was badly knotted and slightly off center. Could this be the same person who had been so contemptuous of "the old man" but now looked exactly like him?

Jim said he was staying with a golfing friend near the Wentworth Club in Virginia Water and complimented us on our cottage and location, as we stepped into the house. Janne started to set out cups and saucers and plates of cheese, crackers, cookies and fruitcake. Cathy was the one who asked her father the question that was on my mind as well, "Where did you get that funny car?" and he said he had borrowed it from a friend as he didn't have one anymore. "What happened to your blue one?" Janne asked, remembering the fancy convertible he'd brought from Switzerland for his first vacation with them in England. "Oh, I left that with Jacqueline," he answered, diving into the plate of cookies in front of him.

This first visit became one of many as Jim found more cars to borrow and more golfing friends to weekend with in the vicinity. It occurred to me that he would have accepted an invitation from me to stay with us, but there was no way that those words could come out of my mouth. My so-called kindness to him was not really for him but for his children and his late mother, and so it came easily. Only in waking moments could I be the big heroine of all time; where he slept I did not want to know.

While the incredibly beautiful birds around our house thrilled me every morning, I had another feathered friend inside our house upsetting me more and more. Noirice had stopped talking. The only noise he made sounded like unhappy grumbling as he'd fly around his cage hour after hour, as though he was angry that

Catina was no longer there, though she hadn't talked to him very much since we moved to the country. Cathy and Janne listened to me politely when I mentioned the problem but their interests were far removed from speaking French to a bird these days. Every day I talked to him as much as I could and even left the radio on in the dining room when I wasn't there; but nothing seemed to help.

Then an idea came into my head. Maybe the French-born Duchess of Bedford would ask the Duke if he'd be interested in having a French-speaking myhna bird in his "Pets' Corner" at Woburn Abbey. When I called Nicole at her stately home, she laughed as only she can laugh and said it would be a wonderful addition insofar as they were getting more and more French family tourists visiting Woburn all the time.

"Besides," she added with a giggle, "We have a myhna bird already whose name is Alfie and he speaks Cockney." She said she couldn't wait to hear what they'd say to each other.

And so one sunny Saturday, Cathy, Janne and I delivered Noirice to his stately home. A Windsor photographer I'd met at a local art exhibition agreed to take us in his station wagon if he could photograph the event, which sounded like "a hoot" to him. The huge cage on wheels that Harrods had made was no problem as it fit on the top of the car and we put Noirice in a small cage to travel on my knees. Nicole greeted us cheerfully and was impressed with Harrods "stately cage" which was put in place before I returned Noirice to his home. Nicole was delighted with him and chatted in French with me while I told her a lot of things he could say. Then Noirice, obviously happy to hear French said, "*Bonjour–bonjour...Ça va, ça va*," and went on with his repertoire while Nicole laughed all the more.

After a tour of the animal kingdom and a cup of tea in one of Woburn Abbey's museum-like salons, we returned to Ascot happy in knowing that our shiny black bird now had French people to talk to and animal experts to take care of him. The photographer sent copies of photos he'd taken plus his bill for his time, work and transportation. The bill was very reasonable and I hoped he could sell a few photos of the new Duchess of Bedford, though the only thing I ever saw in print was an item in a gossip column about me and Nicole headlined "Maggi Gives the Duchess the Bird."

Who would ever dream that Christmas would come to our little English cottage on a country road where I would be preparing all the trimmings for a huge turkey roasting in the oven while Janne set the table for four–with a place for her father. Jim was once again staying with friends nearby but he had invited himself to Christmas dinner with us saying, "Would you mind awfully if I came to have Christmas dinner with the kids?" I said it was alright with me as we'd certainly have more than enough and went about the business of getting everything together.

Champagne...

The Duchess of Bedford greets our French-speaking Noirice in the pets' corner of Woburn Abbey. An item in a London gossip column said "Maggi gives the Duchess the bird."

A few days before that he'd said he didn't have time to buy gifts, but would take Cathy and Janne to Windsor to pick their own presents. They came back loaded down with packages plus wrapping paper and ribbons, saying that even though they knew what they were getting, they wanted to put pretty packages under the tree to open on Christmas morning. I thought that was a good idea and told them they could wrap everything in my office where there was plenty of elbow room.

Jim stood around awhile, talking about himself, as usual, bragging about how many friends he had, places he knew and how many parties he'd been invited to this season right around our territory. (But no Christmas dinner, thought I, and that's why he was coming to our house.) He still harped on about the lousy job he had that he was about to quit, how he kept thinking about taking a "cushy job" in Pennsylvania teaching French at a private school until "the old man dies." His thought processes never ceased to shock me even though I'd brain-rinsed myself not to give my opinions.

When I cut holly from our own tree for table decoration and unpacked one of Grandma Nolan's antique lace tablecloths, I felt a tingling sensation both times–when I was out in the garden and back into the house–she was still with us and sharing this day. Spreading and smoothing the cloth, I could even hear her voice telling me so sweetly that she wanted us to have beautiful things for every room of our *petit pavillon* in Paris. So much had happened, so many changes, and yet I still felt her presence all around me.

On Christmas morning I discovered that Cathy and Janne had gotten their father to let them pick out a gift for me. I had happy surprises of a flowery pink scarf from Cathy and a delicate porcelain rosebud vase from Janne. When Jim arrived later I didn't forget to thank him for making my gifts possible and then, a bit later, I found another surprise. Jim left an envelope on the window sill above the kitchen sink. On the outside was written "for Christmas stuff" and on the inside was a check which more than covered the turkey, trimmings, plum pudding and wine.

Of course, I thanked him properly despite my mixed emotions on this festive day. As much as I tried to analyze Jim's behavior, my thoughts kept confusing or upsetting me, proving once more that I knew nothing about men; especially Jim, who seemed to have a certain satisfaction at seeing me here "in the sticks" wearing any old thing, scraping vegetables in the sink, while he played Lord Bountiful taking the children shopping and placing a check for me on the window sill next to soap, scrub brush and a water glass filled with wild winter blooms.

If the thought came to mind that he was changing, that his gestures were indications of generosity and/or guilt feelings, those ideas were dismissed. Guilt was not one of his complexes; his generosity came more from feelings that he had control over this apron-wrapped woman he'd seen so many times grinning out from celebrity-studded stories in Paris/London newspapers; this woman who'd gained every court fight with him was now on her knees. I'm pretty certain that these were his thoughts in my regard but I had a secret that he'd never guess–I was very happy where I was at this moment and no one could take that away from me. With that in mind I set out to have a lovely Christmas dinner with light-hearted talk and a feeling that Grandma Nolan was by my side.

During our festive turkey-and-trimmings dinner which went on and on Cathy and Janne never missed a chance to tell their father that they loved everything American and would be going there for high school and college as "Mother said so." Jim was in such an expansive mood that it seemed like a good time to talk about it, starting with the need for children to have roots and theirs were in Reading, Pennsylvania. Jim looked like he couldn't believe what I was saying. "You'd live in Reading?" he asked with wide eyes staring through his thick glasses. I repeated that "children need roots," while wondering where Jim thought I'd want to live to raise children...New York? Hollywood? Las Vegas? I knew nothing about Jim and he certainly knew nothing about me. We were even.

When we got up from the table, everyone pitched in to pile the dishes in the kitchen but I shooed them out saying I'd rather arrange everything myself while they amused themselves playing some of the games that awaited under the Christmas tree. This wasn't Maggi-the-martyr time; I actually enjoyed what I was doing; that relaxed me like therapy, while knowing that the better the relationship the children had with their father, the better for all of us. They were getting to know him more and more. It was only after he left that I realized how well. Cathy commented that she found it funny that he never would admit when he'd lost a game they played even though it was right there in front of him. Janne agreed and they went on talking about other things. Later, Janne came to me, pulling on my apron string as she said, "Hey, Mom, you always said you wanted a son so why don't you adopt Dad?"

When the time came for us to leave our little country house in England for our next destination, the U.S.A., I was financially poor but rich in strength, hope and enthusiasm to make a home and start to work again. Cathy, Janne and I went to Harrods to get another photo of us together for our new passport, which was to be our last family document as, after that, they each had their own. How they had grown between Harrods photographs! My daughters were both taller than I; Cathy called me "titch" patting the top of my head, when I was wearing flat shoes. Thinking what changes there had been in our lives since the very first time we'd set foot in this store, I realized that the only thing that hadn't changed was our dependence on Harrods for everything. And now that we were leaving Harrods auction house would be sending their van to Ascot to pick up everything we weren't taking with us–furniture, refrigerator, television, electrical appliances right down to every last dish, pot, pan and wooden spoon–to sell in auction, collect the money, take their percentage and airmail a check to us in Reading, PA.

Jim wasn't around when we packed up but he sent his agreement on the move through his London lawyers to mine and mailed a check to me for airfare, with some left over for expenses when we got there. Cathy and Janne sorted their books, keeping only those they'd won for their essays, good marks and animal rights efforts, boxing the rest, around 150 in all, to deliver to their school in Windsor. Shipping trunks, paintings, filing cabinets and everything too heavy to fly, we still ended up with 34 pieces of unmatched luggage in assorted sizes accompanying us on the airplane.

Arriving in Reading, PA. on an icy winter day in an overloaded Philadelphia station wagon taxi, the driver pulled up in front of the Berkshire Hotel where we'd be while looking for a home. There was a white-collared, black-suited reverend standing there at the curb, intrigued at the sight of all the luggage being unloaded. He asked us how many of those bags were ours and when he heard "all of them," he asked where in the world we came from with all that baggage. As nosy and curious as he was, I liked him, so I answered that we came by way of Paris, France, and then London, England, and then Ascot in Berkshire. He still stood there and then asked, "Were you happy in all those places?" I told him with a nod that we were and he smiled, broadly, saying "Then you'll be happy here because you're bringing your happiness with you."

The old reverend came into the hotel after us, saying that he was also a resident here and hoped to have the pleasure of speaking with us again so he'd like to know our name. When I said "Nolan," he asked the same question we heard from then on everywhere we went. "Are you related to J. Bennett Nolan of Oley Street?" and when I answered that he was my children's grandfather, his face lighted up in recognition while I told myself that my daughters' instant roots were about to take hold.

We found a little house on a tree-lined street in the "shrub-burbs" of Reading, a few blocks from the high school where Cathy and Janne had their first encounter with American education. They seemed advanced in all subjects except science, which might mean the study of leaves and insects to little English dayschool girls, but outer space to USA classmates. From the time of our arrival Grandpa Nolan came around to see us in our new home, staring at bare rooms we'd not yet furnished, while never offering to lend us anything from his huge house crammed from cellar to attic with enough to furnish several houses. I didn't ask for anything either.

Once I saw him looking intently at an empty trunk I'd turned sideways as a makeshift desk for myself in the corner of the dining room. He looked for such a long time at my rickety, old, mechanical typewriter sitting there that I couldn't help but say, "Don't forget, Abraham Lincoln wrote the Gettysburg Address on the back of a paper bag." He turned his back, mumbling "It was an envelope."

Grandpa invited us over to his house a few times in those first months of our arrival, but it amazed me that he was so nervous. He didn't take his eyes off me as though he feared I'd run off with his treasures. Once, however, when I told him I wanted to visit Grandma Nolan's room, he didn't follow me when I showed Cathy and Janne her bedroom and her favorite glassed-in porch where she sat sewing for so many years. Grandpa thought there was nothing of value up here so he let us go on our own. Nothing of value? That's what he thought. As I stood there remembering that lovely woman, I could picture her darning the hours away with that funny sock-mender she owned. Then I noticed her sewing box was still on the table beside her chair and, sure enough, the darner was there as though it awaited her return.

With a big lump in my throat I took it out of the box and held it in my two hands for awhile before deciding to take it with me in memory of my children's loving grandmother. As far as I was concerned, it was the only thing of value in Grandpa's house.

Despite the strained relationship I had with my children's grandfather I could sense his growing interest in Cathy and Janne. Their first report cards from school couldn't help but impress him although he uttered not a word when I put them in his hands. Their good manners in front of his old crony friends invited to his home for a glass of sherry at the same time as we were there must have pleased him as well, though he could not bring himself to say so. Relations would improve with time, I was sure, but we had been there less than a year when he died on a cruise ship just before it docked in St. Thomas.

By then, Jim was doing just what he said he'd do–teaching French in a little Pennsylvania boarding school. When he got the news of his father's death, he quit his job, flew to St. Thomas to bring his father's body back to Reading, and never worked another day in his life.

As soon as Jim's father was gone, he had enough income to make his dreams come true: never work, play golf, collect antique golf clubs, travel, buy a boat and learn bookbinding. His father arranged, however, that Jim could never touch the capital but only the interest, and that eventually the capital would go to Grandpa's church, hospital and college in ways that amounted to monuments to himself. I read the will and thought of the saying "you can't take it with you." Grandpa did.

All Jim's wishes came true but he didn't seem blissful to me as he traipsed around in sloppy clothes, more like his father every day as he spent hours in book-shops and *antiquaires*. He bragged, every chance he got, to anyone who'd listen, that he didn't have to work and he looked down on the poor slobs who did. At the same time, in every city he went to, he got a reputation for being the perennial houseguest with his "any old couch will do" approach when visiting friends. Many different people told me of his overnight and many-night stays. Some seemed delighted with his charming, easy-going company; some felt sorry for him, think-ing he was down and out; but our old friend, Eve from the fifties, was outspoken in her annoyance. Now living in New York, she wrote that Jim got on her nerves, using her living room like a "flop house" whenever he came to Manhattan and always leaving a mess for her to clean up after he was gone.

Every time I heard reports about how he managed to live off others' hospitali-ty and generosity, I felt sorry for him while hoping and praying that our children were learning about the joys of working, getting paid for it and knowing the plea-sure of spending their earnings with the assurance that work would bring them more. So many people I knew who lived on unearned income had never learned this simple fact of life and seemed deeply troubled without understanding why.

Cathy and Janne thrived in their American high school, getting top marks while active in clubs and youth organizations and then went on to greater things. Cathy graduated from Beloit College in Wisconsin (*magna cum laude*, Phi Betta Kappa) in sociology and philosopy, and received a Rockefeller Foundation Scholarship at Harvard after that, taking her first job in the scientific research library of the Massachusetts Institute of Technology (M.I.T.). Later she traded sci-entific research for journalism. Today she's Paris correspondent for the magazine*People* , writing about everything from French President Jacques Chirac to orphans in Rumania to baby elephants in Africa to the 120-year-old woman in Arles to Leslie Caron's gourmet restaurant in Burgundy. Janne got her Bachelor of Arts at Ohio's Antioch College in political science and foreign languages; going on to obtain a Ph.D Masters at the Fletcher School of Law and Diplomacy, specializing in economics and international security. Her first job was in the State Department. At this moment Janne is a permanent fellow at the Brookings Institution "think tank" in Washington, D.C., and is working on her fifth book. Her subjects: power of nuclear strategy, global engagement and ballistic missiles in the Third World, for example.

While Cathy and Janne were off to universities in Wisconsin and Ohio, I worked as women's editor of a newspaper, public relations director of two hotels and then talked the owners of the largest advertising agency in Lancaster, Pennsylvania into starting a public relations division for their existing accounts. They were skeptical, at first, but agreed to let me try at a salary guaranteeing that they didn't have much to lose. It was actually fun looking into old established companies producing such things as chicken feed or artisan-made furniture or prefabricated houses and then writing out uncomplicated, inexpensive methods of solving some of their problems. We put programs in action, impressing both the agency and the account when they saw that PR planning worked.

Before the first year was over, one of our companies gained a government award through our efforts while another got national television coverage for their new multi-million-dollar plant opening and the third consolidated confused employees after a conglomerate merger. What the agency owners viewed as "miracle results" was nothing more than theory learned in New York and Paris put to work in the virgin territory of Lancaster, PA. One agency partner with the marvelous Pennsylvania name of Wagonseller took to calling his new public relations department a "profit center," and I received salary raises without asking for them, which was quite a change after so many years of underpaid journalism.

The historic city of Lancaster seemed an ideal place to settle down so I bought an inexpensive rowhouse dating from the 1700s and fixed it up quite cozily. People I worked with and met along the way were genial. I joined the Lancaster Riding and Tennis Club (finally getting a chance to wear my riding clothes) and became a member of the Lancaster Advertising Club, where I served as president one year. Franklin and Marshall College in Lancaster offered night courses to anyone interested but it took Janne's insistence and help before I had the nerve to fill in the forms. Later, I didn't mind at all when she said "I told you so" as I was quite happy with an "A" in writing and a "B" in literature. When I addressed the college students on career possibilities in public relations, I cut out the newspaper clippings and sent them to my children, like I was the kid and they the grown-ups. What a joy the day I saw my book of poems written with my sister displayed in a bookshop window. It didn't make any money, of course, but the satisfaction was priceless.

Cathy and Janne came home for all holidays and blossomed into very attractive young ladies. (I must admit I had a bit of a shock when I sent them off to college in adorable twin sweater sets with matching skirts and they came home in jeans and oversized shirts with tails flapping in the breeze, but they were the same Cathy and Janne underneath.)

It looked like I was settled for life until one day Janne announced that she couldn't understand why I didn't move back to Paris now that she and her sister were grown. The idea shocked me at first and I told her I thought I should always keep a home for them to come back to whenever they wished. Janne heaved a heavy sigh before saying, "Frankly, Mother, if you lived in Paris you'd see a lot more of us than you do now in Lancaster, Pa."

From that bit of daughterly wisdom came the big move back to Paris after more than ten years away. I'd missed all the general strikes, student riots and upsets of the 60s that had torn Paris apart and shut it down. When I checked into the little Hôtel Duminy on the Rue du Mont Thabor, Mr. Duminy was still there, a little redder in face and rounder in body, but there he was with his family. "My" Paris looked the same from where I was, around the corner from the Ritz. I decided not to try to contact any old friends until I found somewhere to live but I couldn't help myself from making a beeline to the Place Vendôme over to the Ritz and down the long hall to the Cambon side as soon as I could. Everything seemed the same. Claude, the barman I'd known since he was a teenage *chasseur*, greeted me warmly as he led me to "my" table as though I'd never been away, while telling me that Charles Ritz had been asking about me recently and would be happy to have my news.

From the first moment I'd set foot in Paris I had a strong desire to see that beloved *petit pavillon* that had meant so much to me on the Rue du Docteur Blanche and I couldn't keep myself from taking a taxi to Passy, past the Trocadéro, along the Avenue Paul Doumer to La Muette. I asked the driver to let me off on the corner of the Avenue Mozart and the Rue de l'Assomption so I could walk the rest of the way, but when I finally turned into my old street, I couldn't believe the sight: apartment buildings, banks, butchers, pharmacies, grocery stores, dry-cleaning establishments, bakeries and pastry shops, to say nothing of newspaper and shoeshine stands. As I looked up at the crackerbox-like buildings, I couldn't help wondering what I'd find at the end of the street where we once lived.

Closer, I could see that "our" garden wall was still there but, getting nearer, I noticed a huge sign out front. From the opposite side of the street, I read an elegant *affiche* announcing that there'd soon be luxurious apartments of "*grand standing*" on this site.

Below the impressive notice, scrawled in thick, black graffiti were very rude words in French declaring this place to be a "TRAP FOR RICH FOOLS." Crossing over, I saw the heavy garden door was off its hinges and the old enamel plaque number "50" had fallen to the ground where it had obviously been stepped on by heavy shoes. Beyond the broken door I could see a pile of rubble instead of a garden and a windowless house that looked like an empty shell. Stepping through the rubble to "my" tree in the left-hand corner, I thought I was about to cry as I put my hands on the tree trunk. Strangely, instead of tears, a feeling of strength and joy ran through me. Looking back at the little house in weeds and rubble, the message was clear: the past is the past. I picked up the enamel "50" from the fifties as a keepsake as I stepped back onto the sidewalk.

Walking down the street I felt light on my feet and younger than I'd ever felt in my life. How lucky I was to have bright, warm, well-educated and amusing daughters who'd sent me back to Paris, the city where they were born.

Ahead that day were more than twenty years of people-watching, celebrity-reporting and champagne-sipping. I was ready with a smile, even if it turned out to be a whole new cocktail, dinner and ball game.

Who would have believed it? In 1986 on the 40th anniversary of my arrival in Paris, Cathy, Janne, my sister, The Sister, and I celebrated with 200 others at my favorite club, *Cercle de l'Union Interalliée*, which, for short, I've always called "The Club."

Index of Names in *Champagne...and Real Pain*

Index

Index

B orn in San Francisco, California on New Year's Eve in 1922, **Maggi Nolan** arrived in Paris on May 20, 1946 naïve and alone–and has never turned back. As the society columnist for the legendary *Herald Tribune*, Maggi quickly made a reputation for herself in the world of celebrities as well as with an international readership for her candor and wit Mother of two daughters, Cathy (the Paris correspondent for *People Magazine*) and Janne (Fellow at Brookings Institute in Washington, D.C.), **Maggi Nolan** resides in Paris' 8th *arrondissement*, where she is busy on her next book...a surprise.